A HISTORY OF
WOMEN IN RUSSIA

A
HISTORY
OF
WOMEN
IN RUSSIA

FROM EARLIEST TIMES
TO THE PRESENT

BARBARA EVANS CLEMENTS

✣ ✣ ✣ ✣ ✣

INDIANA UNIVERSITY PRESS
BLOOMINGTON AND INDIANAPOLIS

This book is a publication of

Indiana University Press
601 North Morton Street
Bloomington, Indiana 47404-3797 USA

iupress.indiana.edu

Telephone orders   800-842-6796
Fax orders   812-855-7931

♾ The paper used in this publication meets the minimum
requirements of the American National Standard for
Information Sciences—Permanence of Paper for
Printed Library Materials, ANSI Z39.48-1992.

MANUFACTURED IN THE UNITED STATES OF AMERICA

Library of Congress Cataloging-in-Publication Data

Clements, Barbara Evans, 1945-
A history of women in Russia : from earliest times to
the present / Barbara Evans Clements.
p. cm.
Includes bibliographical references and index.
ISBN 978-0-253-00097-2 (alkaline paper) — ISBN 978-0-253-00101-6 (pbk. : alkaline
paper) — ISBN 9780253001047 (e-book) 1. Women—Russia—History. 2. Women—
Soviet Union—History. 3. Women—Russia (Federation)—History. I. Title.
HQ1662.C575 2012
305.40947—dc23   2011045345

1 2 3 4 5   17 16 15 14 13 12

To my mother,
Champe Winston Evans
(1915–91),
a widow who worked the double shift
in the days of *Leave It to Beaver.*

A good wife is more precious than jewels.

THE PRIMARY CHRONICLE

✛ ✛ ✛ ✛ ✛

When the Devil himself has failed, he sends a woman.

RUSSIAN PROVERB

CONTENTS

ACKNOWLEDGMENTS

Many people helped me in the writing of this book. Lynn Benediktsson, Jerry Newman, and Christine Worobec read early versions. Their wise observations and kind suggestions guided me through the rewriting. Shelley Baranowski gave me very useful comments on the finished manuscript and some bucking up when I needed it. So did Jerry Mushkat, whose counsel over many decades has been invaluable. Rochelle Ruthchild and an anonymous reader for Indiana University Press made careful assessments that assisted in the final polishing. Tina Kelley, Pete Newman, and Lynn Benediktsson were there through the years with words of good cheer. I hope all these folks like what they read here. I must also acknowledge my mother, who taught me about love, about coping, and about finding joy in simple things. I dedicate this book to her.

✛ ✛ ✛ ✛ ✛

INTRODUCTION

This book is a brief history of all the women in all the Russias that existed on the far-eastern European plain during the past millennium. That history includes more than one hundred ethnic groups inhabiting what had become by 1800 the geographically largest country on Earth. Their lives across the centuries deserve telling, from the earliest times to the most recent, so this book begins with the Rus of the tenth century and ends in the present day. It concentrates on the Russians, Ukrainians, Belarusians, Poles, Lithuanians, Estonians, Latvians, and Jews who made up the great majority of the population. It also attempts to bring into view the histories of women of smaller ethnic groups, particularly those who lived in the vast territories of Siberia, Central Asia, and the Caucasus that were annexed by the spreading Russian Empire.

Susan Armitage, a historian of women in the western United States, has written, "We do not wish to create a sweet little cameo version of western history that will slip right into the Hisland story. We want to change the way the story is written."[1] Historians who study women in Russia have the same goal. Over the last forty years, they have done much to uncover the realities of women's lives in the Russian past, and thereby challenge the Hisland story. And yet, through no fault of their own, their scholarship remains somewhat ghettoized, resisted or overlooked by many who consider women's history a lesser, didactic, even outdated endeavor. We who write the general histories seek to undermine that resistance by demonstrating that putting women into the history of Russia changes the way we understand the past of all the people of that great nation, women as well as men. Two historians, Barbara Alpern Engel and Natalia Pushkareva, have already done much in their surveys of the history of women in Russia to advance this enlightenment. I hope to add to what they have accomplished.[2]

The Focus of the Study

To that end, each chapter begins with a survey of the political and economic history of the period under examination. Each then poses two questions: What did women do in this time, and what difference did they make? Uncovering what they did requires telling the story of their history as a gender. How did gender values and practices structure their lives, how did they react to these influences, and how did both their reactions and the gender arrangements change over time? Women's beliefs, their roles in their families, their work outside the home, their authority within their families and communities, and the variations in all of these produced by differences in age, ethnicity, marital status, religion, and social rank will occupy much of our attention. Each chapter will also highlight both politically significant women, such as Catherine the Great, and less prestigious individuals whose lives illustrate important themes. Sidebars include pictures and excerpts from primary sources about those women.

It is possible to undertake such a study now because historians and literary scholars have produced so much fine work on the history of women in Russia over the last several decades. Some of these were Soviet scholars, many were British and American, and now they are being joined by a new generation of Eastern and Western Europeans. Synthesizing their findings is a chief undertaking of this book. Included will be citations to English collections of translated primary documents and to translations of my own that bring the voices of the people studied into their own history. The last chapter relies as well on interviews with six Belarusian women, friends and acquaintances of mine whose insights enhanced my understanding of the years since 1991.

This is not a history of gender. Definitions of masculinity and femininity and the norms that followed from those definitions are important subjects in what follows, but this book does not treat women's history as a lens through which to see something else, such as gender. Nor is it a modern variant on the oft-crooned lament about how difficult the lives of women have been across the ages, though it does document the manifold ways in which patriarchal institutions and the hardships of Russian history affected women. Instead it highlights women's agency. All the subordinated people of the past must be approached this way, if their lives are to be understood and the historical significance of those lives is to be appreciated.

Changing the Narrative

Bringing women to the forefront changes the established narrative of Russia's political, economic, and social history. Political history has been the dominant member of that triad, because the government has played a particularly important part in Russian history, and because historians in the European world are heirs to a historiographical tradition that viewed politics as the driver of history. This book puts women into the political narrative of Russian history by discussing their roles in elite politics and in mass movements and highlighting the contributions of important individuals. Tracing women's participation in politics, which was limited by custom and law and yet was often consequential, yields a more nuanced view of political realities than the top-down, male-centered perspective that traditional historiography gives us.

Women's history also teaches that one of the great political differences between Russia and the rest of Europe was the attempts by rulers, from Peter the Great onward, to engineer gender change in Russia. This intervention and public responses to it led in the later nineteenth century to an upsurge of political and social activism by women. Their activism drove revolutionary change forward before and during the Revolution and resulted in the implementation of a sweeping program of political, economic, and social emancipation for women in the 1920s. Soviet policies and women's responses to them in turn made possible the massive industrialization drives of the 1930s and the successful mobilization of the nation in World War II.

Women's history also sheds light on the history of the Russian Empire. Although scholars have studied the ways non-Russian women experienced conquest and colonization, their findings have not much affected the narrative of the colonial process, most of which still consists of discussions of government policy and of the responses of the male leaders of the conquered peoples. In fact, women mattered. Native women in Siberia mediated between their own people and the conquerors, resisting the colonizers in some cases, assisting them in others. Across the Caucasus, Central Asia, and Siberia, women kept ethnic and religious traditions alive. Women were also among the colonizers from the nineteenth century onward, sometimes representing the imperial power, as the wives of governors and communist officials did, sometimes working to improve the lives of native women, as did teachers and physicians, all the while transmitting the gender values of the imperial power. The people of the time recognized the importance of women to colonial interactions; historians have undervalued it.

The prevailing understanding of Russia's economic history is also altered if one puts women in, for then the dependence of the economy on their work becomes a central theme. Throughout Russian history, women's participation in subsistence agriculture was crucial to peasant survival, and therefore to national survival. When industrialization began, they flocked to the factories in greater numbers than did women elsewhere in Europe. Because gender assumptions structured their involvement, women's participation differed from that of men, as did the effects of industrialization on them. The presence of so many women in the paid-labor force had major economic and political consequences, for it affected Bolshevik thinking before the Revolution and Soviet policies thereafter.

Women have been given greater consideration in social history than in other fields, because social history is about daily life and the mores and norms that shape it. Scholars have long recognized the importance of women to these topics, and so women are often included in discussions of Russia's social history. The patriarchal character of gender values is usually commented on as well. Daily life and patriarchy are central themes in this book too. Here they will be considered relevant not just to family and community life, and hence to social history, but also, as the above paragraphs suggest, to political and economic developments. For gender values and norms pervade all human societies, ordering public as well as private worlds. And they have changed across time. So watching the development of gender ideas in Russia and comparing them to gender ideas elsewhere in Europe will illuminate far more than the quotidian. It will make the politics and the economics make more sense as well.

The European Context and Russian Particularities

This book will also fit the history of women in Russia into European women's history. For that is where it belongs. The dominant culture across the centuries was Slavic and Christian, as were most of the people, and their gender values and customs were very similar to those of other Europeans. The significant differences arose from Russia's geography and climate, its people's take on pan-European gender values and norms, its autocratic politics, and its relationship to the rest of the continent.

Russia began on Europe's easternmost frontier, in lands that were cold, vast, and difficult to farm. Frequent conflict among warriors competing for power and territory made life still more precarious. The Russian elite eventually overcame its fractiousness and constructed a centralized government, but it did little thereafter to help the peasants prosper. These enduring realities—a demanding natural environment, a self-aggrandizing ruling class, and a mass of people mired in hardship—meant that, until well into the twentieth century, most women had few opportunities to improve their circumstances.

One of the greatest ironies of Russian history is the fact that the autocratic governments were a major force in progressive changes for women. Beginning in the late seventeenth century, Russia's rulers attempted to alter gender norms, because they believed that in order to make their nation a leading power in Europe, they had to modernize it, and that in turn required weakening patriarchal controls on men and women. To this end, Peter the Great and the tsars who succeeded him greatly expanded education for noble and middle-class girls and permitted women to enter the paid-labor force. Their communist successors proclaimed that women were men's equals and opened up schools and jobs to women from the lower classes. Because so many of Russia's rulers believed that changing women's lot was essential to reform, and because so many educated people, among them many women, pushed the rulers to permit even more change, change, when it came, was extraordinarily rapid and substantial.

Central to that transformation were the interactions between Russia and the rest of Europe. This will be yet another of the major themes of this book. It is already a major one in Russian history, but usually attention is paid to the ways in which Western influence affected Russia's political, economic, and intellectual development. Women's history was also hugely impacted, as Western notions about femininity, domesticity, and women's liberation from patriarchy flowed in, to be rejected, adapted, and fought over by rulers, revolutionaries, peasants, and urban folk. Women's history also contains one of the most important instances of Russian influence flowing outward, for in the twentieth century, Soviet gender values and the government's program of women's emancipation influenced communists, socialists, and feminists around the world.

Conclusions

This book will sum up the scholarship on the history of women in Russia. It will explain the major developments in women's history and the effects of those developments on the history of the nation. It will sketch the lived experiences of women across the generations. It will identify individuals of particular significance. And it will demonstrate how the behavior of individual women and great collectivities of them shaped the history of their land.

It would be impossible to create "a sweet little cameo version" of the history of Russia's women, for most of it is a story of people struggling with poverty brought on by a recalcitrant environment and exacerbated by a rapacious government. But it is also a story of endurance and achievement. In their millions over the centuries, the women of Russia helped build the cultures that survived the hardships. The bravest and luckiest women accomplished extraordinary things—promoted the conversion to Christianity, governed estates, created great art, rebelled against governments, established charities and professions, designed programs to liberate women, built the tanks that rolled into Berlin in 1945, and flew the planes that strafed the retreating Wermacht. Other women exploited their serfs, worked for the secret police, supported whatever status quo prevailed at the time, doted on their sons, and taught their daughters to suffer in silence. The history of all these women, in all its daunting complexity, is a tale worth telling.

NOTE ON DATES,
TRANSLITERATION, AND NAMES

I will adhere to standard practice on these matters, with a few adjustments to make this book more accessible to non-specialists.

Only in 1918 did Russia adopt the reforms in the calendar that had been undertaken in eighteenth-century Europe. Consequently, until that time, Russian dates were ten to twelve days behind those of the rest of Europe. I will use the Russian dates throughout.

In transliterating words from the Cyrillic to the English alphabet, I will employ the Library of Congress system, without the diacritical marks. The differences between that system and others account for occasional differences in spelling between words in the text and the same words in quotations and bibliographic references, e.g. "Baranskaia" (the Library of Congress version) and "Baranskaya" (a common alternative).

Russian names present the thorniest problem for a Russian historian writing in English for a general audience. I have chosen to modify the standard transliteration practices by eliminating the "ii" in the endings of such first names as Mariia. I have kept the "ii" in last names, because doing so distinguishes Russian from Polish and other Slavic surnames. I have also omitted the patronymic middle names that are an integral part of Russian names but are confusing to non-Russians. Finally, I use common anglicizations of the names of famous people, e.g., Catherine II, not Ekaterina.

✛　✛　✛　✛　✛

GLOSSARY

Boyar (feminine: *boyarina*)—the title of members of the elite families that ranked just below royalty from Rus to Muscovite times.

Bolshevik Party—the branch of the Russian Social Democratic Labor Party that seized power in 1917. It adopted the name Communist Party in 1918.

Commune—the organization headed by male heads of household that existed in some Russian peasant villages from Muscovite times through the 1930s. It allocated some farming tasks and handled relations with landlords and government officials.

Duma—(1) city assemblies modeled on the *zemstva,* established in 1870; (2) the national legislature established in 1906 and abolished in 1917; (3) the lower house of the Russian legislature established in 1993.

NKVD—People's Commissariat of Internal Affairs (Narodnyi Komissariat Vnutrennikh Del), the national police agency of the Stalin period.

Politburo—the committee comprising the top leaders of the Communist Party.

Populists—the socialists of the 1870s and 1880s.

Russian Social Democratic Labor Party (Social Democrats)—the Marxist party, organized in the 1890s, that split in the early twentieth century into the Bolshevik and Menshevik factions.

Socialist Revolutionary Party—a party with roots in the populist movement, set up shortly after 1900.

Soviet—(1) in 1905, one of the committees organized in St. Petersburg and other cities to represent the workers and coordinate general strikes; (2) in 1917, one of the elected organizations representing workers and soldiers; (3) from 1918, one of the elected bodies that made up the legislatures of the Soviet government.

Union of Soviet Socialist Republics—the political unit created in 1924 that comprised the republics of Armenia, Azerbaijan, Belorussia, Estonia, Georgia, Kazakhstan, Kyrgyzstan, Latvia, Lithuania, Moldova, Russia, Tajikistan, Turkmenistan, Ukraine, and Uzbekistan.

Zemstvo—an elected assembly, created in the 1860s, composed mostly of nobles and charged with organizing and financing local economic development and social services.

List of Royal Titles (in chronological order)

Prince, princess (in Russian, *kniaz, kniaginia*)—titles held by the ruling families of the Kievan and Appanage periods. The titles continued to be used in later centuries to denote families of ancient pedigree.

Tsar, tsaritsa, tsarevny—in Muscovy and thereafter, the ruler, his wife, and his daughters.

Emperor, empress—titles adopted by Peter I and his successor, who kept the title "tsar," but relegated it to a lesser position, after "emperor" and "autocrat."

Grand duchess, grand duke—the children of an emperor and the wives of a grand duke.

A SKETCH OF THE
HISTORIOGRAPHY

This book is based upon a historiography more than 150 years old. It seems appropriate, therefore, to provide a brief introduction to the development of that historiography. A few examples from the bibliography of each stage in the process will be identified in the footnotes. Those seeking to explore further should begin with Livezeanu et al.'s authoritative *Women and Gender in Central and Eastern Europe, Russia, and Eurasia.* They will also find many useful links on the website for the Association for Women in Slavic Studies, http://www.awss.org.

The study of women's history emerged from the discussion of the woman question in nineteenth-century Russia and developed in tandem with that discussion. As did feminists and their supporters elsewhere, Russian intellectuals produced lectures, articles, and books that analyzed patriarchy. They also celebrated independent women of the past and present. This scholarship stressed Russia's backwardness, pointing to the strictures of *The Domostroi,* the traditionalism of the peasantry, the conservatism of the nobility and the autocracy, and the doleful lot of long-suffering women. When Marxists weighed in in the early twentieth century, they emphasized the economic origins of women's oppression.[1]

Soviet scholars from the 1920s through the 1980s developed the Marxist interpretation into a tale of tsarist oppression and Soviet emancipation. They wrote about the hardships endured by poor women, particularly factory workers, before the Revolution. They chronicled the achievements of outstanding women before and after 1917, and they documented the accomplishments of the Soviet period. Much of this scholarship was supported by solid research into women's education, work, and family lives across the Soviet Union.[2]

The emergence of second-wave feminism in the 1960s increased the interest in women's history among Western European and North American historians. Simultaneously, the Cold War was increasing interest in Russian history. Some of the Russianists discovered that the history of women in Russia was blessed with fascinating individuals and source material. The result was the development of a community of scholars in the United States and the UK who began to publish their findings in the 1970s. Influenced by Cold War theories of totalitarianism and by the Russian and Soviet historiography on women, they stressed the linked oppressions of patriarchy and autocracy in the imperial and Soviet periods. They emphasized as well the open-mindedness of the intelligentsia and paid particular attention to the emancipated women of the pre-revolutionary period. They shared with historians of women in other cultures the goals of documenting women's situation in the past and recovering the stories of significant women absent from mainstream historiography.[3]

As the scholarship on the history of women in Russia developed, historians from across the European world weighed in on a broad range of topics. Social histories of women in the late nineteenth and early twentieth centuries provided sophisticated understandings of peasant and working-class cultures and of the functioning of gender values. The medieval and early imperial periods saw groundbreaking research into law, the role of elite women in politics and family life, witchcraft, and women's spirituality. Scholars also began to pay attention to non-Russian women within the empire. As a consequence, the early emphasis on oppression gave way to more nuanced interpretations of women's responses to their world and put the Russian experience into an international context. All of this work was informed by gender theory and post-modernist attention to discourse. It benefited as well from rapid development of the study of other fields of Russian history. It also brought women's history to the attention of specialists in those fields, so that women's history began to be integrated into the larger narrative of Russian history.[4]

Until the 1990s, historians of women in Russia in the Soviet Union and those working elsewhere had little contact with one another. The Western scholars read the work of the Soviet historians, and some of the Soviets read the Western works that were available in a few libraries. Foreign scholars doing research in Soviet archives got to know Soviet historians interested in women's history. Then the USSR came to an end and contacts between scholars expanded exponentially. Feminist historians across the former Soviet Union (FSU) established gender studies programs, often with the assistance of outside funding; began publishing their work; and by the early twenty-first century were training a new generation of historians of women. These people, most of them women, worked on late imperial topics, such as elite education and feminism, that had been considered suspect in the Soviet period. They took a more critical view of Soviet emancipation than their predecessors. They also adapted those methodological and theoretical approaches from Western scholarship that they found useful. The result was a developing dialogue between Western and FSU scholars that was very enlightening to both sides.[5]

There is still much to be done. The scholarship on the history of women in Russia is meager compared to that on subjects such as the Russian Revolution or the pre-emancipation peasantry. As a result, there are few historiographical debates as yet. Medievalists have discussed the pace at which women converted to Christianity and they have argued over whether changes in women's property rights in the Muscovite period enhanced or diminished the authority of elite women. No major controversies have yet emerged regarding the imperial period. Scholars east and west are presently holding a decorous discussion over revising the critique of the Soviet emancipation project to minimize the stress placed on government manipulation and pay more attention to the responses of ordinary people. These debates should multiply as the historiography continues to develop.

The integration of the scholarship's findings into the larger field of Russian and now post-Soviet history will continue as well. That is a development to which I hope this book, an attempt to synthesize the historiography to date, will contribute.

✛ ✛ ✛ ✛ ✛

A HISTORY OF
WOMEN IN RUSSIA

I

THE WOMEN OF
THE RUS

900–1462

In 950, two peoples at the far-eastern reaches of Europe were pooling their fortunes. They were the Rus, Scandinavians who had ventured south seeking riches, and the Slavs, farmers who had lived in the great expanses of steppe and forest for centuries. The Rus brought to this alliance their skills in warfare, trade, and manufacture; the Slavs provided food and furs. Off and on for decades the two groups made alliances and marriages that brought them into ever-closer cooperation. By the year 1000, Slavs and Scandinavians were merging into one people, whom history would call the Rus, after their swashbuckling leaders.

Most Rus women spent their lives working. In the countryside, they harvested the fields and forests. In the cities, they participated in family businesses. Among the ruling elite, they managed households. Women of all classes also married, had children, experienced youth's pleasures and hopes, and found ways to endure advancing old age. The Rus believed that men should rule women and that young women should obey their seniors. When women became seniors themselves, they required their daughters, daughters-in-law, and sons to honor and obey them. They also advised their menfolk, a custom that, among the elite, led to women becoming political advisers and, on a few occasions, regents.

Rus women's work, family lives, participation in their communities, and spirituality were similar to those of women elsewhere in Europe, because the gender values that structured those practices were pan-European. The differences in their history arose from their existence on Europe's far-eastern frontier. A powerful ruling elite and an omnipresent established church came to them later than they did to other Europeans. So for most of Rus history, the great majority of women were legally free farmers, living in small villages, moving to new lands at will, preserving their customs and their ancient faiths, and trying to stay out of the way of the warriors who lived to trade and fight.

The Kievan Period, Tenth Century to 1240

POLITICS

Most Rus warriors were fair-skinned, blue-eyed, and bearded, like their Viking cousins. In leather armor and pointed helmets, they navigated the broad rivers of their adopted homeland, pursuing a profitable trade in furs, honey, slaves, Persian silver, and fine manufactured goods from Byzantium. They made their capital at Kiev on the Dniepr River in today's Ukraine and hailed the prince who ruled that city as their paramount leader. Though loosely organized, the Rus dominated the commerce of their region and even sent periodic delegations to Constantinople, the sophisticated capital of the Byzantine Empire, far to the south across the Black Sea.

The rules of Rus society were patriarchal. Family affiliations, titles, and property descended through male kin and men held all public offices, secular and religious. Age and social rank figured in the making of gender hierarchies, as they do universally, and so senior men had power over the junior men in their families as well as over all the men who ranked below them in the larger society. Older women had considerable authority over younger female kin and were supposed to receive the respect and attention of their sons and husbands. Widows may have been allowed more autonomy than married women; that was the case elsewhere in Europe and can be documented in later periods of Russian history. Elite women also commanded the obedience of the servants and slaves, male and female, who worked for them. This granting of power according to a woman's age and her status in her family's and society's hierarchy extended to the lower-ranking members of Rus society as well. It would endure throughout subsequent centuries in Russia and across Europe.

Prominent among the early rulers of Kiev were Olga (c. 915–c. 969), a princess who served as regent for her son, and her grandson Vladimir I (ruled 980–1015), later canonized for converting the Rus to Christianity. Vladimir also expanded his home city and increased his control over the hinterland that supplied him with food and trade goods. His successor Iaroslav (1018–54) promoted Christianity, issued the first written law code, and sponsored still more building in Kiev.

Iaroslav did not establish a method of passing power peacefully from one generation to the next. The Rus practiced lateral succession—that is, brothers could claim the title of a deceased brother, and only after all brotherly claims were exhausted did sons inherit. Since princely families were large, this custom often led to prolonged warfare. Shortly before he died, Iaroslav commanded his sons and brothers to promise to abide by a scheme he had devised, one that ranked Rus cities in a hierarchy from Kiev down, and dispersed them as dependencies to brothers and then their sons in order of seniority by birth. His kin duly swore, then broke their oaths after his death. Iaroslav and Vladimir before him had come to power through fratricidal war, and their successors did so as well.

Such violence was common in European monarchies in the medieval period, and primogeniture, the right of the first-born son to inherit his father's title and landed estates, even where securely established, did not guarantee peaceful succession. The special peril faced by the Rus was the presence nearby of nomadic tribes, such as the Pechenegs and Polovotsy, which were eager to take advantage of Rus disunity. Warfare among princes usually led to warfare with the surrounding peoples, disruption of trade, and the pillaging of Rus cities.

And yet, despite periodic eruptions of civil war in the eleventh and twelfth centuries, the Rus population grew and spread across a sprawling territory. This expansion testified to the people's success in wresting a living from the land and trading with their neighbors, but it also exacerbated tensions that plagued the warrior class. As families grew, claims to titles multiplied. Princely families that had settled in towns far from Kiev developed local ties and consequently felt less loyalty to the center. Even politically skilled princes, who managed to rally their cousins' support for defense and trade, could not reverse the consequences of the elite's proliferation and dispersal. By the early thirteenth century, therefore, political bonds between the rulers were growing dangerously weak.

THE LIVES OF WOMEN IN THE COUNTRYSIDE

The Slavic farmers on whom the warriors depended for food and taxes lived in small, stockaded villages scattered across the rolling grasslands of Ukraine and through the forests of today's Belarus and western Russia. These country folk, like peasants elsewhere in Europe, were self-sufficient, feeding themselves by hunting, fishing, keeping livestock, gathering wild foods, and growing grains and vegetables. They made their clothes of flax, wool, and fur, their houses of wood, and their tools and weapons of wood and metal. To clear land for cultivation, they chopped down bushes and trees, burned the brush, and spread the resulting ash to enrich the soil. Then they planted seeds in shallow holes dug in the cleared land. This slash-and-burn agriculture quickly exhausted the soil's fertility, but there was so much land that when the productivity of one field declined, the farmers could move on to another.

The rural folk of the Rus confederation were not serfs, as were so many peasants in Western Europe at the time. Instead, they were free to run their own lives, so long as they paid their taxes. They could even dodge that obligation by relocating to places beyond the reach of the warriors. There were no local landlords, adjudicating disputes and managing agriculture, as in Western Europe, because Rus warriors, true to their Viking roots, spent most of their time at war or on trading expeditions. The farmers only saw them or their representatives once a year or so, when they came around to collect taxes, paid mostly in furs and honey. The rest of the time the men in armor left the peasants alone.

The peasants' relationship to the church was similarly remote, which was another major difference from the situation in Western and Central Europe. The Rus warrior elite began converting to Christianity in the eleventh century, but because the rulers had so little contact with the farmers and because their territory was so immense, it took centuries for the clergy, which worked under warrior sponsorship and with warrior funding, to extend their influence into rural areas. So the peasants kept on worshipping their nature gods and goddesses and lived free of church supervision for most of the Rus period. The church's ability to enforce its will on the countryside would remain weak for centuries thereafter.

Women in the countryside spent most of their time producing the food and clothing that sustained their families. Dressed in homespun linen and wool, they cared for small livestock, grew vegetables, gleaned the fields after the men had reaped the grain, and gathered mushrooms, berries, medicinal plants, and wood for fuel. In their smoky cabins (chimneys were not common until much later), they made clothes, prepared food, and tended babies and young children. Midwives attended births, casting spells to keep evil spirits at bay and welcoming newborns into the world with potions, amulets, and lullabies. Men did the heaviest work—constructing tools and houses, chopping down trees and chopping up firewood, digging wells, plowing, and caring for cattle and horses. This division of labor, an ancient one among the tribes of Europe, was built on the differences in physical strength between men and women and on the fact that women spent much of their adult life pregnant or nursing. By Rus times, it was seen as the natural way of things across Europe. Plowing was men's work, gleaning women's.

THE LIVES OF WOMEN IN THE CITIES

The cities of the Rus confederation boomed in the late eleventh and early twelfth centuries. Many of them were little more than trading posts, but others, such as Kiev and Novgorod, grew into thriving communities graced by substantial churches and palaces. Historians have estimated the population of Kiev at the end of the twelfth century at forty or fifty thousand, which was roughly the size of Paris or London at the same time.[1] In its crowded neighborhoods, artisans crafted weapons and tools, jewelry, enamelware, pottery, glass, and wooden goods. Merchants distributed all this, as well as luxury products brought from Byzantine and Arab lands. Some townspeople, women as well as men, could read, write, and do arithmetic, skills they used in managing their financial affairs. At the bottom of urban society, mostly working for the rich, were slaves, who had come into bondage by being captured in war.

As was common elsewhere in Europe during the medieval period, Rus cities were self-governing, with their own local leaders, town meetings, and common law. When Kievan princes began to exert more control in the eleventh century, townspeople zealously defended their rights. Contemporary chronicles refer to abusive princes being overthrown and even lynched by angry crowds.

MERCHANT WOMEN

The women of the middle ranks of town society supervised housework, shopped, kept financial records, and conferred with their husbands on the management of the family business, as merchant women did elsewhere in Europe. Some owned property in their own names and lent and borrowed money. Their clothes may have been similar in design to those of rural folk, but rich merchant women could afford much finer fabrics, including silk brought in by traders. They also bought imported and locally made jewelry, especially intricately carved combs, silver brooches, necklaces, and gold and silver bracelets and rings. Less affluent women dressed more plainly and lived more simply, selling goods in the markets and working as artisans. Spinning was considered women's work among the Rus as elsewhere in Europe. Some surviving spindles have women's names carved on them.[2]

WOMEN OF THE RULING CLASS

The women of the Rus warrior elite had much in common with lower-ranking women. They too married men of their parents' choosing, for marriage was considered an alliance between families, not a private matter to be decided by the couple. Elite and poor women were expected to be dutiful wives who bore healthy children and worked to support their families' well-being. The women of the warrior class had more luxuries and status than poorer women, of course, and some additional obligations. They were supposed to set pious examples for their communities and to participate in their families' jockeying for power and wealth, that is, in politics.

Elite women's most passive involvement in politics was entering into the arranged marriages that helped establish and maintain good relations between powerful families. Daughters of the princes of Kiev became the brides of foreign kings, which attests to the fact that royalty abroad regarded Rus princes as their equals—and their daughters, therefore, as suitable consorts. Four of the granddaughters of Vladimir Monomakh (ruled 1113–25) married non-Rus princes: Malfrid became queen of Norway, Evfrosinia queen of Hungary, and Ingeborg queen of Denmark, and Dobrodeia married the nephew of the Byzantine emperor.

Elite women were also actively engaged in their families' affairs. This was not unusual in medieval Europe, where politics took place within families and clans. The female relatives of Rus warriors were expected to advise their male kin, and that obligation entailed staying on top of political developments so as to inform brothers, husbands, or fathers of impending treacheries. Indeed, in that turbulent age it might mean death to discount the value of a wife's sharp eyes and attentive ears.[3]

Among the Rus, as among other Scandinavian and Germanic peoples, women were also valued for their peacemaking skills. The *Primary Chronicle,* a history of the Kievan princes written by monks in the twelfth century, tells of a princess trying to mediate between her warring sons. Identified only as Vsevolod's widow, she was the mother of Vladimir Monomakh and grandmother of those four princesses who married foreign royals. In 1097, when her sons and their cousins were vying for the throne at Kiev, she went, with the head of the church, the metropolitan, to urge Vladimir to make peace. "We beseech you, oh Prince, and your brethren not to ruin the land of Rus," she pleaded. Vladimir burst into tears and agreed. "Thus he obeyed her as he was bound to obey his mother," the chronicler intones. She returned to Kiev to beg Vladimir's cousin Sviatopolk, the reigning prince, to reconcile with his enemies. Sadly, her motherly appeals did not end the dispute.[4]

Princesses could not become rulers in their own right. This was the general practice across Europe, although the feudalism of the West did enable a few women who inherited fiefdoms to exercise considerable power. Far more common among the Rus and other Europeans was the custom of widows serving as regents for their minor children or taking up their husbands' administrative duties when the men were away. Seals bearing the names of such Rus women have been unearthed in archaeological digs. We do not know how many regents or temporary administrators there were, but we can identify the one whose political career earned her the greatest fame.

✣ ✣ ✣ *OLGA (c. 915–c. 969)* ✣ ✣ ✣

Olga, the widow of Prince Igor of Kiev, was regent to her son Sviatoslav from 945 to the late 950s or early 960s. She is best remembered for the murderous revenge she took on the Derevlians, perennial enemies of the Rus, after they had defeated and beheaded her husband. The *Primary Chronicle* recounts that the victorious Derevlians proposed to Olga that she marry their prince and thus unite the two warring peoples. It was an offer they expected her, a vulnerable woman, to accept. This proved to be a fatal misunderstanding of her character. Olga buried alive the first group of Derevlian ambassadors who came to arrange the marriage. Then, on the pretext of accepting their offer, she went to the Derevlians' capital, camped outside the city walls, hosted a great feast, and finished the celebration by massacring her drunken guests. She then laid siege to their city. When the townspeople sued for peace, Olga directed each household to give her an offering of three pigeons and three sparrows. They sent them to her, and she ordered her soldiers to tie matches to the birds' feet and light them. Released, the terrified creatures took their flaming burdens home and set the city afire. Thus did Olga avenge Igor and defend the Rus lands from the Derevlians.

This bloody tale is probably a myth. Scandinavian folklore delights in stories of widows exacting hideous revenge. The monk who wrote about Olga's life in *The Primary Chronicle* almost two centuries after her death probably told the story to illustrate her cleverness and courage, and her willingness to use those talents in defense of her people's independence. These were the themes of the rest of his account of her life, which is more solidly grounded in the historical record. He writes about her conversion to Christianity, which is confirmed by Byzantine sources, and her wisdom as a ruler. Olga served as regent for her son for more than a decade, during which time she increased government revenues, improved relations with other princely families, and strengthened ties to Byzantium. The princess

A modern copy of an ancient icon depicting St. Olga.
http://it.wikipedia.org/wiki/File:Helga_Olga.jpg.
Accessed June 27, 2011.

OLGA

The *Primary Chronicle* provides the following account of Olga's conversion:

"Olga went to Greece [Byzantium] and arrived at Tsargrad [Constantinople]. The reigning Emperor was named Constantine, son of Leo. Olga came before him, and when he saw that she was very fair of countenance and wise as well, the Emperor wondered at her intellect. He conversed with her and remarked that she was worthy to reign with him in his city. . . .

When Olga was enlightened, she rejoiced in soul and body. The Patriarch [head of the Church], who instructed her in the faith, said to her, 'Blessed art thou among the women of Rus, for thou hast loved the light and quit the darkness. The sons of Rus shall bless thee to the last generation of thy descendants.' He taught her the doctrine of the Church, and instructed her in prayer and fasting, in almsgiving, and in the maintenance of chastity. She bowed her head, and like a sponge absorbing water, she eagerly drank in his teachings."

SOURCE: SAMUEL HAZARD CROSS AND OLGERD P. SHERBOWITZ-WETZOR, TRANS. AND EDS., *THE RUSSIAN PRIMARY CHRONICLE, LAURENTIAN TEXT* (CAMBRIDGE, MASS.: MEDIAEVAL ACADEMY OF AMERICA, 1973), 82.

also led a delegation of priests and male and female advisers to Constantinople, where she negotiated trade agreements with the emperor and was baptized, with the emperor standing up for her as godfather.[5]

When her son reached his majority, Olga became a powerful royal mother. During Sviatoslav's incessant wars, she governed Kiev and oversaw the rearing of her grandchildren, among them the future Vladimir I. The *Chronicle* portrays Olga as begging her son to convert to Christianity, which he refused to do on the grounds that his men scorned the faith as a woman's religion. "He did not know that whoever does not obey his mother shall come to distress," the chronicler declares.[6] Sviatoslav, ever the valiant and enthusiastic warrior, was killed in combat sometime after Olga's death. Vladimir, who grew up under his grandmother's supervision, did convert, and he decreed that all the Rus should become Christians too.

CHRISTIANITY

Many elite Rus women were converting to Christianity in the tenth century, and probably many of them persuaded their male relatives to be baptized. Elite women across Europe had played this role in the spread of Christianity since Roman times. In the centuries after Olga's death, the new faith slowly spread among the elite, then moved out into the countryside, merging with the pagan beliefs the Rus had inherited from their ancestors. As it became a part of Rus culture, Christianity brought new institutions into women's lives and shaped the gender values of their world.

Vladimir's conversion officially affiliated the Rus with the eastern branch of Christianity. When he converted, disagreements between the church authorities in Constantinople and those in Rome were dividing Christendom into a Catholic West and Orthodox East. The Catholics and the Orthodox agreed on the basic articles of the faith, but differed on a few theological issues, as well as on matters of church organization. These differences would affect the development of Christianity among the Rus, and the hostility between Catholicism and Orthodoxy would also sour the relations between Catholic Europe and the Rus and their successors, the Muscovites.

From Olga's time onward, elite women figured prominently among the converts. They became generous patrons, donating money to build churches and monasteries and to purchase precious liturgical objects such as chalices. Some high-born women also participated, as did men of their rank, in the selection of church officials. A twelfth-century princess, Verxoslava, wrote to the Metropolitan Simon, the head of the Rus church, "that she would like [Polikarp] appointed bishop . . . 'even if I have to spend a thousand pieces of silver'" to get the prelate to agree. Simon quoted Verxo-slava in a letter he wrote to Polikarp. He frankly told the latter that he had refused the princess's request because Polikarp was too ambitious. Simon did not, however, condemn Verxoslava for making the nomination. Rath-er, he considered her efforts to be part of the normal scheme of things.[7]

Not content to influence the church from the outside, women entered it as well. Hundreds, perhaps thousands became nuns in the first few cen-turies after conversion. The Rus believed it desirable for all their daughters to marry, and therefore they did not enroll young girls in convents, as did the western Christians. Instead, most Rus nuns took up the religious life as middle-aged widows. Because Rus monasticism followed the Eastern Orthodox model in being decentralized, and because the Rus elite did not practice feudalism, which granted fiefs to monastic communities, large and powerful convents led by abbesses did not develop in the Rus lands. Rather, Rus nuns lived in small compounds and were supervised by monks from nearby monasteries.

Women were also present in the Rus church as priest's wives. Ortho-dox priests were required to marry, for church authorities believed that having wives would help priests control their sexual urges.[8] By the end of the Rus era, there were priestly families living and working in some vil-lages, where there was little to distinguish the wives officially from other women. They had no liturgical role. Perhaps they held a slightly higher status in the community of village women by virtue of being married to priests.

As Christianity spread, it absorbed some of the older religious ideas of the Rus in a blending process known as syncretism. This merger, often encouraged by Christian missionaries, took place all over Europe as people converted, and among the Rus, as elsewhere, it went on for centuries. In Kiev, Vladimir ordered statues of Perun, the sky god who spoke in thun-der, thrown into the rivers; the Rus later attributed thunder to the Old Testament prophet Elijah. Across Europe, people did the same, transfer-ring legends of dragon-killing warriors to a mythic saint named George, for example. The Rus kept on wearing amulets to repel evil spirits too, only now the amulets were crosses or the likenesses of saints.

An important part of this syncretism was the blending of Rus and Christian gender ideas. Identifying Christian influences on pre-existing Rus beliefs is difficult, because Christian monks wrote the historical documents. That said, there is some evidence that Christianity may have stressed women's sinfulness more than did pre-Christian Rus patriarchy. Orthodox and Catholic churches taught that women were prone to the sin of Eve—that is, that they readily succumbed to temptations, particularly sexual ones, and then seduced men to sin also. Scholars now debate whether Catholicism obsessed more about Eve's fall than did Orthodoxy. What is clear is that Rus monks, like their Western counterparts, excoriated women for leading men astray. In an essay on female vice and virtue written in the eleventh century, an anonymous monk declared, "Small is all wickedness compared to the wickedness of a woman; may a sinner's lot befall her. A wicked woman is a wound to the heart. From woman is the beginning of sin, and because of her we all die."[9]

Christianity paired these wailings about women's wickedness with instructions to women on how to be good. The monk quoted above also wrote, "A virtuous and wise wife is a blessed lot and will be given as a portion to those who fear the Lord." Women who chose sin, often defined as sexual licentiousness and/or rebellion against authority, were evil, dangerous, and far too numerous, he declared, but those who practiced virtue, particularly chastity and service to their husbands, were to be treasured. The best women of all—loving mothers—should be venerated and obeyed. Indeed, there was persistent emphasis throughout Rus writings on the obligation to revere mothers. "Give honor to your mother," the monk advised, "and do her all good so that with joy you will see the Lord and rejoice in this forever."[10]

Closely allied to this veneration was praise of the saints and the Virgin Mary. The Virgin, the most important of the female spirits, was the perfect mother, always merciful, forgiving, long-suffering, gentle, and protective. The Rus came to see her as a powerful figure, ever willing to intercede for her children with the deity. Over the centuries, Mary and the female saints became central to women's faith in Russia, as they were across Europe. There were fewer female saints in the Rus pantheon than in Western Christendom, but those women that were recognized for their sanctity made women feel welcome in the faith and gave a focus to their worship. Their example also reminded the Rus and their descendants that women, despite their frailties, were just as capable as men of receiving the gifts of God's grace and eternal life.

Christianity may also have appealed to women in Rus lands and across Europe because it enjoined men and women to cultivate virtues that were seen as more feminine than masculine. The church declared that both sexes should be pious, kind, selfless, dutiful, contemptuous of worldly riches and ambitions, and non-violent. This meekness did not appeal to the military men who were Europe's political leaders. From Roman times onward, they denounced the faith as a religion for women and cowardly men. Sviatoslav was typical of the warriors in thinking that conversion would make him seem effeminate. In response, the church, ever adept at fashioning compromises to win converts, came up with a set of masculine values tailored for the warriors. The Christian soldier, priests declared, could and should be a ferocious fighter, hunter, and leader of men. But when he came home to his family, he should put away his weapons and his warrior swagger and become a dutiful husband and father, a defender of the poor and weak, a generous patron of the church, and, perhaps above all, the humble servant of all those men, clerical as well as lay, who had power over him. These were the values preached by the Orthodox missionaries who converted the Rus; Vladimir found them persuasive. There was always and everywhere a good deal of space between the ideal and the reality of warrior behavior, but the priests were at least preaching a kinder, gentler masculinity.

LAW

The Rus also adopted Byzantium's legal system and thereby laid a foundation for Russian law that would endure until the 1917 Revolution. The law codes, drawn up by monks working for the princes, defined women's property and inheritance rights as well as men's, set the penalties for crimes against women, and regulated women's access to the courts. The foundational principle of these codes was patriarchal: senior men should rule their families justly and should care for and protect their dependents.

Rus authorities followed the European custom of dividing the laws into two general categories: secular, which included property and criminal law and fell under the jurisdiction of the princes; and ecclesiastical, which included regulation of the clergy, marriage (which was a religious sacrament), sexual behavior, and religious conformity, and was controlled by the church. Some Rus laws that addressed women were more liberal than the laws of other Europeans; some were stricter. Overall, the differences are less significant than the similarities. Unfortunately, the records of Rus courts have not survived, so we know very little about how laws were applied in specific cases. The courts probably concentrated on disputes among city dwellers and their reach into the countryside was probably confined to areas around the cities.

Women's property and inheritance rights were defined in the secular codes. The lawmakers worked with two guiding principles: men were to own most property and women were to be provided for. The codes they drafted required that women receive dowries, which would remain their property after they married, rather than being folded into the marital family's property, as was common in contemporary England and elsewhere. They also stipulated that sons were to inherit the lion's share of their families' holdings. Should a father not will anything to his daughter, her brothers were obliged to provide her a dowry. For their part, husbands were enjoined to leave their wives enough moveable property—precious objects, money, clothing, livestock, tools—and the income from sufficient land to support them for the rest of their lives. They could give them whatever else beyond the minimum that they chose. Widows possessed some discretionary power to determine which of the male heirs would inherit the family patrimony. These laws, which were very similar to those of other Scandinavian and Germanic peoples, were more restrictive than Byzantine rules, which granted sons and daughters equal inheritance rights, and which set definite percentages regarding the inheritances of widows. On the other hand, Rus law compared favorably with that of such Western European cities as Avignon, where daughters were banned from inheriting anything.[11]

The church's marriage laws followed the same principles of asserting the power of fathers and husbands and requiring that that power be limited by regard for the welfare of wives and children. To that end, the law charged parents to obtain the consent of their children to the marriage partners they had chosen for them. This was an improvement over Rus common law and that of other Scandinavians, which did not have such a requirement.[12] Parents who forced their daughters or sons to marry against their will were subject to fines. If a young woman did herself bodily harm rather than submit, the fine was substantial. (Rus criminal law followed the Scandinavian practice of fining wrongdoers rather than imprisoning them.)

Once married, the Rus were to stay that way, for the Orthodox church considered monogamy a commandment from God. Concubinage, common before conversion, was outlawed and remarriage after the death of a spouse was frowned upon. Husbands could request divorces from the church if their wives had committed sexual indiscretions, whereas wives could only petition on grounds that their husbands had done them great injury or attempted to impoverish them. Adulterous husbands were liable for fines. These were also the general principles of Catholic marriage law, but the Western church was less insistent on the "till-death-do-us-part" requirement. Catholic courts would grant annulments if they found that parents had coerced their children into marriage, if the husband was impotent, if the couple were close relatives, or if either partner had another spouse. Catholic law also occasionally permitted legal separation, as Rus law did not, and took a less censorious attitude toward remarriage than did Orthodox authorities, the Rus included.[13]

Rus criminal law mentions women rarely, perhaps because the drafters of the codes assumed that most crimes would be committed by men and perhaps also because female lawbreakers were customarily punished by their male relatives. The jurists did consider crimes against women serious offenses; the first two articles of Prince Iaroslav's *Church Statute* concerned rape and the abduction of a woman by a man. These crimes were addressed also in the secular codes because they were considered crimes of violence as well as sexual offenses. A man found guilty of sexual assault had to pay a fine. There were Europeans, such as those in the Germanic lands and Iberia, who imposed physical punishments for rape, including execution; many others, including the English and French, did as the Rus and levied monetary penalties. The fines varied with the rank of the rape victim. A man who attacked the wife or daughter of a *boyar* (a warrior just below the prince in the social hierarchy) owed the substantial sum of five gold *grivnas* to the victim, and the same to the bishop. The lower-ranking the woman, the lower was the fine.

It is noteworthy that Rus rape statutes required that the fine be paid to the woman herself, rather than to her family, as was common elsewhere. Rus jurists believed that the victim was the most injured party in a rape, for she had suffered great damage to her reputation in addition to psychological and possibly physical trauma. This view grew out of the censorious attitude the Rus took toward sexual indiscretions by women. So important was it to them that a woman be known as virtuous that they considered spreading tales that a woman was promiscuous to be as grave an offense as raping her. So they leveled the same fines for slander as for rape. This concern about reputation and the provision for innocent women to receive restitution themselves were not common across Europe. They would be preserved in the revisions of the Rus law codes for hundreds of years.

The Appanage Period, 1240–1462

POLITICS

In 1237, thousands of Mongol cavalrymen, clad in leather armor and riding small, sturdy horses, trotted onto Rus territory. They had come to stay; their wives, children, slaves, extra horses, and flocks trundled along behind them. Three years later the Mongols had conquered all the princes. Rape was a weapon in their arsenal, as it has been in the arsenals of so many armies; tens of thousands of Rus women probably fell victim to their assaults. Serapion, a thirteenth-century bishop, summed up the disaster when he wrote, "There fell upon us a merciless people who devastated our land, took entire cities off to captivity, destroyed our holy churches, put our fathers and brothers to death, and defiled our mothers and sisters."[14] The Mongols had already cut a swath of conquest from China through Central Asia, but the Rus did not know this, and so they came to see their defeat by the rampaging infidels as God's punishment for their sins.

The Mongols, so brutal in conquest, proved to be tolerant overlords. As long as Rus rulers paid their taxes on time and performed occasional obeisance before the khan, the Mongol king, the Mongols mostly left the Rus rulers and people alone. Indeed, the Mongols who conquered the Rus did not even live among their subjects, as their cousins in China did. Instead, christening themselves "the Golden Horde," they settled in the grasslands along the Volga River, far to the south of the centers of Rus population. There they could pasture their enormous flocks and stay in touch with their people's extended trade networks. They got along amicably with the Orthodox church, despite their own conversion to Islam. Indeed, Mongol rulers practiced religious toleration throughout their vast empire. They did interfere in Rus politics by backing princes who were favorably disposed toward them, and this meddling had consequences for the history of the Rus, but it had little impact on Rus political institutions.

Those changed largely because of developments within the Rus polity that had started long before the conquest. As the Rus expanded across their huge territory in the Kievan period, regions far from the capital city came to contain princely families. Since every son of a prince was a prince, the list of claimants to titles and property kept growing. This was particularly true in the northeast, the forested region that was to become central Russia. The earliest important political centers there were Rostov, Suzdal, and Vladimir. The titular leader of the northeast Rus princes was the grand prince of the city of Vladimir. Galicia and Volynia to the west of Kiev, and Chernigov and Smolensk to the north, also contained ambitious dynasties and a growing population by the early thirteenth century.

This process of territorial diffusion, begun before the Mongols came, continued apace thereafter. Kiev, no longer an economic or political center, slipped into obscurity and was taken over by energetic Lithuanian rulers in the fourteenth century. The Lithuanians also established themselves as overlords of much of the southwestern Rus lands, with the result that only the northeastern principalities remained independent of all outsiders save the Mongols. The Mongols' control over them weakened in the fourteenth century, as internecine warfare between the leaders of the Golden Horde intensified.

"Appanage" is a term from French medieval history that refers to grants, often of land, given by sovereigns to their junior sons. It was adopted by Russian historians as the name of the period from the thirteenth through the fifteenth centuries when Rus lands were divided into a multiplicity of small princedoms. Never does the meekness and forgiveness preached by the monks seem to have fallen on deafer ears than during this time, when the princes employed their armies in almost constant warfare. They betrayed one another to the Mongols; they took oaths that they quickly broke; brothers killed brothers and uncles and cousins. Out of this deadly pursuit of power there emerged by the mid-fourteenth century the Danilovichi, a family that made its headquarters in Moscow. "They were a warrior band," Nancy Kollmann has written, "united in the quest of booty and benefit."[15] The Danilovichi proved to be luckier and cleverer than the other princely families. They were particularly good at cultivating the support of the Mongols and the church. Their most successful prince was Vasili II, who ruled from 1425 to 1462, during which time he completed the subjugation of the other independent princes. With the ascent of his son, Ivan III, to the role of pre-eminent prince in 1462, another political era in Russian history, the Muscovite, began.

SOCIAL AND ECONOMIC DEVELOPMENTS

The freebooting traders of Kievan times had faded into the past by the Appanage centuries, replaced by an elite that derived more of its income from landowning. Scholars debate whether it is legitimate to call these men and their families "nobles." For our purposes it seems appropriate to do so, on the understanding that this term refers to a landed military elite that subscribed to a common code of honorable conduct, treated war-making and law-giving as its birthright, and claimed greater power than before over the peasantry.

Those peasants were bringing more land under cultivation and improving farming techniques, even as the demands of the nobility rose. The peasants believed that the land they farmed and the forests they harvested belonged to them, but their ownership was not recognized in formal titles. They had no legal recourse, therefore, when princes, boyars, lower-ranking military men, and the church claimed ownership of their land. So they went to work for the new landlords. The landlords remunerated the peasants at the lowest possible rate and required them to pay various fees. The princes levied taxes. The frequent warfare and the demands of the Mongols raised all these exactions, and peasants found themselves squeezed by rulers more intrusive and demanding than they had been in Kievan times.

Despite the growing pressure of the rulers, the peasants managed to increase their productivity in the late thirteenth and early fourteenth centuries. Meanwhile, the merchants, who benefited from being connected to the Mongols' vast trading networks, were expanding commerce. The coming of the bubonic plague in the mid-fourteenth century brought new hard times; the death of one-third of the population cut the food supply and slowed trade.[16] By the early fifteenth century, the economy was recovering once again, and by the end of that century it entered a period of rapid growth.

THE LIVES OF PEASANT AND MERCHANT WOMEN

The upheavals of Appanage Rus did not alter gender ideas or the well-established patterns of women's lives. Peasant women still spent most of their time working the land with their families, tending animals and children, and growing, preparing, and preserving food. Merchant women shared with their husbands and adult sons the management of large households, supervising servants and employees, buying supplies, and selling the products of the family business. Less prosperous women worked as shopkeepers, artisans, and weavers. Middle-ranking women also borrowed and lent money. Surviving documents from Novgorod, a major trading city in the northern Rus lands, show them writing letters and keeping accounts.[17]

THE LIVES OF NOBLEWOMEN

We know more about the daily lives of noblewomen in the Appanage period than in Kievan times. They grew up under the care of servants, most of whom were slaves, and their education consisted of learning household management. They and their menfolk were far less likely to be literate than were contemporary nobles in central and western Europe. As teenagers, noblewomen married men chosen for them by their parents. A girl's parents considered themselves successful if they found a groom who was a strong, healthy young man from a wealthy family. Ever mindful of the importance of their daughters' having spotless reputations, parents permitted them little contact with people outside their family circle, so often girls met their fiancés for the first time at their weddings. This practice made a mockery of the law's requirement that daughters consent freely to the grooms chosen for them. Newly married wives moved in with their husbands' families and learned the tasks of managing slaves, overseeing expenditures, and getting along with in-laws.

Women of the princely class were involved in the dangerous politics of their time in the same ways as Kievan princesses had been. Some became victims, captured, ransomed, or killed during the incessant warfare. One of these unfortunates was Konchaka, sister of the Mongol khan Uzbek. In 1316 or 1317, she married Iuri, prince of Moscow and candidate for the supreme title of grand prince of Vladimir. By giving his sister to Iuri, the khan signaled his desire that Iuri become grand prince. Iuri's chief rival, Michael of Tver, laid claim to the throne also, and soon he and Iuri were at war. Michael prevailed and captured Konchaka, perhaps to intensify Iuri's humiliation or perhaps to hold her hostage in order to extract concessions from Iuri. The stratagem backfired: Konchaka died in his custody and Iuri accused Michael of poisoning her. The two princes then headed to the Mongol capital of Sarai to explain to Khan Uzbek what had happened to his sister. The khan believed Iuri. Declaring Michael guilty of the murder of Konchaka as well as other crimes, Uzbek executed him. Iuri became grand prince.

Most of the women active in politics in the Appanage period had happier fates than poor Konchaka. As they had done in the Kievan period, they advised the men in their families, particularly their sons, and participated in arranging marriages for their children. The authority that some achieved is documented in the last testament of the Moscow prince Dmitri Donskoi (ruled 1359–89), a hero of Rus history because he was the first prince to score a major military victory over the Mongols. When he dictated his will in 1389, Donskoi charged his wife Evdokia, a princess from Suzdal, with keeping the peace between their five fractious sons after he was gone. "I commit my children to my princess," he declared. "And you, my children, live as one and heed your mother in all things." He also bequeathed considerable property to his wife and charged her with far-reaching administrative powers over the family patrimony. At the end of his will, Donskoi admonished his sons yet again: "And you my children, heed your mother in all things, and do not go against her will in anything. And if any one of my sons does not heed his mother and goes against her will, my blessing shall not be upon him." Evdokia appears to have been more successful than some of her predecessors; her son Vasili ascended the throne in 1389 without major internecine conflict. She also made a reputation for herself as a woman of great piety and spent a fortune building monasteries and churches.[18]

SOPHIA VITOVTOVNA *(1371–1453)*

Evdokia's son Vasili was also married to an influential woman. She was Sophia Vitovtovna, the daughter of Grand Duke Vytautas of Lithuania.

Although a foreigner, Sophia established herself as an important figure at court, by relying on her own political skills and the reputation of her father, who was a far more powerful and assertive man than her husband. Vasili, it is said, governed in Vytautas's shadow and under his patronage. He demonstrated his respect for his wife by appointing her, in his will, regent for their young son, also named Vasili. So, after her husband's death in 1425, Sophia governed the Moscow lands, advised by female relatives, church leaders, and allies among the boyars at court. After eight years of lobbying and over the objections of Prince Iuri, brother of the dead Vasili, whose claim to succeed was stronger than the young prince's, Sophia and her supporters managed to persuade the khan to appoint Vasili grand prince.

Shortly thereafter, in February 1534, Sophia Vitovtovna presided over the wedding of her son. Iuri's son Dmitri Shemiaka attended, wearing a gorgeous golden belt that he had received as a gift from his father-in-law. Sophia took this as a deliberate insult, for the belt, she had heard, should have been Vasili's. The reasons why are convoluted; Sophia's response was not. She went up to Dmitri and ripped the belt off him. This still graver insult set off a quarter century of civil war between the feuding clans, during which Sophia was captured three times by Shemiaka. Each time he released her unharmed, perhaps because he feared that killing the dowager princess would alienate his supporters. Vasili, on the other hand, he blinded after capturing him in 1446.[19]

Other women came to Vasili's aid. A female servant named Poltinka, who worked for his sister Anastasia, provided intelligence about the disposition of Shemiaka's forces, which were occupying Moscow in 1446. His aunt Juliana then traveled to the city on Christmas Eve, requesting entrance so that she could worship there. When the gates were opened, Vasili's men flooded in and retook the city. In 1449, Shemiaka gave up and went into exile in Novgorod. He died four years later, poisoned, some say, on Sophia's orders. What is clear is that the relentless politicking of Sophia and the occasional assistance of other female relatives helped Vasili become the pre-eminent grand prince.[20]

PROPERTY AND INHERITANCE LAW

As they expanded their land ownership, the elite of the Appanage period also expanded women's property rights. In Kievan times, women could inherit moveable goods, but probably not land. In the Appanage centuries, parents and husbands began bequeathing land to their female survivors. Most of these inheritances were "life estates" given to widows; a recipient received the income from a parcel of land so long as she lived. On her death, it passed to her male heirs. Such "usufruct rights" were commonly employed across Europe because they provided for widows, while guaranteeing that real property would remain in the widows' marital families.

Rus law during the Appanage period also allowed women to inherit land free of any encumbrances. Parents could dower their daughters with land, over which the recipients had full property rights. That is, they could sell, mortgage, and will it. Husbands could also leave land to their wives. Thus when Dmitri Donskoi granted huge acreages to Evdokia in his will, he was acting according to notions of women's property rights that were becoming widely accepted. Anticipating that his sons might claim a voice in their mother's management of her affairs, he wrote, "And I bless my princess with all these my acquisitions, and in these acquisitions my princess is free: she may give them to one of her sons or she may give them for the memory of her soul [to a monastery]. And my children shall not interfere in this."[21]

The right of elite women to own land in the Appanage period increased their role in property management. Married female landowners probably had to defer to their husbands, for land, even if it formally belonged to the wife, was considered a part of a family's overall holdings and thus was properly under the patriarch's control. Widows such as Evdokia, who had been granted both authority and ownership in their husbands' wills, had full managerial authority over their holdings, authority similar to that exercised by those noblewomen in Western Europe who inherited fiefs.

The best known of such widows, other than the princesses, came from Novgorod, a prosperous city in northwest Rus. There, in the fifteenth century, three women, Oksinia Esipova, Nastasia Grigoreva, and Marfa Boretskaia, were among the city's largest landholders. One of these women, Boretskaia, led a rebellion against Sophia Vitovtovna's grandson, Ivan III.[22]

MARFA BORETSKAIA (BIRTH AND DEATH DATES UNKNOWN)

Fifteenth-century Novgorod was a thriving commercial hub. Its merchants and nobles imported woolen cloth, salt, beer, metal goods, and gold and silver from the Germanic ports to the west, and silk, cotton, jewels, spices, and steel weapons from the Middle East. Their most valuable export was fur. They also sold wax, honey, tar, and hides obtained from the city's far-flung hinterland and from trade routes that extended into Siberia. Marfa Boretskaia was born into a boyar family that had grown rich from this trade; she married into another, the Boretskiis.[23] Boretskaia worked with

"Marfa at the Destruction of the Veche,"
as imagined by the late nineteenth-century painter Klavdi Lebedev.
http://en.wikipedia.org/wiki/File:LebedevK_UnichNovgrodVecha.jpg.
Accessed June 27, 2011.

MARFA BORETSKAIA

Lebedev portrayed Boretskaia as a heroic defender of her people against tsarist oppression. The monk who wrote the pro-Muscovy account in the *Novgorod Chronicle* of the fifteenth century saw her differently.

"AD 1471 The Grand Prince Ioan [Ivan] Vasilievich marched with a force against Novgorod the Great because of its wrong doing and lapsing into Latinism [Catholicism]. . . .

That tempter the devil entered . . . into the wily Marfa Boretskaya, widow of Isaac Boretskii, and that accursed [woman] entangled herself in words of guile with the Lithuanian Prince Mikhail. On his persuasion she intended to marry a Lithuanian *Boyar,* to become Queen, meaning to bring him to Great Novgorod and to rule with him under the suzerainty of the King over the whole of the Novgorod region.

This accursed Marfa beguiled the people, diverting them from the right way to Latinism, for the dark deceits of Latinism blinded her soul's eyes through the wiles of the cunning devil and the wicked imaginings of the Lithuanian Prince. And being of one mind with her, prompted to evil by the proud devil Satan, Pimin the [Catholic] monk . . . engaged with her in secret whispering. . . . This Pimin did similarly trust in the abundance of his riches, giving of them also to the crafty woman Marfa, and ordering many people to give money to her to buy over the people to her will."

SOURCE: THOMAS RIHA, ED., *READINGS IN RUSSIAN CIVILIZATION*, 2ND ED., VOL. 1 (CHICAGO: UNIVERSITY OF CHICAGO PRESS, 1969), 44.

her husband, Izak, in managing their lands and marketing their products. She also supervised their employees and ran a large household in Novgorod. Boretskaia did all this without leaving home; it was not considered proper for elite women to travel. When her husband died, she took charge of the business herself. She then expanded it and thereby made her family one of the richest in Novgorod.

Perhaps her commercial success emboldened Boretskaia to become involved in Novgorod's turbulent politics. This unusually independent city was run by a boyar oligarchy. Some office-holders were elected and an all-male city assembly, the *veche,* had a voice in city decision-making. The prince, on the other hand, was a hired gun, who served a limited term as commander of Novgorod's army and was not permitted to live in the city. The boyars were able to maintain this happy arrangement until Ivan III, the grand prince of Moscow, came to power in 1462. Ivan sought to eliminate Novgorod's special status so as to incorporate the city into his expanding kingdom. Marfa Boretskaia was among those who resisted him.

The conflict burst into warfare in 1471. Novgorod's elite families were divided: some wanted to make the best deal possible with Ivan, who, they believed, would prevail eventually. Others, Boretskaia among them, argued that the city should call for help from the powerful Lithuanians. She sent her two sons, Dmitri and Fedor, and her grandson Vasili to the city assembly to argue that if the city chose a Lithuanian to be its prince, that man would bring with him an army formidable enough to defend Novgorod from Ivan. Boretskaia herself may have spoken at the meeting, although it was not customary for women to do so. "We are free people of Great Novgorod," a chronicler records her as shouting, "and the Grand Prince of Muscovy has caused us many offenses and has perpetrated many injustices; but we will be with Kasimir, King of Poland and Grand Prince of Lithuania."[24]

Although the assembly remained divided, Dmitri Boretskii and several other boyars took the field at the head of a Novgorod army. Moscow chronicles record that Ivan III's mother Maria urged her son to accept the challenge. When the Muscovites won, Dmitri Boretskii was captured and executed, but neither the death of her son nor the failure of the Lithuanians to give the help they had promised weakened Boretskaia's resolve. Nor did the fact that Ivan made a peace offer that would have preserved some of the city's liberties. Boretskaia refused to submit even after many other Novgorod families had done so. Her son Fedor fought the grand prince again in 1476, lost, and was taken as a prisoner to Moscow. The next year Boretskaia was driven from her home by a fire that was probably intended either to kill her or to persuade her to submit. Now Ivan was finished with conciliation. He ordered the rebels to leave Novgorod forever. Boretskaia and her grandson were arrested and exiled permanently to Nizhni-Novgorod, a city far to the east of Moscow. Nizhni-Novgorod means "Lower Novgorod." Perhaps this was Ivan's idea of a parting shot. Boretskaia died there.[25]

Assertive noblewomen such as Boretskaia and Sophia Vitovtovna were empowered by gender ideals that prevailed in Rus society and across Europe. Each was a middle-aged, widowed mother when she assumed leadership; each acted in defense of and through her sons. Women were supposed to fight for their children; adult sons, as we have seen, were supposed to obey their mothers. Boretskaia and Sophia also drew authority from their social rank, for female members of elite families were powerful people entitled to command the obedience of everyone lower-ranking than they. Like Olga centuries before, Boretskaia and Sophia Vitovtovna were gritty matriarchs eager to wield their power. There were undoubtedly others whose names we do not know, peasants and princesses, who took maximum advantage of the authority and power that were apportioned to them by law, custom, and fate.

The presence of such exceptional women among the Rus testifies to the opportunities for female agency that existed within European patriarchy. Women, particularly high-born women, exercised authority within their families and communities. In Appanage times, that authority was enhanced by expanding property rights. It bears remembering, though, that the rich and powerful were a tiny minority of Rus society. Most women were peasants, who shared with their menfolk short lives of struggle with the natural environment and the increasing demands of the ruling class.

Conclusions

The history of women in Russia began when Rus adventurers and Slavic peasants created a confederation that proved strong enough to survive for two centuries. Those centuries saw the establishment of patterns in women's lives that would outlast the confederation itself. Elite women managed households and played politics; merchants worked in family businesses; peasants farmed. Christianity slowly spread among them, remaking their understanding of the supernatural and fortifying the protections afforded them in law. The upheavals of Mongol conquest, plague, and political conflict cost many women their lives, without appreciably altering the gender values and norms that structured those lives.

The Rus lands were an unruly frontier by comparison with western and central Europe—that is, they were characterized by vast tracts of unsettled land, minimally defined boundaries, and decentralized politics. Despite the challenges of this world, Rus women lived lives very similar to those of women in English or Saxon lands, because European gender values and mores were as functional on the frontier as in more densely populated, closely governed areas. The similarities would persist in the Muscovite period, but the differences, shaped by the consolidation of monarchical power in Muscovy and by major political, economic, religious, and intellectual change to the west, would grow.

2

THE AGE OF
THE DOMOSTROI

1462–1695

Ivan III, grandson of Sophia Vitovtovna, conqueror of Marfa Boretskaia, great prince of Moscow, referred to himself as "tsar" in correspondence with foreign governments. The term was an ancient one, created in the Balkans from the Latin word "Caesar." By borrowing it, Ivan declared himself heir to Rome's power. It was a ridiculous assertion, for Muscovy in the late 1400s was a small, weak kingdom far from the centers of European power. Ivan and his descendants acted on his aspirations by building a government more centralized and powerful than any of its Rus predecessors. They also greatly expanded the territory they governed and fostered trade and diplomatic relations with other European nations, thereby opening Muscovy to greater contact with the outside world. And they and their nobles reduced the peasantry to serfdom and brought tens of thousands of non-Muscovite women under Moscow's rule.

For women, these centuries were a time of enduring gender ideals and wrenching disruptions. The ideals were set out most famously in *The Domostroi*, a compendium of advice on household management written by an anonymous government official or cleric in the mid-sixteenth century. *The Domostroi* described the elite family as a harmonious mini-kingdom, presided over by a benevolent, wise patriarch and his supportive, authoritative wife. The real lives of most women, princesses as well as peasants, were a good deal grittier than this, but none of the hardships called into question, so far as we can tell, women's notions about themselves or the customs of their daily lives. So women of the peasantry farmed, women of the towns ran the family businesses or worked for the rich, and women of the nobility managed their households and advised their men. This stability in gender arrangements was characteristic of the rest of Europe in these centuries as well.

There were subtle changes afoot among the nobility that, by the end of the seventeenth century, portended far greater changes to come. Low-ranking military officers who lived in the countryside were frequently away on campaign, leaving their wives to take on greater responsibility for managing the estates. Richer women in the cities were doing similar work, but, unlike women in the countryside, they were spending most of their time sequestered within their households. High-ranking Muscovite families believed that decorum required that their women hide themselves from public view, and so the wives and daughters of tsars and boyars rode around Moscow in sealed sledges and sat behind screens in church. By the 1660s, some of the privileged, aware that elite women elsewhere in Europe were freer, began to question their seclusion. Their discontent affected Kremlin politics and may have fueled a schism in the Orthodox Church.

Politics

The Muscovite period in Russian history was a time of expanding territory and government power. The kingdom grew from an estimated 300,000 square miles when Ivan III took the throne in 1462 to 5.6 million when Peter I was crowned in 1682.[1] Governing this extensive territory required the rulers to enlarge the rudimentary bureaucracies they had inherited from the Appanage princes. Their government, small by today's standards, grew sufficiently to achieve the tsars' goals—expanding and defending the realm, maintaining the monarch in power, keeping the peace, collecting taxes, paying bills, and making money from trade. Few European governments of the time attempted more.

The tsars' servitors consisted of nobles, who staffed the military and advised the crown, and civil servants drawn from the clergy and merchantry. To keep these men working effectively together, the monarchs had to cultivate the support of the great boyar families while also attending to the needs of the minor nobility, the church, and the richer townsfolk. "Politics was the personal interplay of elite men, women, and families," Nancy Kollmann has written, "and was shaped by factors such as self-interest, personal charisma, respect for tradition, loyalty to family, and the obligations of honor and dependency."[2] It was a complicated game played by everyone with power, female and male.

From the 1460s to the 1560s, the tsars managed the game quite well. Ivan III (ruled 1462–1505) and his son Vasili III (ruled 1505–33) brought under Moscow's control much of the land that had been in the Kievan confederation. They also prevailed in power struggles with their own siblings, in the process instituting primogeniture to regulate succession to the throne. The economy grew at a healthy pace, particularly in the 1490s. A bloody power struggle marked the childhood of Vasili's son Ivan IV, but when the young tsar began to rule in the late 1540s, he proved to be an intelligent, hard-working reformer.

Unfortunately Ivan spoiled many of his own accomplishments after 1560, when he earned the sobriquet "the Terrible" by turning rapacious and paranoid. His attacks on real and imagined enemies, domestic and foreign, decimated the ruling class, severely weakened the economy, and ushered in decades of political instability. The tsar even killed his heir apparent, an act that resulted in the crown's passing, on Ivan's death in 1584, to a mentally incompetent son, Fedor. A de facto regency ensued under the able boyar Boris Godunov, but when, after the death of Fedor in 1598, Godunov made himself tsar, the social bonds that held together Muscovy's diverse peoples frayed. From 1598 to 1613, a period known as "the Time of Troubles," the poor rose up against the rich, factions of the rich attacked one another, and the Polish king Zygmunt, eager to take advantage of Muscovy's weakness, sent troops supporting pretenders to the throne. Peace finally came when an assembly of nobles, merchants, Cossacks, and a few peasants elected a new tsar, Michael Romanov, the first link in a dynastic chain that would stretch into the twentieth century.[3]

Michael (ruled 1613–45) and his son Alexis (ruled 1645–76) strengthened government, modernized the military, increased trade with the rest of Europe, resumed territorial expansion, and completed the legalization of serfdom. From the late fifteenth century onward, the government had tried to limit the peasants' right to leave the service of their landlords, in order to guarantee the nobles a stable labor force. It issued laws requiring that people pay their debts before moving away, then restricted the time of year that people could move. Still the peasants fled, sometimes to newly conquered territories, sometimes to the land of a noble who had made them a better offer than their current overlord. The government's efforts to tie the peasants down culminated in the *Ulozhenie* of 1649, a law code that included provisions binding peasants to the estates on which they resided for the rest of their lives. Their descendants were to inherit this bondage. Limitations were also put on the peasants' property rights and access to the court system. Monarchs across Eastern Europe were following the same course in the seventeenth century, decreeing serfdom at the behest of their nobilities even as the institution was fading away in Western Europe. Because the *Ulozhenie* ratified an enserfment that already existed de facto for most peasants, it did little to change their everyday lives. That would happen in the eighteenth century, when the landlords began to assert greater control over the people who worked their lands.

The Lives of Poor Women

PEASANTS

Before and after the legalization of serfdom, peasant women in Muscovy lived much as their ancestors had. Girls did chores and took care of younger children. After marrying in their teens, they moved into wooden cabins with their husbands or, more often by the 1680s, into their in-laws' homes. Extended families living together lessened the taxes, which were assessed on households. Women did the lighter gardening work, tended small livestock, prepared and preserved food, and made clothes from linen and wool they grew themselves. Younger ones did all this work while pregnant or nursing, for the babies came along regularly every few years so long as the mothers' health held out.

The patriarchal values according to which peasant women lived were very similar to those described by the author of *The Domostroi*. Senior men and women in peasant families were authoritative figures, who had the life-long right to command the junior members of their families. Wives were supposed to submit to their husbands, fathers-in-law, mothers-in-law, and other senior women and men in the village, and men were encouraged to beat wives to keep them compliant. "A wife isn't a jug," the peasants said. "She won't crack if you hit her a few."[4]

Russian proverbs, some of which date back to Rus times and most of which probably originated among the peasants, also suggest that wives did not always conform to the patriarchal ideal. "It's easier to manage a sack full of fleas than one woman," one complained. Another observed that "the wife rules the husband not with a stick, but with a temper." An awful fate awaited those who succumbed to wifely domination: "A crab is not a fish; a bat is not a bird; and a hen-pecked husband is not a man."

There are enough such laments over the difficulties of controlling women to indicate that those difficulties were not uncommon. And there are also a few proverbs that comment on marriage from a woman's point of view, thereby suggesting that women had their own opinions of husbands' power. "A wife is not an instrument you can hang on the wall when you're tired of playing on it," one asserted. Another observed, slyly, "Even a foolish wife won't tell her husband the truth." A third commented on men's complaints about women: "If only one evil woman lived on earth, every man would claim she was his wife."

Peasant women did more than toil, obey, and talk back. They brightened their lives by singing lullabies to their children and telling them stories about clever boys, good girls, and wicked things that lurked in wild places. They embroidered blouses and icon cloths in the winter, when the fields were frozen. On holidays, they celebrated with feasting, drinking, songs, and dancing. Older women policed the behavior of younger ones and helped them birth their babies. All women, under the tutelage of the old ones, tended the sick and taught each other spells to attract a husband, cure diseases, foretell the future, and ward off the demons that they believed to be lying in wait to harm them. When someone died, women gathered to wash and dress the body, and then sat up all night to mark the passing. Many of the dead were children, especially when epidemics swept through the countryside. At such times women comforted one another with the reminder that their babies had gone on to a better place in heaven. Life on this earth, they believed with good reason, was all too often grueling, uncertain, even cruel.

URBAN WOMEN

Most of the women in Muscovy's cities were poor, a condition they shared with the great majority of urban women across Europe. Muscovite townsfolk lived in wooden cottages clustered along unpaved roads; the rich sheltered in large, walled compounds. Poorer women supported themselves by making consumer goods, keeping taverns, or selling food, clothing, and housewares in boisterous markets near the city center. Some worked as servants. Theirs were precarious existences, given the ups and downs of Muscovy's economy. Unfortunately we know very little about such women because the documents that have survived deal overwhelmingly with the elite. They contain extensive information on only one group of urban poor people, the slaves.

SLAVES

There were a lot of slaves in Muscovy; they constituted perhaps as much as 10 percent of the population, making them more numerous than nobles, merchants, or priests.[5] There were also far more slaves in Muscovy than elsewhere in Europe at the time, because slavery served a very different purpose in Muscovy than it did in Western Europe. In the West, by the sixteenth century, slavery consisted overwhelmingly of the horrific bondage inflicted on Africans sent to colonies in the western hemisphere. In

Muscovy, by contrast, slavery was a state into which people entered voluntarily in order to save themselves from destitution. It was akin to the English practice of indentured servitude, except that it lasted longer. In England, the indentured earned their freedom after a period of labor for their masters; in Muscovy, until the 1590s, slaves were required to remain in bondage their entire lives. Thereafter, the government changed the law so that slaves were emancipated on the death of their owners.

Muscovite slave owners shared with the English, Spanish, French, and Portuguese a preference for male slaves. Richard Hellie has calculated that two-thirds of Muscovy's slaves were men. This was largely a matter of economics: slaves cost more in room and board than they returned in labor value. So the majority of nobles, who could afford only one slave, usually selected a man, because men did more varied work than women. Men could perform menial chores, become household and estate managers, and even serve with their masters in the army. Most of the slave owners—80–90 percent—were also men, because women's rights to buy slaves were limited.[6]

A third of Muscovy's slaves were female, the great majority of them married women who became slaves when their husbands arranged for the entire family, including children, to enter into service. Widows and women whose husbands had deserted them also turned to slavery to save themselves from want, but they were less likely to find buyers than were single men. "The consequence . . . ," Hellie observes, "must have been the death from starvation and related causes of the females for whom a market did not exist." This devaluation of female labor meant that Muscovite slavery, considered as a social-welfare institution, benefited men and married women much more than single females.[7]

Most Muscovite slaves, male and female, performed domestic labor in wealthy households. They gardened, prepared food, made clothing, and tended children. Some also served as maids to the family's women. Although the work was hard, it was not as exhausting or as uncertain in its returns as farming. Slaves were also better clothed, housed, and fed than the rural poor and they had more economic security.

In exchange, they were subject to the power of their masters. Slaves in Muscovy were allowed to marry, which was often not the case in the western hemisphere. As in the West, owners in Muscovy could separate children from their parents by selling them or giving them to a son or daughter who was moving away from home. Hellie argues that Muscovite slave-owners abided by the general belief that slave families should not be so violated. He also finds that female slaves suffered less than women in other slave societies from sexual exploitation by their owners, probably because the Orthodox Church condemned such behavior and levied penalties on it.[8] The fact that there were no economic incentives to produce large numbers of slave children, as there were in the Americas, where slaves did agricultural, mining, and manufacturing work, may also have dampened the ardor of Muscovite masters.

In sum, Muscovite slavery was a good deal less oppressive than many other slave systems, and "freedom" in the larger society was for many a less attractive alternative. This mournful reality is attested to by the fact that oftentimes freed slaves, even those who had run away from masters they did not like, sold themselves back into slavery in fairly short order. Slavery offered a recourse that was less awful than begging or watching one's children starve. The desperation that drove people to slavery has been well documented by Hellie. One of his most chilling findings is the fact that families entering slavery contained very few female children. He speculates that parents who had decided to become slaves killed their daughters, because they believed that doing so would improve their chances of finding owners. It is also possible that they did away with their female babies as poverty bore in on them. After people became slaves, they no longer had to make such dreadful choices, so the families born to married slaves contained natural numbers of girls and boys.[9]

The Lives of Elite Women

The homes in which the slaves labored belonged to a Muscovite elite made up of wealthy noble families and a growing cohort of non-noble court servitors and merchants. In the cities, these people lived in substantial walled compounds containing residential buildings; outbuildings such as kitchens, stables, storage sheds, and smokehouses for curing meat and fish; gardens devoted to vegetables and fruit trees; and wells. Geese, chickens, goats, and pigs wandered around the barnyards and through the trees; the family's cattle and horses grazed on nearby pastures in summer and joined the other livestock in the compound in the winter. The human inhabitants of these mini-farms included the head of household and his wife, their minor children and unmarried adult ones, perhaps a few relatives too poor to live independently, and a household staff of slaves and servants. Working together, they produced most of their food and clothing, tended to their medical needs, and reared their children.

THE DOMOSTROI

The major contemporary source on these households is *The Domostroi,* a book written by a highly placed priest or government bureaucrat in the 1550s to instruct male family heads in managing their domestic affairs. This was no trivial matter, for the anonymous author believed, as did most Europeans of his era (and of ours, for that matter), that the family was the cornerstone of the social order. The welfare of the family, in turn, depended on its being run by a loving, mutually respectful husband and wife, a pair united in work and life. The "master" was the boss, and the author of *The Domostroi* devoted a lot of attention to his tasks. He also believed that the "mistress" made a crucial contribution to family success, and so he painstakingly laid out an idealized pattern of character and behavior for her as well. The resulting book became a classic of Muscovite literature that was still being consulted by Russian readers in the twenty-first century.[10]

The author of *The Domostroi* believed that the mistress should be chaste, obedient, and loving to her husband, stern and commanding to other members of the household, and modest in her dealings with acquaintances. Obedience to her husband was her most important obligation. "Whatever her husband orders, she must accept with love; she must fulfill his every command," the author declared (124). She should also strive to live with him in amity. "A wife should not get angry at her husband about anything, nor a husband at his wife" (143). But the lady of the house was to take on quite other qualities when supervising her female servants. In that role she was required to be a no-nonsense manager. "The wife should . . . teach her servants and children in goodly and valiant fashion," the author wrote. "If someone fails to heed her scoldings, she must strike him" (143). This was not an unusual admonition; physical punishment of disobedient subordinates, be they children, employees, soldiers, or slaves, was widely accepted across Europe. As widespread was the ideal of the elite woman who submitted humbly to her husband's authority and that of others who outranked her, while unflinchingly exerting her own authority over inferiors.

The mistress also had to be competent and hard-working. She had to know how to perform all the tasks of the household, from raising chickens to making clothes, for it was her job to teach younger women and to supervise their work. She had to value cleanliness, in both her personal hygiene and the running of her home. She had to keep a close eye on expenditures. The author of *The Domostroi* had a positive horror of servants' stealing, so he advised the mistress to count leftover fabric scraps at the end of the day before locking them up for safekeeping. He also urged the mistress to set a good example for the servants by getting up before them in the morning, rather than letting them wake her. At the end of the day, he advised, "She should even fall asleep over her embroidery (after she has first said her prayers)" (127).

The mistress's duties included maintaining her reputation outside her family. Wealthy families in Muscovy were as deeply concerned as their Rus ancestors about preserving their honor, that is, their standing as morally, politically, socially, and financially respectable people. The honor of the mistress depended on her behaving correctly in polite company, and so the author of *The Domostroi* provided detailed instructions. "When she visits or invites people to her house, she must still obey her husband's commands. While entertaining guests or visiting, she should wear her best clothes. During meals, she should not drink alcohol. A drunk man is bad, but a drunk woman is not fit to be on the earth" (132). In conversation she must stick to uncontroversial subjects. "With her guests she should discuss needlework and household management, discipline and embroidery. If she does not know something, she may ask the advice of a good woman, speaking politely and sweetly" (132). She should never gossip. These admonitions, it should be noted, were quite similar to those made to elite women elsewhere in Europe.

The author of *The Domostroi* believed that embroidery was a fine public way for a woman to demonstration her mastery of feminine virtues. "If her husband invites guests or his friends, they should always find her sitting over her embroidery," he wrote. "Thus she will earn honor and glory, and her husband praise" (126–27). Perhaps the art of fine sewing seemed particularly feminine, because it produced linens and clothing that were delicate, beautiful, and decorative. Embroidery was also something wealthy women could do while entertaining, thereby demonstrating their industriousness and artistry to their guests. Poor women also embroidered, and in their circles, the ability to produce beautiful things out of humble materials was highly valued as well.

Last in the author's list of the mistress's tasks came mothering. This ordering of priorities was common in Europe in the early modern period because childrearing had to be subordinated to the endless labor of providing for material needs. The necessities of daily existence had less influence over the thinking of church leaders, but they too, when they commented on family life, said very little about parenting. They concentrated instead, as did the author of *The Domostroi,* on the relationship between husband and wife and the good family order that derived therefrom.[11]

When he did address parenting, the author of *The Domostroi* treated both parents as equally involved in their offspring's upbringing. Here he parted company with other sixteenth-century Europeans; most contemporary works on family life portrayed fathers as stern enforcers of discipline, mothers as more tender-hearted nurturers. There is a bit of this in *The Domostroi,* but in his general statement of parenting principles, the author minimized gender distinctions. "If God sends anyone children, be they sons or daughters, then it is up to the father and mother to care for, to protect their children, to raise them to be learned in the good. The parents must teach them to fear God, must instruct them in wisdom and all forms of piety. According to the child's abilities and age and to the time available, the mother should teach her daughters female crafts and the father should teach his sons whatever trade they can learn" (93).

The author adds that girls should be impressed with the importance of preserving their reputations as virtuous maidens and advised parents to begin saving for their daughters' dowries when the girls were infants. In return for this care, the children were to obey and honor their parents throughout their lives and take care of them in their old age.

Spending so much time discussing *The Domostroi*'s treatment of women reflects our priorities, not the author's. He addressed his book to male readers and devoted the lion's share of his attention to portraying the ideal "master." The foundational principles he laid out were similar to those he enjoined for women: "Be obedient and submissive to your superiors, loving to your equals, welcoming and kind to inferiors and the poor" (103–104). As head of household, the master had to serve as guardian of his home, "protect[ing] his people faithfully" (122) and dealing fairly with neighbors and friends. He should practice "good deeds and wise humility," as all Christians should (138). He should be sober, sexually abstemious, hospitable, and charitable. These were ancient masculine virtues; we have seen them prescribed for Rus leaders. The author added a newer emphasis on the importance of service to the monarch that reflected the increasing power of the Muscovite crown. "Fear the tsar and serve him faithfully. . . . Obey the tsar in all things," he enjoined his readers (71).

Within his household, the master's primary obligation was to be a wise patriarch, "teach[ing] and lov[ing] your wife and children" (92). Above all, he should instruct them in Christianity by leading family prayers and attending church "every day" (86). Protestantism and Catholicism were also stressing the religious obligations of the family head in the sixteenth century; the notion had ancient roots in the faith, stretching back to the church fathers. When family members disobeyed, the master was obliged to discipline them, beating them if necessary, in private and without losing his temper.[12] *The Domostroi,* like other such works published across Europe in the early modern period, gave instructions on how to whip disobedient wives and servitors without doing them serious bodily harm.

Also important were the managerial skills of the paterfamilias. He had to be a good organizer of domestic work, a frugal steward of resources, and a smart consumer who bought when prices were lowest. He should not go into debt but rather "live according to his means, thinking ahead, acquiring and spending according to his own true income" (123). If he was a merchant, he should be honest in his business dealings. The master could be pleased with his "justly acquired property," for it was virtuous to "amass property according to Christian law." Indeed, the manual went so far as to state that creating a prosperous household "merit[ed] the life eternal" (122).

This stress on sobriety, thrift, piety, and assiduous husbandry was popular in Muscovy, particularly among the merchants and clergy, to whom the author probably belonged. Such people did not care much for the swashbuckling masculinity of the Rus warrior, and hence the warrior is absent from the pages of *The Domostroi.* Instead there is the homey, comforting vision of a harmonious household headed by its benevolent, diligent patriarch and matriarch. These ideals had widespread appeal, even among the warriors, and so *The Domostroi* quickly became an influential synopsis of Muscovy's gender ideals.

SECLUSION AND WOMEN'S HONOR

The Domostroi does not talk directly about one of the major aspects of elite women's lives in the Muscovite period: their seclusion from public view. The highest-ranking women wore veils when outside their residences, sat behind screens in church, and moved around Moscow in closed carriages or sledges. These customs arose from the notion that elite women should avoid being seen by males who were not members of their families. In large households, women slept in their own separate quarters and were supposed to be very careful about how and whom they entertained. Consequently, foreign men visiting a Muscovite boyar or merchant in his home rarely laid eyes on his wives or daughters. If they appeared at all, it would be to greet their guests in highly ritualized ceremonies, after which they returned to their rooms.

The seclusion of elite women grew out of the Muscovite belief in the importance of shielding high-born women from contact with people who might sully their honor. This concern was not unique to Muscovy. One of the most famous statements of Western European patriarchal values, the instructions of the Goodman of Paris to his young wife, written in the 1390s, declared, "You ought to be moderately loving . . . towards your good and near kinsfolk . . . and very distant with all other men and most of all with overweening and idle young men, who spend more than their means and be dancers." Muscovites, who were even more anxious about women losing their good names than was the Goodman, extended the circle of threatening outsiders to include virtually everyone outside the walls of their well-guarded homes.[13]

Seclusion was also a marker of a family's status. A wealthy upper-class woman did not have to work in the fields or move around the city to make her living. Instead she stayed home, consulting with her husband, supervising her slaves, saying her prayers, and finally, at day's end, falling asleep over her embroidery. "Their chief employment is sewing," declared a befuddled German diplomat named Adam Olearius, "or embroidering handkerchiefs of white taffeta or cloth, or making little purses or some such toys."[14] Olearius had never seen the mistresses at work running their households. He believed that the ladies of the ruling class sat quietly stitching all day—which is just what the author of *The Domostroi* and the elites of Moscow wanted him to believe.

A less restrictive and more widespread expression of the Muscovites' concern about women's honor was their practice of permitting women who felt that they had been dishonored to take their complaints to court. This practice, begun in Kievan times, was unusual in Europe. In many Italian city-states, for example, insults to a woman were treated as insults to her family, and her male relatives brought suit and received compensation. Muscovite law, by contrast, permitted women to sue in their own names, awarded the fines to them as their property, and assessed higher fines for insults to women than for insults to men. A wife who had been insulted received double the fine her husband would have received, and their daughter four times as much.

These differences reflect the fact that women whose reputations were damaged suffered social ostracism greater than that inflicted on insulted men. If they were of marriageable age, their prospects of finding a good match were diminished. To defend themselves against such dire consequences, women of all social classes went to court, bringing complaints that ranged from verbal slander and minor physical assault, such as knocking off a headdress, to major attacks, including rape. Women were complainants in perhaps one-third of honor cases brought before Muscovite courts. Judges took the charges very seriously, investigated assiduously, and often awarded considerable damages to the injured women.[15]

THE ELEVATION OF ROYAL WOMEN

Ivan III and his successors portrayed themselves as divinely favored, powerful rulers. This transformation of the warrior prince into a sovereign tsar required a commensurate elevation of his wife, the *tsaritsa,* and her daughters, the *tsarevny.* Isolde Thyrêt has argued that this was a process of status-building in which the entire royal household participated. In court ceremonies and on icons and embroideries, the women of the royal family presented themselves as the blessed wives of their husbands and the mothers of their people. Tsaritsy prayed to God to bless their husbands, sons, and subjects. They made large, well-publicized donations to the church and the poor. By the reign of Ivan IV, church fathers, drawing on earlier ideals, were also suggesting that the tsaritsa, being female and therefore more naturally humble, submissive, and devout than her manly husband, could tame his cruder impulses and nudge him toward peacemaking.[16]

Portraying the tsaritsy as exemplars of Muscovite femininity and consorts of powerful tsars did not increase the powers granted them by custom. Instead, the royal wives participated in politics in much the same ways as had the princesses of Kievan and Appanage Rus. They advised their husbands, mediated family disputes, arranged marriages, and advanced their sons' interests. Thyrêt has shown that tsaritsy were more likely to become politically involved during periods of instability at court.[17] Sophia Paleologus, second wife of Ivan III, lobbied successfully for her son Vasili to be named successor. The mother of Ivan IV, Elena Glinskaia, served as regent for her three-year-old son after the death of her husband, Vasili III.

The royal mothers lived with their daughters and young sons, ladies-in-waiting, administrative staff, and a host of servants in the Moscow Kremlin's women's palace, a household similar in its organization to those of other elite women, but much larger.[18] The responsibilities of running this establishment were considerable, and some tsaritsy, given the opportunity, willingly applied the skills acquired there to the outside world. When plague struck Moscow in 1654–55 and Tsar Alexis was too far away to supervise the government response, Tsaritsa Maria took over, conducting her own correspondence with city officials. Her tone was that of a self-confident woman accustomed to exercising authority.[19]

She did all this while hidden away from the view of the people over whom she ruled, for the elevation of the royal women did nothing to ease their seclusion. And no women were more walled in than the tsarevny, the daughters of the tsars, for they were prohibited from marrying on the grounds that no Russian was high-ranking enough for them and no suitably prestigious royal foreigner professed the true faith, that is, Russian Orthodoxy. So the grandiose ambitions of the tsarevny's fathers led to life-long spinsterhood for them. We will return to this subject later, when we come to the time when one of those daughters rebelled.

PROPERTY AND INHERITANCE LAW

Muscovy retained the property-ownership customs established for women during Kievan and Appanage times. As in the past, women received most of their property as dowries and inheritances from their parents and they retained full rights over it after they married. Widows often held "life estates" that they managed and from which they received income. When they died, the land passed either to their sons or to other male members of their husbands' families.

Over time, Muscovy's landholding practices became more diverse, requiring jurists to reconcile women's property rights with the new developments. Chief among these was the spread of *pomeste*. This term describes an arrangement whereby the tsars granted land to the men who served them, primarily to the cavalrymen who made up their armies. When pomeste began, the grants were provisional, that is, they lasted only so long as the service. If a man left the tsar's employ, the land reverted to the tsar's control. Over the sixteenth century, pomeste grants and service obligations became hereditary within families. Many nobles also owned land that they had inherited (called *votchina*) and they bought land from other landlords. The Herculean task of adjudicating property disputes in such a complex system was made still more difficult by the expansion of both the nobility and Muscovy's borders. Fitting women into the mix was yet another complication. In 1562, Ivan IV's advisers attempted to simplify matters by decreeing that pomeste and votchina land could belong only to men, and that all men owning such land had to do military service. Women could not receive either type of land in their dowries or inheritances.

This law proved impossible to enforce, because of Ivan's demented behavior. His wars and his purges of the nobility created thousands of widows who needed the income from all their husbands' land to survive. For their part, government officials realized that they needed the widows to keep the estates going in order to sustain the economy. The government therefore suspended enforcement of the ban against women inheriting pomeste and votchina. The importance of elite women's work to the economy had been demonstrated in a particularly brutal way.[20]

The Romanov governments of the seventeenth century were more successful in defining women's property rights. In 1627, Filaret, patriarch of the Orthodox Church and co-ruler with his son, Tsar Michael, renewed the prohibition on widows' inheriting pomeste or votchina estates, but he declared that a husband could bequeath to his wife and daughters land that he had purchased. The decree also contained the generous provision that a wife was entitled to one-quarter of the couple's moveable property. Filaret further ruled that childless widows could receive a share of the income from their marital family's pomeste land and reaffirmed women's long-standing rights to their dowries. His grandson Alexis expanded these provisions in the *Ulozhenie* of 1649, the law code that also defined serfdom. The *Ulozhenie* permitted daughters to inherit both votchina and pomeste land if the family had no surviving sons. It also granted life estates to all widows and unmarried daughters of nobles who had held pomeste land. The effect of these Romanov codifications was to continue the limitation on women's right to votchina land but to expand their claims on estates gained through service or purchase, estates which made up the great majority of land held by the nobility in the seventeenth century.[21]

Assessing how these changes affected elite women is difficult. As yet, historians have been unable even to agree on whether Muscovites obeyed the new regulations and whether the government enforced them. It is easier to assess the laws in the context of contemporary Europe; seen that way, the property rights of elite women in Muscovy were liberal, as Rus laws had been. They were similar to the rights contemporary Spanish women enjoyed, more limited than those granted women in the Ottoman Empire, and far greater than those possessed by women in England, France, the German states, and Scandinavia. Furthermore, rights in these last countries were shrinking as central governments issued new, increasingly restrictive laws governing women's property holding.[22]

ELITE WOMEN IN THE COUNTRYSIDE

The laws were affected, as we have seen, by the important part noblewomen in the countryside played in the management of estates. Their service appears to have increased in the Muscovite period because their husbands were often away. Many cavalrymen were on duty every year from summer through fall, with the result that some couples spent as much as half of their marriages separated from one another. When the husbands were gone, the wives ran the estates, for only the very richest landowners could afford to employ estate managers. This meant that all over Muscovy, noblewomen were in charge during the growing season, when the workload was the heaviest and the need for good management the greatest. These women did not live secluded inside their houses nor did they veil themselves when out of doors, though they usually did stay close to home. Once again, we are not dealing with an exclusively Muscovite phenomenon. Increasingly onerous service obligations for noblemen were increasing elite women's responsibilities and authority elsewhere in Europe in the early modern period.[23]

In the seventeenth century, Kallistrat Druzhina-Osoryin, the son of a provincial cavalryman, wrote a portrait of his mother, Iuliana, that sums up the life's work of such a woman: "She occupied herself diligently with handiwork and managed her house in a manner pleasing to God. She provided her serfs with sufficient food, and appointed each of them a task according to their strength. She cared for widows and orphans, and helped the poor in all things."[24] The author rarely mentioned his father's activities on the estate, and although he stressed his mother's humility and piety, he did not include obedience to his father as one of her cardinal virtues. It was her competence and benevolence that impressed him.

NUNS

Monasteries for women flourished in the sixteenth and seventeenth centuries. The largest of these institutions were substantial walled establishments, containing hundreds of residents and supervised by abbesses, councils of nuns, and administrative officials such as cellarers, who were in charge of food provisioning. Convents also owned estates outside their walls; the land belonging to the Pokrovskii Convent in Suzdal extended across five counties (*uezdy*) and contained twenty-two villages.[25] The female leaders of these convents ran the affairs of their enterprises as secular women ran their households, that is, they remained within the walls, assigning business that required travel to monks who worked for them.

In its organization, Muscovite monastic life was little changed from Kievan times. There were still no highly structured religious orders such as existed in Catholic Europe. Within individual convents, discipline was looser than in the West, allowing more scope for individuals to structure their lives. A woman entering a convent could bring servants to live with her; she could have her own quarters built within the compound; she could do her own cooking and her own washing or have her servants do it. Indeed, a widow could live out her life in a convent without ever becoming a nun.

Women wishing to enter the community did have to pay a fee, as did Catholic women, with the consequence that most of Muscovy's nuns came from the propertied classes. The nuns who performed the physical labor may have been poorer widows who could not support themselves on their inheritances and dowries, daughters from city or countryside whose parents could not find husbands for them, and perhaps also the mentally or physically disabled. From time to time, a few women were banished to convents because they had fallen out of favor with the tsar. But most nuns were widows, in keeping with tradition since Kievan times. Once a woman had fulfilled her familial duties—married, served her husband, supervised the rearing of her children—she was entitled to choose a quiet life of religious devotion.

Was monastic life a little too pleasant? Church fathers occasionally charged that discipline in the convents was lax. They complained about nuns eating expensive food and drinking too much; they hinted at sexual liaisons. Similar complaints were made about monks when clerical reformers attempted to enforce asceticism in prosperous institutions, and the reports of Catholic inspectors to the West bemoaned the same sorts of straying from the abstemious monastic ideal. Undoubtedly there were miscreants, but, sadly, we will never know how much partying was going on in Muscovy's convents. It is clear that most nuns kept up their daily devotions, ran their establishments, and produced beautiful handcrafts, particularly embroidery.

The Hunt for Witches

Fires, crop failures, wars, economic recessions, epidemic diseases afflicting people, animals, and plants—these recurring troubles plagued Muscovites. In the seventeenth century, they also fed a series of witchcraft scares. Witches were a common obsession across Europe in the early modern period, particularly in German-speaking areas, where tens of thousands of people, more than three-quarters of them women, were executed for consorting with the devil. We do not know whether seventeenth-century Muscovy experienced more witch hunts than did the Rus period, but we do know that the Romanov government was more willing and able to document them than its predecessors. So records exist that make it possible to sketch the contours of Muscovite witch-hunting and to compare it to witch-hunts elsewhere. There were significant differences: in Muscovy the scares came far less often, fewer people were accused, and of those, at least two-thirds were men.[26] Witchcraft scares deserve attention, therefore, for they are a well-documented instance of Muscovy's take on European gender beliefs leading to outcomes for women different from those that occurred elsewhere.

The witchcraft persecutions in Central and Western Europe arose out of two developments that never reached Muscovy—the propagation of the doctrine that black magic was the special province of women and the political and religious conflicts of the sixteenth- and seventeenth-century Reformation. The major treatise on witchcraft was *Malleus maleficarum* (*The Hammer of Witches*), published by the German monks Heinrich Kramer and Jacob Sprenger in 1486. *The Hammer* declared that witches held midnight gatherings in hidden places to worship Satan and have sexual congress with him. Satiated, they then went out to do their beloved's evil bidding. Because they had renounced the true faith, witches were heretics. So when rooting out heretics became an obsession during the Reformation, that obsession begat the search for witches.

Muscovite clerics burned heretics too, but they did not indulge in elaborate, sexualized fantasies about witches, perhaps because they and their Rus predecessors had never laid as much stress as Catholic monks did on women's sexual transgressions. Consequently the Orthodox Church did not spread tales of weird sisters coupling with Satanic goats, Muscovite law did not consider witchcraft heretical, and Muscovites continued to believe, as their ancestors and most Europeans had long done, that men were just as capable of black magic as women.[27]

Muscovites did accept the widespread European idea that the world was full of good and evil spirits and of special people who could manipulate those spirits for good and evil purposes. Diseases, they thought, had supernatural as well as physical causes, and so healers treated the sick with potions, many of which were medically efficacious, and with spells, which could have a powerful placebo effect. Ordinary people also used magic to foretell the future, persuade a reluctant lover, or punish an enemy. The line between good white magic and bad black magic depended on who was drawing it. A wife's love potion, sprinkled onto her husband's food to perk up his libido, could be seen by the husband, if he spent the following three days throwing up, as an attempt to kill him. Moreover, Muscovites believed that diseases in people, plants, and animals were as likely to be caused by magic as cured by it.

Witchcraft scares were set off in Muscovy, as elsewhere, by stresses in a family or community. Food shortages, epidemics, hostilities between neighbors, rumors of mysterious strangers seen on the roads could—but rarely did—lead to accusations. Usually communities dealt with the accused on their own. People beat suspects, ran them out of town, even killed them. Sometimes they took their accusations to the courts. The government and the church defined witchcraft as a crime of violence or social disruption, not heresy, so the convicted were subjected to the same penalties as those convicted of comparable non-magical crimes. People found guilty of murder were put to death; Valerie Kivelson has estimated that 10 percent of the accused met this fate. Those convicted of less lethal enchantments were exiled to the borderlands, where male convicts were required to serve in the armies guarding the frontier.[28]

Folk healers and community outsiders were among those most frequently accused in the witchcraft scares of the seventeenth century. Muscovites and their Rus ancestors had long distrusted the self-proclaimed magicians who traveled from village to village, entertaining people with conjuring tricks. When a witchcraft scare began, therefore, villagers turned on itinerant minstrels and peddlers. If the latter happened to be non-Muscovites, they were still more likely to rouse suspicion. Folk healers were also vulnerable because they used magic in their work. Since many of the minstrels, peddlers, and healers in Russia were men, men made up a large proportion of those accused of witchcraft. Furthermore, these categories often overlapped—that is, many folk healers were itinerant non-Muscovites.

Most women who came under suspicion had gotten involved in disputes with family members or acquaintances that had escalated into accusations and counter-accusations of black magic. One of the commonest charges was that a relative, friend, or neighbor had cast a spell that caused evil spirits to enter a woman's body and possess her. Women convinced that they had been possessed lost their appetites, had seizures, or went into trances in which they barked like dogs or hissed like geese. Christine Worobec and Valerie Kivelson have found that these women's families and friends often cared for them tenderly and labored to cure them by exorcisms. Those accused of causing the possession encountered no such merciful treatment. Some of them—how many is unknown—had in fact taken the very risky course of attempting a little white, or black, magic. The case of a peasant widow named Katerinka is a case in point.[29]

KATERINKA (c. 1600–?)

In 1628, Katerinka was a servant of the wife of Prince Fedor Eletskoi. She lived in the Eletskois' house on their country estate, and she was not happy with her employers. The prince and princess were required by law to arrange a marriage for their widowed maid, but they refused to do so or to permit her to marry a man of her own choosing. So Katerinka began sleeping with Mikitka, a cook in the household. When the prince learned of her disobedience, he punished Katerinka with beatings. That was, *The Domostroi* tells us, a master's prerogative, indeed, his obligation. It did not have the desired effect of showing Katerinka the error of her ways.

Soon afterward, the princess fell ill and miscarried. Muscovites believed that miscarriages sometimes resulted from spells cast on the mother, so when the princess lost her baby, she and the prince suspected Katerinka, whom they already distrusted. The angry prince began beating her anew, this time to extract a confession of witchcraft. At first, Katerinka accused her lover Mikitka of casting a spell on the princess. When a search of her room turned up packages of suspicious powders and grasses, she identified them as cosmetics. The beatings continued until Katerinka confessed. The prince took her to the authorities and accused her of witchcraft, whereupon she renounced her confession.

The maid maintained her innocence until court interrogators turned to torture. Tsarist officials employed beating, burning with red-hot irons, simulated drowning (better known now as waterboarding), and stretching on the rack. They soon induced Katerinka to confess again, this time to putting something in the princess's food, but not of causing the miscarriage. She said that a folk healer had told her that if she gave the princess a magical salt, the princess would drop her opposition to Katerinka's marrying. "And I took about a pinch of that salt from Baba Oklulinka," she testified, "and I gave her for that salt a headdress. . . . And that salt all went into the princess's food. . . . And I gave the princess that salt . . . because she had a grudge against me. But I never intended to bewitch the princess. And unfortunately, the illness started, and she miscarried the baby, but not from bewitchment."[30]

We do not know the court's ruling. The records end with Katerinka and Mikitka still under arrest. The old healer, Baba Oklulinka, who had also been arrested, died in jail. Valerie Kivelson has speculated that the two lovers might have been released eventually, for judges sometimes freed those accused of witchcraft if they found that confessions had been coerced by masters. Confessions extracted by the courts' torturers were not subject to the same consideration.[31]

Katerinka had much in common with accused witches in Central and Western Europe. Many of the latter were also poor widows without large families to defend them. Some of them had sought to increase their influence over others by dabbling in magic, and thereby incurred the enmity of neighbors or employers or family members. We do not know how many Katerinkas there were in Russia or even whether Katerinka was guilty. What is clear is that widowhood, which sometimes conferred great authority on a wealthy woman, could doom a poor one to still greater poverty and vulnerability. Katerinka reminds us of another universal reality: strong-willed women, particularly poor ones, had to choose their battles carefully.

Women of the Conquered Territories

Muscovy's expansion brought tens of thousands of non-Slavic, non-Orthodox people under tsarist rule. Ivan IV annexed Kazan (1552) and Astrakhan (1556), thereby pushing the kingdom's boundaries south almost to the Black Sea. He also gave his blessings to expeditions into Siberia. In the reign of Alexis (1645–76), a substantial portion of today's Ukraine came under Muscovite rule; and by 1700, the tsars had laid claim to all of Siberia. These annexations accelerated the transformation of Muscovy from a small kingdom at the edge of the East Slavic lands into a huge, multi-ethnic empire. They also complicate the task of studying the history of women in Russia because, from the 1600s onward, the Muscovite government claimed as its subjects dozens of ethnic groups. To describe the histories of all these conquered peoples is neither possible nor desirable in a work of the present sort, but some value may be found in an attempt to open up here, and to discuss again in later chapters, the significant interactions between the imperial homeland and the women brought under its rule.

The first major distinction that emerges from an examination of the relationship between Moscow and its new, non-Muscovite subjects is this: conquest had little impact on the gender ideas of people with close historical and cultural connections to the Muscovites, such as those who lived in Ukraine. This is not to say that conquest was an inconsequential event for the women there. The seventeenth-century wars in that region between the Poles, Cossacks, Muscovites, and Tatars killed thousands and devastated the economy. Women suffered as women usually do in war: some were butchered, others were assaulted, robbed, and raped, some were successfully defended by their menfolk, most struggled to protect themselves and their children, and a few performed extraordinary acts for which they were celebrated. In 1654, a woman named Zavisna, the wife of a Cossack commander, refused to surrender her town to besieging Poles after her husband had been killed. Instead she did away with many of the attackers by hurling a torch into the munitions dump. The explosion also killed most of the town's defenders, Zavisna included.

In mid-century, the Cossacks of central Ukraine established an autonomous government and abolished serfdom. Thereafter, the Cossack elite began to claim increased prerogatives, which brought elite women greater status and more comfortable lives and peasants a renewal of serfdom. This process of social differentiation continued into the 1700s, but had little effect on the gender ideas or practices that governed women's lives in Ukraine. Siberia was another story: what happened there was very similar to the concurrent European conquest of the Americas.

Muscovite and Cossack trappers, traders, and soldiers ventured into Siberia in the sixteenth century seeking furs, Muscovy's most lucrative export. They entered a vast territory inhabited by perhaps as many as 220,000 indigenous people.[32] The hundreds of Siberian tribes are often classified, as are native people in North America, according to their languages: the Finno-Ugric peoples of the west; the Turkic and Mongol peoples of the south and east; and the far-northeastern groups, including the Chukchi and Eskimos, who are related to native Alaskans. In the more northerly latitudes, Siberians lived by herding, hunting, and gathering. Many were nomads who followed the reindeer in their seasonal migrations. Those living in the south cultivated crops and bred horses, sheep, and goats. Nomadism was common there as well. Closely tied by history and culture to the Mongols, the southern Siberians, of whom the Yakuts and Buryats were the largest groups, were formidable warriors.

There were strong similarities in the beliefs and social organization of the many Siberian groups when the Muscovites came. Although Islam and Buddhism had made inroads in the south, the majority of Siberian natives had preserved their age-old animistic religions; they worshipped the forces of nature and the spirits that lived in the trees, rivers, and sky. Particularly revered was the Siberian brown bear, cousin to the North American grizzly. Shamans helped the Siberians communicate with the spirit world and tended them when they were sick. The Buryats and Yakuts, who had learned about powerful rulers from the Mongols, had strong clan structures and social divisions. Most of the other indigenous peoples lived in small communities and delegated leadership, when necessary (during a communal hunt, for instance), to respected elders. They did not need complex class structures or highly developed conceptions of property to wrest a living from the frozen land.

The gender notions of the Siberians were also more egalitarian than those of their conquerors. As did many of the native peoples of the Americas, they granted leadership within families and clans to senior men and gave older women more authority than younger ones. Men did most of the hunting and fishing; women collected and processed plants for food and medicine. Siberian women also worked with men in butchering and drying the catch. Men, women, and children watched over domesticated animals; among the Tungus of central Siberia this included training reindeer to be ridden and milked. Women made clothes out of animal skins or fibers, and tended babies. Parents arranged their children's marriages, exchanging both bride price, paid by the groom's family, and dowry. Strict rules prohibiting marriage between members of the same clan were common, as was the practice of men having as many wives as they could support.

There were significant variations from group to group. Elderly women of the Chukchi, Itelmens, and Koraks of the Pacific coast conducted religious rituals in concert with senior men. Similarly, Tungus women of the Lake Baikal region served in the honored position of shaman and acted as heads of their households when their husbands were away. On the other hand, people who had more complex class structures and greater contact with other patriarchal cultures, such as the Buryats and Yakuts, made stricter distinctions between women's roles within and outside the family, and granted men more authority.

The Muscovite invasion of Siberia was a catastrophe for the native peoples. They fought back, but Muscovy prevailed for the same reasons the Spanish, Portuguese, French, and English prevailed in the Americas: the invaders enjoyed military superiority; they were merciless; and they brought with them diseases—especially smallpox, tuberculosis, measles, and influenza—against which the native peoples had no immunity. Once they had conquered a group, the Muscovites and the Cossacks exacted tribute in the form of furs, particularly the much-prized sable, black fox, and marten. When the animals were trapped out, which occurred in the more accessible areas by the end of the 1600s, the invaders switched to requiring monetary payments.

From time to time the tsarist government denounced the exploitation of Siberian tribes, but it could do little to stop it. Officials working thousands of miles from the capital cast in their lot with the exploiters, selling trade goods at exorbitant prices, hiking taxes, spreading disease, hunting fur-bearing animals to extinction, chopping down forests, and polluting waterways. When Muscovites began settling permanently in Siberia, the displacement of the native peoples began.

The gruesome parallels between the conquest of the Americas and that of Siberia extend to the consequences for women. James Forsyth has written, "Wherever the Muscovite invaders went, it was women and girls that they seized first of all in their assaults upon the native inhabitants."[33] Initially some Siberians permitted the newcomers to have sex with native women, because this was an accepted gesture of hospitality. But soon they found that the conquerors considered themselves entitled to such favors. Muscovites and Cossacks also grabbed women and children as spoils of war, holding them hostage to compel tribes to submit, enslaving them, or even trading them for furs. When the invaders built settlements, they forced captive women to do the work of wives. This began a process of native women leaving their communities to settle among the Europeans and give birth to children with ties to both cultures. These women may have played the role of cultural intermediaries, helping to ease tensions between the conquerors and conquered. Because many Cossacks and Russians soon moved on, native wives could also find themselves abandoned or passed to other men. All these practices, from rape to intermarriage, occurred in the western hemisphere as well.[34]

Native men who resisted were often killed; those who survived suffered a continuing assault on their masculinity. First their standing as warriors was diminished by their inability to fight off the conquerors. Then they were forced to trap furs for the Muscovites, which left them less time to provide for their families. Some of the native men became dependent on the conquerors for food because their traditional lands had been despoiled or claimed by Muscovite settlers. The result was a profound demoralization that expressed itself in alcoholism and apathy.

The conquerors could not devastate all of Siberia, for the land was vast and the people were resourceful. Along the southern frontier, the tribes of the Lake Baikal region were able to limit the damage because they were more numerous, organized, and prosperous than the smaller peoples of the north. They were also effective soldiers, and their long-standing contacts with Central Asia and China may have strengthened their immunity to the diseases the Muscovites brought. Some of the more ferocious peoples, such as the Chukchis of the Pacific coast, managed to keep the Muscovites at bay for more than a century. Others, such as the nomadic Tungus, headed off into remote terrain that was harder for the conquerors to penetrate. By 1700, although Muscovite rule was established in Siberia and immigrants from Muscovy made up at least half the population, there were still great tracts where native peoples pursued their traditional ways of life relatively undisturbed.

Extraordinary Women in Troubled Times

The history of Muscovy is pockmarked by upheavals. The worst of these was the Time of Troubles (1598–1613), a period of political and economic instability that climaxed in a vicious civil war. A much shorter and less catastrophic uprising occurred in the 1670s when a former slave, Stenka Razin, led an army of Cossacks, peasants, and urban poor up the Volga in an attempt to overthrow the government. Even as Razin's army surged along the river, moreover, a religious dispute was producing fiery confrontations between tsarist officials and defiant members of a new sect called the Old Believers. In all these conflicts, a few women played leading parts.

It had long been common across Europe for women to join in riots, rebellions, and wars. Muscovy was no exception to this rule. In Pskov in 1581, townswomen defended the city against Polish troops by firing artillery at the attackers, pelting them with rocks, and finally, in the words of a chronicler, "hurl[ing] themselves against the remaining enemy troops in the tower, fighting with all the arms given them by God." Women also joined Stenka Razin's revolt. Most did the chores usually assigned to women by armies: they cooked and nursed the sick and injured. A few also fought. The most famous of the female warriors was Alena Arzamasskaia, a nun from the town of Arzamas east of Moscow, who ran away from her convent in 1669 and, dressed like a man, led a unit in Razin's army. Her fate echoes that of a more famous female soldier, Joan of Arc: she was captured, tortured, convicted of being a bandit and impersonating a man, and burned on a pyre. Practicing witchcraft did not condemn one to death by fire in Muscovy, but participating in a major uprising against the tsar did.[35]

In the politics of the elite during Muscovy's warring times, women took the traditional parts of advisers, promoters of the fortunes of their menfolk, and pawns. Of the handful of women prominent enough to make it into the accounts of observers and participants, two deserve special mention, one because she was a pawn of unusual resourcefulness and the other because she was a founder of the largest schismatic movement in Russian history.

MARFA NAGAIA (c. 1560–1610)

Deeply involved in politics during the Time of Troubles were three tsaritsy: Irina Godunova, wife of the Tsar Fedor and sister of Boris Godunov, the regent from 1584 to 1598 and tsar from 1598 to 1605; Maria Godunova, Boris's wife; and Marfa, the last wife of Ivan IV. Of the three, Marfa had to be the most adroit, because her situation was the most perilous. She relied on the rooted reverence for royal women and also on her own political skills to navigate the troubled waters she first entered when, as a girl named Maria, she married Ivan the Terrible.

That marriage went better than she might have expected, given Ivan's predilection for disposing of his wives. Maria was his seventh; he had exiled two of her predecessors and was rumored to have poisoned three. His first wife may have been poisoned by others. Maria managed to outlive her murderous husband, but when he died in 1584, he left her in an uncertain situation. Their marriage violated church law, which permitted only three marriages in a lifetime, so Maria was not legally tsaritsa in the eyes of the church, and her son Dmitri had a questionable claim to the throne. Godunov, the regent, decided to exile the problematic mother and son to Uglich, a town far from Moscow and its court politics. In 1591, Dmitri suddenly died. Godunov sent investigators to determine the cause of death; they reported back the unlikely tale that the boy had accidentally cut his own throat. When Tsaritsa Maria protested that her son had been poisoned on Godunov's orders, the regent commanded her to become a nun. Upon taking her vows, Maria became the nun Marfa. Seven years later, Tsar Fedor died without heirs and Godunov became tsar.

Marfa was living in a remote convent when, in 1603, a Muscovite soldier named Grigori Otrepev popped up in Poland claiming to be her dead son. He gathered an army, and in 1605, shortly after Godunov died, seized Moscow and was crowned Tsar Dmitri. To validate his claim, the new tsar sent for Marfa. She came to Moscow and publicly swore that Otrepev was her long-lost son. Isaac Massa, a Dutchman then living in Moscow, understood her reasons for lying. "It was not surprising that she recognized Dmitri as her son, even though she knew full well that he was not. She lost nothing thereby; on the contrary, she was thereafter considered a tsarina, treated magnificently, and led to the Kremlin, where she was given the convent of the Ascension as her residence. There she lived as a sovereign."[36]

When a boyar group led by Vasili Shuiskii overthrew Otrepev in 1606, Marfa had to change her story. Now she announced that her son had actually died years before and that she had been forced to swear that the pretender was Dmitri. "She said she had merely acted out of fear," Massa reported, "and in her joy at her deliverance from her sad prison [the remote convent to which Godunov had banished her], she had not known what she was doing." Shuiskii soon had the corpse of the real Dmitri brought to

Moscow so that he could hold a public viewing to establish once and for all that the boy was dead. Again Marfa took her place onstage. In front of a crowd presided over by church and government officials, she looked into the coffin and declared, in awed and prayerful tones, that her son's body lay there, as fresh as it had been on that sorrowful day fifteen years before when she had laid him to rest. Christians believed that holy people did not decay after they died. So Marfa was testifying that Dmitri had graduated into sainthood. Massa, who attended this ceremony, was no more taken in by it than he had been by Marfa's certification of Otrepev. He noted that only Marfa and a very few of the highest-ranking clergy were permitted to view the blessed remains.[37]

Marfa's career as Dmitri-checker was not yet over. A few years later another False Dmitri knocked at her door. She again agreed to testify that her boy was back. Marfa was spared another staged renunciation, because she died in 1610, before the Second False Dmitri was overthrown and a new dynasty, the Romanovs, came to power.

Years later, another Marfa, this one the mother of Tsar Michael Romanov, donated money for the perpetual saying of prayers for Marfa's soul. It was not unusual for the mother of a tsar to so honor another, but Romanova may also have been motivated by sympathy for Marfa. Romanova had also been forced to become a nun by Boris Godunov, because her husband Fedor had lost a round in the power struggles of the Time of Troubles. She too had lived in remote monasteries, under orders never to return home and from time to time in fear for her life and that of her son Michael, who lived with her. She could understand why Marfa had told so many lies, and perhaps she thought a few extra prayers would help her soul avoid damnation.[38]

FEODOSIA MOROZOVA (1632–75)

Fifty years after Marfa's death, Feodosia Morozova became a leader of a schism that permanently split the Russian Orthodox Church and created a new sect, the Old Believers, that continues to this day. The dispute that gave rise to this rupture began in the 1650s when church leaders ordered revisions in the liturgy. The proposed changes, which included using a different number of fingers when making the sign of the cross, introducing a new spelling of Jesus' name, and some editing of church interpretations of Christian doctrine, seem innocuous today. Seventeenth-century Muscovites, however, considered them to violate the correct practice of Christianity. The church leaders who ordered the changes believed that they were removing errors that had crept in because the Turkish conquest of Byzantium had diminished contact between Muscovy and the centers of the Orthodox faith in Greece. Unfortunately, many Muscovites, lay and clerical, disagreed. They believed in the sanctity of the uncorrected practices and became convinced that the Devil was behind the revisions. Soon a charismatic priest, Avvakum, began to speak against the reforms, and long-standing discontent with the religious leadership in Moscow began to coalesce into rebellion.

Georg Michels has found that "women formed a strong numerical majority among early Old Believers" and that the work of its first female converts was "absolutely crucial to the formation and survival of early Old Belief." His words remind us of the equally important role played by women in Christianity's establishment among the Rus. In both eras, the Kievan and the Muscovite, the earliest and most influential female converts, in the first case to a new faith, in the second to a sect within that faith, came from the wealthier households.

To join the new sect was to rebel not only against the church, but against the tsar. Alexis reacted by demanding recantation. Some women returned to the fold; others defied him. Two abbesses, Elena Khrushcheva and another whose name has survived only as Marfa, made the Moscow convents they headed into bastions of the new sect. After the authorities fired Khrushcheva from her position, she traveled around Muscovy proselytizing. She found shelter with wealthy widows who were promoting Old Belief among their peasants. One of the most rebellious of these widows was Evdokia Naryshkina, the aunt of the Tsar Alexis's second wife. When, in the 1670s, the tsar sent guards to confine her in her house, Naryshkina rushed at the commander of the detachment and grabbed hold of his beard, thereby gravely insulting his honor. Later she escaped captivity by leading her family across a swamp. The group remained at large in a forest encampment until the tsar's soldiers tracked them down in 1681.[39]

The best known of the early Old Believer women was Feodosia Morozova. She became one of the heroines of Russian history, praised in pamphlets written shortly after her death, hailed as a rebel by nineteenth-century revolutionaries, and honored as a holy martyr by Old Believers to this day. There was little in her early life that foreshadowed such a heroic biography. Morozova was born into one boyar family, the Sokovnins, and married into another, the very rich, very prominent Morozovs. She enjoyed a happy, albeit short, marriage with her husband Gleb, with whom she had one son, Ivan. In 1662, Gleb died and Morozova took charge of their extensive properties. "She may have owned eight thousand serfs and had three hundred slaves in her household in Moscow alone," Margaret Ziolkowski writes. Morozova supervised all these people from luxurious rooms overlooking gardens where peacocks roosted in the trees. She took particular interest in the piety of the peasants on her estates, ordering priests to make sure their parishioners attended church regularly.[40]

In the early 1660s, Morozova began to criticize the reforms in Orthodoxy. When the Old Believer priest Avvakum returned from exile to Moscow in the mid-1660s, she invited him and his family to stay with her. Soon Morozova was taking in other schismatics and speaking out in opposition to the tsar. Alexis confiscated some of her estates in punishment, but he also attempted to conciliate her, perhaps because Morozova was lady-in-waiting to his wife, Tsaritsa Maria. At first Morozova appears to have wavered in her support for the schismatic movement, but as the years passed she grew more determined. She converted her sister Evdokia to the cause and enlisted the covert support of her brothers. In 1670 she secretly became an Old Believer nun.

Convinced that she was doing God's will by defending the old practices, Morozova was willing to martyr herself and her loved ones. When her uncle urged her to consider the welfare of her son, who was at mortal risk because of her behavior, she replied, "If you wish, take my son, Ivan, to *Red Square* and give him over to be torn to pieces by dogs and try to frighten me. Even then I will not do it [accept the reforms]. . . . Know for certain that if I remain in the faith of Christ to the end and am fit to taste death for the sake of this, then no one can steal him from my hands."[41] Ivan subsequently died, perhaps murdered, and Morozova grieved for him, but she did not regret her decision, for she believed she had chosen the righteous path. God would restore her son to her in heaven.

Nor was Morozova intimidated by the powers arrayed against her. Contemporary accounts detail her self-righteous and insulting behavior toward top churchmen. She is reported to have told a group of interrogators, "It is fitting, there where your liturgy is proclaimed [during church services], to engage in a necessary function and to vacate the bowel—that's what I think of your ritual." She was only slightly more polite to the tsar, to whom she wrote in 1670, "It does not befit the sovereign to harass me, poor servant that I am, because it is impossible for me ever to renounce our Orthodox faith that has been confirmed by *seven ecumenical councils.* I have often told him about this before."[42]

By this point, Morozova was courting martyrdom. In 1671 she finally exhausted Alexis's patience by refusing to attend his wedding to his second wife, Natalia Naryshkina. (Morozova's protector, Tsaritsa Maria, had died.) Tired of Morozova's obstreperousness and wanting to send a message to her fellow schismatics, Alexis ordered her arrested, along with her sister Evdokia and another female supporter, Maria Danilova. The three women were held in the Novodevichy convent in Moscow, where many boyar women visited them to express support.[43] The tsar then exiled the three to more distant convents, even while continuing to offer them clemency on the condition that they accept the reforms. They refused. Finally, in the fall of 1675, incarcerated in a deep pit far outside Moscow, Morozova, her sister, and their friend died of starvation.

Morozova was not the only Old Believer martyr. Hundreds, perhaps thousands of members of the sect emulated the fate of their hero, Avvakum, who was burned at the stake in 1682. When threatened with arrest, they gathered in groups and set themselves on fire. After decades of intermittent, violent confrontation between the authorities and the schismatics, the conflict subsided. The Old Believers became a permanent sect within Russian Orthodoxy, officially outlawed but persisting. The faith endures to this day inside and outside Russia, women's contributions to its survival continue, and Morozova remains a revered figure in its pantheon.

She was a most remarkable woman. Not only did she refuse to submit to the formidable powers arrayed against her, but she also worked to develop the theology of Old Belief. "Feodosia was assiduous in the reading of books," Avvakum wrote, "and derived a depth of understanding from the source of evangelical and apostolic discourses." She argued matters of faith forcefully with the church leaders sent to question her and also with other Old Believers, including the egotistical Avvakum. Even more remarkably for a Muscovite woman, she wrote religious tracts. After her death, Avvakum praised her intellectual fortitude: "When the time came, Feodosia put aside feminine weakness and took up masculine wisdom."[44] She was manly in her intellect, he wrote, and in her resistance to the authorities. That Morozova had transcended the supposed limitations of her gender was the highest praise Avvakum could bestow on her.

The history of Christianity is full of women rebelling against state and church authorities in defense of their understanding of the faith. Perhaps one explanation of this phenomenon is that religion was virtually the only source of power and authority through which women could hope to stand on an equal footing with men. Most female saints were women who had resisted the pressure of evil officials and unsympathetic families, willingly gone to horrible deaths, and then reportedly ascended to heaven to live with God. Some of these martyrs, for example the Muscovite favorite St. Paraskeva, patron saint of married women and housework, were as defiant and assertive as Morozova. The tales of all these female religious rebels

Feodosia Morozova as imagined by
the nineteenth-century painter Vasili Surikov.
http://en.wikipedia.org/wiki/File:Boyarynja_Morozova.jpg.
Accessed June 27, 2011.

FEODOSIA MOROZOVA

In 1669, Morozova was at odds with Avvakum's sons, Ivan and Prokofii. Warned by Avvakum that "it will go badly for you [unless you] . . . make peace with my children," Morozova wrote to Avvakum's wife, Anastasia. After repeating her charges against the sons, she concluded:

"Little mother, I have sent you fifteen roubles for whatever need you may have, and I sent eight roubles to the little father [Avvakum]: two for the little father alone and six for him to share with Christ's fraternity. Write to me whether it gets to them. And from now on don't allow your children to read others' letters, make them swear that from now on they won't read my letters and the little father's. Christ knows that I am as happy with you as with my own birth mother. I remember your spiritual love, how you visited me and nourished my soul with spiritual food. Formerly you really were happy with me and I with you, and truly I am as happy as before. But your children have turned out to be real spiritual enemies of mine. . . .

Forgive me, a sinner, little mother, you and Ivan and Prokofii, in word, deed, and thought, for however I have grieved you. Ivan and Prokofii, you have greatly grieved and vexed me, because you wrote against me and others to your father. . . . Forgive me, my beloved mother, pray for me, a sinner, and for my son. I beseech your blessing."

SOURCE: MARGARET ZIOLKOWSKI, ED., *TALE OF BOIARYNIA MOROZOVA: A SEVENTEENTH-CENTURY RELIGIOUS LIFE* (LANHAM, MASS.: LEXINGTON, 2000), 89–90. REPRINTED BY PERMISSION OF ROMAN AND LITTLEFIELD PUBLISHING GROUP.

inspired women across Europe to join heretical movements in the medieval period and to break with Catholicism altogether during the Reformation. Some of the new Protestant sects of Central and Western Europe were as dependent on the support of prosperous women as were the Old Believers in Russia. Morozova was probably ignorant of the Anabaptists and the Quakers, among whom women figured as founders, but she undoubtedly was versed in the hagiography of the early Christian female martyrs.

She probably took inspiration also from Muscovite customs that permitted women to express their piety outside the confines of the family and the convent. It was common for Muscovite women, peasants as well as nobles, to go on pilgrimages to the shrines of saints. A few became "holy fools" who traveled and preached from village to village. Some devotees of St. Paraskeva got together on Fridays to parade through their communities, singing the saint's praises and calling on other women to quit their work and join them. The church was suspicious of this kind of spontaneous, unregulated religiosity. In 1551, delegates to a church conference complained, "False prophets, men and women and maidens and old grannies wander among parishes . . . , naked and barefoot, with loose hair and dissolute, shaking and beating themselves."[45] The Muscovite church was too loosely organized to repress the grannies, and so the shaking and beating continued, helping to pave the way for later conversions to Old Belief.

Morozova was inspired by the female saints; she was empowered by her rank. Because she was a boyarina, she could turn her home into a center of schismatic activity and build her authority as a leader of the movement. Her status emboldened her to defy the tsar; she knew that he would hesitate to strike down a woman from a leading family. Her sense of her own authority also empowered her to lecture Avvakum, which roused class and gender resentments in the priest. Angrily he wrote to her, "Are you better than we because you are a boyar woman? . . . Moon and sun shine equally for everybody . . . and our Lord has not given any orders to earth and water to serve you more and men less."[46] Avvakum kept telling her over the years that she should submit to him because he was a man and a priest. He had to repeat these orders because she continued to assert herself.

All the Old Believer women, lay and clerical, risked social ostracism at best, death at worst. It was no small thing in Muscovy to refuse to obey the tsar and the priests, especially if one was a woman. So the great majority of women did not do it. Instead, they remained within the established faith and were probably horrified by the rebellion. When they heard about Naryshkina pulling her jailer's beard or Morozova refusing to obey the tsar, they must have wondered how these women could so dishonor themselves. Who would ever speak to them again? Who would marry their daughters? Some devil must have possessed them. Otherwise they could not have forgotten that honor lay in being modest, stay-at-home, dutiful mistresses.

And yet, among the horrified majority there may also have been a few who admired the defiance of the Old Believer women. For discontent about the restrictions on elite women was spreading in Moscow by the time of the schism. Perhaps it helped to fuel the schism. After the death of Alexis in 1676, it certainly affected Muscovy's politics at the highest levels.

Kremlin Women

CHANGE IN THE WEST

This desire for change arose among the highest-ranking Muscovite women. By the last decades of the seventeenth century, some of them had learned that they were more confined than elite women elsewhere. They came by this information from tales spread by foreigners living in Moscow as well as from imported books. Their enlightenment was part of a larger exchange between Muscovy and Central and Western Europe, ongoing throughout the seventeenth century, that accelerated under Tsar Alexis.

Muscovites had always traded with merchants from the west, as had the Rus before them. By the seventeenth century, those merchants were coming from a region that was being transformed by political, economic, and cultural change. Centralized, bureaucratized monarchies had developed. Merchant capitalism, backed by the monarchs, was producing manufactured goods and expanding international trade. Intellectual life, which had flourished since the twelfth-century development of the universities and court patronage of the humanities, bloomed into the Renaissance in the fifteenth and sixteenth centuries, leading to major scientific discoveries and promoting formal education. Technology was also advancing: artillery and primitive rifles were revolutionizing warfare, while the printing press permitted the dissemination of new ideas to an increasingly literate elite, among whom middle-class people figured prominently. The Reformation, even while producing major wars and witchcraft persecutions, promoted literacy as well as critical examinations of Christian doctrine by clerics and lay people alike.

These developments are the reasons why historians see the medieval phase of European history as ending in the fifteenth century and the early modern period beginning in the sixteenth. The intellectual, economic, and political currents spread into eastern Europe, affecting first those areas long in contact with the West, such as Poland and Bohemia, and then lapping at the gates of Muscovy. Tsars Michael and Alexis knew that the other Europeans had more effective armies than theirs, so they brought in foreign military advisers to teach the new weapons and methods to their troops. They and their courtiers also bought the latest luxury goods, including fine textiles and ingeniously automated clocks, from merchants come to Moscow. And they listened to stories about life among royals elsewhere. They heard that queens and countesses did not spend their lives cooped up in their houses, that they rode unveiled around their capital cities, that they wore beautiful, light, brightly colored silk dresses to elegant parties, where they danced with men they were not married to.

Although he presented himself as a pious traditionalist, Tsar Alexis was willing to bend the rules governing royal women. He was an unusually attentive father to his six daughters—Evdokia, Marfa, Sophia, Ekaterina, Maria, and Feodosia.[47] He expected them to be politically informed, and when away on military campaigns he sent them detailed reports.[48] He also took the unprecedented step of permitting his third daughter, Sophia, to study with his sons' tutor, an erudite monk named Simeon Polotskii. And he chose as his second wife a young woman who had experienced, by Muscovite standards, a permissive upbringing. The tsar's open-mindedness enabled Sophia, his daughter, and Natalia, his wife, to become important political actors.

NATALIA NARYSHKINA (1651–94) AND SOPHIA ROMANOVA (1657–1704)

Natalia Naryshkina was the niece of Evdokia Naryshkina, the Old Believer who had lived in the woods rather than submit to the tsar. The Naryshkins were one of the liberal families: they studied foreign languages, entertained foreign visitors, decorated their homes with imported luxuries, and allowed their daughters to learn to read. They also permitted them to socialize more freely than *Domostroi* custom would permit. When they decided, in 1670, to send Natalia to live in Moscow, they put her under the supervision of another liberal family, the Matveevs. Artamon Matveev, the family head, was a close adviser to the tsar. Alexis was now a widower, for his wife Maria had died in 1669, and when Matveev introduced his new ward to the monarch, Alexis was delighted by her outgoing ways. In January 1671 they married and on May 30, 1672, Tsaritsa Natalia gave birth to a son, who was christened Peter.

A contemporary portrait of Sophia in royal regalia.
http://en.wikipedia.org/wiki/File:Sophia_Alekseyevna_hermitage.jpg.
Accessed June 27, 2011.

SOPHIA

Dressed in clothes like these, Sophia presided over ceremonial events at court. The Swedish ambassador, Kersten Gullenstierna, described being received by her in 1684:

"Sofia was seated on her royal throne which was studded with diamonds, wearing a crown adorned with pearls, a cloak of gold-threaded samite lined with sables, and next to the sables was an edging of lace. And the sovereign lady was attended by ladies-in-waiting, two on each side of the throne . . . and by female dwarves wearing embroidered sables and gold sable-lined cloaks. And the lady was also attended in the chamber by several courtiers and at the sides there also stood Prince Vasily Vasilevich Golitsyn and Ivan Mikhailovich Miloslavsky."

SOURCE: E. LERMONTOVA, SAMODERZHAVIE TSAREVNY SOFI ALEKSEEVNY, PO NEIZDANNYM DOKUMENTAM (IZ PEREPISKI, VOZBUZHDENNOI GRAFOM PANINYM) (ST. PETERSBURG, 1912), 44; QUOTED BY LINDSEY HUGHES IN *SOPHIA, REGENT OF RUSSIA, 1657–1704* (NEW HAVEN: YALE UNIVERSITY PRESS, 1990), 189.

Surviving accounts do not reveal how well Natalia got along with her many stepdaughters, but they indicate that she brightened life in the Kremlin. Jacob Reutenfels, a German living in Moscow, wrote of the new tsaritsa, "She is evidently inclined to tread another path to a freer way of life since, being of strong character and lively disposition, she tries bravely to spread gaiety everywhere." Alexis entertained his young wife by opening a theater, where plays on Biblical and classical themes were performed. This was an audacious innovation, for the church disapproved of playacting and thought still less of pagan mythology. The royal family also traveled more often than in the past to its various estates. A particular favorite was a model farm at Izmailovo where the tsar experimented with windmills and glassblowing, while the ladies interested themselves in the gardens.[49]

This idyllic period lasted only five years. In 1676 Alexis died at age forty-seven. His fourteen-year-old son Fedor succeeded him and, despite his youth and chronically poor health, managed to carry out his duties competently until 1682, when he too died. The royal family was plunged into crisis. There were two Romanov heirs, Ivan, the fourteen-year-old son of Maria, and Peter, the ten-year-old son of Natalia. Ivan, the rightful heir, was physically and mentally disabled. Peter was healthy, strong, and precocious, so it seemed reasonable to some in the Kremlin to proclaim him tsar.

The choice outraged the *streltsy,* units of the standing army that were already unhappy because the government was not paying them on time and was extending their terms of service on the frontiers. It is not known whether anyone from the royal family helped to foment rebellion among the streltsy. What is certain is that some of the soldiers mutinied after the announcement of Peter's elevation. Gangs of streltsy rampaged through Moscow, attacking those who supported Peter and murdering several of Natalia Naryshkina's relatives.

Sophia, the educated tsarevna, stepped forward to lead the peacemaking and promote her own political fortunes. She played a major part in the negotiations that resolved the conflict, calming angry delegations of armed men and on at least a few occasions saving people from execution. Peace was restored by making concessions to the soldiers and declaring Ivan and Peter co-rulers. Thereafter, throughout the summer and fall of 1682, Sophia was involved in consolidating a new ruling coalition based on her mother's family, the Miloslavskiis. From this politicking she emerged, at the age of twenty-five, as regent for her younger brothers, even though there was no basis in tradition for an elder sister to assume that position. The surviving tsaritsa, Natalia, was entitled to become regent, but her family had been decimated by the streltsy attacks, leaving her without powerful supporters at court. So she retreated with her son Peter to estates outside Moscow, while her stepdaughter gathered the reins of power.

The ambition and audacity of Tsarevna Sophia are astonishing. Nor only did she have no right to become regent, she was supposed to live her life out of public view. Tsarevny occupied lavish quarters within the woman's section of the Kremlin, they owned estates outside of Moscow, and they controlled their private incomes and household staffs. Their good works included attending church services, patronizing the church, donating to charities, and embroidering icon cloths. In short, they had the privileges and obligations of all wealthy women, with the enormous exception that they were never to be wives or mothers.

Sophia decided to do otherwise, ruling Muscovy from 1682 to 1689 and ably continuing her father's foreign and domestic policies. Assisted by a skilled diplomat, Vasili Golitsyn, Sophia negotiated a treaty with Poland in 1686 that gained Muscovy territory in Ukraine, including Kiev. By affiliating Russia with the Holy League, an anti-Turkish alliance of Poland, the Holy Roman Empire, and the Venetian Republic, Sophia broke down some of her government's hostility toward its neighbors, thereby laying the foundation for the diplomacy of Peter I. She also fostered the continuing development of art and architecture in Moscow.[50]

While exercising a tsar's power, Sophia presented herself to her courtiers and subjects as a pious, righteous tsarevna. She continued to live in the women's quarters of the Kremlin, went to church regularly, and donated generously to convents, especially the Novodevichy in Moscow. She did not marry, though she may have had a romantic relationship with Golitsyn. She also held court, in a manner befitting a tsar, not a tsarevna.

Sophia liked ruling Muscovy, and as the years passed, she sought ways to institutionalize her position. After the 1686 treaty with Poland she claimed the title "autocrat," formerly reserved for male rulers, and ordered coins decorated with her image. In 1687 her supporters began circulating a proposal to have her crowned co-ruler with Ivan and Peter. Portraits portrayed her wearing a crown and ermine-collared robe, or holding the symbols of sovereignty, the orb and scepter. Court poets sang her praises. She went no further than this, for fear of alienating her brothers and powerful boyars.[51] Perhaps she was also deterred by the fact that Golitsyn, whom she sent off to war in Ukraine, did not win victories that would have bolstered her reputation. When he returned from a second campaign in the summer of 1689, Sophia's regency suddenly ended.

The dramatic events of August 1689 are well documented. Sophia hoped to glorify her adviser as a great conqueror, though the fact that he had mostly led his army on fruitless marches was well known. To that end, she expected that her seventeen-year-old half-brother Peter would perform the usual ceremonies welcoming Golitsyn back from the war. Peter, at the urging of his advisers, refused. Sophia demanded that he do so, rumors began flying that she intended to arrest Peter, the younger tsar fled to the sanctuary of a monastery, and in the stand-off that followed, Sophia's supporters deserted her. On September 7 Peter ordered the tsarevna stripped of her title "autocrat" and remanded to the Novodevichy Convent. Her ruling days were over.

No woman could have kept power once a legitimate, healthy tsar was old enough to challenge her. Sophia managed as long as she did because she possessed extraordinary political skills and because Peter was an immature teenager. Having ordered her to spend the rest of her life in comfortable confinement, her half-brother left her alone. Then, in 1698, the streltsy revolted again. Peter suspected that Sophia was involved, even though investigations turned up no evidence to prove it. After an angry meeting at which he accused her of treason and she denied the charges, Peter imposed on Sophia the time-honored punishment of disgraced royal women—taking the veil. She became the nun Susanna. To remind her of the importance of loyalty to him, Peter ordered that the bodies of three of the streltsy conspirators be hanged outside the tower in which she lived. There the corpses dangled through the winter. The tsar also issued instructions limiting the number of visits Sophia could have with her sisters. His one-time regent lived out her life in the beautiful precincts of Novodevichy, died there in July 1704, and was buried in the convent grounds.

And what of Natalia, Peter's mother, the effervescent tsaritsa who had stepped aside when Sophia made herself regent? From 1672 onward, Natalia lived with her son at the royal estate at Preobrazhenskoe, managing the household and avoiding politics. She did not subject Peter to the confinement and supervision imposed upon young tsars who lived in the Kremlin, and so the boy played war games using live ammunition, frolicked with foreigners, and studied occasionally, when his tutor was sober enough to teach him. There is little evidence that he spent much time with his mother. Natalia did arrange his marriage when he was seventeen. Curiously, she chose Evdokia Lopukhina, the daughter of a conservative noble family. Evdokia had been brought up in seclusion, so she and Peter were ill suited to one another. One wonders why Natalia, once an outgoing young woman, should have selected a retiring maiden for her rambunctious son. The tsaritsa died in 1694 and so did not live to see her boy abolish the seclusion of elite women.

Conclusions

The lives of women in the Muscovite era, like those of earlier periods, were shaped by the politics and economics of their times. The strengthening of the central government produced warfare that made more difficult the lives of some women. The establishment of serfdom legalized the subjugation of the peasantry. The tsars' empire-building had devastating consequences for many native women in Siberia and brought women from scores of different ethnic groups under Muscovite rule and into contact, however remote, with Muscovite moral and social norms. The tsars also increased contacts with the rest of Europe, which led, by the reign of Alexis, to an easing of the seclusion of elite women.

Amid the instabilities fostered by these changes, gender norms held firm for most of the women of Muscovy. The elite values of the time were summed up by the author of *The Domostroi,* who promoted the notion that an ideal family was one in which everyone knew her or his place and all worked together to meet their material and spiritual needs. Muscovites extended these ideals to society as a whole, seeing the tsar and tsaritsa as master and mistress of the realm, presiding over a gigantic household in which the powerful took care of the needy, men guided and protected women, women served and cared for their families, and all obeyed those above them. This vision legitimated the ground rules by which women lived their lives. As in the Rus centuries, the rules empowered older women, particularly elite ones, even as they sustained boundaries beyond which women trespassed at their peril. By the end of the Muscovite period, a few women were pushing against those boundaries. The age of *The Domostroi* was drawing to a close.

3

EMPRESSES AND SERFS

1695–1855

Peter I, known to history as Peter the Great, believed that he had to change elite women in order to transform Muscovy into a modern, powerful Russian Empire. He began by ordering them to put away their heavy kaftans and veils and order dresses of German design. Though his strong-willed sisters Maria and Ekaterina refused to get new wardrobes, many other women in the circles around the throne happily acceded to the tsar's demands. The tsar also commanded his female subjects to attend court festivities with men, and thereby began abolishing the seclusion of elite women. These decorative reforms set in motion much more substantial changes in privileged women's lives over the next century and a half. The gender ideas of Western and Central Europe, which were in ferment during these years, flowed into Russia, where they changed Russian ideas and were changed in their turn. Education for girls and women expanded. Revisions in property laws permitted elite women to buy ever more land. By 1850, Russian noblewomen were attending boarding schools, reading scholarly journals, publishing poetry and short stories, running charities, and managing estates.

This transformation was limited. In 1850, women still owed obedience to their older relatives and to their husbands; they had to have their spouses' permission to travel on their own; they could not divorce. They could not attend the universities or enter the professions that were beginning to develop. Still more significant was the fact that women's opportunities improved only among the elite, who made up less than 10 percent of the population. The great majority of women were serfs, whose bondage became ever more onerous.

The pressure for reform was growing. By the 1840s social critics were attacking the constraints on elite women and criticizing serfdom. In the early 1850s a few connected the two issues, denouncing the bondage of women and serfs as dual consequences of Russian patriarchy and calling for the abolition of both. When Alexander II took the throne in 1855 and encouraged a wide-ranging discussion of reform, therefore, the intelligentsia was ready to put "the woman question" on the agenda. The age of Peter the Great and his eighteenth- and nineteenth-century successors may be seen as a time of important changes in the situation of elite women and as the seed-time of a still more transformative era in the history of all women in Russia—the later nineteenth century.

Peter I, 1682–1725

Natalia Naryshkina's iconoclastic son began to rule in his own right in the mid-1690s. Over the next thirty years, he and his ministers expanded the country's borders and inserted themselves into the foreign affairs of Central and Western Europe. At home they converted the military to a standing army, founded the Russian navy, and reorganized the government. They promoted economic growth. They reduced the power of the church by putting civilian administrators in charge of its revenues and limiting its influence at court. They abolished slavery and began collecting the "soul tax," a levy on male peasants that increased government revenues. Finally, and most importantly for women's history, Peter and his advisers sought to transform Russian noblemen into progressive, well-educated executors of the royal will and noblewomen into cultured, decorative helpmeets.

This effort to engineer gender change was not unique to Russia. In Europe and elsewhere, there was a long history of governments shoring up their power by promoting revisions in gender values. Augustus, the first Roman emperor (reigned 27 BCE–14 CE), trumpeted the virtues of the dutiful Roman matron as part of his campaign to present his regime as restoring traditional values. In the early modern period, the governments of Qing China, Tokugawa Japan, the Ottoman Empire, and Louis XIV's France attempted to shape the character of their subjects, particularly their ruling classes, by emphasizing revised ideals of masculinity and femininity. The Chinese and Japanese did as Augustus had, and claimed to be restoring values corrupted by their predecessors. Peter took a different tack, condemning Muscovite traditions for making his servitors conservative and lethargic and their womenfolk prisoners in their own houses. As foils to these dismal stereotypes, he promoted idealized gender conceptions heavily influenced by Central and Western European ideals. By so doing, Peter made foreigners and their notions about men and women the official standards by which to measure Russia's elite.

ENERGETIC MASCULINITY

Peter's first priority was the men of his ruling class. Piety did not matter much to him, nor did the old markers of status, such as family pedigree and wealth. Instead he endorsed a hard-working, open-minded, and above all, energetic masculinity, which he modeled literally and figuratively. Peter dressed in plain suits of Western European design much of the time, kept his hair short and his face clean-shaven, and ordered his nobles to do the same. He befriended and sometimes promoted to high office men from all walks of life. He took up boat-building, collected scientific specimens, beat the drum in parades, and pulled teeth. He moved the capital from Moscow, which he saw as a bastion of the old order, to a new city that he founded on the Baltic Coast and named St. Petersburg. Much of this, while expressive of his character, was calculated to impress. Peter was seeking to inspire the nobles to be like him so that they would work with him in improving Russia. He would set the agenda, for he did not question the autocratic power he had inherited. Nor did he see any contradiction between forcing his followers to shave their beards and urging them to exercise initiative.[1]

PETER'S REFORMS FOR WOMEN

Peter believed that elite women should participate in his make-over of the ruling class. So he ordered his female courtiers to wear clothes of foreign design, to participate in public ceremonies, and to dance, drink, and play cards at court parties. This delighted some women, horrified others. French dresses, cut low to reveal cleavage, were embarrassing to women used to clothes that covered them from head to toe. One could also develop a serious case of the shivers wearing them in St. Petersburg's newly built and drafty palaces. Still more unsettling were the boisterous parties at which the wives and daughters of the court were required to dress up in costumes and frolic with the men. Some of Peter's more adventurous ladies enjoyed themselves. Most noblewomen were probably, at least at first, appalled.

More women may have approved of his 1702 reform of marriage customs. As we have seen, parents in Muscovy arranged marriages with the interests of the family in mind. By the seventeenth century, the ancient Rus rule that they had to obtain the agreement of the future bride and groom was rarely followed, and it was not uncommon for couples to meet for the first time at their weddings. Peter did not approve, probably in no small measure because he had taken an immediate dislike to Evdokia Lopukh-ina, the wife his mother had chosen for him. Instead, he thought that prospective spouses should be permitted some voice. Undoubtedly this was a feeling widely shared by other people damaged by unhappy marriages. So the decree of 1702 granted parents the right to choose partners for their children, but gave the children a right of refusal. Couples had to be permit-ted to meet during a six-week betrothal. If either party decided against the match, parents were prohibited from forcing it to occur. Furthermore, the decree permitted a groom to refuse to marry a woman with a physical dis-ability. There was no similar "escape clause" for brides. Peter reinforced the decree in the 1720s with additional regulations outlawing forced marriages.

The marriage decree reflected and promoted attitudes already pres-ent among elite Russians. Notions about marriage had begun to change in the second half of the seventeenth century, a change detectable in a small but growing secular literature that featured stories in which true love triumphed over all obstacles. The nobility was beginning to believe that marriage should be more than synchronized teamwork, more than a prospering alliance built on duty, piety, and hard work. It should sustain the partners emotionally. Peter's marriage law gave legal recognition to the newer concept that marriage would work better if the spouses found one another desirable. The tsar himself acted on this concept by divorc-ing his wife and living with, then marrying, a lower-class woman named Martha Skavronska. On converting to Orthodoxy, Martha took the name Catherine.

Peter's sisters, although they honored many Muscovite customs, in-cluding the requirement to remain single throughout their lives, supported their brother's efforts to engage women in Russia's new social life. Maria took the unprecedented step of traveling abroad to attend the wedding of her niece in 1717, ignoring her brother's complaints about having to pay the expenses of the huge entourage that accompanied her. Natalia moved to Peter's new capital and set about promoting Peter's reforms as well as oc-casionally supervising his children. She also sponsored a theater, for which she wrote at least one play, organized a choir, and perhaps composed songs. When she died in 1716, Natalia left behind sixty-one paintings, one hun-dred books, mostly about religion, and several wardrobes full of dresses cut to foreign patterns.[2] Her sister-in-law, Tsaritsa Praskovia, widow of Ivan V, also subsidized a theater. Much of the tsarevny's patronage was devoted to arts with a religious theme, and so it would not be accurate to describe them as departing radically from Russian traditions, which had long en-couraged rich women to promote religion. But now such women increasingly could, and did, use their fortunes to encourage arts new to Russia, such as theater.

Peter did not challenge the fundamental values that defined women's natures and duties. Nor did he advocate limiting the power of senior men. *The Honorable Mirror of Youth,* an etiquette manual published in 1717, advised its female readers, "You must acknowledge your own weaknesses, frailties, and imperfections, and be humble before God and consider your fellow beings more than yourself."[3] Gender change is often accompanied by such reaffirmations of core values. In contemporary France and England, the same emphasis on female frailty prevailed, and the few women in the West who aspired to be artists or writers were often reminded that their role was to appreciate the works of men, not to create their own.

Peter's involvement of noblewomen in social life did promote an understanding among the highest ranks of the nobility that women should be something more than the dutiful housewives of *The Domostroi.* Their wishes were to be consulted by parents arranging their marriages; their husbands were to permit them to chat with, even flirt with, other men. They were to embody, literally, a femininity that was on public display, and this was a major change from the seclusion of the past. Furthermore, Peter's reforms and the examples of his sisters and his court became the foundation on which subsequent generations of elite women built for themselves a significant position in Russia's secularizing elite culture. Central to that process were two of Peter's female successors, the empresses Elizabeth I and Catherine II.

The Age of the Empresses, 1725–96

It was another of Peter's reforms, a change in the law of succession, which permitted women to rule Russia for most of the eighteenth century. In 1722 Peter decreed that each emperor[4] should choose his own heir. When he died three years later without doing so, his edict enabled court factions to promote the fortunes of two women. Catherine I, Peter's wife, became his successor as a result of the machinations of Alexander Menshikov, Peter's powerful minister and her former lover. She died in 1727, and a rival clique overthrew Menshikov and put Peter's grandson on the throne. That young man ruled as Peter II for three years. After he succumbed to smallpox in 1730, he was succeeded by Anna, the daughter of Peter's half-brother, Ivan V.

Empress Anna was a lazy, frivolous woman who presided over a government noted for corruption, exorbitant taxation, and unsuccessful military adventures. A childless widow when she took the throne, Anna did not remarry thereafter, so when her health weakened in the later 1730s, her courtiers began casting around for an heir. The empress insisted on maintaining the succession through the descendants of her father Ivan, and settled on her niece, Anna, the daughter of her late sister, Catherine. Anna moved to St. Petersburg with her German husband and in August 1740 gave birth to a son, whom she named Ivan. Shortly thereafter Empress Anna died and the infant was proclaimed tsar. Anna's former advisers settled in to govern for a good long time, their puppet king being still a babe in arms. They did not reckon on the opposition mounting against them, particularly within military regiments stationed in the capital. Nor did they reckon on Elizabeth, the daughter of Peter and Catherine.

During the reign of her cousin Anna, Elizabeth had passed herself off as a woman interested in hunting, dancing, expensive clothes, and nicely uniformed officers. The ruse worked; the clique surrounding the infant tsar Ivan underestimated her. Aided by subsidies from the French and Swedish governments, which saw Anna's ministers as pro-Prussian, Elizabeth gathered a faction of powerful supporters. In November 1741 she led a coup in which the little Ivan VI, his parents, and his supporters were arrested. Elizabeth then had herself proclaimed Russia's new empress.

ELIZABETH I (born 1709, ruled 1741–61)

Elizabeth seized the throne intending to rule, and rule she did for twenty years. She was not a hard-working monarch ablaze with new ideas, as her father had been. Rather, this tall, slim woman preferred hunting, travel, and parties to policy-making. But Elizabeth was committed to many of her father's innovations in government, foreign affairs, and cultural and social life. Like her counterparts elsewhere in Europe, she promoted higher education (the University of Moscow was established in 1755), subsidized academicians, supported the publication of scholarly journals, and patronized the national Academy of Sciences, founded by her father. She fostered the development of the arts as well, hiring French and Russian theater troupes to perform for her court and commissioning Italian architects to decorate St. Petersburg with the delicate pastels of rococo architecture.

It was as an exemplar of new fashions in social and cultural life that Elizabeth had her greatest impact on elite women. She spent vast amounts of money on herself and her palaces. Famous for changing her dress three or four times in the course of one ball, she ran up enormous bills with Paris dressmakers and jewelers. She also ordered ornate furniture by the wagonload. This conspicuous consumption furthered the popularization of imported luxuries and, perhaps more important, of the West as the source of all that was stylish. Elizabeth also promoted the Western custom of wealthy women patronizing the secular arts and education.

Her courtiers believed that the empress was secretly married to one of her favorites, an army officer named Aleksei Razumovskii. Officially, she remained single. Intending never to give birth to an heir, Elizabeth appointed her nephew Peter to that position shortly after she took the throne. The young man was the son of Elizabeth's sister Anna and a minor German ruler, the duke of Holstein-Gottorp. After bringing Peter to St. Petersburg to live with her, Elizabeth chose as his bride-to-be a fourteen-year-old princess named Sophia, from the little German principality of Anhalt-Zerbst. Sophia moved to Russia in 1744. When she was baptized in the Russian Orthodox church, she took the name Ekaterina. We know her as Catherine the Great, one of the most remarkable rulers in European history.

CATHERINE II (born 1729, ruled 1762–96)

Sophia of Anhalt-Zerbst would not have become Catherine the Great had she been the modest, unassuming princess that Elizabeth thought she was. She came from a large but not very loving family; in her memoirs, Catherine portrayed her mother Johanna as distant and abusive and said virtually nothing about her father.[5] She had received the education customary for German princesses—tutoring in French, religion (hers was Lutheranism), literature, philosophy, music, and drawing. After her marriage to Peter in August 1745, Catherine settled down to the life preordained for her; within a few years she began to chafe at its limitations.

Chief among her discontents was her unhappy marriage. Catherine found her husband juvenile and crude; he found her haughty and prim. The intellectual differences between the two were profound as well, for Catherine was interested in books and the arts, Peter in military matters. In her memoirs, Catherine said the marriage had soured because Peter had never loved her. This rejection made her "more or less indifferent to him," she wrote, "but not to the crown of Russia."[6]

By the early 1750s the two were entertaining themselves with lovers. This was common practice in the courts of eighteenth-century Europe; indeed it was expected that royalty and their courtiers, locked for life into marriages with spouses chosen for them, would have extramarital affairs. The relationship between Catherine and Peter was unusually hostile, even by the relaxed standards of the era, and by the end of the 1750s the two were rarely speaking to one another. "I let him do as he wished and went my way," Catherine wrote.[7] She had performed her prime obligation in

Catherine in youth and in maturity.
Picture Collection of the New York Public Library.

CATHERINE THE GREAT

In her memoirs, Catherine wrote this description of her talents:

"I used to say to myself, happiness and misery depend on ourselves;
if you feel unhappy, raise yourself above unhappiness, and so act that
your happiness may be independent of all eventualities. With such
a disposition I was born . . . and with a face, to say the least of it,
interesting and which pleased at first sight, without art or effort. My
disposition was naturally so conciliating that no one ever passed a
quarter of an hour in my company without feeling perfectly at ease
and conversing with me as if we had been old acquaintances. Natu-
rally indulgent, I won the confidence of those who had any relations
with me, because everyone felt that the strictest probity and goodwill
were the impulses that I most readily obeyed, and, if I may be allowed
the expression, I venture to assert on my own behalf that I was a true
gentleman, whose cast of mind was more male than female, though,
for all that, I was anything but masculine, for, joined to the mind
and character of a man, I possessed the charms of a very agreeable
woman."

SOURCE: ALEXANDER HERZEN, ED., *MEMOIRS OF CATHERINE THE GREAT* (NEW YORK:
APPLETON, 1859), 319–20.

1754 when she gave birth to a son, Paul. (She later wrote in her memoirs that Paul was the son of courtier Sergei Saltykov.) The estrangement of the royal couple troubled Empress Elizabeth, who occasionally attempted to mediate between them. Mostly the empress avoided the pair and devoted herself to rearing Paul and his sister Anna, born in 1757 of an affair with Stanislaw Poniatowski, future king of Poland. Catherine rarely saw her children.

In late December 1761 the empress died and Peter III ascended the throne. He was not popular with many of the powerful at court, and he made things worse by pursuing controversial domestic and foreign policies. He may also have contemplated exiling Catherine to a convent so that he could marry his latest lover, Elizaveta Polianskaia. These proved to be fatal mistakes. In June 1762, after giving birth to a baby fathered by her current lover, Grigori Orlov, Catherine organized a coup against her husband. Peter was arrested, and church, military, and government leaders proclaimed his wife "autocrat of all the Russias." A few days later, Peter was murdered by his captors. The same fate soon befell the former tsar Ivan VI, now a man in his early twenties who had spent his entire life as a prisoner.

Catherine's audacity in seizing power in her own name is astonishing. A foreigner who had no powerful relatives at court, who was subject to the absolute authority of an empress who did not like her much, who had made an enemy of her theoretically powerful husband, Catherine was nonetheless able to cultivate allies among the cliques and clans of Elizabeth's court. When the moment came to act, she chose to make herself reigning empress rather than taking the more cautious and time-honored path of becoming regent for her son Paul, despite the fact that important people at court favored that latter arrangement. She prevailed because she was a far more able politician than her hapless husband. Ambitious, intelligent, pragmatic, and duplicitous, Catherine devoted the rest of her life to governing Russia. Her overriding mission was to maintain herself in power, and at that she succeeded magnificently.

Catherine owed her success in part to her skillful blending of contemporary European ideas about queens with much older Russian notions. An ethnic German whose first language was French, Catherine presented herself as a sophisticated member of cosmopolitan European royalty. She urged her nobility to study the ideas of the Enlightenment, that is, the new thinking about politics, economics, and education that was making a stir elsewhere. Catherine's interest in Enlightenment thought was genuine, and her espousal of it enabled her to pose as a modern-day Athena bestowing Western culture on her subjects. This image of the modernizing monarch appealed both to those courtiers who wanted to be perceived as social leaders and to educated people who admired Western thought. Catherine emphasized her own enlightenment by corresponding with leading intellectuals abroad and liberally patronizing the development of Russian arts and sciences.

The empress also exploited more traditional Russian ideas about royal women. She publicized her devotion to Russian Orthodoxy and she portrayed herself as deeply solicitous, in a very feminine way, of her people's well-being. Catherine appeared often in loving concourse with her son Paul while he was a child. At court, she played the kindly mistress, wielding power with tact and generosity. As she aged, she encouraged her people to think of her as "Matushka," Little Mother. This term of endearment was used throughout Russia not only by children but also by subordinated people, such as serfs, when addressing noblewomen whom they served. By claiming to be Russia's Matushka, Catherine clothed herself with those qualities of benevolence, piety, authority, and maternal care that had long been attached to Russia's royal women.[8]

Assessing Catherine's more concrete accomplishments has occupied generations of historians. Most have agreed that she further developed the innovations of Peter I in government, trade and commerce, intellectual life, and the arts. Catherine introduced such progressive measures as inoculation against smallpox and the abolition of capital punishment. She eased the central government's demands on the nobility and confirmed the elite's political and economic prerogatives in her "Charter to the Nobility" (1785). Noblemen as a result spent less time in government service and could devote more of their energies to managing their estates. Catherine's foreign policy impressed observers at home and abroad: she expanded Russia's borders, won minor wars with Poland, Turkey, and Sweden, and maintained her empire's standing among the Great Powers.

Her critics argue that the empress talked a far better game than she played. Her foreign policy was financially extravagant and rapacious; it also complicated the governing of Russia by bringing into the empire still more ethnic groups hostile to their Russian overlords. She avoided dealing with her country's most pressing problem, serfdom, even though she recognized it as a moral evil and an obstacle to economic development. She did nothing to improve the situation of serfs on private estates or on the extensive lands owned by the crown and the royal family. Indeed, when she awarded tens of thousands of acres of state land to private owners, she increased the burdens borne by the peasants on those lands. Power was Catherine's lodestar, her critics assert. To them, her oft-stated admiration for Enlightenment humanism was simply part of a public relations campaign aimed at building her reputation.

These disputes can never be fully resolved, for the record of Catherine's life will support a variety of interpretations. As regards the history of elite women in Russia, her reign figures as a time of significant progress. It was remarkable in her era for a monarch, even a female one, to have a set of policies concerning women. Catherine did; and moreover she directly addressed women's education and their role in the arts and intellectual life. She even appointed a woman to head the Academy of Sciences.

SCHOOLING FOR GIRLS

Catherine began laying the foundation for a system of education for girls soon after she seized power. There was much to be done, for Russia had only a few private schools for female pupils. In 1764 the empress ordered the establishment in St. Petersburg of the Smolny Institute, a public boarding school for noble girls that was designed to set the standard for other such institutions. At the same time she authorized the creation of a school for girls from the middling classes, the Novodevichy Institute, located on the grounds of the Moscow convent where Tsarevna Sophia had been imprisoned. The Smolny curriculum included courses in history, languages, literature, mathematics, manners, religion, and that safeguard of feminine virtue, embroidery. The Novodevichy offered a less academically rigorous curriculum and tutored its students in household management and crafts such as sewing. Catherine also established a foundling home in St. Petersburg in 1763. It contained a maternity ward for unmarried mothers and an orphanage for abandoned children. The girls living there learned trades and received dowries when they graduated to improve their marriage prospects.

Over the following decades, publicly and privately funded schools, many of them coeducational, proliferated. By 1792 there were 302 public schools spread across the European part of the empire, enrolling 17,178 students, of whom 1,178 (7 percent) were girls.[9] Far more upper-class girls were being educated at home by governesses and tutors. Comparable figures for female education elsewhere in Europe are difficult to come by, but the patterns were similar: there were schools catering to the propertied classes; most young women were educated at home. Higher education was closed to women everywhere. Few monarchs, other than Catherine, were making any effort to promote education for girls.

The Smolny Institute was her flagship institution, and Catherine supervised its administration herself, visiting the premises occasionally, corresponding with students, and requesting pedagogical advice from Enlightenment luminaries such as Voltaire. The teachers, all of whom were women for the first twenty years of the school's existence, emphasized to their charges that education was a privilege granted them by the beneficent empress. Inspiring curiosity and developing rationality had been the goals Peter had identified for the education of men; Catherine was now seeking to do the same for women. She was not a radical on the subject of women's education; she justified it with the Enlightenment argument that women had to learn to think clearly in order to be good mothers and good subjects of enlightened monarchs. She also declared that educated women would be more self-controlled, and hence more modest, devout, and self-sacrificing than ill-educated ones. Thus did the eighteenth-century advocates for women's education turn to their uses the ancient notion that women's irrationality led them to sin.[10]

Twenty years after the institute's founding, Catherine decided to lay more stress on training its students to be good wives and mothers. New government instructions emphasized the importance of teaching young women to be actively involved in rearing their children and reaffirmed the importance of women's accepting the power structure of the family. In terms reminiscent of *The Domostroi,* the empress wrote, "Everyone in the household, that is, the lady of the house, the children and the servants, must love the head of household or master as a benefactor or guardian."[11] As if to symbolize this sharp new emphasis on the patriarchal order, the government replaced the female staff at the Smolny with male teachers.

Historians are still debating whether the instructions of the early 1780s represent a shift in the educational goals of the Smolny, or whether they simply made more explicit values that had been assumed from the founding of the institute.[12] It is clear is that Catherine's pronouncements, so redolent of *The Domostroi,* were also quite in tune with, indeed had been influenced by, the thinking of the leading European pedagogue in the second half of the eighteenth century, Jean-Jacques Rousseau. The fact that Catherine herself had not lived a life devoted to family was an irony lost on the monarch. She always thought of herself as a dutiful wife and mother who had done her best for an idiot husband and an ungrateful son. They had failed her, not she them.

She did believe that elite women should be active members of Russia's Enlightenment culture, and here she set a powerful personal example. She read widely, patronized artists and writers, and wrote essays, poetry, plays, and memoirs. To press home the message that women could play an important part in the development of the Russian intelligentsia, Catherine appointed Princess Ekaterina Dashkova to head the St. Petersburg

Academy of Sciences in 1782. The next year she named Dashkova founding president of the Russian Academy, an institution devoted to the study of the Russian language. These were extraordinary positions for a woman to hold, but Dashkova, as Catherine knew, was an extraordinary woman.

EKATERINA DASHKOVA (1743–1810)

She was a widow in her forties when Catherine chose her to head the two academic institutions. A member of the aristocratic, cultivated Vorontsov family, which had provided high-ranking servitors to the tsars for generations, Ekaterina had married Mikhail Dashkov when she was sixteen. Their happy union lasted only five years; the prince died when he was just twenty-eight years old. Thereafter Dashkova concentrated on managing her property, rearing her son and daughter, and playing court politics. She proved far more skilled at finance than at parenthood or political intrigue. Although she was an important member of the conspiracy that brought Catherine to power, Dashkova soon fell from the empress's favor, perhaps because she quarreled with Catherine's lover, Grigori Orlov, and his influential brothers.

Throughout her life, Dashkova admired and emulated Catherine. Like the empress, Dashkova was independent and ambitious. In 1805 she wrote that she had decided as a teenager "to become all I could be by my own efforts." She prided herself, with reason, on her intellect. "There were no other two women at the time," she wrote, "apart from the Grand Duchess [Catherine] and myself, who did any serious reading."[13] To continue her education (her formal schooling had consisted of tutoring in languages and deportment), Dashkova journeyed across Europe in the 1770s, meeting royalty and famous intellectuals, admiring the great art of Western Europe, and cultivating her knowledge of science, literature, and philosophy. She enrolled her son Pavel in the University of Edinburgh, then a major center of European science and moral philosophy, and lived with him there, soaking up the vibrant cultural life of that city. Dashkova returned to Russia in 1782 well versed in the ideas of the Enlightenment and well known to its leading lights abroad.

Catherine chose Dashkova to head the Academy of Sciences because she wanted to send a message about women's intellectual capacities. She also believed that Dashkova could bring order to that poorly run organization. The princess proved up to the task, straightening up the academy's finances and broadening its curriculum. Dashkova also took a leading role in compiling the etymological dictionary of Russian that was published by

Ekaterina Dashkova in court dress.
Notice the medal bearing Catherine's portrait.
http://en.wikipedia.org/wiki/File:Vorontsova-Dashkova.jpg.
Accessed June 27, 2011.

EKATERINA DASHKOVA

Dashkova prided herself on her relations with her serfs. In her memoirs, she described a reception to welcome an Irish friend, identified only as "Mrs. Hamilton," to one of her estates.

"I organized a village fete for my friend, which pleased and affected her and the memory of which will remain with me so long as I live. A village had been newly built a few miles away from Troitskoe [one of Dashkova's estates]. I had all the peasants who were going to dwell in it gathered together, all dressed in their best clothes, embroidered by the women, as is the custom with us. The weather was gorgeous, and I made them dance on the grass and sing Russian songs. My friend, who had never seen or heard anything like it, was delighted with it all—the songs, the dances, the women's dresses. Russian dishes and drinks were not forgotten, and the whole formed such a truly national picture and was so novel for Mrs. Hamilton that she enjoyed it more than the most magnificent Court entertainment I could imagine.

At the moment when these good people were about to drink my health I presented my friend to them as the person to whom their respect was due, told them their new village must be called 'Hamilton' after her, and wished them all kinds of prosperity in a place which bore so dear a name. I then presented them with a gift of bread and salt and sent them away so happy and grateful that the memory of that day is still preserved in the little colony."

SOURCE: DASHKOVA, E. R., *THE MEMOIRS OF PRINCESS DASHKOVA*, TRANSLATED AND EDITED BY KYRIL FITZLYON, INTRODUCTION BY JEHANNE M. GHEITH (DURHAM, N.C.: DUKE UNIVERSITY PRESS, 1995), 218.

the Russian Academy, edited two literary journals, wrote articles on various scholarly subjects, and composed several plays.

Upper-class women across Europe were participating in the Enlightenment as patrons, writers, and scholars. Dashkova matched and in some ways surpassed this elite company in the range of her interests as well as in ambition and achievements. No other woman of her time headed a university-level academic institution. Dashkova was empowered by the long-standing Russian practice of granting autonomy and authority to high-ranking widows, and also by the presence on the Russian throne of another innovative woman. They both used their power to promote the development of their country's intellectual life and women's participation in that life.

Catherine fired Dashkova in 1793 because the princess had authorized the publication of a play that the empress—spooked by the French Revolution—found subversive. Dashkova retired to her estates and devoted herself to enlightened agriculture. She believed that serfdom was a necessary institution, arguing that it protected peasants from rapacious government officials and guaranteed the nobility a livelihood. She also believed, despite much evidence to the contrary, that sensible nobles would usually treat their serfs well. "A landowner would have to be crack-brained to want to exhaust the source of his own riches," she wrote in her memoirs. Dashkova acted on her beliefs by personally managing her estates, even, we are told, working alongside the peasants. Martha Wilmot, an Anglo-Irish woman who lived with Dashkova in the first decade of the nineteenth century, left this description of the energetic princess: "She feeds the cows, she composes music, she sings and plays, she writes for the press, she shells the corn, she talks out loud in Church and corrects the Priest . . . , she talks out loud in her little Theater and puts in the Performers when they are out in their parts, she is a Doctor, an Apothecary, a Surgeon, a Farrier, a Carpenter, a Magistrate, a Lawyer . . ."[14]

Change for Noblewomen in the Eighteenth Century

Dashkova's accomplishments reflected developments in elite women's lives that spread outward from St. Petersburg during the eighteenth century. By Catherine's reign, the gender segregation of the Muscovite era lingered on only in provincial areas far from the major cities. Nearly everywhere, girls from noble families were being educated, mostly by tutors hired by their parents. Women in families attuned to the new arts and ideas read for pleasure, played musical instruments, attended plays, and drew sketches of the countryside.[15] While these pleasant additions to daily life spread through the provinces, noblewomen were also expanding their property rights.

PROPERTY RIGHTS

Women's property rights were defined in various government statutes and debated in Russian law courts throughout the eighteenth century. Revisions of inheritance law remained true to the provisions of the *Ulozhenie* of 1649: widows were entitled to one-seventh of their husband's real property and one-fourth of moveables. A daughter whose parents died intestate could claim one-fourteenth of her parents' real property and one-eighth of the moveables; parents could choose to make more generous bequests in wills. The law did not address the question of whether daughters' dowries should be considered part of their inheritances. That issue was contentious, because counting dowries as inheritances meant that women would receive less when their parents died. The courts usually ruled that dowry property should not be subtracted from inheritance shares.[16]

Russian judges in the eighteenth century also repeatedly reaffirmed the long-standing principle that women, regardless of their marital status, could control their property. In 1753 the imperial Senate, Russia's highest court, ruled in a landmark case that a woman did not need her husband's consent to sell an estate that belonged to her. In effect, the senators were stating that women had the same ownership rights as men. Although consistent with Russian tradition, this ruling was remarkable in the context of eighteenth-century Europe. In most countries, particularly the larger ones, medieval customs that had granted women considerable control over their dowries and inheritances had given way in the early modern period to law codes that gave husbands control of, and often ownership of, their wives' property. In Britain, for example, the legal principle of couverture decreed that in marriage, "the husband and wife are one person in law; that is, the very being or legal existence of the woman is suspended during the marriage, or at least is incorporated and consolidated into that of the husband."[17] Because of couverture, an English wife required her husband's agreement to sign a contract, file a civil suit, or execute a will, and she had little recourse should a profligate spouse gamble away all her property. By comparison, a Russian wife was practically a free agent.

The property rights of Russian noblewomen were also strengthened in the eighteenth century by a redefinition of the landholding rights of their class. In the aftermath of Peter I's abolition of pomeste and votchina, nobles argued successfully in court cases and petitions to the government that an individual landowner possessed full title to an estate. The government could not confiscate land if an owner defaulted on his obligation to serve the state. Nor could the government require an owner to obtain the consent of his or her extended family before selling land. It was significant that Russian jurists and litigants made no gender distinctions in these new arguments, and they also appear to have been quite blind to the attractions of couverture, eschewing its importation into Russian law.

Perhaps noblewomen themselves pressured the lawmakers to preserve their rights, for even as the jurists drafted the laws and the judges interpreted them, noblewomen were exercising those rights more energetically than ever before. Widows had long been involved in the real estate market; now married women became more engaged as well. Michelle Marrese has found that 20 percent of the female sellers of land in the 1710s were married women. By mid-century, that figure had more than doubled, to 46 percent. One hundred years later, married women were 63 percent of the female buyers of land and serfs. Marrese has estimated that by 1860 women comprised a third or more of the buyers and sellers.[18]

In the eighteenth century, women also participated more directly and more often in other legal transactions. They attended sessions of the courts and signed their own names to sales contracts, rather than sending male representatives to perform such tasks, as they had done in the past. Some women sued estranged husbands or other family members over property disputes. Foreign observers were astonished by the autonomy of propertied women. Martha Wilmot, Dashkova's friend, wrote in her journal in 1806, "The full and entire dominion which Russian women have over their own fortunes gives them a remarkable degree of liberty and a degree of independence of their Husbands unknown in England."[19] The persistence of women's property and legal rights in Russia was one important instance in which the preservation, and indeed expansion, of traditional principles worked to women's benefit.

FAMILY VALUES

Notions about family life were more affected by ideas flowing in from Western Europe in the eighteenth century. We have already seen that Peter I endorsed the principle that spouses should share emotional intimacy as well as household management. This principle gained widespread acceptance in the eighteenth century. In 1767, Natalia Dolgorukaia (1714–71), who belonged to the top ranks of the nobility, summed up the new stress on conjugal love in her description of her marriage. "It seemed to me that he had been born for me and I for him," she wrote of her husband Ivan, years after his death, "and it was impossible for us to live without one another." Theirs was an alliance of soulmates; "I was a comrade to my husband," she fondly recalled.[20]

Similar sentiments appear in the correspondence of other noblewomen. Olga Glagoleva has analyzed the way eighteenth-century wives addressed their husbands in letters. Early in Peter's reign, women writing to their spouses emphasized their subordination. "To my sovereign Ivan Ivanovich," wrote Maria Kireevskaia in 1716, "be healthy my sovereign Ivan Ivanovich for many years, please my sovereign have a letter written to me about your perennial health." Glagoleva and Mary Cavender have found that by the end of the century, the tender terms "friend" and "angel" had replaced "sovereign."[21]

Older patriarchal ideas persisted. Dolgorukaia saw herself as her husband's comrade, not his equal: she believed that it was her duty to devote herself completely to him, while his was to serve as her lover, protector, and moral instructor. "I had everything in him," she wrote many years after his death, "a gracious husband, and father, and teacher and seeker after my salvation."[22] Dolgorukaia proved her devotion to Ivan by following him into Siberian exile after he ran afoul of Empress Anna's favorites.

If a wife did not have such a loving marriage, she owed it to God and her family to make the best of things. A widow named Iakovleva, who headed her household and managed a small estate, made this clear to her thirteen-year-old daughter Anna in 1769, shortly before she arranged Anna's marriage to a much older man. "And when God blesses you with a husband," the widow declared, "then respect your husband as your master, obey him, and love him with all your heart, even if he acts badly toward you. Know too that he was given to you by the Lord: the good for making you happy, and the bad to test your tolerance. If you bear all of this with humility, then you will have submitted to the will of God and not humanity."[23]

Noblewomen were also expected to be lovingly submissive to older family members, both before and after they married. In their memoirs, Dolgorukaia and Anna Labzina, Iakovleva's daughter, profess deep affection for their marital families, especially their mothers-in-law. Each portrays herself as an innocent young bride afraid to leave her mother and go to live with people whom, as Dolgorukaia put it, she was "not accustomed to." Both women came to love some of their new kin. Labzina, whose marriage to her first husband was desperately unhappy, threw herself on the mercy of her in-laws, and they responded with kindness. "I will never forget their love and affection, " she wrote, "especially that of my brother-in-law, who, upon seeing my youth and simple nature, endeavored to treat me warmly." Labzina also relied heavily upon her mother-in-law, whom she remembered as "my . . . consolation and solace."[24] This latter comment may be particularly instructive. Eighteenth-century court cases suggest fairly regular friction among sisters-in-law and brothers-in-law but rather less between parents and children. Perhaps the long-standing Russian belief in the importance of respect for elders limited the conflict between generations.

THE BEGINNINGS OF THE CULT OF DOMESTICITY

During Catherine's reign, Russians who followed intellectual trends in Western Europe became aware that a powerful critique of the Enlightenment was brewing. Dominant systems of ideas and behavior often provoke reactions, resulting in the diversion or even the temporary choking-off of liberating energies, which may emerge only many decades later in altered forms. Such was the case with the Enlightenment, which generated so many theories of liberation, rationalism, and progress, and yet which ended in the later eighteenth century in a reaction that touted the worth of traditional customs, religion, romantically intuitive ways of knowing, and revised gender values.

This counter-revolution played itself out in women's history through a critique launched against the Enlightenment's impact on women's education and social behavior. The Swiss philosopher Jean-Jacques Rousseau, by his own testimony solitary and egocentric, was the pioneer of this critique. Rousseau and a growing number of like-minded social critics began by charging that noblewomen were spending too much time socializing and dabbling in intellectual activities. Partying, they asserted, led to immorality, and reading to addled female minds; the dreadful result was that women were neglecting their children and encouraging their husbands' frailties. How else to explain the rampant immorality, especially among the frivolous, decadent aristocracy? But there was a remedy. Women could play a crucial role in getting society back on the right track by devoting themselves to their homes and families. Safe within the domestic circle, far from the corruptions of the public world, they could cultivate their natural piety, teach their children to be moral people and good citizens, and provide support to their husbands. By building stable families, women would contribute to stability in the society at large.

For centuries Europeans had believed that ideal women devoted themselves to their menfolk and their families. The cult of domesticity updated those core ideas in response to the political and social realities of the eighteenth century. But it contained new ideas too, chief among them its assertion that women possessed an innate sense of right and wrong. And this was important, for earlier gender codes, as we have seen, taught that women were less capable of understanding morality than men were. Proponents of the cult of domesticity strenuously disagreed, maintaining instead that women could serve as moral guides for their husbands and children. They argued that the ideal women was a loving, self-sacrificing, pious anchor of happy families and rearer of the next generation of pious, ethical citizens. They valued women's economic contribution to their families' welfare less than thinkers of the past, perhaps because the development of markets and manufacturing in Western Europe was reducing the amount of income-generating work that was performed in the homes of the propertied.

Early in the nineteenth century, the cult of domesticity became the dominant European conception of women's nature and roles, even though its prescriptions for homemaking and childrearing could only be followed by the small minority of women who did not have to contribute to the economic support of themselves and their children. We have already seen its influence at work in late eighteenth-century Russia, in Catherine's revision of the curriculum of the Smolny Institute. The cult of domesticity was also proclaimed by Russian writers, particularly poets, during Catherine's reign. The empress sent mixed messages on women's domestic mission, for she was also deeply committed to their participation in intellectual and cultural life. Her successors, particularly her conservative grandson, Nicholas I, emperor of Russia from 1825 to 1855, were another story.

Romanov Domesticity, 1796–1855

POLITICS

In 1796, Catherine died. Her son Paul seized the powers of autocrat eagerly and issued strict regulations to his courtiers and military. Paul was peevish; he had lived too long under the thumb of his unloving mother. He sought to undermine her reputation in a variety of ways, one of which was the publication of a new law of succession in 1797 that prohibited women from inheriting the crown ever again. Unfortunately, Paul's political skills resembled those of his father more than his mother, so he made enemies, especially among the military high command. In 1801, army officers murdered Paul in his bed and thrust his son Alexander onto the throne.

Alexander I (ruled 1801–25) was an intelligent, thoughtful man, steeped in the Enlightenment. In the early years of his reign he reformed the government and the law code and improved the administration and funding of higher education. Alexander also joined the European-wide coalition fighting Napoleon, suffered defeats, but distinguished himself in 1812 by refusing to surrender, even after the French occupied Moscow. The Russian army thereafter played an important part in Napoleon's defeat, and Alexander entered the peace negotiations that followed as one of Europe's most highly regarded monarchs. On his return to Russia, he pursued conservative domestic policies.

In November 1825, the forty-eight-year-old emperor suddenly died of natural causes, possibly typhus. The succession was muddled, for Alexander was childless. His younger brother Nicholas took power, then immediately had to suppress a revolt by an army faction, the Decembrists, that was calling for a constitutional monarchy. The Decembrists were easily routed, but the existence of revolutionary sentiments within the military elite alarmed Nicholas, already a conservative by temperament and training.

For thirty years, he labored to keep democratic ideas from penetrating Russia, while continuing the policies of his predecessors. He promoted elite education and government reform, in hopes of making both elite and government into instruments of his will. He maintained a huge army. This required raising government revenues, which in turn led the emperor to consider abolishing serfdom, for he and many of his advisers believed that the bondage of the peasantry inhibited economic development. And, to his credit, Nicholas also thought that serfdom was morally indefensible. In 1842 he described it as "an evil, palpable and obvious to everyone." "However," he added, "to attack it now would be, of course, an even more disastrous evil."[25]

Thus torn between the old evils that he knew and new ones that he dared not foster, Nicholas spent his reign trying to limit the consequences of his own reforms, while pursuing a foreign policy that caused him to be seen abroad and at home as an aggressive reactionary. He funded the universities, but clamped them under strict controls to prevent faculty from teaching pernicious subjects. He presided over a huge expansion in the number of books, newspapers, and magazines imported to and printed in Russia, but had them censored. Ultimately he failed to maintain control over the minds of his ruling class. By the 1840s, proposals for major reform were circulating among intellectuals and government bureaucrats. In 1853, Nicholas blundered into the Crimean War with Britain, France, and the Ottoman Empire. It was a disaster for the Russian army and a demonstration of the nation's military and economic inferiority to the Great Powers. In February 1855, before peace could be made, Nicholas died of pneumonia. He left behind an intelligentsia seething with new ideas and an heir, Alexander, who was committed to major reforms.

EMPRESS MARIA (1759–1828) AND
EMPRESS ALEXANDRA (1798–1860)

Nicholas was a happy subscriber to the variant of the cult of domesticity that prevailed among the European nobility. It may seem odd that the cult, which arose within a bourgeois critique of the aristocracy, won fans among aristocrats. It did so perhaps in part because, especially after the French Revolution, such people were afraid to be out of step with the cultural changes of the time, on which the middle class was having increasing influence. The cult also appealed to the nobility for the same reason it appealed to lower-ranking folk: it was based on an ancient vision of family life in which man provided and woman served. The cult valued her emotional service more than her physical labor, which was a shift of emphasis from earlier gender ideals, but a shift only. The notion of the gentle, all-forgiving, virtuous mother preached by the cult had been present for centuries in the idealizations of the Virgin.

Because the cult was rooted in these widely accepted universals and because it held out promises of loving families and sheltering homes in a time of rapid, unsettling economic and political change, it traveled easily. It was picked up by conservative rulers, such as Nicholas, who saw its potential to shore up the status quo; by republican Americans, who believed that mothers could teach democratic values to the citizens of the new United States; and later in the nineteenth century by nationalists from Wales to Poland, who granted women a central role in preserving ethnic identity. Feminists made use of the cult as well, arguing that women should be permitted to apply their moral sense and housekeeping skills to social improvement. After Europeans disseminated it around the world, non-Europeans as remote from one another as Hindu fundamentalists and Chinese communists incorporated its ideas into their worldviews. Even as all these devotees adapted the cult of domesticity to their cultures and objectives, its core ideas about women remained remarkably stable. Their influence endures in the twenty-first century.

The nobles' variant of the cult arose in the late eighteenth and early nineteenth centuries from their own critique of the customs of family life in their class. Many of these people agreed with bourgeois critics who charged that aristocratic parents paid too little attention to their children. Catherine the Great shared these discontents, and in the memoirs she wrote in the 1790s, she portrayed herself as a lonely child, dominated first by an autocratic, self-absorbed mother who slapped her for the least misbehavior, then by Empress Elizabeth, who was still more distant and controlling.[26] The ideal of a sympathetic, attentive mother had tremendous appeal to people who had had such childhoods. Catherine complained about her own mother while being a distant and demanding mother herself, which may explain why her son Paul was drawn to the cult of domesticity.

So was his wife Maria, whose parents, the duke and duchess of the German principality of Württenberg, had brought her up to believe in the importance of loving relations between royals. Maria married Paul in 1776, after his first wife died in childbirth; the young people had the good fortune to love one another. An energetic woman, Maria remodeled the couple's palace at Pavlovsk, outside St. Petersburg, patronized charities, attended the many court ceremonies and religious observances, and painted, embroidered, carved cameos, and played several musical instruments. Maria enjoyed her heavily scheduled life, first as grand duchess, then as empress, but she also believed that she should be an attentive and affectionate mother. So she oversaw the education of eight of her ten children (her eldest sons, Alexander and Constantine, were reared by Catherine) and kept in close touch with all of them when they were grown. She also commissioned poets to sing her praises as a loving mother, and she stressed her devotion to family by undertaking extended periods of mourning for deceased relatives and having monuments constructed to commemorate her parents and husband. All this was sincere, and it served as a repudiation of her mother-in-law Catherine, with whom she had a frosty relationship. It also gave the royal stamp of approval to the nobles' variant of the cult of domesticity.

Maria remained true to the ancient principle that marriage among royals must serve the purpose of preserving the dynasty. So she was disappointed when her oldest sons, Alexander and Constantine, could not reconcile the promptings of their hearts with their obligations as princes. Alexander barely tolerated the wife that had been chosen for him and, perhaps as a consequence, had no children. Constantine insisted on marrying his beloved, a Polish noblewoman who was not of royal rank. Then he renounced his claim to the throne. Fortunately for the house of Romanov, Nicholas, Maria's third son, did not disappoint. He contracted a love match with Princess Charlotte of Prussia, and she became an empress who personified the ideals of the cult of domesticity even more perfectly than her formidable mother-in-law.

Christened Alexandra on her baptism into Orthodoxy, the new grand duchess set about having babies and developing her reputation as a frail, shy consort. In part this image arose because Alexandra was in fact a retiring woman who lacked Maria's self-confidence and energy. It also reflected a shift in the aristocratic cult of domesticity, away from the culturally accomplished women of the late eighteenth century to a more emotional, even childlike, ideal. Artists portrayed Alexandra as a pale, willowy, and serene woman, swathed in gauzy dresses and hung with ropes of pearls. Courtiers declared reverently that she had taken an oath never to use the word "command." Court poets portrayed her as radiating happiness. "Near her all our thoughts are song!" crooned Vasili Zhukovskii. Perhaps this was not mere sycophancy. Nicholas wrote to Alexandra after twenty years of marriage, "God has bestowed upon you such a happy character that it is no merit to love you."[27]

Nicholas and Alexandra, like their British counterparts Queen Victoria and Prince Albert, were deeply committed to one another and to being good parents. The emperor was a devoted husband who considered his wife both friend and confidant. The empress returned his love in full measure. Breakfasting with his family frequently, the emperor expected his children to tell him about their lessons and whatever else they were doing. The family also often dined together. A bevy of nannies and tutors did the work of rearing the children, but Nicholas and Alexandra's brood were far closer to their parents than their predecessors had been.

Government spokesmen publicized the royal family's happy home life to promote the popularity of the emperor, tapping into deep affinities within the Russian public, elite and poor folk alike. The image of domestic felicity conveyed in pictures, poetry, and public appearances was reassuring and endearing. By presenting it as in tune with ideas fashionable in the great capitals of Europe, Nicholas's publicists also portrayed the monarch and his consort as cosmopolitan enlighteners of their people, a role played by all the Romanovs since Peter.[28] There were older ideas at work in the campaign as well. Emphasizing Nicholas's dutiful and loving attention to his children reinforced the notion that the emperor was also the caring father of his country. Catherine had done the same when she portrayed herself as the enlightened empress and as Matushka.

THE ASCENDANCY OF THE CULT OF DOMESTICITY

Nicholas did not have to coerce his subjects into accepting the cult of domesticity; it already had many devotees among the elite when he took the throne. Mary Cavender has found late eighteenth-century letters in which Russian nobles praised mothers who instructed their families in ethical behavior. We have already seen the increased emphasis in these decades on more loving, less patriarchal relations between husbands and wives. In the early nineteenth century, government officials turned to the ideas of the cult for ways to control criminals exiled for life to Siberia. The men should marry, officials believed, because loving wives tamed men's unruliness and inspired them to behave better. The exile would also "find a helpmeet in his wife, who will uphold and increase the comfort of domestic life through her own activity," an 1827 report declared.[29]

The dissemination of cult ideas continued throughout Nicholas's reign, as the bookstores filled with housekeeping guides, cookbooks, etiquette manuals, and edifying literature and poetry, some published in Russia, some imported from abroad. A typical description of the perfect wife appeared in an 1846 collection of essays for young people, written by Maria Korsini, a graduate of the Smolny Institute: "Her dominion is kindness and gentleness. She looks after the domestic tranquility of her husband. . . . She raises her babies and is the first to pronounce for them the name of God and to make them pray. She also ensures that the servant performs her duties and that quietude and peace reign in her house. A woman is given inexhaustible patience, which helps her to endure the screams of children, lack of sleep, and many minor domestic unpleasantries."[30]

This version of the cult is adapted to the life of the average noblewoman, for it emphasizes household management, as the royal version did not. Royal women supervised their staffs, but this was not an activity for which they were widely praised. More important was their symbolic position as consort of the emperor and mother of his children and, by extension, of the nation. It was quite otherwise with noblewomen, whose primary responsibilities included running households, and so Korsini harkens back to *The Domostroi* in the importance she attaches to "ensuring that the servant performs her duties." Novels, short stories, and diaries from the period suggest that there was still a good deal of the steely mistress of *The Domostroi* in real married noblewomen. Managing domestic chores and possibly their own estates required them to be authoritative.

There were other differences between the Nicholaevan cult of domesticity and the more bourgeois versions ascendant in Western Europe and North America. Chief among them was a different emphasis on the importance of separating woman's sphere, the inside and private, from man's, the outside and public. The notion that women belonged in the home, away from the temptations and dangers of the wider world, was an ancient one among Europeans, as well as among Arabs, Turks, Chinese, and other peoples. We have seen it in *The Domostroi,* and in the Muscovite seclusion of elite women. Nineteenth-century Russian advocates of the cult of domesticity, however, never carried that idea to the extremes of those contemporary British or Germans who wrote obsessively about the importance of women staying home. Now it was the Western Europeans who were harping on women's seclusion.

This difference arose from differences in economic and social development in Western and Eastern Europe. In the West, especially the northwest, the growth of commerce and manufacturing led to a physical separation of urban residences from workplaces. By the end of the eighteenth century, more and more men were working away from home, which had not been the case in earlier times, when workers and bosses lived and labored in the same buildings. This development was idealized as the cult of domesticity was formulated. Home came to be seen as a refuge from the moral and physical squalor of public spaces. Soon this idealization was put in service to the social agenda of the middle class. Desirous of distinguishing themselves from the nobles who still outranked them in status and the artisans and peasants from whom many of them sprang, these people, particularly the English ones, defined middle-class "respectability" as requiring that women spend most of their time in their residences, as nobles did not and poor people could not. The Russian nobility in the early nineteenth century had no such social anxieties. Nor did the physical separation of workplaces and residences exist in Russia, either in the preindustrial cities or in the countryside. Hence the version of the cult that they created laid far less stress on the physical locations of men's and women's "separate spheres" than did middle-class variants elsewhere, which resulted in less attention being devoted to policing elite women's behavior when in public.[31]

The Russian cult of domesticity also differed from the Western European bourgeois one in its definitions of masculinity. Thus far we have not discussed the cult's prescriptions for men, and, indeed, they are often overlooked by historians. This is unfortunate, for the cult of domesticity had quite a bit to say about men, as all gender codes do, and what it said was very influential. Western European proponents of the cult sang the praises of the hard-working husband who provided for and loved his family, disciplined his children, and supervised their education, especially that of the boys. To the larger world, he set an example of rectitude and rationality. These values moved quite easily to Nicholaevan Russia, where they merged with Peter's energetic masculinity. Nicholas's government preached that the men of the ruling class should be educated, self-disciplined, dutiful, modest, pious, and hard-working. But public life might toughen them too much, deadening their capacity for fellow-feeling and perhaps even corrupting their morals. (This was a key idea of the cult.) Hence they needed good wives waiting at home to soothe and advise them. This synthesis of imported and inherited masculine ideals reflected, as Peter's gender ideas had, the character of the monarch as well as his agenda for his servitors.[32]

Nicholas's notions about masculinity and those proclaimed by opinion-makers in Western Europe differed most significantly in that his were more autocratic, theirs more democratic. The masculine ethos popular among the middle and, increasingly, the working classes argued that a man should be judged not according to his social rank, his family's connections, or how well he subordinated himself to the authorities, but on his own merits and by his own accomplishments. He could be considered successful if he was a good family man who did well in business or the professions. This leveling individualism, which suited Western Europeans, especially the British and their North American cousins, could never win the favor of authoritarian rulers such as Nicholas. He stayed true to older patriarchal ideals of obedience, service, and class and believed in the importance of duty, especially the duty to serve the tsar.

Nicholas could not keep the cult's more democratic version of masculinity out of Russia, though. It crept in among those elite men who dreamed of political change and rejected what they saw as the servility demanded of them by the autocrat. They valued rationality, education, integrity, social responsibility, diligence, and independence of thought. Like Peter the Great, they also put stock in energy and initiative. During Nicholas's times such men were few. There would be many more of them during the reign of his son Alexander.

NICHOLAEVAN FAMILY LAW

The cult of domesticity was the soft, persuasive voice of Nicholaevan gender discourse. When the law spoke, it sternly reaffirmed the enduring rules of patriarchy. *The Collection of the Laws of the Russian Empire,* issued in 1832, declared, "[The] wife is obligated to obey her husband as the head of the family, to live with him in love, respect and unlimited obedience, and to render him all pleasure and affection as mistress of the household." A husband's duties were "to love his wife as his own body, to live with her in harmony, to respect and defend her, and to forgive her insufficiencies and ease her infirmities."[33]

This statement of general principles was attached to a short list of specific obligations drawn from older Russian laws. William Wagner has pointed out that the *Collection*'s medieval origins are reflected in the fact that it was mostly concerned, as *The Domostroi* had been, with prescribing duties and stressing the importance of submission to authority.[34] Husbands were required to support their wives. Wives were required to live with their husbands, unless those husbands were sentenced to exile in Siberia. The law of common residence was reinforced by another regulation that forbade women from holding passports in their own names. Passports were the identification cards of imperial Russia. Since women could not obtain them, they had to have their husbands' or parents' permission to live apart from their families or to travel. Married women also required the consent of their husbands before they could take a job. Both spouses were forbidden to injure one another physically or involve one another in criminal acts. The latter requirement was far more likely to be enforced than the former, for Russian custom and Russian people of all social ranks, as we have seen, had long tolerated the beating of wives and children, so long as it did not result in serious injury, and sometimes even when it did.

The 1832 law code preserved ancient patriarchal principles regarding the relations between parents and children as well. Parents were required to support their minor children; children repaid this care by giving their parents lifelong obedience. The laws declared that dutiful children should accept uncomplainingly whatever punishments their parents administered. Disobedience was defined as a crime, and particularly objectionable were failing to support aged parents financially and marrying without parental consent. A young woman or man who eloped could be disinherited and brought up on criminal charges.

Marriage law still fell under the jurisdiction of religious authorities in this period. Gregory Freeze has found that, as the Orthodox Church enlarged its administrative apparatus in the eighteenth century, it became better able to enforce its definitions of monogamy. By Nicholas's reign, consequently, Russian divorce procedures were among the strictest in Europe. Orthodox prelates declared that the only justifiable grounds for dissolving a marriage were adultery, abandonment for many years, impotence, or exile to Siberia. Even when these conditions existed, obtaining an annulment was time-consuming and expensive. For example, to gain an annulment on the grounds of sexual incapacity, a plaintiff had to provide evidence that his or her spouse's impotence arose from physical causes and had existed prior to the marriage. Testimony from physicians was required, and if the wife was the plaintiff, she had to also have a doctor certify that she was still a virgin. If a woman did obtain an annulment, she had no right to custody of her children or financial support from her former husband.[35]

Roman Catholic and Lutheran authorities in the Russian empire also prohibited divorce and rarely granted annulments. Indeed, Christians across Europe in the nineteenth century opposed divorce because they still believed, as they had for centuries, that marriage was a union created by God during the wedding ceremony. To dissolve it was to go against God's will. The pain experienced in an unhappy marriage was no different from all the other suffering of life, Christians were taught. Suffering was a necessary means to the end of learning how to be patient and dutiful; it brought one closer to Christ, who had suffered agonies for humankind's sake. So a bad marriage was to be endured humbly, with the hope that things would improve if people stuck it out long enough. Labzina's mother and in-laws told her precisely this in the eighteenth century. Christian and Jewish authorities also argued that marriage was the bedrock institution of society; peace in the larger community depended on peace within the family, family tranquility depended on orderly relations among family members, and order depended on patriarchal power, whether or not it was exercised benignly.[36]

EDUCATION

The proposition that elite women could best meet their family obligations if they were formally educated was widely accepted in the early nineteenth century, and schooling for propertied girls continued to expand. Tutoring at home remained the predominant method, but by 1845 thirty-six boarding schools for girls, called "institutes," had been founded. In 1843 the church began opening schools for the daughters of priests, and private organizations and individuals also endowed schools. All these institutions emphasized the preparation of their students to be wives and mothers. As in the past, the curriculum varied according to the social class of the pupils: there was more stress on the arts in schools for noble girls, more stress on learning trades in those for the less privileged. The 1827 rules and regulations for a school for middle-class girls declared, "The purpose . . . is to teach the students to be good wives, solicitous mothers, and exemplary mentors for their children, and to teach them the skills they need to be able to provide for themselves and their families by means of their own hard work."[37]

In memoirs, graduates of the boarding schools paint portraits of their teenage years that are similar to those created by other nineteenth-century Europeans. They report feeling terrified when, at age eight or nine, they first entered the institutes that would be their homes until they graduated at age sixteen. This was more than the usual anxiety of a child on the first day of school, for many of these girls were beginning a long separation from their families. Contact with relatives was not encouraged even for pupils whose families lived nearby, because Russian pedagogues believed that the shaping of girls into moral young ladies proceeded best without distraction. Years passed before those from provincial families returned home.

The schools were spartan. Sophia Khvoshchinskaia, a graduate of the Smolny, remembered her first impressions: "The longest of corridors, enormous classrooms, endless dormitories, staircase upon staircase. A spacious and bleak place after the crowded coziness of home."[38] Many alumnae complained about bad food, stifling rules, lazy instructors, and autocratic matrons who supervised the dormitories. But they did form deep attachments to other girls and to the more admirable teachers. By the time they graduated as teenagers, many girls had come to consider the institutes their homes, and they found it wrenching to leave their friends. "Spare me from describing our final farewells," wrote Nadezhda Sokhanskaia in 1847–48. "It all seems even sadder to me now. Where have you gone? What has become of us? How much that was fine and beautiful has disappeared, perhaps forever, never to return!"[39]

Across Europe, the curriculum of women's education in the early 1800s was often criticized for being insufficiently rigorous. Religion, embroidery, and social graces were taught to girls, while boys studied classical languages and mathematics. This educational inequality was galling to those who did not consider women innately inferior to men intellectually. In Russia as elsewhere, however, the education available to elite women did foster the participation of those women in the nation's growing secular culture. From the reign of Catherine on, noblewomen were reading poetry, novels, and magazines as well as devotional texts. By the 1820s they were also attending lectures, plays, and poetry readings.

PHILANTHROPY

One of the great ironies of women's history in nineteenth-century Europe is the fact that the cult of domesticity, which prescribed women's concentration on their homes and families, was used to justify ever greater involvement by elite women in the world beyond those homes. Philanthropy, a highly organized type of charity, was one of the first, most popular, and most enduring of their many ventures. We have seen that elite women had long been expected to help the poor. The rapid social changes of the time, particularly the growth of slums in the cities of northwestern Europe, convinced some that traditional benevolence (giving alms to beggars, taking in homeless people, making donations to the church) was no longer sufficient. So charitable societies were established across Europe. Female philanthropists often focused their energies on urban poor women and justified their engagement by arguing that the virtuous upper-class woman had a religious duty to rescue her less fortunate and more corruptible sisters by giving them financial assistance and educating them to be self-supporting, pious, and virtuous.

The prejudices and condescension of nineteenth-century philanthropists should not blind us to the great social evils they were trying to alleviate. Crime, epidemic diseases, alcoholism, and prostitution bedeviled nineteenth-century cities, and poor women struggled as well with awful living and working conditions. In the first half of the century, the need was less severe in Russia than in Western Europe, because Russia had yet to experience the Industrial Revolution, which swelled urban populations and urban problems. But the situation of poor women in Russia's cities was compelling, nonetheless.

The foremost advocate for philanthropy aimed at women was Empress Maria, Nicholas's mother. This redoubtable woman was running so many charities when she died in 1828 that a government agency, the Department of the Institutions of Empress Maria, had to be created to oversee them all. The empress also inspired her daughters-in-law to become philanthropists. Elizaveta, the wife of Alexander I, established the Women's Patriotic Society in 1812 to work among those injured or displaced by the Napoleonic Wars. It continued on as a sponsor of girls' schools after the wars ended. Alexandra, Nicholas's wife, allocated funds to several charities and paid close attention to the operation of the Smolny Institute. Still more energetic was her sister-in-law, the Grand Duchess Elena, a German princess who was the wife of Michael, Nicholas's younger brother. Elena funded charities and schools, and became an advocate of the emancipation of the serfs.

The example of Maria and her daughters-in-law was widely followed. Adele Lindenmeyr has written that setting up a charity became "virtually part of the job description of the wives of high-ranking state officials."[40] By the 1830s, "Ladies' Charitable Societies" in Moscow, St. Petersburg, Riga, Tver, and other provincial cities were distributing food, clothing, and money to the needy. Prison societies were sending members into the jails to pass out warm clothes and nutritious food, teach basic literacy and numeracy, and read the Bible aloud. Other groups sponsored schools and workhouses in which poor women learned marketable skills, particularly needlework. Their philanthropy was part of an increasingly wide-ranging involvement of elite women in public life.

WOMEN IN THE INTELLIGENTSIA

Also part of that involvement was women's participation in one of the most important developments of the Nicholaevan era, the emergence of the reform-minded intelligentsia. The foundation for this participation was laid by Catherine. In her day it consisted mostly, as it did in Western Europe, of wealthy women sponsoring male thinkers and writers. This was not one of Catherine's innovations; rich women had been supporting the arts in Russia since Peter's reign. The new development of Catherine's reign was the salon, weekly gatherings hosted by women at their homes during which people debated political questions or talked about the arts. Salons were all the rage across Europe during the Enlightenment; Russia's first one met at the home of Varvara Iushkova in the city of Tula in the 1790s. There some of Russia's best poets debuted their latest works. The heyday of salons in Russia came during Nicholas's reign, when Iushkova's daughter, Avdotia Elagina, led a salon in Moscow that met for more than thirty years and played an important part in generating the political and intellectual movement known as Slavophilism. In St. Petersburg, Grand Duchess Elena, the philanthropist, held a salon at her palace on Thursdays, to which she invited the leading lights of Russian culture, as well as distinguished foreign visitors. Dozens of other noblewomen sponsored salons in the capitals and other major cities in the first half of the nineteenth century.

A few women also joined the ranks of Russia's writers during the reign of Catherine II. The empress herself, as noted earlier, wrote plays and essays. Following her example, dozens of women became poets. Most wrote light, entertaining verse, but the most ambitious, for example Ekaterina Sumarokova and Ekaterina Urusova, undertook the more difficult task of publishing lyric poetry on classical themes. Such poetry was accepted by educated readers, perhaps in part because male poets were wary of provoking Catherine's disfavor by publicly denigrating women's intellectual abilities.

The female writers of the Nicholaevan decades did not receive as warm a reception, for now the ruler was a man who viewed female intellectuals with suspicion, a suspicion shared by many of Russia's male writers. The critique of intellectually accomplished women propagated by the cult of domesticity fed this suspicion. A loving wife could provide the inspiration for a talented man, she could serve as "the radiant guiding star of his life," as the literary critic Vissarion Belinskii put it in 1835.[41] But a woman who tried to be a writer herself, particularly a writer of serious fiction or poetry, took the immodest step of entering a world created by and for men, a world for which she was not suited intellectually or spiritually. She would fail, her work would be inferior, and she would end up a pathetic or ridiculous curiosity.

These prejudices, which prevailed across Europe, repressed the literary efforts of several generations of women. In Russia, as elsewhere, most of those who wished to write devoted themselves to autobiographies, diaries, and letters that they shared only with family members. Others took the course of Avdotia Elagina, the salon hostess, who translated foreign works of history and ethnography. Elagina also served as editor for the poet Vasili Zhukovskii. Still other women published works on topics considered appropriate to their gender, such as housekeeping, childrearing, etiquette, fashion, and religion. Maria Korsini's essays for young people, discussed above, are an example of this sort of women's writing. It was acceptable because it dealt with matters best left to women, such as manners and babies, and because it inculcated the virtues of domesticity.[42]

A few female writers of fiction and poetry did publish their works in the Nicholaevan era, and several of them were bold enough to launch a frontal attack on patriarchal ideas. By the 1840s, Sophia Khvoshchinskaia (whose memoirs of the Smolny Institute were quoted above), her sister Nadezhda, and Elena Gan, among others, were criticizing the triviality of elite women's education, the intellectual and emotional poverty of their home lives, and the evils of their being dominated by their fathers and husbands. In 1844, Karolina Pavlova, author of splendid poetry as well as fiction, summed up the consequences of these controls in her description of the typical young noblewoman: "By now Cecelia was 18 years old, and was so used to wearing her mind in a corset that she felt it no more than the light silk one which she would take off at night. That is not to say that she had no talents; she certainly did, but they were modest ones. . . . She sang very prettily and drew very prettily too."[43]

Similar complaints about the vacuousness of women's education were circulating among reform-minded people across the European world in the 1830s. A critique of the patriarchal principles at the heart of the cult of domesticity was developing, centered at first on education and married women's subjugation to their husbands. Russian female writers and the intelligentsia to which they belonged took it to their collective hearts and thereby demonstrated their close connection to the continental currents of opinion regarding women.

Peasant Women under Serfdom

All the changes we have noted in women's situation in this period were important. They brightened the lives of contemporaries and they paved the way for still more significant changes later. Confined to the nobility, however, they affected less than 10 percent of the women of Russia. Most women were serfs, and the improvements in elite women's lives during the eighteenth and early nineteenth centuries did not benefit them. Instead, their servitude intensified.

THE DEMANDS OF SERFDOM

Serfdom, the binding of peasants to lifelong service to the landowners on whose estates they were born, developed across Eastern Europe in the early modern period, long after it had waned in the West. By the eighteenth century it was practiced in Russia, many of the eastern German principalities, Poland, the Austrian Empire, and the Balkans. Serfdom then came under heavy criticism during the Enlightenment, and by the mid-nineteenth century it had been abolished almost everywhere. The Austrian Empire was one of the last to end it, in 1848. This left Russia alone in preserving an institution widely considered unjust and economically backward. Nicholas accepted these criticisms, but feared the destabilizing effects of emancipation.

His fears were warranted, if only because there were so many peasants in Russia. In Nicholas's time they constituted 85 percent of the population. Their numbers had increased from an estimated 9 million individuals in 1697 to 32 million in 1857. Half of these people were females. A majority were serfs. They included ethnic Russians (the majority), as well as Polish, Ukrainian, Belarusian, and Baltic peasants. A small minority of the serfs worked in mining and manufacturing. The rest farmed.[44]

The least oppressed were state and crown serfs, who belonged to the government, the royal family, and, until 1762, the church.[45] They constituted a little less than 50 percent of all serfs in the eighteenth century, a bit more than that in the nineteenth. The state was a less demanding master than the nobles, and so state and crown serfs paid lower dues and taxes and were supervised less closely than were the so-called seigniorial peasants, who lived on nobles' estates. The government also made efforts to improve the situation of its serfs. In 1801 it permitted them to own land and go into business as traders or factory owners. Thereafter periodic efforts were made to ensure that these serfs had adequate amounts of land.

The bondage of the peasants who served nobles was worse, because they had to meet most of the demands the government made on state, crown, and seigniorial serfs as well as those made by their landlords. The government taxed them and required them to perform occasional services such as repairing roads or supplying horses and wagons to the army and postal service. They had to turn over some of their young men for lifelong service in the military. And they had to provide their village priests with plots to farm, pay them to perform christenings, weddings, and funerals, and bear some of the cost of maintaining church buildings.

These exactions were laid on top of those imposed by the landowners. The landowners were entitled to a substantial share of the crops grown on the estates and could also require serfs to do construction and maintenance and work as house servants. Furthermore, seigniorial serfs were governed by their masters. Landowners had to give permission for a serf to travel away from home or marry a serf who belonged to another master. Serfs who misbehaved could be exiled to a distant estate or, in the case of men, sent into the army. Landowners could also discipline serfs by beating them with a vicious multi-thonged whip called the knout.

The few laws limiting the nobles' power were rarely enforced. Landowners bought and sold serfs, even though such transactions were illegal. They arranged the marriages of serfs without the consent of either parents or brides-to-be. Sexual relationships, consensual and abusive, between serfs and masters were common. Murdering serfs was illegal, but Catherine issued laws that denied serfs the right to take complaints against their landowners to the courts. Brutal landowners could be brought to justice only if other landowners reported them to the authorities.

By the nineteenth century, one third or more of Russia's landowners were women, many of whom, in keeping with tradition, personally managed their properties. Did they exercise their powers differently from men? The reports are mixed. There were exemplary female landowners such as Ekaterina Dashkova, the earnest believer in serfdom who toiled alongside her peasants. In the early nineteenth century, Sophia Stroganova established a village school and supervised the improvement of farming on her estates. She was one of the few female members of the Free Economic Society, which publicized progressive farming techniques. Dashkova's and Stroganova's polar opposite was Daria Saltykova, who was convicted of murdering thirty-eight of her serfs in the late 1760s.

Between monsters like Saltykova, who appear to have been few, and progressive women like Dashkova and Stroganova, also exceptional, the majority of women probably lay. In her memoirs, Anna Labzina praised her mother's solicitude for her serfs, and suggested thereby that such solicitude was expected of women. Nineteenth-century memoirists speak of affectionate relationships between house servants and their owners, especially between nannies and the children they tended. But literary sources also speak of the routine abuse of serfs, particularly house servants, by their mistresses. All this evidence is too anecdotal to support reliable generalizations about gender differences. It does document the virtually unlimited power female and male landowners held over the people who provided their daily bread.[46]

VILLAGE ORGANIZATION

Peasant villages ranged in size from a few dozen households to as many as several hundred. Smaller communities were more common in northerly areas; larger villages prevailed in Ukraine and the Black Earth and steppe regions southeast of Moscow. In addition to the peasants' houses, large villages might contain a church and, by the early nineteenth century, a tavern or a small store. The fields farmed by the peasants lay around the villages, as did pastures, forests, meadows, streams, and rivers. One or more dirt roads ran through the communities and away to the world beyond.

Peasants lived in small wooden cottages roofed with thatch or timber, surrounded by a fenced yard containing a shed or two, a vegetable garden, a cow or goat, some chickens, and perhaps a few pigs. The buildings, livestock, and tools belonged to the family, as distinct from the land, which was the landowner's. Most dwellings had a main room furnished with a stove used for heating and cooking, benches, and a large table. There were also shelves and chests, the latter including those belonging to the women of the family, in which they stored their dowry linens and clothes. In the holy corner, a candle-lit icon draped with embroidered cloths stood on a high shelf. During the winter, livestock sheltered in a lean-to built against the side of the house or were stabled on the ground floor, while the people lived in the rooms above. Families added bedrooms as their families grew, if they could afford to. Most villages had a common well or two, from which the women carried home the household's water; some of the larger families dug wells in their yards.

The peasants had structured their ways of farming and governing their communities to meet the demands of their overlords. The village was collectively responsible for producing crops and paying taxes and dues, so it made sense for the households in the community to pool their labor. Communal farming in turn required commune leaders. Chosen from and by the male heads of households, these men conducted negotiations with outsiders—landowners, estate managers, tax collectors, and military recruiters. They also made the major decisions about managing common areas, chiefly meadows and forests, and about farming the fields. The fields were divided into strips and assigned to families according to the number of able-bodied workers in each household. Because families changed over time as a result of marriages, births, deaths, and the military draft, the elders periodically had to reassign the fields, in a process known as "repartition."

All these practices reached their fullest development in the central Russian region. In the borderlands, looser controls prevailed because distance weakened the government's reach, because the government and landowners wanted to attract settlers to these regions, and because the non-Russian inhabitants—Ukrainians, Lithuanians, Baltic Germans, Belarusians, Poles, and a host of less numerous peoples—had different customs of village governance and landowning. Over the decades, serfdom's controls tightened in the south and west, but the commune and land repartition remained commonest among the Russians.

Most Russian landowners took a less direct role in managing their estates than did their contemporaries elsewhere in Eastern Europe. They were content to let the peasants make most of the farming decisions, run their village affairs, and police one another. Wealthy aristocrats such as Dashkova, who owned dozens of estates scattered across the empire, rarely even saw most of their properties. They entrusted management to bailiffs and stewards, most of whom came from the peasantry. Less affluent nobles, who were the great majority and who lived near their serfs, also tended to delegate substantial authority over day-to-day affairs to the elders in the villages. This lightened the workload for the landowners, and it lightened as well the burden of their control over the peasants.

PEASANT PATRIARCHY

Senior men ran their families and the villages. This reminds us that patriarchy regulates not just the relations between women and men but also those among men. Male peasants in Russia lived at the bottom of the power structure, so the list of people they had to obey was a long one. It included the landowner and his or her adult family members and representatives, any other nobles—male and female, old and young—that they might encounter, churchmen, and government agents. Within peasant families there was a hierarchy as well, with older men outranking younger ones. Indeed, many male peasants spent much of their lives under the control of their fathers or uncles, for most peasants were in their forties before they became heads of their own households, and few lived to be seventy. Elsewhere in Europe and in North America, sons chafing under their fathers' power in this period demanded farms of their own or left the countryside for the cities. Serfdom denied most peasants in Russia these options.

Individual men fell short of the ideal of submission to those with authority over them, of course. There were sons who fought with their fathers and insulted their mothers. Peasants also cheated the landowner and lied to the tax collector. Opposition to senior men in the village was not often tolerated, and young men critical of their elders' authority had to comfort themselves with the hope that they would live long enough to become family heads themselves. They could also take solace in their right to command the obedience of their wives and the younger members of their families.

The peasants' code of masculinity praised attributes that served the community. Men were expected to be skilled at farming, physically strong, and hard-working. Piety was highly regarded, as were frugality, courage, and cleverness. Peasants were encouraged to be good comrades with men their own age, both to facilitate harmony in the village and to build the alliances that would knit together the next generation of elders. A peasant man owed his wife protection and hard work; he owed his children support; and he also served as the boys' taskmaster and instructor in the duties of manhood.[47]

For their part, women were enjoined to obey older men, the men of their own generation within their family, and older women. They were also taught to be pious, diligent, and skilled at women's work. Noblewomen lived under the same rules, but the prescriptions of feminine submission, as always, were leavened among the nobility by the prerogatives of class and age. Noblewomen, while submitting to their social equals and superiors, exercised power over all those below them in the social hierarchy. A peasant woman's sphere of autonomy and authority was much smaller. Peasant women did own property, mainly their dowries, and they were entitled to inherit a "widow's portion" of about one-seventh of their husbands' property. They could not run estates or manage their finances independently.

Peasant women could aspire to become the senior women of their households. The *bolshuka* (literally "the big one") wielded significant authority over her children, daughters-in-law, and grandchildren. Among the peasants, as among the nobility, mothers were entitled to great respect from their male and female children, and their opinions and wishes were to be listened to. They also supervised the labor of the younger women in the household and were accustomed to ruling junior females with an iron hand. Widows could also become household heads. Rodney Bohac has found that between 1813 and 1861, women headed one-third of the households in the villages of Manuilovskoe, a large estate in Tver province north of Moscow.[48]

Widows who headed households with grown male children could, with luck and hard work, keep their families together. Those left only with underage youngsters faced a far bleaker future. The work was simply too grueling for one adult to manage on her own. "I had to learn to take complete charge of the household myself, as well as raise two small children," lamented an aged peasant named Iguminshcheva in the 1890s.[49] Other families were unlikely to lend a hand because the peasants believed that it was a waste of resources to help a weak family limp along. The best course, they thought, was for a woman to find herself another husband, and that was the path that most young widows took.

FAMILY LIFE

The Russians were more insistent on getting people married and keeping them that way than were many other peoples in Europe. We have seen this as early as Appanage times, expressed in the belief that only older, preferably widowed women should become nuns. Under serfdom, the government assessed taxes according to the number of work teams in a household, and defined a work team as a husband and wife. Unmarried men were not given land allotments, and landowners punished families with unmarried adult children. In the late eighteenth century, V. G. Orlov, a wealthy nobleman, summed up prevailing attitudes in instructions to his estate managers: "It is highly necessary for all girls of marriageable age and bachelors who have achieved manhood to enter into marriage. This is an act pleasing to God; it safeguards morality and wards off many vices." The landowner specified fines to be levied on parents who did not arrange for their sons to be wed by age twenty-five, their daughters by twenty.[50]

Few peasant parents required such coercion, for they agreed that marriage was essential to social order and family productivity. Since most villages were small communities where people knew each other well, it was probably often the case that parents began considering how to pair off their children long before those children reached marriageable age: sixteen to eighteen for the girls, eighteen to twenty for the boys.[51] If the village was very small, peasants searched for marriage partners in neighboring villages, and so would periodically arrange gatherings to introduce eligible young people to each other. When a boy's parents had decided to make an offer to a girl's family, matchmakers, usually women who were related to the prospective groom, helped negotiate the marriage contract. That contract specified the contents of the bride's dowry and the size of the fee (bride price) to be paid by the groom's family to the bride's to compensate them for the economic loss they would suffer when their daughter left home. After the wedding, a bride moved in with her husband's family. If wife and husband came to love one another, that was all to the good, but if they did not, their relatives expected them to do their duty by living together with a minimum of acrimony.

Peasants took a cautious attitude toward romantic love and sexuality. They condemned homosexuality and policed the boundaries of masculine and feminine. Men judged effeminate were persecuted. Heterosexuality the peasants sought to confine within the bounds of marriage, but they were not as abstemious as the church wanted them to be. Indeed, peasants in the Russian Empire had one of the highest birthrates in Europe. They punished extramarital sex, because they considered it sinful and also because it caused trouble between families and thereby disrupted village life. Lovemaking by unmarried youths drew the least severe response; there were some occasions, such as the midsummer holiday of St. Ivan Kupala, when parents turned a blind eye as their children paired off for long walks in the woods. Also given fairly wide latitude were betrothed couples. The same cannot be said of adulterers, who drew upon themselves very public censure. Tabooed also was sexual misbehavior within families—incest, adultery between in-laws, sexual abuse of daughters-in-law and children. All such offenses were defined as crimes in church law, but perpetrators were rarely brought to the authorities. Rather, the peasants preferred to mete out their own punishments, which ranged from shaming to physical assault. Because the villagers themselves policed sexual offenses, it is impossible to determine how common such crimes were.

We also know very little about the emotional side of peasant family life. Anthropologists studying peasants around the world have found that children are looked after by and form attachments to many relatives and neighbors. Their parents, occupied with the unending demands of subsistence agriculture, welcome this diffusion of responsibilities and its consequent dilution of emotional ties. Anecdotal evidence suggests that this was the case in Russia as well. Yet the sources also document deep attachments between mothers and their children. This is hardly surprising in a culture that venerated maternal love and enforced maternal authority. In many parts of Russia, girls sang laments when they were betrothed, mourning the fact that they were moving from the loving protection of their mothers to strange new families where people might not be so nice to them. The same fears appear in the memoirs of the noblewomen Labzina and Dolgorukaia.

Less direct evidence of peasant mothering comes from the descriptions of nannies in nineteenth-century memoirs. The common practice was for noble children to be given as infants into the care of a nanny, usually a servant who might herself be married with her own children. The nanny was the child's constant companion, taking care of all its physical needs, teaching manners and morals, and accompanying the child on journeys. Many memoirists remembered feeling closer to their nannies than to their mothers; they portrayed these women as kind, loving caregivers and stalwart defenders of their charges. This evidence suggests that peasant women believed a good mother was a strong, no-nonsense guardian of her children. If she had the time, when work was done, she would also sing lullabies and tell fairy stories.[52]

Alliances between women were crucial to the well-being of individual peasant women, families, and the community. Within the family, daughters worked together, took care of younger siblings, and shared confidences. Girls also struck up lasting friendships with girls from other families, and grown women relied on one another's support during the mundane tasks of daily life and in moments of special celebration or crisis. Women gathered together to birth babies, excluding men. Women also nursed one another's families through illnesses, and when death came, they washed the bodies of the dead, dressed them, then kept vigil until the funeral and keened laments, as their ancestors had done for generations.

WOMEN'S WORK

Women's lives were patterned by the seasons, as are those of all farmers. In the winter, which lasted five months even in southerly regions, women occupied themselves with handcrafts, particularly spinning, weaving, and sewing. They gathered together to do this work, and sometimes young men came around to serenade them and to chat with the teenaged girls. Women, men, and children also fed and watered the livestock and mucked out the animals' bedding. There was always cooking and washing to be done, water to be hauled, livestock to be fed, cows and goats to be milked, eggs to be gathered, cheese and butter to be made, and children to be supervised. Women, particularly the older ones, also nursed sick people and animals, and helped out at the birth of babies in the bathhouses or barns. Holy days required attendance at church. Peasant women also whiled away the long winter nights telling fantastic tales about demons and angels, evil spirits that lurked in the rivers, clever peasants, and talking animals.

When spring broke up the ice in the rivers and brought green shoots to the fields, the pace of village life quickened. First came Easter, the major holiday of the Christian year. Women baked special breads that village elders presented to the landowner, along with salt and eggs, to symbolize the life and fertility that returned with the spring. The landowner responded with gifts of food. The community then attended a long mass in the village church, and afterward held a feast at which musicians played and young people danced, dressed in their holiday clothes. With Easter concluded, the peasants turned to planting. The work eased up a bit in June, after the seed was sown, but by July the hay was ready to mow. From that point until early September, families walked out to the fields at first light, which came very early in these northerly latitudes, and toiled there through the long summer days to bring in the harvest.

The traditional division of labor persisted under serfdom, with regional and ethnic variations. Men did the sowing, because the peasants associated it with the male function in conception. In some Russian villages, the first stalks of ripe grain were cut by an elderly woman of good character—probably because the Earth was conceptualized as a female force that had to be supplicated by a virtuous, grandmotherly woman before its bounty was taken. The peasants still assigned men the heavier work such as plowing and fencing, and women the lighter, such as gleaning the rye fields and reaping oats, flax, and hemp. The terms "heavy" and "light" are relative, for hours of bending over to pick up stalks of grain or cut flax left backs aching and hands bleeding. Women also prepared the day's food for the harvesters and sometimes went back to the villages to fetch it during the dinner break at midday. Mothers of babies brought them to the fields, swaddled and strapped to backboards, then set them aside in the shade, to be nursed when they cried. Little ones too small to help out with the work were looked after by girls as young as eight.

After the fields were shorn, the peasants processed the fruits of the harvest. Women and men threshed the grain, a laborious process that sometimes continued into the winter months. Women also pickled cabbage, beets, cucumbers, and mushrooms, and dried berries and mushrooms. This work had begun in midsummer, as the first produce and wild plants ripened. Women also prepared raw cabbages, onions, garlic, carrots, and radishes for storage in root cellars. There were fish to salt, and chickens and hogs to butcher. When most of this work ended in October, village women settled down to the slower rhythms of winter.

SPIRITUALITY

We have already seen that Muscovites believed that the supernatural world played a very real part in their daily lives. Their descendants in imperial Russia, nobles and peasants, felt the same. Peasant women believed that God, Jesus, and the angels watched over them, doling out temptations, rewards, and punishments. The Virgin hovered near God's throne, interceding for sinful humans and sometimes coming to Earth to reveal herself. The saints also looked out for ordinary people, and women felt that the female saints, headed by the Holy Mother, paid special attention to them. There were shrines scattered across the Russian Empire to which peasant women made pilgrimages to pray and to seek healing from a miracle-working icon or a holy monk or nun.

Peasant women in Russia believed, as did peasant women all over Europe, that evil spirits were active in their world. Satan headed a huge company of demons and sprites who were at best mischievous, at worst dangerous. Demons possessed people and made them ill. Nasty female spirits, the *rusalki,* lay in wait in the rivers to attack the unsuspecting. The peasants also continued to believe that sometimes their neighbors used black magic against them.

Poised between benign and malicious spirits, peasant women endeavored to propitiate both. They prayed in the approved Christian way, wore crosses, and kept candles burning in the icon corners of their houses. They dabbled in white magic, preparing potions and making up spells and incantations. At certain places—bathhouses, crossroads, forests, and riverbanks—and at certain times—during childbirth, at midnight, on midsummer's eve—the barrier between the natural and the supernatural weakened, raising the risk of evil enchantments. So women passed down through the generations defensive spells and prayers. One, to be said by a mother over a child about to set out on a journey, concluded, "And may you be, my child, protected by my strong word . . . in the night and at midnight, every hour and half-hour, on the road and on the path, sleeping and waking, from the evil force, from unclean spirits; may you be kept safe from sudden death, from grief and misfortune; may you be saved on the water from drowning, guarded from being burned in fire."[53]

The church deeply disapproved of much of this, seeing it as a survival of pagan superstitions, which it was. The spells to ward off evil spirits very likely came down from the distant past when the ancestors of the Slavs and the Rus were animists. Over the centuries, the beliefs and the spells had persisted, veneered with Christianity. This mixture of pagan and Christian ideas was common throughout the rest of Europe, for everywhere peasants were vulnerable to a host of calamities, from bad weather to disease, the natural causes of which they poorly understood. Magical beliefs provided explanations and offered ways of coping, as they still do for people around the world.

Russian peasant women also sometimes beat their children, quarreled, flirted with one another's husbands, passed on poisonous gossip, lied, and stole. In short, they were no more consistently virtuous or consistently selfish than any other group of human beings. In general, their ways of doing things were well adapted to the exigencies of their situation. That the population and food production of rural Russia increased steadily during the period 1700–1861 is a testament to the ingenuity with which peasants, female and male, responded to their demanding environment.

Urban Women

There were many other groups of women in the expanding Russian Empire. Within the Russian heartland, towns contained, as they had for centuries, artisans, laborers, market vendors, and small traders. At the top of the urban pyramid were the merchants, whose tax burdens and economic privileges were set out in government charters. Russia's merchantry never enjoyed the corporate rights that had defined the merchants of France or England as important members of their societies since the medieval period. Furthermore, in the eighteenth and early nineteenth centuries, Russia's economy did not experience the rapid expansion that fostered the growth of cities and empowered the middle classes in Western Europe. Consequently the merchants remained politically insignificant and wedded to Muscovite traditions well into the nineteenth century.

The lives of poorer women in the cities ran along traditional tracks as well. They participated in the economic ventures of their families as urban women had in past. Most lived in households containing nuclear families, that is, parents and minor children. The homes of wealthier merchants also included live-in servants and employees. Senior women managed the housework, as had their predecessors in the era of *The Domostroi*. Poorer women sold wares and food in public markets, worked in taverns, and assisted male artisans in manufacturing consumer goods such as textiles, tools, and utensils. Poverty was an endemic problem that particularly afflicted widows. Daniel Kaiser has found that such women made up 55 percent of the urban poor in ten Russian cities in the early eighteenth century. Some of those women received help from relatives or charities, although not enough, evidently, to raise them out of poverty.[54]

Women of the Conquered Territories

Territorial expansion continued throughout the first 150 years of the imperial period, with the result that by 1861 the Russian Empire was the largest nation on Earth, covering a land mass three times the size of the continental United States. Peter added to Russia today's Latvia, Estonia, and Lithuania. Catherine annexed southern Ukraine, the Crimea, Belarus, and central Poland. Alexander I laid claim to Finland. Throughout the eighteenth century the colonization of Siberia continued. In the nineteenth, Russian armies, officials, and traders pushed southward into the Caucasus and southeastward into Central Asia, the region north of Afghanistan and Iran.

The consequences of this expansion for non-Russian women followed the patterns established in the seventeenth century. In Siberia, native women coped, some by moving with their people into lands the Russians had not penetrated, others by marrying Russian husbands. The third path, the one taken most often, was to attempt to meet Russian demands while preserving native culture. For example, the women of Tungus, a people who lived near Lake Baikal, continued, as they had done for centuries, to herd and milk the reindeer every day, make deerskin coats and boots, clean, and cook, while the men hunted and processed the kill. They produced more of their warm, weatherproof coats after the Russian advent than previously, and traded them to the Russians for tea, flour, sugar, salt, tobacco, and alcohol. The groups that succeeded best at this accommodationist strategy were the peoples of southern Siberia, who had a long history of dealing with outsiders. In the Caucasus and Central Asia, Russian incursions were as yet too limited to affect the great majority of women.

Russian rule strengthened serfdom in the western borderlands and consequently increased the hardships of women's lives there. The change was particularly severe in Ukraine, where the peasants had known a period of freedom in the seventeenth century. In the eighteenth, the increased power granted the Ukrainian nobility by the Russian crown came at the expense of the peasantry, whose labor dues were increased. Catherine the Great also gave enormous swaths of Ukraine to private landowners who imposed onerous requirements on the peasants. The burdens of Russian rule fell less heavily on peasants living in Polish territory, for the mournful reason that serfdom was already quite severe there. In the nineteenth century, the government actually eased the exactions of Polish serfdom, in an effort to court peasant support against the rebellious Polish nobility. The nobles of the Baltic states of Latvia, Lithuania, and Estonia, influenced by liberal ideas flowing in from Central Europe, were more enlightened, less exploitative serf-owners, despite the establishment of Russian rule.

Annexation by Russia did not substantially alter the patterns of women's lives in Polish, Baltic, Belarusian, and Ukrainian territories, mainly because Russian gender values and practices were very similar to those of the conquered peoples. This correspondence was closest among the elites, who communicated with one another and imbibed the same influences from Central and Western Europe. Where there were differences, in inheritance laws for example, the Russian government did not challenge local gender arrangements, because officials believed that doing so would stir up unrest. A notable example of this unwillingness to interfere occurred after the Polish Rebellion of 1830–31, when Nicholas I abolished the autonomy of the government in Warsaw, but refrained from diminishing the authority of Catholic ecclesiastical courts over marriage and divorce.

The Beginnings of Russian Feminism

Disasters have a way of forcing people to re-evaluate the status quo. For the Russian nobility and intelligentsia, the Crimean War was such a disaster. In 1853 Emperor Nicholas I blundered into war with the Ottoman Empire; in March 1854 Britain and France came in to support their Turkish ally. After victories in the Balkans, Russian troops withdrew to the Crimean peninsula and there dug in for months of nasty siege warfare. The army, made up of noble officers and peasant draftees, was poorly led and even more poorly equipped and supplied. Filthy conditions and the resulting diseases killed more men than did combat. In a showdown with the Great Powers, in whose ranks the Russian leadership wanted to be included, Russia had come up painfully short.

As the casualties mounted, Russia's female philanthropists gathered to help. Grand Duchess Elena organized and funded the Community of Sisters of Mercy of the Exaltation of the Cross, a group of 163 nurses, mostly young noblewomen, led by a physician named Nikolai Pirogov. Empress Alexandra sponsored another group of volunteer nurses, all widows. The women made the long journey to the Crimea, and there performed heroically, even when under fire. Their devoted service was widely publicized at home, a Russian answer to the praise being heaped on Florence Nightingale in the British press.

Nicholas died in 1855. His son Alexander, who had been involved in discussions of reforming Russia during the 1840s, assumed the throne and soon declared that he intended to make major changes, chief among them the emancipation of the serfs. To rally public support, the new emperor invited the intelligentsia to discuss what needed to be done. While most writers were concentrating on serfdom, a few brought up the inequalities that plagued women. Doctor Pirogov, who had returned from the Crimea impressed with the work of the nurses there, weighed in with articles calling for women's education to be improved so that they could contribute more to society. Soon afterward, Maria Vernadskaia, a magazine editor, moved beyond Pirogov's argument: "A woman can feel, can think, can crave education, can understand the desire to be useful in some way. Finally a woman can work and toil for her own benefit as well as for the benefit of the public. No one would repudiate this, but then is it necessary to devise separate principles of morality and honor for women, to prescribe special duties for them, to restrict their education, and, finally, even to ascribe to them certain special virtues and vices? If woman is the same sort of being as is man, then the principles of honor and morality should be the same for both."[55]

These were the ideas of liberal feminism, developed in the United States, Great Britain, and France in the 1840s, and publicized widely by the English liberals Harriet Taylor and John Stuart Mill in the early 1850s. Some Russian intellectuals were well acquainted with the critiques of patriarchy that had led to feminism. They were particularly drawn to the argument that slavery in the western hemisphere and the subordination of women across the European world both derived from Europe's oppressive patriarchal institutions. Russia had no slaves, but it did have a peasantry in bondage, so it was easy to argue that Russian patriarchy had produced both serfdom and women's inequality, and that both social ills must be addressed. When Emperor Alexander invited a discussion of reforms, improvements in women's situation were quickly proposed. A woman should be educated so as "to be useful" (Pirogov's argument), but also "for her own benefit," because—and here was the truly new idea—she was "the same sort of being as is a man." The "woman question," as the discussion of reforms for women was called across Europe, was now on the agenda of the Russian intelligentsia.

Conclusions

Between 1695 and 1855, Russia's government opened up new opportunities for elite women that many women welcomed. They bought land, exercised their legal rights, became educated, and joined the intelligentsia. They also participated in the importation and adaptation of the cult of domesticity, thereby elevating women to a central role in their families' emotional lives even while reaffirming the importance of wifely submission.

All these changes enriched the lives of noblewomen. They did little to improve the situation of the peasants or of poor women in the cities and the conquered territories. As the reign of Nicholas ended, a few educated women and men had come to believe that much more needed to be done for all the women of the empire. They would work for solutions to the woman question in the decades that followed, even as emancipation of the serfs, industrialization, and urbanization challenged traditional understandings and made finding solutions more pressing.

4

INDUSTRIALIZATION AND URBANIZATION

1855-1914

From 1855 to 1914, the Russian economy grew rapidly and so did the cities. Peasants freed from serfdom crowded into factories; merchants and shopkeepers expanded their businesses; apartment blocks went up, as did tenements. Between 1811 and 1914, the percentage of Russia's people living in urban areas rose from 6.6 to 15 percent, with much of this increase concentrated in the metropolises. Moscow had swelled to more than a million inhabitants by 1902; St. Petersburg was home to more than 2 million in 1914.[1] Now women of all ranks of life had to cope with the problems and the possibilities created by the Industrial Revolution in its Russian incarnation.

Women's experiences of and participation in the economic and social developments of the last decades of imperial Russia depended on their social position, ethnicity, religion, place of residence, and individual experience. The standard of living rose for some women in the middle ranks of urban society, and the cities filled with new amenities, such as opera houses, theaters, and, by the early twentieth century, electric lighting. Influential noblewomen organized a feminist movement that set up charities and persuaded the government to admit women to higher education. Although, as in the past, improvements in education benefited the nobles first, they now spread to more girls from the middle ranks of Russian society, the working class, and the peasantry. Female graduates of the new schools then established a women's presence in the growing professions, particularly teaching and medicine

Most of these changes seemed, once again, to leave peasant women behind. They made up 80 percent of the female population in the late imperial decades, and as the twentieth century dawned, most were still living much as their ancestors had, despite the fact that Alexander II had abolished serfdom in 1861. Their awareness of the outside world was expanding, though, for the menfolk, returning from jobs in the cities, told them about the latest styles in clothes, entertainment, even courtship. More significantly, poor women were playing a crucial part in industrialization. They filled in on the farms when the men went off to work in the cities, and they did a substantial share of the new cottage industry in the villages. Peasant women were also one-third of factory workers and the great majority of the house servants in the growing cities. Russian industrialization depended on their labor in the late nineteenth century, as it would continue to do throughout the twentieth.

Political and Economic Change, 1861–1917

The Emancipation granted seigniorial, state, and crown serfs personal freedom, and divided farmland between peasants and landlords. Ownership of the land went to village communes or, in regions where communes did not exist, to individual families. Like most political compromises, the Emancipation was received grudgingly. Peasants believed that they had been given too little land and that their taxes were still too high. Nobles resented losing property that they considered rightfully theirs and they feared that they would not be able to support themselves on what they had left. The aftermath of Emancipation fed these resentments, for the income of lower-ranking noble families plunged, even as most peasants continued to struggle with poverty.

The Emancipation was the centerpiece of a program of reforms begun under Alexander II and continued by his son Alexander III (ruled 1881–94) and grandson Nicholas II (ruled 1894–1917). Government ministers overhauled the judiciary by creating additional courts, improving legal procedures, and introducing trial by jury. They established the *zemstva* (the singular is *zemstvo*), assemblies elected at the district and county levels to promote local economic development, education, and health care. They reformed the military and encouraged industrialization. They also maintained the government's autocratic power, censored the press, and harassed critics.

The transformation of the economy bred problems that the bureaucrats were unable to solve. Poverty continued to plague city and countryside alike. Factory work was grueling, dangerous, and poorly paid, and the government did little to improve conditions. Doctors, lawyers, teachers, and engineers labored to upgrade social services as well as infrastructure, but when they lobbied for input into government decision-making or requested greater freedom for their professional organizations, they usually received a frosty response from the authorities.

The government also bungled foreign policy. In the late nineteenth century, being a great power was more expensive than ever before, because industrialization had led to mechanized armies and navies. In view of the empire's already enormous size and economic underdevelopment, Nicholas II should have stayed out of the increasingly hostile competition between the colonial powers in the 1890s. Instead he increased military spending and meddled in China and Korea. The latter folly led to war with Japan, which intensified domestic unrest and, in 1905, produced uprisings across the empire. Yielding to the pressure, Nicholas agreed to the establishment of an elected legislature, but after protests subsided, he refused to share power with it. He then blundered into World War I in 1914. That colossal error, coming on top of so many others, brought on the Russian Revolution in 1917.

The Woman Question in the Reign of Alexander II

FORMULATING THE ANALYSIS

In the early years of Alexander's reign, Russian intellectuals launched a thoroughgoing consideration of what was called in the nineteenth century "the woman question." What was woman's nature, they asked? How should society be reformed so that women could fulfill their potential? If emancipated, what should women do with their lives? Maria Vernadskaia, the foremost female participant in this discussion, was a liberal feminist, that is, an advocate of the ideas publicized in the early 1850s by Harriet Taylor and John Stuart Mill. Women should be given the same education as men, she declared, because they were entitled to it as "equal beings." Then they would justify their emancipation by making a positive contribution to society. "If society would only realize," Vernadskaia wrote, "that women must be useful, that they must work, that they are created not just for pleasure but also for serious activity—then women would take an equal place to men in society and would have equal rights, for anyone who works for the benefit of others is entitled to having a place in society commensurate with his or her contribution to it."[2] Vernadskaia also made the argument, around since the eighteenth century, that well-educated women would be better mothers and more interesting companions to their husbands.

After Vernadskaia's death in 1860, other Russian intellectuals, among them Evgenia Tur and Avdotia Panaeva, the editors of progressive journals, and M. L. Mikhailov, a poet and political radical, kept the discussion of the woman question going in the press. So did two novels, Ivan Turgenev's *On the Eve* (1860) and Nikolai Chernyshevskii's *What Is to Be Done?* (1863). These books became the most widely read Russian answers to the woman question.

Both novels portray young women who break free from parents and conventions in order to dedicate themselves to doing something "useful" for society. Elena, the twenty-year-old heroine of *On the Eve,* confides to her diary, "To be good is not enough; to do good—yes, that is the main thing in life. But how to do good?"[3] She finds her mission in marrying a Bulgarian revolutionary and taking up his struggle to free his homeland from Turkish rule. Chernyshevskii's central character, Vera, makes a marriage of convenience with a university student, which frees her from the control of her parents. She then seeks to "do good" by running a sewing workshop for poor women and studying medicine. She also falls in love, at which point her accommodating husband goes off to the United States to learn about the emancipation of the slaves. Abandoned in the eyes of the law, Vera gets a divorce and marries her true love; the happy couple then works among the poor.

Turgenev and Chernyshevskii presented the emancipation of Elena and Vera as morally good, both for the women and for the men who help them and are thereby also emancipated from Russia's unjust patriarchy. Learning how to treat women as equals and to support their independence was part of becoming an ethical male citizen, Turgenev and Chernyshevskii argued. And, for both authors, the liberation of their heroines served another, implicitly greater, good, which was the improvement of the situation of the poor. Feminists across Europe made the same arguments, but the Russian intelligentsia were more insistent than intellectuals elsewhere that women who gained independence must use it to promote social justice. It was a credo that several generations of activist women would take to heart.

RUSSIA'S FIRST FEMINIST MOVEMENT

The discussion of the woman question in the 1850s gave rise to campaigns for reform. The "big three" of this first generation of feminist activists were Anna Filosofova, Nadezhda Stasova, and Maria Trubnikova. They came from the elite, as did many other European feminists. Anna Filosofova belonged to an eminent intelligentsia family, the Diaghilevs. Her husband, Vladimir Filosofov, was a political liberal and official in the Ministry of

War. Stasova was the daughter of court architect Vasili Stasov, who had sternly impressed on all his children, girls as well as boys, the admonition, "A man [*sic*] is worthy of the name only when he is useful to himself and others."[4] Stasova never married, choosing rather to devote herself to caring for an ill sister and then, after that sister's death, to feminist advocacy. Trubnikova was a philanthropist as well as an editor, with her husband, of *The Stock Exchange News*.

In the 1860s, Filosofova, Stasova, Trubnikova, and thousands of other feminists in St. Petersburg, Moscow, and several provincial cities concentrated on helping poor urban women and improving education for girls. Modeling their organizations on philanthropic societies, which many of them had participated in, the feminists set up governing committees to coordinate projects and collect donations. Bazaars selling foods and handcrafts were particularly popular fund-raisers.

POOR RELIEF

The feminists' efforts among the urban poor also followed paths laid down by the philanthropists. To help women upgrade their job skills, feminists organized workshops. In 1863 the Women's Publishing Cooperative in St. Petersburg taught forty women how to print and bind books. Volunteers also established night and Sunday schools that gave lower-class women instruction in basic literacy and numeracy. The Society for Cheap Lodgings, set up in 1859 in St. Petersburg, arranged inexpensive housing for single women. It continued to operate into the twentieth century. Many other projects were short-lived, for they were plagued by the problems that bedeviled all volunteer organizations in Russia. Government officials were often suspicious and unhelpful; fund-raising was difficult; clients drifted away; patrons became discouraged because the immensely time-consuming charities helped few women.

EDUCATION

Russia's first feminists enjoyed far greater success in their other endeavor, improving the education available to girls from the nobility and the middling ranks of society. There was widespread agreement among the elite by the 1850s that Russia needed more secondary schools for girls. Furthermore, critics, including many in government, argued that the curriculum of the boarding schools was academically weak, with too little attention given to subjects such as history and languages, too much to those perennial staples of women's education, manners and embroidery. This was true in schools across Europe, for the influence of the cult of domesticity was everywhere producing education that concentrated on preparing girls to be pious, dutiful wives and mothers. The Russian government was one of the first to buck that trend when, in 1858, A. S. Norov, minister of education, ordered the establishment of more rigorous secondary schools for girls. To preserve the class distinctions established by Catherine II, he decreed that new schools for the daughters of merchants and artisans, which came to be called *progymnasia,* would teach literature, languages, and religion, as well as some vocational courses, while the *gymnasia,* established for noble girls, would concentrate on the humanities.

It was typical of Alexander II's reforms that local people were expected to get the projects under way themselves, following government regulations and guidelines, with minimal government funding. As regards educational reform, feminists, philanthropists, and local government officials did just that, working together to raise money, rent buildings, and hire faculty for the new secondary schools. Professors from the universities advised on curriculum design. By 1868, ten years after Norov's decree, the volunteers had established 125 secondary schools, which enrolled more than ten thousand girls.[5] Most were urban day schools, not boarding schools, and most students came from families that could afford to pay the tuition. Also by 1868, the curriculum of the gymnasia had been expanded to include more science and a year of education courses. Graduates who completed the full eight years of study were qualified to work as private tutors or teachers in the first four grades of the gymnasia and progymnasia. The progymnasia continued to offer less science and more vocational courses in their three-year program.

The popularity of the new schools inspired more improvements. The administrators of the much-maligned boarding schools strengthened their curricula and opened secondary day schools. In the 1880s the church established diocesan schools that offered a six-year program emphasizing religious instruction. They proved to be quite popular with daughters of the clergy.

Through the subsequent decades, enrollments in girls' secondary schools grew; by the 1890s they were educating 79,000 pupils per year. This was a small fraction of the millions of girls in Russia, most of whom were peasants, but it represented substantial progress for the young women lucky enough to be able to attend. The new schools also testified to the progressive attitudes of many of Russia's parents and educators. Germany, by contrast, although renowned for the quality of its educational system for males, had less than 200 secondary schools for girls in 1871, all offering the watered-down curriculum of the "finishing school." French public schools did not provide college-preparatory classes to girls until 1924.[6]

Feminists and their supporters also succeeded in establishing colleges for women. In the 1860s, Russia had universities in Kazan, Kharkov, Kiev, Moscow, St. Petersburg, and Vilnius, none of which, in keeping with the European-wide practice, admitted women. The feminists, unable to change that policy, got permission to set up "higher women's courses," private colleges staffed by volunteer professors and funded by donations and tuition. The most prestigious of these were the Bestuzhev Courses in St. Petersburg, named after their first director, history professor K. N. Bestuzhev-Riumin. Founded in 1878, the Bestuzhev Courses enrolled more than seven hundred students annually for the first eight years of their existence.[7] The women studied at night in a boys' school. At first the faculty concentrated on the liberal arts, then added science and mathematics. The four-year program became the equivalent of a university's course of study, with the important qualification that Bestuzhev graduates were prohibited from receiving degrees. The minister of education in the late 1870s, D. A. Tolstoi, took a dim view of women in higher education and had only grudgingly approved the creation of the courses. He refused all requests to give them degree-granting authority.

By the early 1880s higher women's courses had also been founded in Kazan, Kharkov, Kiev, and Moscow. Christine Johanson has found that 60 to 70 percent of the students in the Bestuzhev Courses in the early years were of noble rank; by the 1880s the daughters of merchant families had increased their enrollment to a third of the student body. In Kiev, women from the middling orders made up a still larger percentage of students.[8] The life of a *kursistka,* as the students were called, was not easy: the courses were demanding and tuition was high. Female students, unlike males, were not eligible for government scholarships, and there were few jobs available to help them augment their incomes. Girls whose parents could not afford to support them struggled to find patrons who would pay their tuition and endured bad housing and food. That thousands persevered until they completed the courses testifies to their thirst for higher education.

The feminists scored successes as well in their campaign to open admission to medical schools to women. Across Europe, socially conscious women were trying to become physicians, because they saw healing the sick as a high calling particularly suited to women. These were feelings that Chernyshevskii expressed in his fictional Vera, who studied medicine.

The resistance to women becoming physicians was strong, however. Male physicians anxious to raise the status of their profession denigrated traditional medicine, much of which had been practiced by women, and lauded the superiority of university-trained physicians. Women could not become such physicians, these promoters of "scientific medicine" argued, because of their inferior intellects. Such attitudes, prevalent all over the European world, led Russian government officials in the late 1860s to deny feminist petitions to admit women to medical schools.

Turned down at home, several hundred women from Russia journeyed west to study medicine at Zurich University, which had opened its doors to women in 1865. Soon government spies were sending back reports that the Russian students were picking up radical political ideas, which was true. Alarmed, the government ordered them to return home in May 1873. Most left Switzerland, but as many as one-third soon enrolled in other European universities. For the rest of the century, Russian medical students would make up the majority of female students at the university in Zurich.[9]

Russian feminists were quick to point out to government officials that this problem would not have arisen had women been permitted to study medicine in Russia. Minister of Education Tolstoi responded in typical foot-dragging fashion: he ordered a study of the feasibility of including medical training in the higher courses. Then the feminists turned to Dmitri Miliutin, the minister of war and a supporter of women's education. They knew that he would be receptive because he had said as much to leading feminist Anna Filosofova's husband Vladimir, who worked for him. On receipt of the feminists' petition, Miliutin agreed to the establishment of a separate curriculum for women at the army's medical school in St. Petersburg. This curriculum evolved over the 1870s into a five-year program as rigorous as the male one. Female graduates received a degree and the title "Woman Doctor" (*Zhenskii Vrach*). By 1882, less than ten years later, more than two hundred students had completed the training. Again, Russian women were ahead of those elsewhere. In that same year there were only twenty-six female physicians in England.[10]

VARVARA KASHEVAROVA-RUDNEVA (1844–99)

Russia's first female physician, Varvara Kashevarova-Rudneva, received her medical degree in 1868, several years before the establishment of the women's medical courses. Kashevarova's origins were humble and her early life would have defeated many other girls; that she became one of the first female physicians in Europe was a testament to her intelligence and persistence, and to the support available to such women from some members of the intelligentsia.

Kashevarova was a Jewish orphan from the Belarusian region who spent her childhood in the temporary custody of various families, some friendly, some abusive. Along the way she managed to learn to read and write. At twelve she ran away to St. Petersburg, hoping to find work there. An army officer and his wife adopted her, but before long she perceived that her new father was grooming her to be his mistress. She escaped when she was fifteen by marrying Nikolai Kashevarov, a merchant much older than she. Three years later, Kashevarova left her husband and enrolled in a school for midwives.

Despite the fact that she had never attended school before, Kashevarova sailed through the midwifery courses. She also earned the support of Veniamin Tarnovskii, a prominent professor and specialist in venereal diseases. Soon Kashevarova was complaining to Tarnovskii that her classes were too rudimentary. She wanted to learn more. "I thought," she wrote in her memoirs, "that even if I were not as able as I had so often been told I was, I was at least confident of my capacity for hard work and my eagerness to learn. Nor had God stinted in giving me a strong will and great determination."[11]

With the support of Tarnovskii and other professors, Kashevarova found a way. In Orenberg province, far to the southeast of Moscow, there was an army garrison plagued by venereal disease. The soldiers and the local Bashkir people were infecting one another, but the Bashkirs would not let the male military doctors have contact with their women. Kashevarova and her supporters persuaded army administrators to admit her to the army medical school in St. Petersburg so that she could become a physician to Bashkir women. Even with that authorization, she fought resistance from some faculty and bureaucrats throughout her five years of study. Permission to take the final examinations had to come from Minister of War Miliutin himself. When Kashevarova received her diploma in 1868, her fellow students celebrated by carrying her around the hall. People agitating for women to be admitted to the medical schools, including her mentor Tarnovskii, cited her as an example of what women could achieve if they were given the opportunity.

Kashevarova's accomplishments were extraordinary for any woman, let alone a Jewish orphan with no connections in St. Petersburg save those she made for herself. The appointment to Orenberg never came through, so she

Belarusian peasants posing in the fields, circa 1900.
Peasants much like these came to Varvara Kashevarova-Rudneva's rural clinic.
Picture Collection of the New York Public Library.

VARVARA KASHEVAROVA-RUDNEVA

In her memoirs, Kashevarova-Rudneva remembered her years as a country doctor:

"In 1881 I acquired a small plot of land (343 acres) in the Valuisky district of the Voronezh province. There in the steppe, far from any village (the nearest hamlet was almost a mile from my farm), I built a house, opened a dispensary, and began to treat the rural population. Before long I acquired a reputation for tens of miles around, and patients came to see me from far and wide. I lived in the countryside for about eight years. I wanted to repay my stipend [at medical school] with service to the people . . . in my native land.

While I was living in the countryside I wrote and published: 1) a review of Professor Lazarevich's book *The Works of Women* . . . ; 2) a popular account of the female organism (1884); 3) my autobiography . . . ; 4) an article entitled 'Toward the History of Women's Medical Education in Russia' . . . ; 5) two articles entitled 'Country Notes' . . . ; 6) in 1892 the second edition of my book *The Hygiene of the Female Organism*. . . .

In March 1886 my rural home burned down because of a servant's carelessness; by some miracle I escaped death. Although I later built another small house for myself, I was then afraid of living alone in the steppe, and two years after that disastrous fire I sold my farm to the peasants through a bank and left the countryside for good."

SOURCE: TOBY CLYMAN AND JUDITH VOWLES, ED., *RUSSIA THROUGH WOMEN'S EYES: AUTOBIOGRAPHIES FROM TSARIST RUSSIA* (NEW HAVEN: YALE UNIVERSITY PRESS, 1996), 184–85.

continued her studies and in 1876 received the degree of medical doctor, the equivalent of a Ph.D. She also wrote scholarly papers and enjoyed a second, happy marriage with one of her professors, Mikhail Rudnev, who died in 1878. Unfortunately the sexist abuse that had always plagued her continued and the conservative press caricatured her as a freak. In the 1880s Kashevarova wearied of battling her persecutors and moved to the countryside. She opened a clinic for the poor and wrote her memoirs and a book, *The Hygiene of the Female Organism,* that was published in multiple editions. Kashevarova was living outside St. Petersburg when she died in 1899.[12]

STRENGTHS AND WEAKNESSES OF FEMINIST ACTIVISM

The strengths and the weaknesses of Russia's feminist activism derived from the nation's politics. The autocratic government was an enormous obstacle. Russian feminists worked for years to get permission to set up the higher women's courses; they could not persuade the authorities to award degrees to graduates. Feminists in the United States, on the other hand, did not require government permission to establish dozens of independent, degree-granting, private women's colleges in the second half of the nineteenth century. In the 1880s these institutions enrolled eighty thousand women, and by 1890 women were 36 percent of American undergraduates.[13] First Amendment freedoms allowed American feminists to publish journals and newspapers and hold meetings and marches—all activities that were strictly prohibited to social activists in Russia. American and British feminists also managed to ease legal restrictions on divorce, a reform Russian feminists did not even attempt, because they realized they could not overcome the resistance of church authorities. Established churches were an obstacle to reform across Europe, it should be noted.

Autocracy did have one advantage over democracy: it could be a powerful patron to those with access to its top leaders. The federated structure of American government enabled feminists to achieve reforms in progressive municipalities and states, but made nationwide successes extremely difficult. By contrast, Russian feminists who had the backing of important government officials could achieve much in a very short time. The medical schools for women and the expansion of secondary education for girls are cases in point. The problem was that what the tsarist government gave, it could also take away. Alexander II's successor, Alexander III, was an arch-conservative who did not approve of higher education for women. In 1888, he shut down most of the higher courses and closed the women's medical school. He permitted the Bestuzhev Courses to continue, probably because they had powerful sponsors. Higher education for women only expanded again a decade later when Alexander's son Nicholas II permitted it.

More reliable, indeed crucial to the feminists' successes, was the support of the intelligentsia. In *On the Eve* and *What Is to Be Done?* Turgenev and Chernyshevskii defined the moral man as one who renounced his masculine prerogatives and supported women in their efforts to escape patriarchy. Many reform-minded men took that principle to heart, propagating the argument for women's emancipation, assisting the feminists in their projects, and teaching in the women's courses. Among the instructors at the Bestuzhev Courses was D. I. Mendeleev, the chemist famous for creating the periodic table of the elements. Hundreds of male teachers, writers, zemstvo officials, and other professionals organized schools for girls, provided grants to students, and helped graduates obtain white-collar jobs.

Their support should not be exaggerated. We have already discussed the prejudice against female writers during the reign of Nicholas. Resistance to reform benefiting women persisted within the intelligentsia throughout the late imperial period. These qualifications notwithstanding, the support that many educated people gave to those reforms and the priority many of them accorded to women's issues were extraordinary in late nineteenth-century Europe.

THE ORIGINS OF RADICALISM

Members of the intelligentsia had been criticizing patriarchy and autocracy since the reign of Nicholas I. Indeed, many well-educated people believed that intellectuals were morally obligated to criticize social injustice. Alexander II raised their hopes when he committed himself to freeing the serfs, but by the mid-1860s, disillusionment with the Tsar Reformer had set in. Emancipation had not given the peasants as much land as many had hoped it would, and Alexander had brutally repressed an uprising in Polish territories in 1863–64. A few educated people decided that Russia would only be a just society when autocracy itself was overthrown. For them, reformism turned into radicalism.

The first radicals of the 1860s were the nihilists, so named by Turgenev because some of them professed to believe in "nothing" (*nihil* is the Latin word for "nothing"). The nihilists actually had quite a few beliefs, most of which involved rejection of the status quo. This collection of several thousand privileged young people, most of them living in St. Petersburg, declared that the first step toward progressive social change was self-transformation. The individual must reject the parasitical, indolent lifestyle of the nobility and become honest and socially responsible. This meant dedicating oneself to work benefiting poor people, such as medicine or teaching. It also meant that men and women should live together as equals, which required men to treat women as comrades rather than sexual objects. A few nihilists acted on these principles by organizing communes in the cities; the one founded by writer Vasili Sleptsov in 1863 included women. The nihilist movement in general and the communes in particular were the inspiration for Chernyshevskii's *What Is to Be Done?*

Sleptsov's commune was tiny, only seven people, and notorious, for Russians considered it scandalous for unrelated, unmarried women and men to live together. The nihilists were quite happy shocking people; they wanted to be publicly outrageous. Like the hippies and stoners of twentieth-century America, the nihilists, particularly the female ones, paraded their rejection of the establishment through the streets. The women cut their hair short, wore blue-tinted spectacles, and smoked cigarettes. They proclaimed their devotion to reason and science and scorned tradition, sentimentality, and religion. Romantics in their public display, rationalists in their pronouncements, the nihilists achieved their main objective, which was to challenge the complacency of the comfortable.

Their rebellion was short-lived. By 1865 nihilism had become a fad among elite young people, many of whom adopted the dress code but not the commitment to reform. Serious nihilists were embarrassed and annoyed by their own disciples. They were also frustrated by the fact that their self-transformations had had no effect on Russia's great injustices. Nihilism was already losing popularity in 1866, therefore, when a radical student attempted to assassinate the tsar. Thereafter the police cracked down, driving most nihilists into quiescence and a few into revolutionary socialism.

These revolutionaries—often referred to as "the Populists" in English-language histories—were young people from the middle and upper ranks of Russian society who dreamed of a popular revolution in Russia that would abolish the old order and establish in its stead an egalitarian society. Vera Zasulich, one of the medical students in Zurich in the early 1870s, remembered her friend Sophia Bardina telling her, "We should direct all our resources not toward ameliorating the plight of isolated individuals, not toward doctoring individual cases, but rather toward the struggle to subvert the social institutions that are the source of all evil. We must struggle against man's exploitation of man, against private property, against inheritance rights. All of these must be abolished."[14]

In this quotation we see both a key difference between Russian feminism and radicalism and the ease with which an impassioned young woman might move from one to the other. Feminists and revolutionaries had a lot in common: most were well-educated people from the nobility and many favored sweeping political and economic change. Russia's first feminists sought to improve women's situation through mobilizing the support of government officials and propertied people. Populists such as Bardina and Zasulich sought to remedy the problems of all of Russia's people by rousing those people to overthrow the monarchy and replace it with democratic institutions modeled on the village commune. These were the ideas of utopian socialism, first formulated in France, now shaped by the Populists into a prescription for peasant revolution.

Having formulated their socialist credo, the Populists attempted to teach it to the poor. Members of the Chaikovskii Circle in St. Petersburg proselytized workers. In 1874, several thousand Populists spent the summer in the countryside spreading their ideas among the peasants. These campaigns roused little popular support, for villagers and workers scoffed at vague appeals from privileged young people. The police were better listeners. They began rounding up Populists in large numbers, and in the late 1870s put several dozen of them on trial.

Suppression discouraged many Populists and drove on a hardened few. In the late 1870s a group called People's Will began planning the assassination of Alexander II. Among the leaders of this group was Sophia Perovskaia, the daughter of a general. She and her comrades argued that a direct strike at the heart of imperial power would show the Russian people that the tsar was an ordinary mortal, not, as they had been taught, a demigod. When the people saw that he was as killable as anybody else, they would rise up against the repressive regime. On March 1, 1881, Perovskaia and her comrades succeeded in killing the emperor, but no great revolt followed. Instead, most people reacted with horror and the police quickly caught the assassins. Perovskaia became the first female revolutionary executed in Russia.

To any student of the "Victorian Age" in Europe—a time when most privileged women lived highly sheltered and conventional lives—it must come as a surprise to learn that women were highly visible members of the Populist movement throughout the 1870s: fully 20 percent of those arrested for "going to the people" in 1874 were women, and women made up as much as one-third of the leadership of Land and Liberty, the organization from which People's Will sprang.[15] This was a prime indicator of the Russian intelligentsia's receptivity to women's emancipation; radical groups in the rest of Europe had far fewer female members.

Still more surprisingly, many Russian liberals, that is, those who favored incremental reform achieved by non-violent means, saw the female Populists as heroic martyrs. They did so because the line between reformers and revolutionaries was a fine one, easily crossed, Russia's injustices being so great and its government so recalcitrant. That government inadvertently promoted sympathy for Populist women by putting some of them on trial in 1877 and 1878. Surrounded by police and prosecutors, the women seemed frail, yet defiant. Perhaps the most eloquent was Sophia Bardina, who declared that she had become a revolutionary to help the poor and who warned, prophetically, that one day "even our sleepy and lazy society" would avenge itself on its oppressors.[16] Her testimony was published abroad and circulated in manuscript throughout Russia. Poets later celebrated the female revolutionaries and art dealers sold portraits of the executed Perovskaia.

This admiration was rooted in traditional notions about noblewomen sacrificing themselves for the unfortunate. Barbara Alpern Engel has shown that many female Populists felt a religious obligation to fight for social justice, even if it cost them their lives. "There are times," wrote Vera Zasulich, "there are entire ages, when there is nothing more beautiful and desirable than a crown of thorns." Zasulich also professed a more modern, more feminist motivation. "And then the distant specter of revolution appeared, making me equal to a boy," she wrote. "I, too, could dream of 'action,' of 'exploits,' and of the 'great struggle.'"[17] Chernyshevskii's Vera had made the same connection between improving Russia and emancipating herself. Future generations of women would do so as well.

The formulation of the woman question in the reign of Alexander II and the projects launched to change patriarchal institutions set the pattern for the rest of the imperial period. Feminists would struggle for reforms while socialists would seek to inspire the poor to revolt. Individual women would move back and forth between the two perspectives or keep a foot in each camp. Traditionalists would excoriate everyone seeking to alter woman's God-given roles as wife and mother. Meanwhile the government would pursue policies that destabilized traditional gender ideas and practices.

Peasant Women after Emancipation

THE EMANCIPATION

The Emancipation Statute of 1861 established procedures for making the peasants independent farmers and incorporating them into the political system as free people. State and crown peasants—those in bondage to the government or royal family—received title to the acreages they had tilled before Emancipation. The division of farmland between landlords and peasants proved more difficult. Negotiations mediated by government agents resulted in most Russian villages of seigniorial peasants—those in bondage to landlords—receiving a little less than half the landlords' land. Ukrainian peasants received still less. In Belarusian and Polish provinces, where most nobles were Polish, the government, angry over the Polish uprising of 1863–64, granted the peasants a larger share. The government paid the landlords for the land they had lost, then required the peasants to reimburse the government with what were called "redemption dues," essentially a publicly financed, forty-nine-year mortgage.

In central Russia, land ownership was transferred to the village commune, not to individual households. Families continued to farm collectively and to repartition the fields periodically. In areas without communal traditions—Ukraine, parts of Siberia, the Urals, and the northwestern borderlands—individual families owned their own fields. Taxes were still assessed by household, and if a man went to work in the city, he remained on village tax rolls and had to contribute his share to his family's payment. Everywhere, the tasks of tax collecting and governance that had fallen to the landlords under serfdom were assigned to village assemblies composed of senior men. Elected peasant courts were established to resolve disputes that could not be handled within the community.

The Emancipation, so long dreamed of by Russia's serfs, did not end poverty in the countryside. Agricultural productivity rose; by the turn of the twentieth century, 20 percent of the wheat on the world market and 43 percent of the barley came from Ukraine.[18] But this growth did not lift most peasants out of poverty, because the government had burdened them with high taxes, and the landlords, many of whom were also hard-pressed, paid them as little as possible for their labor and charged them as much as possible for the land they leased. At the same time, an expanding peasant population meant more mouths to feed. And so, in 1900, Russia's rural people were still coping with grueling labor, periodic food shortages, and epidemic diseases.

For women, this meant the old ways of doing things continued little changed. Across the empire in the early twentieth century, peasant women were still stooping over the land in the fall to gather the dropped grain. Wife-beating was still an everyday occurrence. The poverty and the patriarchy endured even as the sort of work women did expanded, schooling became available, and ideas and products made in the industrializing cities showed up in the villages. These changes marked the beginning of a long transformation in the lives of peasant women that would continue into the second half of the twentieth century.

PEASANT WOMEN AND THE LAW

Emancipation did not alter peasant women's property rights. Throughout European Russia, peasants stuck to the custom of giving sons equal shares of whatever property the family possessed and daughters far less—sometimes nothing at all. Shortly before World War I the national law was revised to grant daughters equal rights with sons in their families' moveable property. The rule that women were entitled to inherit only one-seventh of the land was retained until the Revolution. A widow who had lived for a long time in her in-laws' household could expect continuing financial support from that family, but she had no claim to any of her husband's patrimony, unless he had made specific provisions for her in a will. Only a widow who had lived with her husband in their own household, instead of in his parents' home, was entitled to receive a share of his property, usually between one-seventh and one-fourth.[19]

Peasant women's property consisted mainly of their dowries, which now often included cash and factory-made goods, their tools, clothes, linens, bedding, personal items such as combs, and storage chests. Peasants in most of European Russia also believed, as did many Europeans, Americans, and Canadians, that women owned the money they made selling handcrafts and foods such as mushrooms, fruit, eggs, and dairy products. Many women in Russia saved the small amounts they earned this way for their daughters' dowries. In keeping with long-established precedents, local and national courts consistently upheld peasant women's rights to their property, even ruling on occasion that a wife could not be forced to pay her husband's debts out of her own resources.

The reforms gave peasant women access to the civil and criminal courts, which led to surprisingly large numbers of them appearing before the judges as plaintiffs. To the township courts, women brought complaints about their neighbors and their relatives. Christine Worobec has shown that, "in the provinces of Vladimir, Iaroslavl, Moscow, and Tambov, . . . 64 percent of the inheritance cases . . . involved women." Beatrice Farnsworth's study of township courts in four provinces between 1866 and 1872 found that women participated in 32 percent of all cases. Most of these disputes concerned debts peasants owed to one another. Women also brought claims against their neighbors for theft, damage to property, and physical and verbal assault. The medieval notion that women could, and should, seek legal remedy for insults to their honor was still quite alive in the Russian countryside in the late nineteenth century. Some women also dared to sue their husbands and in-laws. Farnsworth has found that almost one-third of the family disputes involved a daughter-in-law accusing her in-laws of mistreating her. A few women sued their husbands for non-support or, more commonly, for physical abuse. Some also filed petitions for divorce with the church courts.[20]

The church denied most of these, and peasant judges often refused even to consider women' complaints against their husbands. But notable instances have been found of judges acting on the ancient notion that the law should protect women. Ethnographer Olga Semenova Tian-Shanskaia recorded, "Not long ago a woman from a remote village was able to have her husband flogged at the township office for his refusal to live with her." To make such an appeal required going to higher authorities than the village elders, an audacious move few peasant women were willing to make. That any did so testifies to the fact that some women were not as submissive and long-suffering as the stereotypes proclaimed them to be.[21]

EDUCATION

In the second half of the nineteenth century, the church, local governments, and the zemstva opened primary schools in the countryside. There was much to be done, for Russia, progressive in its education of elite women, lagged far behind more prosperous countries, such as Germany, in providing schooling for the poor. For their part, peasants resisted the idea of formal education for boys because they thought it was a waste of money. Boys should be working, not studying. In the last decades of the century, many peasants came to understand that literate sons would get better jobs in the cities and promotions in the army. They could also help their parents handle their financial affairs. So by 1900, the number of poor boys attending primary schools had grown considerably.

Peasants thought that daughters, on the other hand, could learn all they needed to know from the women of the village. "If you send her to school, she costs money; if you keep her home, she makes money," one man observed in 1893. School administrators also believed that the education of boys was a priority. Most were supportive of enrolling girls, but, when faced with overcrowded facilities, they granted preferential admission to boys. Consequently, far fewer girls than boys enrolled in primary schools, and those girls that did so were likely to drop out before completing the three-year course of study in reading, writing, and arithmetic. This disparity weakened as the century drew to a close, as parents became less resistant and more schools were built. Ben Eklof estimates that by 1910 perhaps 40 percent of peasant girls had had some formal education.[22]

HEALTH CARE

Village healers still provided most of the health care in the countryside in the late nineteenth century, and the rates of maternal and child mortality were among the highest in Europe. Peasant mothers died in childbirth more frequently than women in the cities, where better care was available, and more suffered from the chronic illnesses, such as prolapsed uterus, that resulted from multiple pregnancies. For children, the consequences were still more dire: half of them died before their fifth birthdays. The healers, most of whom were women by this time, could treat some injuries and minor illnesses effectively, and they knew how to help with uncomplicated childbirths. But they understood very little about the causes of disease and infection, and therefore remained powerless to stop epidemics that occasionally swept through the villages. They also promoted unhygienic customs. Midwives encouraged mothers to soothe their infants by giving them rags stuffed with solid food to suck on. Although the midwives did not invent these microbe-laden pacifiers, which spread gastro-intestinal infections, they encouraged their use and thereby contributed to the deaths of tens of thousands of babies every year. By contrast, David Ransel has found far higher survival rates among babies born to Muslim mothers, who fed only breast milk to infants.[23]

The attempts by the government and the zemstva to improve rural health care were insufficient to the huge task and were impeded by public resistance. Kashevarova, the country's first woman doctor, struggled to earn her patients' trust, because most peasants did not believe that doctors could help them. In fact they were often correct; nineteenth-century "scientific" medicine was almost as inefficacious as the traditional sort. Peasant women were particularly suspicious of midwives trained at programs like the one Kashevarova attended. And Kashevarova herself found the courses oversimplified and too short. The young, inexperienced graduates then came into the villages as strangers and tried to convince peasants that they knew more about birthing babies than the grannies who lived there. They also refused to help out with the housework while the new mother recuperated from childbirth, as traditional midwives did. So peasants often refused the services of the few professionally trained midwives that ventured into the countryside; in 1900, village women were still assisting in 98 percent of rural births.[24]

NEW WORK FOR PEASANT WOMEN

Industrialization and urbanization expanded markets and created new kinds of manufacturing that enabled peasant women to increase the amount of non-agricultural work they did. For centuries, some had been making handcrafts for sale; now production of those goods rose rapidly. By 1912, 8 million women, children, and men were engaged in this work. Women and girls specialized in beadwork, embroidery, and the making of gloves, lace, straw hats, and knitted goods. It was not uncommon for an eight-year-old to knit a pair of socks a day. Many women did more than one craft, switching from straw hats in the spring to embroidery in the fall, as the demand for products changed with the seasons. There were also enterprising peasant businesswomen who bought machinery to knit socks or stitch gloves and then set up small workshops staffed by neighbors. Some of these women prospered.[25]

Women and girls also worked in cottage industry, that is, manufacturing performed in the villages for city-based companies. This practice had developed in Western Europe in the fifteenth and sixteenth centuries; there women had made up the majority of the work force. Men were more involved in Russia, but the specialties employing women were similar across the continent. They were particularly likely to be engaged in weaving cotton cloth and bleaching linen, and they also wound thread onto bobbins for use in textile mills, assembled the paper mouthpieces of cigarettes, and made bootlaces.

The division of labor and the pay scales of cottage industry were gendered across Europe. In Russia as elsewhere, men worked in more mechanized manufacturing; in the textile industry, they ran the power looms, women the hand looms. The hours were long—thirteen or more per day for weavers—the pay was low, and women were even more poorly paid than men. In cottage industry, as in handcrafts, some peasant women became entrepreneurs who supplied the raw materials, supervised workers in the villages, and then delivered products to buyers in the cities. The income from all this work was a welcome contribution to the family pot, and it could be earned while the families continued to farm.

Other peasant women fostered children abandoned by their parents to state orphanages. The numbers of such children grew hugely in the second half of the nineteenth century across Europe, because the booms and busts of industrializing economies left many people unable to provide for their children and because urban women were having more out-of-wedlock births. There were years when as many as 17,000 children were turned in to the central orphanage in Moscow. The facility in St. Petersburg handled thousands of babies and young children as well. After 1870, zemstva-established orphanages in the countryside were also sheltering abandoned children. To ease the strain of caring for so many, administrators organized foster-care programs that placed children with peasant families. In the peak years, the Moscow orphanage alone was supervising the foster care of 40,000 youngsters.[26]

Foster mothers were paid for their labors, which included breast-feeding the babies and rearing older children along with their own offspring. Here too, enterprising peasant women provided the intermediary services on which the system depended: they collected abandoned children for delivery to the orphanages, recruited women as foster mothers, brought babies from the orphanages to the countryside, and delivered the foster mothers' monthly stipends. Although the stipends were low, there were villages in the poorer regions around Moscow that derived most of their non-farm income from caring for abandoned children. Elsewhere, taking in a child supplemented the family income and provided extra hands to work in the fields, if the children survived. Most did not; victims of neglect from birth, foster children were very vulnerable to the diseases that carried off peasant children.[27]

Many peasant women also worked away from their villages after Emancipation. In Poland by the first decade of the twentieth century, an estimated hundred thousand women were doing field labor on other people's farms. Across the empire, such women made up 25 percent of the female paid-labor force. Some of these field hands were young, single women whose relatives could work the family plots without them. Others were widows and wives of men who were disabled or absent; they leased their land to others so that they could work full-time for wealthier employers. This made more sense than farming alone or with young children, even though the demand for field hands was seasonal and women were paid less than men.[28] Other women became house servants or nannies, jobs that often paid better and were less wearing.

MIGRATION TO THE CITIES

More men than women left their home villages looking for work, particularly before 1900. In Moscow province, one of the most industrially developed in Russia, 76 percent of men were working away from their villages in the years 1898 to 1900, compared to 32 percent of women. Forty-eight percent of the women who had left their villages took jobs within their own district; 63 percent of the men had gone to jobs farther afield.[29]

This was a continuation of customs developed under serfdom, when it had been common for young men to do artisanal work such as carpentry away from home during the winter and to travel around selling handcrafts at fairs. Emancipation freed the peasants to leave without the landlord's permission and industrialization and urbanization opened up many more jobs, with the result that young men left for longer periods than in the past. Most planned to work in the cities, send the bulk of their earnings back home, and after some years return to farming. Their wives and children stayed in the countryside and worked the land with older family members; the migrants came home at least once a year to help with the harvest and to renew their passports. This arrangement—men on the move to better-paying jobs, families keeping the farms going in the ancestral village—was common across Europe in the nineteenth century and it occurs in many places around the developing world today.

The consequences for women in Russia were mixed. The males' departure meant that women who stayed behind had more work to do. Data collected in several Moscow districts in 1910 showed that women had taken up plowing and mowing, traditionally men's chores.[30] Some absent husbands defaulted on their promises to send money home or disappeared from their families' lives altogether. On the other hand, migrants who kept their promises made very important contributions to the family income, and women who lived in areas of large out-migration may have enjoyed better health because they had fewer pregnancies.

IMPORTS FROM THE CITIES

The flow of people between city and countryside gradually changed peasant attitudes and village life. Rural folk had long believed that cities were places where treacherous strangers lay in wait to cheat them. Now they also knew that the factories were producing useful and attractive things. Peasant women liked the soft, colorful cotton cloth and thread, the sharp pins and needles, and the sturdy pots and pans. In a good year they could spend a little of the money they made with their handcrafts on luxuries such as ribbons, hats, shawls, mirrors, combs and brushes, toys, printed pictures to hang on the walls, and musical instruments. Tea, though expensive, became a favorite drink.

Migration also affected the social life and power structure of the villages. Being on their own bolstered the self-confidence of some of the migrant workers and made them feel superior to country folk. When they, and army veterans as well, came home, they were less willing to accept the authority of village elders and of peasant customs. Some migrants insisted on choosing their own brides, rather than having their mothers choose for them. Young husbands pressed for a division of family property before their fathers died so that they could move out of their parents' houses into ones of their own. Younger women welcomed the assertiveness of the young men, because it weakened the control of mothers and mothers-in-law as well as patriarchs.

These were small changes when measured against the considerable power the elders still possessed in the last decades of the imperial period. Fathers and mothers continued to command obedience from their adult sons and to watch closely the behavior of their daughters. Girls had to be careful how they flirted with stylish young men from the cities, lest they wake up one morning to find the boys departed and their family's gate smeared with dung or tar, a message to everyone in the village that here lived a girl who had ruined her reputation. Furthermore, the man who defied his parents would not necessarily brook defiance from his wife. In many provinces the marriage ceremony still ended with the bride affirming submission to her new husband by kneeling at his feet.

Women in the Cities

WORKING-CLASS WOMEN

Some peasant women joined the tide of men surging into the cities in the late nineteenth century. They headed out in small groups for places where they had friends who could help them find housing and jobs. This female migration grew from a trickle in the 1880s to a substantial flow by 1910. The percentage of women among the peasants living in Moscow increased from 40 percent in 1871 to 65 percent in 1902; the corresponding figures for St. Petersburg were 30 and 48 percent. In Warsaw, women constituted a slight majority of migrants.[31] Need and opportunity drove these female pilgrims. Young women sought to work for a few seasons, then go home and marry. On the other hand, widows, most of whom left the villages because they could not survive there without their husbands, came to town intending to stay. There were also some married women, although a smaller percentage than elsewhere in Europe, who moved to the cities to join their husbands. It was commoner, as we have seen, for wives to remain in the countryside with their children.

DOMESTIC SERVANTS

Many of the female migrants became servants. Domestic service was the greatest employer of urban women all over industrializing Europe in the nineteenth century, because the rising incomes of middle-class families enabled more people to hire household help and because housework was easy for a peasant newly arrived in the city to learn. In 1890 there were 87,777 women working as domestic servants in St. Petersburg, an increase of 59 percent since 1864. The number of men in domestic service had remained constant over those decades. In 1900, servants were a majority of the blue-collar female labor force across the empire; the 1897 census recorded that 1,621,755 women were working as servants. This percentage fell slightly in the next decade, as better-paying factory and service jobs opened up.[32]

Most servants worked as the sole employees of families of moderate means who lived in apartments. Single-family houses were common only in smaller cities or towns. In an era before electrical appliances and flush toilets, the maintenance of clean, comfortable homes required the combined energies of servant and female employer. For the servant, the pay was low, days off were rare, and some bosses were stingy with food. Few servants had rooms of their own; most slept in a corner of the kitchen or under the stairwell. "The 'masters' paid a pathetic pittance and demanded that they give them their whole souls," wrote P. Lapteva, a servant in St. Petersburg in the early 1900s.[33] Most servants were also isolated from other workers, who might have provided support, and were in constant contact with employers who had the power to abuse them.

The souring of relations between servants and employees is documented by the fact that servants were more likely than other working women to be accused of theft by their employers. Perhaps employers blamed them unfairly when things went missing. Perhaps domestics who stole were more likely to get caught than were other kinds of workers. Servants were also subject to sexual exploitation by the families they worked for. At best, such contacts, when discovered, led to the servant's being fired. At worst, a woman became pregnant before she was let go. Bearing the stigma of unwed motherhood, she would then find it difficult to get another position. Not surprisingly, female servants did what they could to end unwanted pregnancies. Of all the occupational groups in urban Russia, domestics had the highest rates of conviction for the crimes of infanticide and hiding the body of a newborn. They were also the women most likely to turn their babies over to foundling homes.[34]

Luckier, more careful servants became valued employees, and, sometimes, deep affection developed between them and the families they served. If a woman was a trusted member of the family, she achieved secure employment, at least as long as she was able to do her job, and emotional connections to replace those she had left when she moved to the city. Her subordinate position may not have bothered her as much as it would have a woman from more privileged origins, for lower-class women in late imperial Russia were treated as inferiors in whatever line of work they followed. Working for an upper-class family was at least familiar; it was what the serfs had done for generations.

FACTORY WORKERS

Women were a large and growing presence in Russia's industrial labor force in the late imperial period. In the 1880s, they were 22 percent of factory workers in the industrializing regions of central Russia. Their largest employer was the textile industry: 37 percent of its workers were female. Other industries with large proportions of female workers were papermaking (36 percent) and tobacco processing (47 percent). These percentages increased in the following decades. In 1914, 59 percent of textile workers were women. An estimated 662,620 women worked in all of Russia's factories that year, making up 32 percent of the factory work force. Their numbers had increased 59 percent since 1901. By contrast, female workers were only 19 percent of the German industrial labor force in the 1910s, and American women would not reach 20 percent until 1920.[35]

There were so many female factory workers in Russia because Russia was poor. The enduring struggle of the peasants to sustain their growing families drove many women to the factories. Managers, believing that women were more docile, soberer workers than men, were happy to employ them in work that they were physically strong enough to perform. Many believed that women were also better at tasks requiring fine manual dexterity, such as cigarette manufacturing, and at traditionally female work, such as sewing. They could also be paid less than men. Rose Glickman has estimated that in Russia, factory women's wages were one-half to two-thirds of men's, because they received lower wages even when they did the same work as men and because they were banned from holding more skilled, better paid jobs. All these exigencies and motives prevailed elsewhere in Europe, but in the more prosperous regions, rising wages for male workers enabled more married women to leave the paid-labor force. Russian manufacturers also built factories in the countryside, particularly around Moscow, which made it possible for women to walk to work every day while continuing to live in their home villages. By 1900, roughly half of factory workers labored in these rural enterprises.[36]

Everywhere, in country and city, wages and working conditions were among the worst in Europe. Shifts of thirteen hours, six days a week, with very short breaks to eat and to use the toilet, were common. Factories were poorly ventilated, filled with loud, dangerous machinery and harmful chemicals, and lacking adequate water supplies, toilet facilities, and medical care. Until 1903 few companies provided disability insurance; in that year the government required employers to fund such insurance, but permitted them wide latitude in the awarding of benefits. Pension plans were non-existent, as was unemployment compensation. The availability of work fluctuated with the business cycle, and workers were fired at the whim of the bosses.

For its part, the government lacked the will to improve the situation. An 1885 law that outlawed night work for women and children is a case in point: the fines it imposed for violations were low; inspections to assess compliance were episodic; and management found ways around the regulations. The same combination of bad laws and worse enforcement undermined an 1897 law that limited the workday for adults to 11½ hours. Consequently, youngsters aged twelve to fourteen routinely put in nine-hour days in textile mills in the early twentieth century. And women, toiling twelve hours or more per shift, grew old before their time. L. Katenina, a physician who studied female factory workers in Kostroma province in 1913, reported, "A woman worker of fifty who has worked at the factory thirty or more years frequently looks ancient: she sees and hears poorly, her head trembles, her shoulders are sharply hunched over. She looks about seventy years old."[37]

Russian employers were much like those in nineteenth-century Manchester or Pittsburgh. They had a huge pool of workers at their disposal and many unskilled jobs to fill, so they could keep wages low and workers dependent. The Russian government, like governments elsewhere, wrung its hands periodically over the workers' hardships, but usually acted to support businessmen in the belief that building the economy was the prime imperative. When workers began to strike in the 1870s, and then organize unions in the 1880s, the government responded with force. By issuing regulations it did not enforce and stifling worker activism, the government guaranteed that the workers would eventually blame it, as well as the factory owners, for their miseries. That led to a combative, easily radicalized labor movement.

Working-class women in Russia, like their counterparts elsewhere in Europe, were less willing than men to get involved in strikes or unions. To explain this quiescence, Russian revolutionaries and liberals, like their counterparts elsewhere, declared that women were "backward," by which they meant that they were ignorant, religious, and conservative. The truth was more complicated. Working-class women were at the bottom of the labor hierarchy. If they protested, they would be fired. If fired, they might be blacklisted, which meant that no other factory would hire them. Being permanently unemployed would leave them destitute. This was no groundless fear; in 1912 there were fifteen thousand female beggars in Moscow.[38] Moreover, many single women in the factory workforce saw their employment as a short-term necessity that would end when they married. Why take risks when one was going to leave after a few months or years? As for married workers, they were too burdened by domestic responsibilities to have time for labor activism, and they were still more likely than single women to fear losing their jobs because they had children to support.

Women also avoided unions and strikes because men wanted them to. Many male workers did not even want women working in the factories, since their presence, it was believed—with some justification—brought down wages and cost men jobs. Leadership in the workplace and in the labor movement was seen by men, and many women, as a male prerogative. In the fall of 1905, female workers did join men in a massive general strike that engulfed Russia's major cities, and a few women served on the St. Petersburg soviet, the strike coordinating committee. In the following years the government legalized unions, but this did not change gender arrangements. Even the overwhelmingly female textile workers' union had male leadership. These attitudes prevailed everywhere in the industrializing world. As a consequence, even in the far more progressive United States of 1920, women, then 20 percent of the industrial labor force, were only 8 percent of union members.[39]

SERVICE WORKERS

Service workers were the third largest category of blue-collar female employees in urban Russia. They included laundresses, cooks, waitresses, charwomen, dressmakers, seamstresses, tailors, salespeople, and market vendors.[40] The laundresses, seamstresses, and dressmakers worked the longest hours under the most difficult conditions. Bathed in steam floating off vats of boiling water, laundresses stirred and lifted heavy loads of wet clothes. Garment-makers bent over sewing machines or did hand sewing in poor light. Their work was seasonal, so they were often laid off for weeks at a time. Although the majority of women in these jobs were peasant migrants to the city, a growing number had been born in the cities—a sign of the growth of the urban working class.

Another sign of the times was the increasing number of saleswomen. Working in a shop became a prized occupation for working-class women, because it was less grueling than factory or sweatshop jobs. It was also considered more prestigious: saleswomen were literate, they dressed well by comparison with factory workers, and they were taught the manners and tastes of their customers. Russia was later than France and Britain in hiring women as shop assistants; only 7 percent of its workers in that occupation in the early twentieth century were female. These women were more likely than factory workers to have been born in the city, and their wages, although only half those of male shop assistants, were higher than those of domestics and many unskilled factory workers.[41]

LIVING CONDITIONS

Living conditions for the urban poor were as bad as the working conditions. Construction of new housing lagged far behind the growing demand, so many people crowded together in fire-trap, bug-infested tenements and barracks. Others built shantytowns in the suburbs. Outdoor latrines served as toilets. Water for washing and cooking had to be bought from vendors or drawn from neighborhood wells, then hauled inside. Rents for even these dreadful accommodations ate up workers' pay. Social services that might have eased the difficulties, such as affordable medical care and daycare for children, were virtually nonexistent. Highly underdeveloped also were sewer systems, garbage disposal, street lighting, fire and police departments, and urban transit. The government's efforts to improve conditions were typically half-hearted and ineffectual. And so the workers, especially the women, who were responsible for housework, developed coping skills for the cities. Polina Novikova grew up among such women, and, in her old age, she wrote about them.

POLINA NOVIKOVA (1896–at least 1974)

Novikova had been born in a village. Her father was a textile worker in Tver who, after some years, moved his family to the city. Polina's mother became a textile worker too, as did Polina when she was twelve. Before that, she worked as a babysitter. Looking back many decades later on her

Workers standing in line at a soup kitchen in St. Petersburg, circa 1905.
Among such people, Polina Novikova spent her childhood.
Picture Collection of the New York Public Library.

POLINA NOVIKOVA

Novikova described, years later, her work in the textile factories. To put her wages in context, it is useful to know that a 1908 study found that an unmarried worker living on her own needed a minimum of nineteen rubles a month to cover food and housing costs.[1]

"The work in the factory was hard: long shifts, dust, heat, no time off. Women sometimes gave birth at the looms. Women often got sick from the exhausting work and the poor nutrition; they died early. Women workers rarely lived more than forty years. My first boss died from consumption.

I signed up at the Zaloginskii factory at twelve. I worked with other girls sorting rags and scraps in a damp, dark cellar. I received three rubles a month. At fifteen they assigned me to train at the loom, and at sixteen I became a textile worker. Textile workers at the Zaloginskii factory received eight to ten rubles a month. When a woman worker complained to the director about the low pay, he replied:

'Where there's a swamp, there'll be frogs. Where there's work, people wanting work will be a dime a dozen.'

After getting some experience, I moved to the Berg factory, where, working three looms, I received twelve to thirteen rubles a month."

SOURCE: P. A. NOVIKOVA, "TRI SESTRY," *BEZ NYKH MY NE POBEDILI BY* (MOSCOW: POLITIZ-DAT, 1975), 44. TRANSLATED BY BARBARA CLEMENTS.

---

1. Glickman, *Russian Factory Women*, 115.

childhood, Novikova remembered the barracks in which her family lived as a place of hardship and mutual support.

> Two or three families huddled together in one room, divided from one another by cotton curtains. There were cradles over the beds; on the beds were dirty sheets, potatoes, washtubs—there wasn't anywhere else to put them. There was one table for two families. While one family ate, the other one waited in the hall. Day and night there was stink, stuffy air; the bedbugs, the cockroaches, tormented us. We could only buy the cheapest cuts of meat once a month. We usually boiled plain cabbage soup or made "mess soup," water with bread and onions crumbled up in it. . . .
> Despite such awful conditions, the workers valued the barracks. They . . . had central heating and a common kitchen with a big Russian stove, where you could cook anytime. When they left for the factory, the women workers would put a pot on the table [in the kitchen] with potatoes or cabbage soup. The cook would put it on the stove, for which each family paid her ten kopeks a month.[42]

Novikova was not one of the submissive women workers; instead she spoke up about the ways foremen mistreated women workers. Before long, revolutionaries had invited her to their clandestine meetings in the woods, and she and her sister had thrown in their lot with them. After the Revolution, Novikova worked full-time for the Communist Party, specializing at first in propagandizing female factory workers.

WORKING WOMEN'S HOUSEWORK

Housekeeping in the cities was less demanding than in the countryside, because women did not have to grow their own food and because they prepared very simple meals, such as the soups Novikova remembered. Women were in charge of laundry and cleaning as well, but as they had few clothes and lived in small spaces, this work was minimal. Many couples did not even cohabit after they married because housing was in short supply and also because employees had to live within walking distance of their work. Public transit, where it existed, was too expensive for the working poor.[43]

The birth of children increased women's domestic duties. Most employers granted no maternity leave, so female workers did as their peasant foremothers had done: they stayed on the job until the onset of labor and returned to work as soon as possible after giving birth. Some employers let women bring their babies to the factories and nurse them during breaks, but most did not. Mothers therefore entrusted their children to the care of neighbors, often neighboring children like Novikova. Women who could not make such arrangements left their children alone at home. This unavoidable neglect and the prevalence of diseases in the crowded, unsanitary cities produced mortality rates among poor children that were even higher than in the countryside. Childhood was also shockingly short. Novikova was one of millions of girls who began working as a babysitter when she was eight and then signed on at the factory when she was twelve.

Many female factory workers preferred to quit their jobs when they became mothers so that they could care for their children. In Russia the working class was so poor that only 20 percent of workers' wives in the first decade of the twentieth century could afford to make that choice. Most of the women in this select group were married to metalworkers, printers, and other highly skilled, relatively well paid workers, but Barbara Engel has found that some wives of poorly paid workers were housewives as well.[44]

Because they had more time to devote to domestic work than did working women, housewives made more comfortable homes for their families, prepared more nutritious meals, and reared healthier children. Many also worked part-time to supplement the family income. Running a boarding house was particularly popular because women could combine cooking and washing for renters with the work they were already doing for their families. A famous example is writer Maxim Gorky's grandmother, Akulina Kashirina, who took in boarders after the family's dyeworks burned down. "My grandmother sewed and got the meals and dug in the garden, bustling about all day long like a huge top driven by invisible springs," Gorky remembered. Housewives also made handcrafts or took in piecework such as gluing cigarette mouthpieces. Although this extra labor made for long days and earned very little, it helped sustain the family and enabled the wife to stay home.[45]

FEMALE LAWBREAKERS

Some urban women turned to illegal activities to make life easier. Crime in urban Russia was gendered in a pattern common across Europe then and now: women committed fewer crimes than men and far fewer violent crimes. Most of the female lawbreakers in Russia were, not surprisingly, poor, and among those convicted of misdemeanors, many were single young people or widows. The most common offenses were theft, fencing stolen property, dodging taxes, and breaking government regulations, such as the domestic passport laws. Women rarely were accused of felonies such as armed robbery, assault, or murder. When they did turn violent, they kept the crime in the family, killing their husbands, other family members, or newborn infants. Women also fell afoul of laws particular to the Russian Empire. A woman could be charged with "resistance to authorities" if she yelled at tax collectors or police. She could be found guilty of participating in "uprisings" if she protested price increases at the shops or refused to disperse when police arrived to break up a neighborhood fight.[46]

The illegal activity that engaged the most women in late imperial Russia was prostitution. This was the case across industrializing Europe, for the cities were full of recently arrived single women and men far from home. Tens of thousands of prostitutes were plying the trade in Russia by the first decade of the twentieth century. They worked in big and small cities, especially those with army or navy bases. Although prostitution was officially a crime, the government tolerated and regulated it. Other European governments were taking the same approach at the time, because they believed, as Europeans had for centuries, that prostitution provided an outlet for male lust, and thereby kept men from preying on "virtuous" women.

Russia modeled its policies on those of France. In two hundred cities across the empire, prostitutes were permitted to work if they registered with the police and lived in licensed brothels. The madams of these establishments, who had to be middle-aged women, were charged with maintaining clean, crime-free businesses. The brothels were inspected regularly and the workers were tested for disease. Those prostitutes found to be infected had to report to hospitals for treatment and quarantine. Because there was very little effort to treat diseased clients, because drug therapies were primitive, and because so many prostitutes operated outside the brothels, the system did not prevent the spread of syphilis and gonorrhea. Nor did it protect prostitutes from abuse by pimps, madams, and customers. Furthermore, Laurie Bernstein has found that even the brothel workers managed to escape supervision by the authorities.[47]

Prostitution in Russia, as elsewhere, was a business of the poor. The well-appointed establishments that catered to wealthy men and the elite prostitutes who enjoyed discreet lives of luxury were exceptional. Most prostitutes in the brothels and on the streets were young, illiterate peasant migrants to the cities. Their customers were mostly workers, soldiers, and sailors. Since the cities were full of men living away from their families, there was no shortage of customers.

Asked why they become sex workers, prostitutes in Russia gave the same answers as French or English ones. Some said that they had been lured into the trade by persuasive seducers. Others said that they took it up as a way to get through periods of unemployment, then went back to legal work when hiring there picked up again. Among the seasonal prostitutes there were married women who engaged in the trade with their husbands' knowledge. Still others said that they found the work easier than hauling tubs of wet laundry or tending a thundering cotton loom. It also paid better, and the madams provided plenty of food, drink, and pretty clothes.

The longer women stayed in the demimonde of the brothel and back alley, the harder it was to leave, because of the stigma attached to prostitution. People in Russia believed that having sex for money was sinful and that the woman who sold herself was worse than the man who bought her services. This double standard, common across Europe, meant that prostitutes got little sympathy from other working-class women. Occasionally, the general hostility would boil over into violent attacks on brothels by people in the neighborhood. Prostitutes themselves appear to have shared some of the disgust for their business. They had very high rates of alcoholism and drug addiction, as well as disease. In 1888, government statisticians reported that 60.5 percent of the prostitutes of St. Petersburg had venereal diseases.[48] When their physical attractions faded with age and infirmity, some prostitutes learned legal trades or found husbands; some may have returned to their villages or moved to other towns to start over. The less fortunate joined the beggars haunting church steps.

THE BENEFITS OF THE CITY

Poor women's situation in the cities improved somewhat by the turn of the twentieth century. There were more public elementary schools and Sunday schools taught by volunteers; parents were more willing to let daughters attend them. An estimated 46 percent of urban females aged nine to forty-nine were literate by 1897, as compared to 13 percent in the countryside. In 1911, girls made up 45 percent of students in primary schools in the urban areas; and in 1914, one-third of female factory workers could read and write. These skills improved women's job qualifications and enabled them to negotiate better the transactions of urban life.[49]

Working-class women were also having more fun in Russia's cities. They read aloud to one another cheap novels featuring exotic adventure tales and steamy romances. They shared magazines and newspapers. They also enjoyed looking at expensive clothes on display in shop windows and finding treasures at second-hand clothing stalls in the open-air markets.[50] There were parks to stroll in, outdoor puppet shows, theaters, circuses, zoos, museums, and even, on the eve of World War I, movies.

URBAN WOMEN OF THE MIDDLE RANKS
AND THE NOBILITY

THE URBAN MIDDLE

The people who benefited most from industrialization were those in the middle of urban society. Enterprising individuals and families built factories, invested in mining and smelting, and developed Russia's stock exchanges. Others joined the professions and became leaders of municipal governments. The women of these successful capitalist families lived much as did wealthy noblewomen. Varvara Armand, the wife of a textile magnate, was typical. She managed the household staffs and budgets of the family's city residence and country estates, supervised her children's French governess, supported charities, attended church and the theater regularly, and entertained often at home. The growing presence of such people within Russia's elite was yet another sign of the weakening hold of the nobility on economic and political power.

There were also middle-class women who headed their own businesses. A few inherited large companies: Marfa Morozova ran textile mills built by her deceased husband. More typically, women owned small businesses. Catriona Kelly has found that 8 to 15 percent of the members of the merchant guilds in the second half of the nineteenth century were women, most widows with children. They came from all the various nationalities of Russia; Jews were particularly well represented. Here too the gendering of the Russian economy was quite similar to that of other European countries, that is, women owned businesses in the fashion and hospitality sectors. They ran dry-goods stores, dress and millinery shops, boarding houses, and hotels. Some also sold other women, or rather their services, for many brothel keepers were women of the lower middle class. Women from more prosperous families owned and managed rental property, particularly in the major cities. In Moscow at the turn of the century, 60 to 75 percent of those listing their occupation as "rental landlord" were women; in Warsaw the figure was 57 percent.[51]

The majority of women in Russia's middling ranks were housewives. By the later nineteenth century, some of these women belonged to prosperous, conservative merchant families. They avoided the cosmopolitan circles frequented by Varvara Armand, preferring to live quietly within their large houses. Most housewives from the middle ranks of urban society were far poorer people who devoted themselves to caring for their families. Cooking alone was arduous, for middle-class women prepared more elaborate meals than did working-class women. They bought some necessities, such as bread, but most dishes had to be made from scratch. Meat was sold in chunks; chickens came with feathers attached. Soups were made daily, cakes required long beating (two hours for gingerbread, according to a popular cookbook) and careful oven preparation. If the family owned a small business, such as a tavern or workshop, the wife of the owner might also keep accounts and cook for the employees. Life in the middle was precarious, and an injury to the breadwinner or a downturn in the economy forced many a middle-class woman into the paid-labor force.

THE NOBILITY

The last decades of the nineteenth century brought substantial change to some noblewomen, while barely touching others. Those in remote rural areas were the least affected. They, like the wives of some merchants and most peasants, continued living as their mothers and grandmothers had. More changed were the lives of those noble families that spent much of their time in the cities. Wealthy noblewomen managed their urban homes in the winter and summered on great country estates. Poorer ones did their own housework, with the help of one or two servants. Some, by 1900, were also working outside the home, and this movement of privileged women into the paid-labor force was one of the most important developments in late imperial Russia.

THE PROFESSIONS

Russia maintained its position as a European leader in education for elite women in the late nineteenth century. The number of secondary schools increased, and in the 1890s the higher courses were permitted to reopen. The Bestuzhev Courses in St. Petersburg and the Guerrier Courses in Moscow were the main programs before 1905; after that year programs were established in Dorpat, Kazan, Kharkov, Kiev, Novocherkassk, Odessa, Tbilisi, Tomsk, and Warsaw. All offered a liberal-arts curriculum. By 1910, the Bestuzhev, Kiev, Odessa, and Warsaw courses had law schools (women could practice criminal, but not civil, law). Kiev and Odessa gave medical training, and Kazan and Moscow offered theology programs. Russia also had a private engineering college for women founded in 1906 by Praskovia Ariian, a feminist journalist. All this expansion increased the enrollment of women in higher education to twenty-three thousand in 1911. By contrast, Oxford and Cambridge, the premier universities of Great Britain, permitted only a thousand women to audit classes in 1910; none was allowed to take exams or receive degrees.[52] Thousands of Russia's educated women went on to professional work between 1871 and 1914, some because they had to support themselves until they married, others to make careers.

✢ ✢ ✢ *EDUCATION* ✢ ✢ ✢

Most found jobs in teaching, as did most educated women across Europe in the second half of the nineteenth century. Close to 90 percent of Russia's teachers by the turn of the century came from the middling ranks, from the daughters of the clergy, and from the nobility; far more male teachers were of peasant origins, reflecting the greater availability of education to peasant boys. Most of the female teachers in Russia, as elsewhere, worked in elementary schools, because of their supposed natural affinity for children. Proponents also argued that teaching would prepare young women for motherhood. For its part, Russian officialdom believed that female teachers were less likely to be infected with seditious ideas than were males. Consequently the government legalized the hiring of female teachers in 1870, included pedagogical training in the curricula of the secondary schools, and granted teacher certification to graduates.

As the school system expanded, so did the number of female teachers. In 1880, 4,900 women were employed in rural elementary schools; by 1911 their numbers had risen to 65,101. By that latter date 62 percent of the teachers in peasant schools were women, and women were a substantial percentage of elementary- and secondary-school teachers in city schools. Women with teacher certification also worked as governesses; in 1902 there were thousands of such private teachers in Moscow alone. Closely allied to teaching was working in libraries; by the end of the nineteenth century, most librarians in Russia were women.[53]

Because teaching was seen as a preparation for motherhood, female teachers were required to quit their jobs after they married in order to devote themselves to their own children. Such rules were common across Europe and in the United States as well. Therefore most female teachers—73 percent of elementary-school ones in Moscow in 1911—were single, compared to 22 percent of male teachers. There was a fairly high dropout rate as well, because pay was low and hours long. Many of the women who stayed on in the schools into midlife did so because they enjoyed their work and saw it as a service to the poor.[54]

✢ ✢ ✢ *MEDICINE* ✢ ✢ ✢

Medicine employed the second largest number of educated women in Russia, and in this Russia was unusual. The medical courses for women, closed by Alexander III in the 1880s, were reopened in 1897. The St. Petersburg Medical Institute for Women became the premier institution, and in 1904 its graduates were granted all rights possessed by male physicians except appointment to the higher-ranking administrative or academic positions. The number of female physicians expanded most rapidly after 1905, growing by 113 percent between 1905 and 1910. By 1910 6 percent of physicians in Russia were female, one of the highest such percentages in the European world. Seventy-five percent of Russia's female physicians practiced in the cities, where they managed to earn almost what men did. The few who worked among the peasants struggled with pitiful resources, village resistance, and lower salaries than male physicians.[55]

Still greater numbers of women trained to be feldshers and midwives. Feldshers delivered basic medical care, much as paramedics and physicians' assistants do today. In Moscow in 1902, 64 percent of the feldshers were women. They were paid about the same as teachers and skilled factory workers. An even greater number of women were midwives. By 1905, four thousand students were studying in the more than fifty public and private schools of midwifery in the Russian Empire and more than ten thousand midwives were practicing, mostly in cities. Twenty-five percent of midwifery students in 1910 were Jewish, which testifies to the fact that becoming a midwife enabled a young woman to move outside the Pale of Settlement in western Russia to which Jews were restricted. Jews were also strongly represented among female physicians: 24 percent in 1889 were Jewish.[56]

Other women worked as nurses, pharmacists, and dentists. Nursing as a profession grew out of the "Sisters of Mercy" societies set up in the reign of Nicholas I. Over the following decades, newly created groups, funded by philanthropists and influenced by the work of Florence Nightingale in England, improved training programs. By the 1890s, nursing was emerging as a female profession in the major cities of Russia. Pharmacy was growing as well; the government had opened training to women in 1889. Perhaps because setting up a small business was difficult for a woman, pharmacy was an overwhelmingly male profession. Even in Moscow, a city with high levels of women's employment, only 5 percent of pharmacists in 1902 were female.[57] Dentistry was a similarly small, primarily urban occupation, to which women were admitted from the 1880s onward.

✛ ✛ ✛ *OTHER WHITE-COLLAR EMPLOYMENT* ✛ ✛ ✛

Additional white-collar jobs opened to women because the growing economy was increasing the demand for educated workers, even as the realization spread that women were good employees. They could be paid less than men, they were perceived as more docile, and they were both able and willing to learn new skills. Most of the hires were in clerical and service work, fields that were becoming feminized throughout Europe. When telephone systems were installed in Russia's major cities, women were hired as switchboard operators. Accounting was also a growing field for women: 5 percent of bookkeepers in Moscow in 1902 were women, 21 percent in 1912.[58]

Women also worked as writers, editors, and independent scholars. Twenty percent of those identifying their profession as "writer" or "scientist" in Moscow in 1902 were women; by 1912 that percentage had increased to 37 percent.[59] There were also more female novelists and poets than ever before, and more female performers in theater, opera, and ballet. Women figured prominently as well among the artists who created the Russian avant garde.

Gender Ideas in the Late Nineteenth Century

All these changes—the movement of women into the paid-labor force, the increasing numbers of housewives in the cities, the development of female-dominated professions, the ongoing discussions among the educated and in the mass media of the woman question, the growing opposition to the status quo—led to the development of a generation of female activists whose multifarious contributions to late imperial society will be the subject of the next chapter. They also affected Russia's version of the cult of domesticity. The dominant ideals stood firm: women were still supposed to manage their households efficiently, exercise loving supervision over their children, obey their husbands, and set a moral example to all family members. Natalia Grot, a noblewoman, enumerated the female virtues in this description of her mother: "Her intellect was outstanding, remarkable for a woman, and her feelings were deep and strong. She was composed, usually quiet, and rarely expressed herself. Her thinking was exquisitely noble and elevated, and her devotion to my father and her family was immutable. A careful, energetic housekeeper with a great sense of practicality, she restrained my father's enthusiasms."[60]

Many members of the Russian elite in the late nineteenth century espoused the child-centered conceptions of parenting that were gaining popularity among propertied Europeans. Parents were advised to focus less on discipline and more on fostering children's emotional and intellectual development. They were also to spend more time with their offspring. Grot summed up this revised ideal as she remembered her childhood in the early nineteenth century: "Our family life in the country was patriarchal, full of love, peace, and piety, and for us children, lively activity and merriment. Our parents and grandparents always put us first."[61] Grot did not seem aware that "putting children first" was a new idea, one that would have appalled a traditional patriarch.

Grot's belief that the ideal woman was a frugal steward of family resources was also being undermined. Across Europe in the late nineteenth century, the upper-class woman was urged to show off her husband's economic success by elaborately decorating herself and her home. Russian writers produced scores of housekeeping manuals instructing women in this new consumerism. Magazines carried advertisements and articles on the latest fashions in clothing and home décor; mail-order catalogues made these goods accessible even in faraway Siberian cities. Women were also counseled on how to display themselves in public. An 1890 etiquette book advised female theater-goers, "It is permissible to look freely through one's lorgnette at the stage. However, it is better for young women to look primarily at the actresses, and they should avoid watching the love scenes or looking at low-cut gowns. Moreover, they should refrain from looking frequently around the hall through their lorgnettes; their role is to stimulate delight and admiration."[62]

This late nineteenth-century elaboration on the cult of domesticity, prevalent across Europe in the fin de siècle, was for the propertied, not the poor. A working-class woman might see the delightful ladies gliding up the steps of the Bolshoi Theater in Moscow, she might even have dressed her mistress for such occasions, but she knew that the lessons on stimulating admiration were not meant for her. When a working woman shopped, she bought necessities. As for nurturing children, she counted herself lucky if she could keep hers alive. Mother love was still highly regarded in her neighborhood, as was a mother's authority. So were strength, endurance, diligence, and frugality, all the ancient ideals of womanhood.

Notions about working-class masculinity were developing in the cities. Among skilled men, such as printers and metalworkers, there was a desire, shared with their counterparts elsewhere in Europe, to distinguish themselves from the newly arrived migrants from the countryside who made up the majority of urban workers. Prompted by self-help manuals, these elite workers argued that men should be assessed according to long-standing masculine ideals, such as diligence, mastery of work skills, and ability to provide for their families, and also according to their compliance with urban standards of cultured behavior. Working men should treat women with kindness and spend time off with their families rather than their drinking buddies. They should bathe regularly, learn how to use a handkerchief rather than wiping their noses on their sleeves, speak grammatically, eschew vulgarities and profanity, and read books and newspapers. For workers all over industrializing Europe in the late nineteenth century, this conception of the "respectable worker" was part of an agenda of social mobility. If men of humble origins worked hard, many believed, and if they acquired education and social polish, they could get out of the slums and into the ranks of the prosperous and successful.[63]

Many women of all social ranks approved of the notion that husbands should treat wives with more consideration. Their longing for a kinder, gentler masculinity is documented by the huge increase in the number of women in the Russian Empire who sought to end their marriages in the late nineteenth century. Between thirty and forty thousand women petitioned the government for legal separation from their husbands between 1884 and 1914. In 1893, 88 percent of the petitioners for separation were women, and of that group, 80 percent were city residents who had been born peasants. In Lithuania, women made up 60 percent of the plaintiffs for divorce, and 45 percent of them were from the middling ranks of urban society, the working class, and the peasantry. Elsewhere in the Russian Empire, more Muslim women than ever before were requesting marital dissolution.[64]

Barbara Engel and Gregory Freeze have found that women asked to be freed from husbands who, they charged, had been abusive tyrants instead of respectful, loving companions. "My husband," one complainant declared, "in everyday life is extremely insufferable, a despot, nit-picking, and coarse." A few women made still more radical claims, saying that they wanted to end their marriages so that they could "live completely free in all respects." Legal separation and divorce were still very difficult to obtain, so women who sought it were unusually determined and perhaps unusually abused. The fact that they came from all Russia's social classes and included Catholics, Muslims, Orthodox, and Protestants suggests that the belief that marriage should be based on love and comradeship was spreading in the cities, as was the idea that a wife should be able to liberate herself from a husband who mistreated her. Barbara Engel has found that two-thirds of these women lived in St. Petersburg and Moscow, a testimony to the liberal atmosphere of the two capitals and the greater access there to legal help.[65]

Women in the Borderlands

THE WESTERN BORDERLANDS

Industrialization and urbanization surged through Poland, Latvia, Estonia, Lithuania, Belarus, and Ukraine in the late imperial period, producing many of the same effects for women as in central Russia. The small city of Gomel in Mogilev province, in the southeast of today's Belarus, is a case in point. There were no large factories in Gomel, but its location at a railroad junction made it a regional commercial center, and by 1900 its population had swelled to thirty-seven thousand. The amenities of the new economy followed. In the first decade of the twentieth century, middle-class women in Gomel entertained themselves with dinner parties and visits to restaurants, the opera, and the theater. The tango was the current rage. Shopkeepers sold sewing machines, complete with lessons on how to do the latest stitches. The town also offered newspapers, magazines, libraries, and public lectures. There were five schools for girls, including a gymnasium headed by a woman, and two music schools. Most of Gomel's women were housewives; the female paid-labor force consisted of forty-three teachers, twenty-seven doctors and feldshers, and a small working class of servants and service workers. The city had several brothels staffed by Jewish, Belarusian, Russian, and Polish women. Ethnicity was the major divider of Gomel's population: 60 percent of the city's people were Jewish, followed by far lesser percentages of Belarusians, Poles, Russians, and Ukrainians.[66]

THE JEWS

The great majority of the Jews in the Russian Empire lived in the western borderlands, because that was where their ancestors had lived and because the government limited Jewish settlement in the Russian heartland. Most were urban folk who worked as artisans, entrepreneurs, and traders. In major cities such as Kiev, Odessa, Vilnius, and Warsaw, as well as in smaller ones such as Gomel, Jews made up a third or more of the population. Men were the religious and community leaders; women worked alongside their menfolk to provide for their families. Among the most devout Jews, wives often were the main breadwinners, while husbands devoted themselves to religious study.

Jewish women's lives were similar to those of their Christian neighbors. The small numbers of rural women did the same sort of farming as other peasants. Urban women worked in family businesses. Jewish women were less likely than non-Jewish ones to become factory workers. They preferred seamstressing and shopkeeping. Women who could afford not to work outside the home became housewives, but the late nineteenth-century cult of domesticity, with its emphasis on mothering and the decorative arts, did not make much headway among the Jews of the Russian Empire. Rather they continued to give high priority to work skills, much as did Christian working people.

The expansion of education opened up new opportunities for Jewish women. Because Jewish religious schools admitted only boys, girls went to public elementary and secondary schools, as some boys did also. There they studied the arts, humanities, and science of the dominant Christian culture. This may explain the fact that more Jewish women than men converted to Christianity as adults. It definitely explains the large percentage of Jewish female students in the medical schools noted earlier.[67]

Some of these students joined revolutionary parties. Waves of anti-Semitic persecution pulsed through the Russian Empire in the late nineteenth century, inspiring some Jews to emigrate and others to join the Zionist movement, which sought to establish a Jewish homeland in Palestine. Most Zionist organizations did not welcome female members; the socialists, who advocated gender, religious, and ethnic equality, did. By 1900 the Russian Social Democratic Labor Party contained an all-Jewish organization, the Bund, based in the western borderlands. One-third of its members were women. There were also many Jewish women in the Menshevik wing of the Social Democrats and in the Socialist Revolutionary Party. These small, illegal organizations grew in significance as revolutionary sentiment spread.

THE POLES AND UKRAINIANS

Alexander II and his successors oppressed the peoples of the western borderlands and so provoked nationalist responses that affected the lives of women and shaped gender ideas. The government was particularly hard on the Poles because they had rebelled so often. After the 1863–64 uprising, it tightened bureaucratic controls in Polish lands and required that Polish schools teach, in Russian, a curriculum stressing Russian history and Russian intellectual and cultural achievements. The Poles resisted this "Russification" by organizing a campaign to preserve their culture, in which women played central roles. Mothers were enjoined to teach their children the history, language, and values of their people and to maintain Polish customs, rituals, and religion in their homes. This conception of women as nurturers of national identity was not original with the Poles. Nationalists across Europe were promoting it in the nineteenth century.[68]

The effects on women were mixed. The drive to maintain Polish culture enabled energetic women to organize charities and private, Polish-language schools. But the nationalist ideas in the cult of Polish womanhood also slowed down the dissemination of feminist ideas from Russia. Because the woman question was a major concern of the Russian intelligentsia, it was automatically suspect among Poles, so any criticism of patriarchy could be denounced as a betrayal of heroic, beleaguered Polish men and a threat to the preservation of the nation. Reformers and conservatives alike, backed by the church, inveighed against improved education for girls, on the grounds that it would undermine women's devotion to their families.

The development of nationalism among Ukrainians had similar consequences for elite women. Some organized higher women's courses; others participated in philanthropy; still others set up *hromada* (community) societies that promoted Ukrainian cultural studies and vernacular literature. All justified their activism as motherly efforts to preserve the culture of their people. Ukrainian women in Galicia, a province of Austria-Hungary, where the political climate was less oppressive, were able to advocate for women's rights without incurring as much resistance from their male allies in the nationalist movement.[69]

SIBERIA

The greatest change to Siberia in the late nineteenth century was a massive influx of migrants from the western part of the empire. Between 1896 and 1912, almost 2 million people moved from European Russia to Siberia, with the result that, in 1900, native people constituted only 11.5 percent of the 9.4 million inhabitants of Siberia. Many of the new people came seeking freedom and economic opportunity in a land that was too vast and far away to be controlled by the central government. Similar dreams called pioneers to the American West in the nineteenth century, and the American frontier nourished more egalitarian gender relations, with the result that women gained political rights first in Western states. Some of the immigrants to Siberia believed the same about their frontier, that the women of their families were more independent and the men less controlling than those in patriarchal Old Russia.[70] This greater autonomy for women did not translate into an energetic feminist movement, perhaps because the great distances and brutal climate inhibited communication of ideas and the building of organizations.

The relationship that developed between native women and European immigrants is comparable to that between natives and immigrants in North America. In both immense regions, the native people were a tiny and shrinking minority confronting an influx of European settlers. In both Siberia and North America, the immigrants were mostly men until late in the century, when families of farmers started coming. We know very little about the interactions between the peasant newcomers and the native women in the Siberian countryside. Did the natives help the arrivals cope with the demanding environment by teaching them how to use medicinal and edible plants, as native women did in North America?

More can be said about the women who came to Siberia's growing cities. Most were the wives of government officials, engineers, and entrepreneurs. They occupied themselves with housework and childrearing, and many also undertook, as women were doing in North America, to "civilize" the frontier. This was a well-established role for European women in colonial areas. The cult of domesticity in its imperial version called on European women of upper-class origins to serve as agents of European culture in non-European areas. They were to model feminine virtue in their family lives and promote European values in the community at large. In so doing, they would lift up the native people, whom Europeans perceived as inferior intellectually and morally. They would civilize as well European men, who were especially prone in colonial or frontier areas to go astray.

Privileged women in Siberia took this mission to heart. They built well-appointed homes in the cities and worked together to organize libraries, literary societies, public lectures, opera houses, and theaters. They supported the establishment of primary and secondary schools, staffed by male and female teachers. They lobbied successfully for the building of medical schools that trained female feldshers and physicians. These projects created agreeable European enclaves in Siberian cities such as Irkutsk and strengthened cultural connections between Siberia and the European heartland. They improved education for girls and promoted women's employment in the professions. They also promoted the dissemination of European gender ideas among the native people.[71]

The natives applied their well-honed coping skills to their interactions with the rising tide of Europeans. Peoples in the remotest regions moved father into the fastnesses of mountains or tundra. The Buryats, Yakuts, Tungus, and some of the smaller tribes in the south continued their generally harmonious relationship with the Europeans. Those who lived in cities became more Russified, and some sent their daughters to the newly opened elementary and secondary schools. They also welcomed manufactured goods, such as needles and fabrics, which were coming east from Russian factories.

Christianity continued to spread among Siberians living close to European settlements, because of energetic missionary efforts by the church. Muslims and Buddhists resisted the priests, but many animists took the Christian saints into their pantheon of spirits, worshipping both Christ and the spirits of the forest. This syncretism was one in which native women played an active part, while keeping their ancestral beliefs alive. In 1900, female shamans were still ministering to their people among the Tungus, the Nivikh, and many other tribes.

THE CAUCASUS AND CENTRAL ASIA

Although the Russian army conquered the Caucasus and Central Asia in the second half of the nineteenth century, daily life and traditional values in both regions went on little altered. The many peoples there, although differing from one another in history, religion, and lifestyle, depended on patriarchal customs and clan affiliations for their social organization. Senior women exercised authority in their families; senior men governed their families and the communities beyond them. So it was primarily the men of the various groups who interacted with the Europeans who came to rule them. For their part, Russian government officials did not meddle with local customs, although they were critical of patriarchal practices such as veiling. The women who accompanied these men settled in Caucasian cities such as Tbilisi and Baku, and some participated in the "civilizing" mission of establishing schools and theaters.

Conclusions

The late nineteenth century brought more rapid change to women's lives than had any previous period in Russian history. Emancipation freed peasants from the rule of the landlords, and industrialization offered them new products and new ways to make a living. The opening up of blue- and white-collar jobs brought hundreds of thousands of women into the paid-labor force. Women's labor in turn played an important part in building manufacturing and expanding commerce and social services.

The intelligentsia's discussion of the woman question was energized by these developments and affected them. Feminist agitation brought substantial improvements in women's education. Dedication to personal liberation and public service impelled young women from the propertied classes into the professions and into the revolutionary underground.

So by the end of the nineteenth century, the government had fostered industrial development, improved education, and overseen the enlistment of women in the paid-labor force. None of this had ameliorated the poverty of the great majority of women. A rising generation of female professionals, many of whom were dedicated to helping the poor, came to believe that the government was an obstacle to necessary reform. The discontents of all these women in the last decades of imperial Russia pushed the country toward still greater change and, finally, to revolution.

5

ACTIVIST WOMEN AND REVOLUTIONARY CHANGE

1890–1930

The Russian Revolution began in February 1917 with a demonstration by poor women in Petrograd, Russia's newly renamed capital city. On February 23, textile workers took to the streets to protest food shortages and the war that had cost so many of them their husbands and brothers. They were answering the call of socialists and feminists to mark International Women's Day with meetings and marches. Dozens, then hundreds of women came out of their tenements and factories. The swelling crowds marched through the streets, they yelled for bread and an end to the war, and they defied the police that tried to keep them out of the city center. Crowds milled around shouting their discontents until sunset and were back again the next morning. Ten days of demonstrations followed, during which troops sent to disperse the people joined them instead and committees of Duma delegates met to form a new government. On March 3, under pressure from his generals, Nicholas II abdicated.

In 1910, the Socialist International had named February 23 (March 8 on the Western calendar) Women's Day, meaning it should be a time to demonstrate for women's rights, and so the protests that swept Russia's capital on that day in 1917 are known as the Women's Day March. It became a much-celebrated milestone in an era of female activism that began in late nineteenth-century Russia and continued into the Soviet period. "Activism" is defined here as participation in such public institutions as the church, government, political parties, professions, trade unions, and voluntary organizations, particularly participation aimed at achieving social, political, or cultural change. The late nineteenth century was a time of rising female activism throughout the European world. Nowhere was that activism more consequential than in Russia. There women broadened the discussion of the woman question, expanded the feminist movement, made major contributions to the arts and sciences, helped to build public education and social services, energized the churches, and strengthened the labor movement and revolutionary parties. This activism led directly to the February 23 uprising.

The 1917 revolution promised still more, because it brought so many women into politics, spread the message of women's equality, and empowered the Communist Party, which was committed to major reforms in gender values and practices. A heady, wide-ranging discussion of what equality was and how it could be achieved followed. Professional women went to work in the ministries of the new government and scholars documented the obstacles hindering poor women's participation in the public world. Operatives from the women's organization of the Communist Party (the *Zhenotdel*) fanned out across the country to inform lower-class women of their new rights, teach them to read and write, and engage them in building social services that would ease their burdens. The scale of the changes undertaken and the participation of women in them were unprecedented in Russia and throughout the European world.

The communist activists, who belonged to a party that was as autocratic as the monarchy it had overthrown, found, as their predecessors had, that autocracy was a powerful and demanding patron. Communist leaders, although willing to do much more than any other government of the time, believed that their main emphasis had to be on economic reconstruction. And so in 1930, when they undertook a massive program of industrialization, they declared the emancipation of women complete, closed the Zhenotdel, and summoned women to the factories. Female activism continued thereafter, but within limits set by the dictatorship.

Women's Activism, 1890–1914

Female activists in the run-up to the Revolution included academics, actors, artists, factory workers, feminists, journalists, nuns, peasants, physicians, socialists, and teachers. They ranged in their political opinions from monarchists to revolutionaries. Collectively, they entered terrain dominated by men and established a presence for women that would endure long past the Revolution. They also changed the places they entered, enlarging women's role in the churches, expanding philanthropy, and broadening the aesthetic of the avant garde. The feminists and socialists among them put the woman question on the political agenda of those seeking to reform and of those seeking to overthrow the tsarist system.

THE NEW NUNS

We begin with Orthodox nuns who revitalized monastic life in late nineteenth-century Russia and in the process "feminized" it. Religiosity, particularly among women, is often associated with political conservatism, and nuns with subordination to male authority, so it may seem mistaken to include the surge of women into the church in a discussion of social activism. But how else can one classify the existence of dozens of all-female communities, created by women despite resistance from church leaders, and practicing a new kind of philanthropy in Russia?

Across the continent, many women were feeling a religious vocation in the nineteenth century, and so they flocked to new Protestant sects and to new Catholic religious orders. When similar urges to a more pious life struck women in Russia, there were few convents for them to join, because Catherine the Great had limited the number of monastics in an effort to cut the costs of maintaining them. Devout women had to improvise, and so, beginning in the late eighteenth century, they organized their own "women's communities," wherein they could pray together and support themselves by raising food and selling handcrafts. For decades the church took a dim view of this effort to get around the limitations on convents. Then, in the mid-nineteenth century, energetic lobbying by a few supportive bishops and abbots gained official recognition for the communities and permission to open more convents. There followed a huge increase in the number of women religious, most of it occurring after 1890. By 1914, there were seventy-three thousand Orthodox nuns and novices in Russia; they constituted an astonishing 77 percent of all Orthodox monastics.[1]

The nuns of the late nineteenth century and the communities they established broke with traditions in important ways. Most of these nuns were single women from the peasantry, not the widows of noblemen, as nuns had been through the centuries. In part this was because Emancipation enabled rural people to leave their villages and male out-migration made it harder for women to find marriage partners. Furthermore, convents no longer charged admission fees, nor did they require sisters to pay for their room and board, as they had in Muscovite times.[2]

Those enabling conditions alone do not explain the prodigious expansion of convents and communities in the late nineteenth century. That growth occurred because tens of thousands of women in Russia who wanted to be nuns took the initiative. They established communities run according to communal principles that gave no privileges to noblewomen, grew their own food, found ways to raise money, and spent years petitioning for recognition by church authorities. Many of the women's communities eventually became convents through this process. The most enterprising of these convents administered farms, maintained chapels for visitors and pilgrims, and sold embroidery, icons, and holy bread. The women religious also expanded the social mission of convents. They performed the traditional charity of providing shelter to pilgrims and the destitute, and they also practiced modern philanthropy, establishing almshouses, hospitals, and schools for girls.[3]

In Polish lands, a large religious movement also developed among women. When the tsarist government closed most Catholic convents in the aftermath of the Polish uprising of 1863–64, women's communities modeled on the Russian ones sprang up in their stead. They lived a quasi-illegal life for decades, supported by the laity and by Catholic authorities. Out of these communities came the Mariavite movement, an organization of thousands of urban nuns who ran soup kitchens, cooperative workshops, and daycare centers.[4]

THE NEW PHILANTHROPISTS

Laywomen were important contributors as well to the expansion of philanthropy in the late imperial decades. This was a time when philanthropy across Europe was ceasing to be the purview of privileged volunteers and becoming professionalized. In the early 1890s, the municipal government of Moscow took an important step in that direction by creating "guardianships of the poor," staffed mainly by volunteers who got to know needy families, provided assistance and referrals to social services, stayed in touch to see how the people were getting on, and reported to the government on slum conditions. These were Russia's first social workers; two-thirds of them were women. Within a few years, the national government established the National Guardianship to set up workhouses and workshops that provided lodging and job training to the needy. Wealthy women raised money to support the workhouses and found markets for the goods manufactured by the residents. The Guardianship's employees also fanned out to rural areas, bringing food, organizing public-works projects that provided employment, and running daycare centers for peasant children. Teachers and female landowners enlisted in all these efforts; they were particularly valuable in the daycare programs.[5]

Female philanthropists also continued to work in private organizations. The Russian Society for the Protection of Women provided low-cost housing, medical care, and job training and publicized the problems of poor women, particularly prostitutes. The Red Cross, staffed by many female volunteers, set up nursing courses. Local charitable societies across the empire supported free clinics and libraries, midwifery and nursing schools, night and Sunday schools, and public lectures. In working-class neighborhoods, they also founded "people's houses" similar to the settlement houses of Great Britain and the United States.

SOPHIA PANINA (1871–1956)

One of the most famous of the people's houses was run by Sophia Panina in St. Petersburg. A noblewoman, Panina had inherited an enormous fortune; after a brief, unhappy marriage, she turned to full-time philanthropy. "My interests," she wrote many years later, "were concentrated on questions of general education and culture, which alone, I was deeply convinced, could provide a solid basis for a free political order." In 1903 Panina took over leadership of a people's house in the working-class Ligovskii district of St. Petersburg and began building it into an energetic presence in the neighborhood. The institution provided activities for children, a cafeteria, elementary education and vocational training, a medical clinic, meeting rooms, public lectures, a reading room, a savings bank, temporary housing, and a theater. Counselors were available to give advice on legal problems.[6]

Panina saw herself as a no-nonsense, hands-on manager who was offering poor people opportunities to improve their lives. She was demanding and bossy and, like so many of the assertive noblewomen in Russia's past, she expected to get her own way. Often she did. Her dedication to the neighborhood, her generosity, and her effectiveness earned the respect and gratitude of her clients. They called her center "Panina's House." It became a model for similar institutions across the empire.[7]

THE ARTISTS

Women substantially expanded their participation in Russia's arts and letters in the late nineteenth and early twentieth centuries, and by so doing overcame much of the misogynistic prejudice against them. This was the Silver Age of Russian high culture, created by innovative poets, playwrights, theater directors, actors, dancers, and artists whose work drew international attention. A significant few of these innovators were women.

WRITERS

Some female writers of the late imperial period continued to talk about the situation of women under patriarchy, while others explored new styles in fiction and poetry. The so-called "realists" wrote about the difficulties that female professionals experienced in the work world and also considered the lives of women in the urban middle and lower classes, as well as the peasantry. Female poets developed innovative ways of exploring women's feelings about love and the spiritual world. Marina Tsvetaeva and Sophia Parnok were the most daring; they wrote love poetry to one another.

Women worked as journalists, editors, and publishers too. Scholars have recovered the names of 447 female journalists; undoubtedly there were many more whose articles were published without a byline.[8] They wrote for all the various types of periodicals—women's magazines, the so-called "thick journals" read by the liberal intelligentsia, and newspapers. The situation of female journalists was similar to that of women in the other professions, that is, most held the lowest paying, least secure jobs, but there were exceptions. Alexandra Davydova edited the journal *Severnyi vestnik* (Northern Herald) and founded the children's magazine *Mir bozhii* (God's World). Ekaterina Kuskova and Ariadna Tyrkova were among the founders of the socialist journal *Osvobozhdenie* (Liberation), which they both wrote for and helped smuggle into Russia. After 1905, feminists also produced a series of periodicals.

DANCERS, SINGERS, AND ACTORS

More women than ever before were in the performing arts, and a few became international stars. Anna Pavlova is widely regarded as the greatest ballerina of the early twentieth century because of her technical skills and consummate artistry. Russia's most popular singer was Anastasia Vialtseva, a peasant who started out in provincial theaters. "The Incomparable One" did not have a first-class voice, but she was such a terrific performer that theater owners around the country had to hire extra security for her concerts, to prevent her fans from rioting.[9]

Stardom was somewhat harder for actresses to achieve, even though the Russian theater flourished in the last decades of imperial Russia. Maria Andreeva and Olga Knipper were members of the repertory company at the Moscow Art Theater, a group that invented a naturalistic style that revolutionized acting across Europe. They were well paid, while most female actors struggled to make a living. All women performers were also plagued by the public's continuing belief that going on the stage testified to a woman's lack of modesty and therefore probably also meant that she was sexually promiscuous. Some were; finding a well-heeled lover was one way to survive.[10]

PAINTERS

It was more difficult for women to become painters, for they were not admitted to the government's art academies. They could study at schools that trained drawing teachers and at two institutions, the Stroganov School in Moscow and the Stieglitz School in St. Petersburg, that taught the applied arts of embroidery, lace-making, porcelain painting, jewelry-making, and engraving. Some of the graduates of these programs then found an opening to painting careers when a rebellion against Russia's stuffy art establishment began in the 1890s. Female painters contributed works to exhibitions sponsored by private organizations such as the Moscow Society for the Lovers of Art. They studied with the prominent painter Ilia Repin. Consequently, when the Russian avant garde developed in the 1900s, it included five women—Alexandra Ekster, Natalia Goncharova, Liubov Popova, Olga Rozanova, and Nadezhda Udaltsova—whose paintings, book illustrations, stage sets, costume designs, and short films broke down boundaries between artistic media and pushed beyond conventional notions of representation. Their works now hang in galleries around the world.

THE ACADEMICIANS

Throughout these decades, the intelligentsia supported women who wanted to work in fields hitherto closed to them. Its members hired female journalists, published women's poetry, and invited female painters to submit works to art exhibits. They could not, however, alter the rules of Russia's universities. Government officials, who had only grudgingly permitted the expansion of the higher courses for women, would not admit female graduates of those courses to advanced study or appoint women to professorial rank until after 1907.

So hundreds of women became independent scholars. We have already mentioned *The Hygiene of the Female Organism,* written by Varvara Kashevarova, which went through multiple editions. So did *Intellectual and Moral Development of Children from the First Appearance of Consciousness to School Age,* by Elizaveta Vodovozova. Still another physician, Maria Pokrovskaia, crusaded for reform in the treatment of prostitutes, publishing a book in 1902, *The Medical-Police Supervision of Prostitution Contributes to the Degeneration of the Nation.* Less prominent women also labored away in their communities. In Siberia, physician and teacher Anna Bek headed local education societies and did research on childhood development. Women also joined the scientific expeditions that studied Siberia's plants, animals, and native peoples.[11]

SOPHIA KOVALEVSKAIA (1850–91) AND
MARIE CURIE (1867–1934)

It is not surprising, in view of all this scholarly activity, that the two most accomplished female academics in Europe in the late nineteenth and early twentieth centuries came from the Russian Empire. Sophia Kovalevskaia, the daughter of a liberal Polish/Russian family, was the first European woman to earn a Ph.D. in mathematics. In the 1870s, she studied in Berlin with the eminent mathematician Karl Weierstrass, who recognized her talent and persuaded his colleagues to waive the rules and grant her a doctorate. For years thereafter, Kovalevskaia applied for university positions in Russia and was turned down. Finally in 1883 she was appointed to the faculty of the University of Stockholm. Kovalevskaia wrote major papers on differential equations (one theorem still bears her name) and on the revolution of a solid body around a fixed point. By the late 1880s, she was being widely hailed as an intellectual phenomenon—Europe's only woman professor in one of the most intellectually demanding fields, mathematics. She received the prestigious Prix Bordin in 1888 and was elected by leading academics in Russia to the Russian Academy of Sciences the following year. Still, no Russian university was permitted to hire her. Kovalevskaia was trying again to secure a professorship in her homeland when she died of an upper respiratory infection in February 1891. She is buried in Sweden, under a headstone paid for by the students of the Bestuzhev Courses.[12]

Marie Curie had to overcome similar obstacles. The daughter of Polish teachers in Warsaw, she enrolled in the Sorbonne in Paris in the early 1990s, and within a few years had completed her doctoral degree in physics. In collaboration with her husband Pierre Curie, she had also isolated two elements, polonium (named in tribute to Poland) and radium. Curie's subsequent research on radium transformed the understanding of the structure of the atom and led to the development of the x-ray as a diagnostic tool in medicine, as well as to radiation treatments for disease. The resistance at the Sorbonne to appointing her to a professorship ebbed after she was awarded the Nobel Prize in physics in 1903. Curie became the first woman to teach at that university; in 1911 she received her second Nobel Prize, this one in chemistry. Unlike Kovalevskaia, Curie did not seek to return to the Russian Empire. She became a French citizen.

Sophia Kovalevskaia in 1880.
http://en.wikipedia.org/wiki/File:Sofja_Wassiljewna_Kowalewskaja_1.jpg.
Accessed June 27, 2011.

SOPHIA KOVALEVSKAIA

Kovalevskaia saw herself as blazing a trail into academe that other women would follow. In 1882 she broke Russian law by lending her passport to the sixteen-year-old sister of a friend. The girl used the passport to leave Russia, over her parents' objections, and study abroad. Kovalevskaia explained her decision to put herself in legal jeopardy in a letter to another friend:

"Is it really possible not to stretch out one's hand, to refuse to help someone who is seeking knowledge and cannot help himself reach its source? After all, on woman's road, when a woman wants to take a path other than the well-trodden one leading to matrimony, so many difficulties pile up. I myself encountered many of these. Therefore I consider it my duty to destroy whatever obstacles I can in the paths of others. According to her brother, this girl has unusual capabilities in the exact sciences. Who knows, maybe she'll become a prominent scholar!"

Two years later, Kovalevskaia wrote to a friend,

"The new mathematical work I recently began intensely interests me now, and I would hate to die without discovering what I am looking for. If I succeed in solving the problem on which I am now working, my name will be listed among those of the most prominent mathematicians.

According to my calculations, I need another five years to get good results. But I hope that in five years there will be more than one woman capable of taking my place here, and I can devote myself to other urges of my gypsy nature."

SOURCE: ANN HIBNER KOBLITZ, *A CONVERGENCE OF LIVES: SOFIA KOVALEVSKAIA, SCIENTIST, WRITER, REVOLUTIONARY* (BOSTON: BIRKHÄUSER, 1983), 166, 186. REPRINTED BY PERMISSION OF SPRINGER PRESS.

In their talent, ambition, and commitment to their chosen fields, Curie and Kovalevskaia had much in common with the other activist women of late nineteenth-century Russia. Many of them were reared in educated families that encouraged their daughters' intellectual aspirations. Curie and Kovalevskaia married and had daughters, were widowed early, and continued their work while rearing their children. They were aided by support from their families and the intelligentsia, as were many other activist women, and by the spread of emancipatory ideas from the intelligentsia to the wider urban world. In this changing milieu, such women accomplished extraordinary things. The celebrity of some of them also testified to the emergence of a public happy to applaud talented women.

But the limits were always there. Kovalevskaia was knocking on the doors of Russian universities long after she was a prize-winning academic in Western Europe. The difficulties arose because patriarchal ideas were still powerful in Russia, particularly within the reactionary, obstructionist government. Frustrating also was the enormity of Russia's problems. Doctors worked themselves to exhaustion, and still diseases carried off half the babies. Teachers toiled in the villages, and still most peasant women could not write their own names. Some concluded that such "small deeds," as they were derisively labeled, were insufficient.

THE POLITICAL ACTIVISTS

The surge of political activism by women began in the 1890s and continued, with ebbs and flows, right up to the women's march that set off the Russian Revolution. It was centered in the European region of the empire and was part of the unrest rising across the society. Tens of thousands of women, poor as well as privileged ones, became involved. They were united in their desire to improve the lives of women and the poor, but divided over whether to work in women's groups or join ones led by men, whether to concentrate on women's issues or pursue multiple agendas, whether to seek incremental changes or revolution. So their activism was multifarious and their arguments with one another heated.

FEMINISTS AND SOCIAL DEMOCRATS, 1890–1904

The 1890s were an encouraging decade for feminists across the European world. Particularly in the United States and Britain, female philanthropists and professionals from a variety of organizations worked with male allies to persuade governments to institute child-welfare agencies, improve education for girls and women, provide pension plans for widows, and issue protective labor laws and public-health regulations. The feminists among these activists built large organizations that campaigned for women's suffrage.

These successes encouraged two veteran Russian feminists, Anna Filosofova and Nadezhda Stasova, to join with pediatrician Anna Shabanova to establish the Russian Women's Mutual Philanthropic Society in 1895. Sophia Panina was an early board member as well. The society's charter was modeled on those of the women's clubs then springing up in the United States, which were dedicated to educating their upper-class members and to philanthropy. Many of the American clubwomen were also feminists who supported the suffrage movement. The Russian society's members, several thousand women in the capitals and in provincial cities, could not pursue the vote in Russia, for the government would not permit it, so they contented themselves with charities—clothing banks, daycare centers, housing for single women, job training programs, medical clinics—and with expanding higher education for women. This agenda was similar to that of the 1860s, and their accomplishments were comparable to those of that period as well. Their work among the poor helped the small number of people it reached; their greatest successes came in improving higher education.

Another, much smaller group of female activists were also organizing in the 1890s. They were the Social Democrats, Marxists dedicated to leading the workers to revolution. Early in the decade, female Social Democrats in St. Petersburg attempted to spread their message about capitalist and tsarist injustices to working-class women. One of the most energetic of these Social Democrats was Vera Karelina, a textile worker; the presence of women like Karelina was a new development in the socialist movement, which had hitherto attracted women from the middling ranks and the nobility. Karelina and a few like-minded comrades argued that working-class women could become radicalized. Most Social Democrats were skeptical. Women, they believed, were far less likely than men to listen to the revolutionaries, because women were more ignorant and conservative. As evidence, they pointed to the fact that women were usually more reluctant than men to join strikes. Karelina argued that properly trained propagandists could get women to listen. Her argument was strengthened when, in 1895 and 1896, female factory workers did go on strike in St. Petersburg. The government broke up the protests, but the groundwork had been laid among female workers and Social Democrats for future engagements with their bosses and the autocracy.

THE REVOLUTION OF 1905

The political temperature rose at the turn of the century. Worker unrest boiled up in a new round of strikes in 1901, in which women participated. In 1902 and 1903, thousands of university students, male and female, demonstrated in Moscow, St. Petersburg, and elsewhere, and the liberal press, professional societies, and zemstvo organizations began publicly criticizing the regime. The government attempted to curry favor by letting the liberals talk and by setting up trade unions for the workers, run by the police but permitted to represent the workers to their employers. It also decided to stir up patriotism by going to war with Japan in 1904.

The war went badly, and then the experiment in government-controlled unions blew up. In the fall of 1904, one of these unions, the Assembly of Russian Factory and Mill Workers of St. Petersburg, headed by a priest named Georgi Gapon and an executive committee of workers that included Vera Karelina, had thousands of members. A thousand or so were women, organized into chapters based in working-class neighborhoods. As the winter came on, the assembly was growing increasingly critical of the regime's ineptitude and intransigence.

In December, when strikes spread again through the factories, Gapon drafted a petition calling for improved working conditions, higher wages, the eight-hour day, an end to the war, and universal suffrage. On January 9, 1905, a sunny, cold Sunday, the priest led a huge crowd to the Winter Palace to present the petition to the emperor. "Many male and female workers thought then that the tsar would listen to them and not let the factory owners harm them," wrote Anna Matveeva, a servant who set out for the palace that morning. But the emperor did not receive them; he was not even there. Instead the marchers were met by soldiers who opened fire. Terrified people fled the Winter Palace Square into the crowded streets beyond, where they were charged by mounted Cossacks and shot at by snipers. Matveeva ran with the rest, forgetting afterward how she got away, but remembering the carnage. "For a long time," she wrote twenty years later, "the cries and moans stayed in my ears, the horror of death in my eyes, especially the cries of the children, the shots, and the curses." Hundreds were killed, many more wounded, and the government followed up by arresting demonstrators.[13]

This massacre, soon christened Bloody Sunday, infuriated and emboldened liberals and radicals alike, and the year that followed was marked by strikes, demonstrations, and violent confrontations between police, soldiers, and angry crowds. Trade unions and political parties organized and the press broke free of censorship. Peasants attacked noble landowners. The fury at the government was fed by humiliating news from the war, which the Japanese were winning. In October, a general strike shut down the major cities. Nicholas II was forced to issue the October Manifesto, promising most of the reforms the Bloody Sunday marchers had called for. Protests then abated, as the nation awaited the establishment of a more democratic government and the government cracked down on revolutionaries.

Working-class women participated in the 1905 revolution by demonstrating and striking. They joined newly formed unions of metalworkers, printers, railroad white-collar workers, shop assistants, textile workers, and tobacco workers. They also organized all-female unions of laundresses in the capital and servants' unions in Kiev, Nizhni-Novgorod, Rostov-na-Donu, St. Petersburg, and Tbilisi. In the fall, working-class women elected female representatives to the soviets, committees representing workers, in Ivanovo-Voznesensk and St. Petersburg.[14] The women who became union members and soviet delegates were few in number, but they and the many female strikers showed that some poor women were far less docile than the government, the factory owners, and the revolutionaries had assumed.

When peasant women joined the turmoil of 1905, their activism was more traditional than that of urban women. Peasants across Russia rose up against their landlords, demanding the renegotiation of leases on the land they farmed and attacking people they perceived as exploiters. Women were in the crowds that marched on landlords' houses and merchants' shops, as they had been in peasant uprisings in the past. Indeed, there was a long tradition across Europe of peasant women joining men in such rebellions. Female activists in Russia's cities were cheered by the willingness of peasant women to protest; conservatives considered it a sign of the end of civilization.

Feminists rose up too in 1905. The Philanthropic Society redoubled its petitioning for improvements in women's education and employment, but now their methods seemed too cautious to many feminists. Some of these women came together in Moscow in late winter to form the Union of Equal Rights. The leaders included doctor of laws Anna Evreinova, historians Anna Miliukova and Ekaterina Shepkina, journalist Liubov Gurevich, teacher Maria Chekhova, and writer Zinaida Mirovich. Quickly the union set up a national board of directors based in Moscow and St. Petersburg and promoted the establishment of chapters in other cities. By the end of 1905 the organization had eight thousand members, most of them professionals in their twenties and thirties.[15]

At the founding convention of the Union of Equal Rights in April, delegates approved a platform that declared their general objective to be "the attainment by all women of political and civil rights identical with the rights of Russian male citizens, with the goal of improving the legal and economic situation of women."[16] Specifically, the platform called for universal suffrage, equal opportunities for females in education and employment, equal treatment of women in reform of the peasant commune, protective labor regulations, and an end to government regulation of prostitution. The platform also advocated constitutional monarchy, civil liberties, the right to organize and bargain collectively, improved working conditions, self-government for ethnic minorities, and the abolition of all laws discriminating on the basis of religion or nationality. By including these reforms in its platform, the Union of Equal Rights affiliated itself with the liberal movement, and more particularly with the Union of Unions, a coalition of professional and trade-union organizations. Some feminists doubted the wisdom of working closely with mostly male political groups. They believed that the Union of Equal Rights would be more effective if it maintained its independence. The majority of its members disagreed, arguing that it was both prudent and principled to ally with others.

The politics of 1905 put that argument to the test. Union feminists made the vote a primary objective, as suffragists in Western Europe and the United States were doing. They got support from the socialists and sought the endorsement of liberals as well. To that end they lobbied the zemstva and their municipal counterparts, the *dumy* (the singular is *duma*). Although individual members of these organizations were receptive, national conferences of zemstva representatives reacted with indifference or hostility. Some delegates argued that women should stay home and take care of their families. Others accepted the justice of women having the vote, but said that advocating it now was dangerous politically. The countryside was awash in peasant rioting, these men argued; no need to stir up the villages further with talk of women's rights. Feminists denounced the hypocrisy of espousing Russia's liberation, then limiting it to one-half of the population.

Lobbying political parties was one element in the union's strategy for the revolutionary year. Members also reached out to peasant and proletarian women, encouraging them to draft petitions, write letters to newspapers, and hold meetings on the woman question. They helped organize a union for domestic servants in Moscow. During the general strike in October, Union of Equal Rights members collected donations for the strikers and held their banners aloft at protest meetings. All this activity built support among other political groups. By early 1906, Rochelle Ruthchild writes, "as a result of feminist lobbying, representatives of the rural and urban local governments, the professional, trade and peasants unions had included women's suffrage planks in their platforms."[17]

The political fortunes of the feminists waned in 1906. Delegates to the new national legislature, the Duma, refused to endorse women's suffrage, which, in the end, mattered little, because the government soon reasserted its power. It dismissed the legislature, then rewrote the election law to ensure that future ones would be compliant and powerless. It also arrested opposition leaders. The Union of Equal Rights was one of many organizations that saw its membership shrink dramatically; it disbanded in 1908.

FEMINISM AND TEMPERANCE

Even as feminists struggled to keep going after 1905, the Russian temperance movement flourished. Across Europe in the late nineteenth and early twentieth centuries, the crusade against alcohol was a major cause for activist women and men. Temperance advocates bemoaned drinking's negative effects on men's health, on their work performance, and on their families, who were often abused and impoverished. They also linked drunkenness among women to that other social evil, prostitution, and more generally to what many saw as the moral depravity of the slums. To remedy the situation, proponents of temperance advocated limitations on the sale of alcohol and educational programs to teach the poor about its evils. And they mobilized to promote their agenda. Some female temperance advocates worked with men; others set up all-female groups. In 1910, the largest of these, the Women's Christian Temperance Union, founded in the United States, enrolled 235,000 members in its home country, 157,000 in Britain, and many more in chapters across Europe, South America, and Japan.[18]

Russia's temperance societies claimed 100,000 members at the same time, but they contained smaller proportions of women, and very few of them were all-female. The greatest activism was in Finland and the Baltic states, where Protestant women held conferences and conducted petitioning campaigns. There also was activism among peasant women, groups of whom petitioned local, provincial, and national government leaders to shut down liquor stores and taverns in their villages. When they got no satisfactory response, some of these women marched to the offending establishments, drove out the staff, and padlocked the doors.[19]

Largely absent from the temperance movement in Russia were feminists and other female activists from the intelligentsia. Patricia Herlihy argues that these women stayed away because they chose to concentrate on what they saw as the economic and political causes of excessive drinking. Maria Pokrovskaia, a leading feminist and frequent participant in discussions of alcoholism, was typical. More important than limiting alcohol sales or persuading men to take abstinence oaths, in her view, were improving poor women's working and living conditions and getting all women political and economic equality.[20] This was a common position among Western European and American feminists too, but the alliance formed in the West between feminists and temperance advocates, although uneasy, was effective in promoting the interests of both groups. Russian feminism might have been stronger had it been able to make such an alliance.

FEMINISTS AND SOCIALISTS DEBATE
THE WOMAN QUESTION, 1906–11

Feminist organizations labored on after 1906. The Women's Mutual Philanthropic Society continued its work, and in 1908 a new group, the League for Women's Equal Rights, was organized. There was a small feminist press, and popular magazines ran stories on women's rights. Meanwhile, professionals and philanthropists applied feminist arguments to deliberations on a range of social issues. In discussions of prostitution, reformers argued that equality for women in education and employment would reduce the poverty that drove girls into the brothels. In debates over abortion, physicians and criminologists made the truly radical argument that women should be able to choose whether or not to have children.

In 1908, Anna Filosofova and Anna Shabanova of the Philanthropic Society won permission to hold the First All-Russian Congress of Women in St. Petersburg. Their goal was to bring feminists and other social activists together to develop a consensus on what needed to be done. One thousand and fifty-three delegates, most of them well-educated women from feminist organizations, philanthropies, professional societies, and women's clubs, attended. The majority were ethnic Russians; the other Slavic peoples and the Jews were represented. The delegates met for six days, holding sessions on education, philanthropy, the situation of peasant and working-class women, and women's participation in politics. The meeting generated networking between the activists as well as useful analyses of the topics discussed.

It also bought to the fore ideological and strategic disagreements between liberals and socialists that had existed as early as the 1870s and had caused dissension within the Union of Equal Rights in 1905. The conferees generally agreed on what women's equality should consist of, but differed sharply on the causes of their inequality and the ways to end it. Socialist delegates to the congress, some of them factory workers, believed that women should work with men to achieve political change, which meant, although they could not say so openly, women should join socialist parties. Feminists argued for an independent feminist movement, while agreeing that the situation of working-class women cried out for redress. The result was a good deal of acrimonious discussion, culminating on the last day of the congress in an argument over a suffrage resolution that provoked a walk-out by some of the socialist delegates.[21]

One of the most irreconcilable of the socialists was Alexandra Kollontai, a noblewoman who had studied at the Bestuzhev Courses, then become a journalist and a Social Democrat. Kollontai had recruited the worker delegates and helped them put together their speeches. She herself could not appear at the congress, because the police were after her. Instead she fled to Germany, and there, shortly after the congress, published a four-hundred-page polemic, *The Social Bases of the Woman Question,* that laid out the socialist indictment of feminism and subjected Russian feminism to scathing criticism. This book marked Kollontai's debut as one of international Marxism's most important commentators on the woman question.[22]

At the heart of the Marxist critique of feminism lay a dispute over the origins of women's inequality. Feminists saw patriarchy as a fundamental evil; Marxists and other socialists considered it to derive from the economic organization of society. Women's subordination to men, they argued, had begun in the distant past when a male elite had established control over private property. That control enabled the propertied to oppress those who did not own property, which in turn led to the development of patriarchy. Capitalism, by pulling women out of the family and into the paid-labor force, was inadvertently breaking down their subordination, but the process could only be completed after the power of all patriarchs—kings, nobles, priests, capitalists—had been broken and a socialized economy had been constructed. People would then organize a society based on perfect equality and cleansed of all discrimination. To get to this new world, women had to work with men in socialist parties, not pursue their own separate, divisive agendas.

When feminism developed into a mass movement in the late nineteenth century, Marxists began to consider ways to counter its influence among working-class women and progressive intellectuals. The German Social Democratic Party, the largest Marxist party in Europe, took the lead in 1891 by endorsing a sweeping agenda of reforms for women, borrowed from the feminists and from the social-welfare policies of the conservative German government. They included the vote, civil and legal equality, publicly funded maternity care and childcare, and regulations mandating working conditions to protect women's health. The last are commonly referred to as "protective labor laws." The German Social Democrats also set up a women's auxiliary, led by Clara Zetkin, the goal of which was to spread the socialist message among working-class women. Zetkin was an ardent propagandist of the socialist critique of feminism, because she believed it, because she wanted to persuade working-class women to reject feminism, and because she wanted to prove her bona fides to the men of her party.

Kollontai had been inspired by the activism of working women in 1905, and she had seen the feminists' outreach to poor women as a threat. So she had gone to Germany in 1906 to consult with Zetkin and had returned to Russia convinced of the rightness of the German strategy and tactics. The fact that there were more than ten thousand women in the Social Democratic and Socialist Revolutionary parties in 1907 and perhaps three thousand in the feminist organizations suggests that many political activists shared her doubts about feminism.[23]

After the Women's Congress, the League for Women's Equal Rights and the Philanthropic Society soldiered on. In 1910 they persuaded the Duma to pass a revision of the inheritance law that granted women equal rights to inherit moveable and urban property; they were only permitted a one-seventh share of rural land. Reform in the marriage law, initially requested in a Philanthropic Society petition of 1912, finally emerged from the Duma in 1914. The new law broadened the grounds on which wives could obtain legal separations and permitted them to seek education and employment without first obtaining their husbands' consent. The law also granted married women the right to carry their own passports, if their husbands agreed. It took four years of lobbying to get these modest reforms out of the Duma, which testifies to the patience, dedication, and energy of the feminists and explains the revolutionaries' conviction that the obstructionist regime had to be overthrown.

FEMINISTS IN THE BORDERLANDS

Even as feminists in the Russian heartland struggled for minor victories, women in Finland became the first in Europe to gain the vote in national and local elections. Finnish feminists won their suffrage campaign because of the unique political situation of their small country. The Finns had come under the rule of the tsars during the Napoleonic Wars but had never suffered the intrusive oversight imposed upon other borderland peoples.

Instead, Alexander I granted them a constitution that permitted considerable political and cultural autonomy. A well-educated people with close ties to Sweden and a strong desire to differentiate themselves from their Russian masters, the Finns developed a very progressive intelligentsia. In 1870, Helsingfors University granted full admission to women; coeducational schools followed in the 1880s. That decade also saw the formation of the first Finnish feminist organization and the extension of the right to vote in municipal elections to women. Finland's liberal politics raised the hackles of Nicholas II, and in 1899 he abolished the Finnish constitution.

Finns responded with a resistance movement in which significant numbers of women participated. They claimed a place by arguing that women, as mothers, were guardians of the national culture. Polish and Ukrainian nationalists used this proposition to justify women's staying home; among the Finns and the substantial Swedish minority in Finland it became an argument for women's participation in politics. Alexandra Gripenberg, a leading feminist, made the case succinctly in a speech to the Finnish legislature in 1897: "Femininity is motherhood in the deepest meaning of the word. That this be given its true value in that greatest of all homes, society, is the primary task of women's rights work."[24]

By 1904 an energetic Finnish Union of Women's Rights was working closely with Social Democratic and liberal groups to push for the return of Finnish autonomy. The movement grew still stronger in 1905. A successful general strike in October persuaded the tsar to permit Finns more self-rule, and during the politicking that followed, feminists pressed their case for women's suffrage. In the spring of 1906, a newly elected Finnish assembly drafted a constitution, accepted by Nicholas II in July, which called for the establishment of a unicameral legislature chosen by all citizens over the age of twenty-four.

The tsar accepted the constitution, Rochelle Ruthchild argues, because he wanted to mollify Finland while he worked on suppressing opposition in the imperial heartland. Once the political climate cooled, he tried to bring the new parliament under his sway. He did not repeal the constitution, perhaps because he feared stirring up more trouble. And so Alexandra Gripenberg was elected a delegate to the new legislature. In 1909 that body passed sweeping improvements in women's property rights and access to education and employment.[25]

Nationalism also fostered women's engagement in the public world elsewhere in the borderlands in 1905 and thereafter. In Lithuania, the Lithuanian Women's Organization took as its goal "equal rights for women and men in an autonomous Lithuania." This activism caught the attention of the Catholic Church and in 1907 it established the Lithuanian Catholic Women's League, from which the most liberal feminists were excluded. The editors of the league's journal advocated improvements in women's education and employment, as well as legal and civil rights. Ukrainian and Baltic German women's organizations adopted similar programs. The endorsement of women's rights by male religious and nationalist leaders indicated how far public opinion in the Baltics had moved on that issue in the early twentieth century.[26]

The democratic spirit of 1905 had no such outcome in Polish lands. There nationalists and the church responded to feminists' call for women's rights by insisting that women's highest duty was to rear patriotic children. They also denounced feminists as separatists who undermined the cause of Polish independence. In 1907 a group of Polish feminists led by Paulina Kuczalska-Reinschmit broke with the nationalists and formed a Union for Women's Equality modeled on the Russian Union for Equal Rights. This union held a women's congress, published a journal, and publicized a suffrage movement in the southern Polish lands that lay within the more democratic Austro-Hungarian Empire. The Polish press was also full of articles on the woman question between 1905 and 1912. This activism appears to have had an effect on public opinion, for in 1918, when Poland won its independence, women's suffrage was included in the new constitution.[27]

MUSLIMS DISCUSS THE WOMAN QUESTION

There was also an energetic discussion of the woman question going on among the Muslim intelligentsia of the Russian Empire, which was centered in Baku in Azerbaijan and in the Tatar communities of the Crimea and of Kazan, a city southeast of Moscow. By the turn of the century, many of these people had accepted the idea that modernity required easing traditional restrictions on women, particularly those regarding education, marriage choice, and social life.

The intellectuals who led this discussion of the woman question called themselves Jadidists, a name taken from the Turkish word for "new." They were inspired by the efforts of Turkish thinkers to reconcile democratic political ideals and nationalist conceptions of women's roles in cultural preservation with Islamic law and teaching. Foremost among the Jadidists was a Crimean Tatar named Ismail Ben Gasprali, who called for Muslim women to play an enlightening role in their families and societies. To do so, he argued, they had to be formally educated. His daughter,

Shefika Hanim, edited a bimonthly magazine for women, *Alem-I-Nisvan* (Women's World), which publicized the philanthropic activities of Muslim women's organizations and informed its readers about progressive developments among Muslim women elsewhere.

In Baku the husband-and-wife team of Jirza-Jalil Mammed-Qulizadeh and Hamideh Javanshir pushed the argument further by criticizing Muslim patriarchal customs. In their journal *Molla Nasreddin*, they called for women to be liberated from veiling, seclusion in their homes, polygyny, and physical abuse by the men of their families. More cautious voices spoke up in a journal called *Ishigh* (Light), published by Mustafa Bey Alioglu and Hadija Hanim Subhankulova-Alibeova. The male and female contributors to this publication muted their criticism of patriarchy, while urging women to organize. Their discretion did not mollify all the Islamic authorities. When he heard about *Ishigh*, Mullah Muhammad Amin, a prominent Baghdad cleric, declared ominously, "The end [is] truly near, since women not only read newspapers but contribute to them."[28]

The mullah might have thought the end had already come if he had flipped through the pages of *Suyumbike*, the most feminist Muslim periodical in the late imperial period. *Suyumbike* was published in Kazan, a city with a major university, higher women's courses, and a lively community of Muslim feminists. Its editors called for women to participate in public life and criticized Islamic patriarchalism. In 1914, a few Muslim women from Kazan who were students in St. Petersburg took their calls for reform to the Muslim delegates to the Duma. They were rebuffed, but the very existence of Muslim feminism in 1914 attested to how far the woman question had come since Vernadskaia wrote her articles in the 1850s.[29]

FEMINIST ACHIEVEMENTS

Across the empire, feminists scored successes in the last decades of the tsarist regime. They expanded women's education and improved their legal rights. They re-energized the discussion of the woman question by publicizing the international feminist agenda—suffrage, legal and civil equality, educational and employment opportunities, improvements in maternity care and childcare, protective labor legislation—and by developing their own analysis of the situation of women in Russia. Feminists also spread the call for women's rights to working-class and peasant women. In all these efforts they worked closely with other progressive people from the intelligentsia, thus continuing the alliance forged in the 1860s. That alliance strengthened after 1905, when governmental intransigence on reforms for women enhanced the appeal of those reforms to progressives.[30]

The grandest goals—suffrage and civil and legal equality—could only be achieved in tiny Finland, because the government was resolutely opposed to such major change and because feminism remained a small movement that enjoyed limited support. That said, it should be noted that the huge suffrage societies of Great Britain, despite their base in a powerful middle class and their much greater freedom to advocate for their cause, also failed to get the vote in these years, because the resistance to woman's suffrage was powerful even in democracies. Russia's feminists kept the woman question at the forefront of reform discussions in the early twentieth century and managed to win some of their battles. They also survived the demoralization that set in after 1905, and when the Revolution came, they would expand their movement with a rapidity that would surprise even themselves.

WORKING-CLASS ACTIVISM AND THE
SOCIALIST RESPONSE, 1912–14

After 1905, protests subsided and women workers, along with their menfolk, went back to the daily grind. The newly legalized trade unions admitted, and some even recruited, female members. Most women stayed away, as they were doing across Europe. They did so for long-standing reasons: they were afraid of the price of activism; they could not afford the dues; they were occupied with their children; they thought women did not belong in unions; they did not want to brave hostility from men. Rose Glickman has estimated that this kept female membership in the trade unions at 10 percent, even though women were 30 percent of the industrial labor force. But that 10 percent was important. Female union members got a political education, built their self-confidence, and became leaders among the women with whom they worked. A few also got involved in the revolutionary movement, supporting the socialists by going to meetings and circulating pamphlets. In these years, working-class women among the Social Democrats increased from less than 10 percent of the female membership to roughly one-quarter.[31]

Some Social Democratic women in Russia and abroad, where many had fled to avoid arrest, were paying close attention to working women's activism. They noticed that women were once again striking during worker unrest in 1912–14. Some of these strikes were huge: eleven thousand women walked out of a St. Petersburg rubber factory in March 1914 to protest the fact that the toxic chemicals with which they worked were poisoning them.[32] This resurgence inspired Social Democratic women, particularly several dozen in the Bolshevik faction of the party, to reach out to working women through organizing clubs for them and publishing articles about their lives. In 1912 Konkordia Samoilova, an editor of the newspaper *Pravda*, ran a column called "The Life and Labor of Women Workers." In 1913, she held Russia's first celebration of International Women's Day. It was well attended. In 1914, she and several dozen other female Social Democrats, including Kollontai, launched two magazines aimed at working-class women. All these projects reached few women and were shut down quickly by the police. Their greatest significance is that they brought together the people who would formulate and lead the Bolshevik party's program of women's emancipation after 1917.

The Hardship and Anger of World War I

In August 1914 Nicholas II committed his country to war with Germany and Austria. Russia had neither the economy nor the leadership to prevail, and so soldiers died by the millions. As men were drawn away to the front, women filled in on the farms and in the factories. Between 1914 and 1917, the percentage of female workers in the industrial labor force rose from 26 to 43 percent. More privileged women joined the war effort by collecting donations, making bandages, knitting socks, and converting their homes into temporary hospitals for the wounded. Thirty thousand women worked on committees organized by the zemstva to gather supplies for the army and care for displaced persons. Eighteen thousand served as army nurses. Others signed up to be clerks, military cooks, drivers, and laundresses. Feminists in Russia, as elsewhere, also lent a hand, hoping that their contributions would strengthen the case for women's rights.[33]

A smaller number of women—probably a few hundred—served in the army. Most got in by disguising themselves as men, and a few obtained permission to enlist by petitioning Nicholas himself. They came from all walks of life, peasants to princesses. These women gave various motives for putting themselves in harm's way—defending their country, avenging relatives who had died in the war, going on a great adventure, getting away from the confines of being a woman. Male soldiers usually figured out the sex of those who were pretending to be men, but a few made it through the entire war undiscovered. Dozens received medals for heroism, and the exploits of a few were widely publicized by the press at home and abroad. Among these were two pioneers of Russian aviation, Evgenia Shakhovskaia and Nadezhda Degtereva, who took their biplanes into the skies to spy on German forces.[34]

As the war ground on, women loyal to the regime did their best to strengthen morale. Empress Alexandra and her four beautiful daughters, dressed in starched white nursing uniforms, were photographed tending wounded soldiers. Nuns prayed for the health of the tsar's family, as well as for the troops at the front. Church bells tolled to remind Russia of God's eventual mercy. These appeals to faith could not still the laments of grieving mothers and wives or ease their burdens. At the front, the soldiers were dying: 3 million by the end of the war, 2.7 million more missing in action or captured.[35] At home, the mood darkened. In 1914 avant-garde artist Natalia Goncharova published a book, *Mystical Images of War*, which celebrated Russian patriotism; in 1916, her friend Olga Rozanova publicized the horrors of the front in a series of fevered linotypes and collages titled simply *War*.

The anger, widely shared, led to strikes, which women joined, and to less conventional protests. In Central Asia, women who were usually sequestered in their homes came out to demonstrate against the conscription of their men to work at the front. In European Russia, peasant and working-class women launched a campaign of market riots. The economy was straining to meet the demands of the war, causing consumer goods and food to grow scarce and prices to rise. Peasant and working-class women did the shopping for their families, so they were the ones who came to the markets to find that prices had gone up overnight. Some paid quietly or went away disappointed. Others asked the merchants to cut prices. When they refused, women seized goods and sometimes beat up the merchants and wrecked the stores. In the town of Kineshma in Kostroma province in the early summer of 1916, a dispute that began in a shop escalated into a crowd of four thousand women charging through the market demanding that all the vendors lower their prices.[36]

Soldatki, the wives of soldiers, were often instigators of and participants in these riots, because they felt particularly aggrieved. The government promised them benefits to make up for the loss of income they suffered when their husbands were drafted, then failed to come up with the funding and the clerical staff to get the payments out regularly. Standing around waiting to receive their money, soldatki grumbled to one another about a system that asked everything of them and gave them so little. Sometimes they decided to do something about it. In June 1916, a group of soldatki in the village of Morshansk, Samara province, asked a shopkeeper to sell them cloth at prewar prices. When he refused, they grabbed bolts of fabric, ransacked the shop, and surged off to attack another one.[37]

In the fall of 1916, anger was also building among the privileged in Russia. The press and Duma delegates openly criticized the government, singling out for special condemnation the emperor and empress. Alexandra, Danish by birth, was a devoted wife and mother, but she had never been good at cultivating the support of her subjects, and so was perceived as aloof and foreign. She had worsened her reputation by becoming dependent on Grigori Rasputin, a scruffy, corrupt Siberian mystic. Widespread rumors accused the empress of being a spy for Germany and Rasputin's mistress. In December 1916, cousins of the tsar tried to restore the reputation of the monarchy by killing the Siberian and dumping his body in the Neva River.

This desperate gesture did nothing to calm the unrest. Poor people in Petrograd[38] were hungry and bread, the staple of their diets, was growing scarce. Women queuing up at bakeries in the damp, dark mornings talked to one another about the hard times, spread rumors about bakers selling better loaves to rich families who could pay more, and cursed the emperor and empress for not taking care of the people. Sometimes when the stores ran out of bread, the women broke windows and threatened the shopkeepers. A worried police official reported to his superiors in January 1917, "One spark will be enough for a conflagration to blaze up."[39] The spark was struck on February 23, when working women took to the streets en masse and set off the uprising that brought down the tsar.

Women in the 1917 Revolution

After Nicholas abdicated, a committee of Duma delegates created the Provisional Government, intended to serve until the election of an assembly, called the Constituent Assembly, which would draft a constitution for a new, republican Russian government. The Provisional Government tried to keep the bureaucracy functioning and the war effort afloat, while the uprising against the tsar spun into a revolutionary effort to destroy the old political order. Crowds looted police stations and drove tax collectors out of town, peasants seized landlords' property, workers took over factories, and soldiers organized committees to speak for them in negotiations with officers. In the cities, democratic organizations sprang up, the most important of which were the soviets, elected assemblies of workers and soldiers. Political parties—the Bolsheviks, Kadets, Mensheviks, Socialist Revolutionaries, and many others—pledged to work for freedom and social justice.

The politicians that benefited most from the Revolution were the Bolsheviks, the left wing of the Social Democratic party. They called for an end to the war, the granting of the landlords' land to the peasants, improvement in food supplies, and the transfer of power from the Provisional Government to the soviets. They also built a strong, well-led organization based in the working class and the army. When, in October 1917, the Bolshevik leadership ordered its troops to overthrow the Provisional Government, the latter could not rally an equally powerful corps of defenders. On October 25 (November 7 on the Western calendar), Vladimir Lenin, the head of the Bolsheviks, stood before a national meeting of representatives of the soviets and declared a new government, based in the soviets and led by the Council of People's Commissars, which was composed mostly of Bolsheviks. The first stage of the Russian Revolution was over.

WOMEN'S ACTIVISM

Many revolutions, by weakening social norms and controls and broadcasting calls to equality and freedom, have opened up new opportunities for women; the Russian Revolution was one of the most liberating. In the cities, women marched in demonstrations and joined political parties and trade unions. In the countryside, peasant women participated in the confiscation of the nobility's property. Women also developed their own independent activism. Shoppers continued to press their demands on merchants. Women workers held meetings to discuss their problems, particularly low wages and sexual harassment. Some workers, such as the laundresses of Petrograd, unionized. Most poor women stayed away from all these activities, because they were afraid to get involved and because they needed to concentrate on feeding themselves and their children, but more women than ever before were politically active, and their uprising empowered cadres of female leaders.

The first off the mark were the feminists of the League for Women's Equal Rights, who began lobbying the Provisional Government in March. Now their years of work bore fruit, for women from all classes were joining them to demand that women's rights be on the agenda of a democratizing Russia. On March 19, Poliksena Shishkina-Iavein, a founder of the league, and Vera Figner, a veteran revolutionary, led a demonstration of thirty-five thousand women to the Taurida Palace, headquarters of the Provisional Government and the Petrograd soviet. They called on the leaders of both bodies to write women's equality into the laws of the new Russia. The men who came out to meet them declared their support for women's rights. The feminists kept up their lobbying thereafter, and by midsummer they had achieved their major objective. The Provisional Government issued an electoral law that granted the right to vote and to run for office to all men and women twenty years of age and older. Tens of thousands of women voted in local elections in the following months, as well as in the elections to the Constituent Assembly that were held in the fall. The Provisional Government also opened the legal profession and the civil service to women, and abolished the rule that only men could serve on juries. The feminists had won, in a few months, reforms they had sought for more than a decade, and in so doing had put Russia at the forefront of European nations in the political rights it granted women.[40]

THE WOMEN'S MILITARY MOVEMENT

Feminists also promoted one of 1917's most publicized developments in female activism—the "women's military movement."[41] Russia was still at war with Germany, and many feared that the Germans would take advantage of the political instability to invade the Russian heartland and stamp out the fledgling democracy. Feminists saw an opportunity in this perilous situation. If women joined the army, they could demonstrate that they were willing to shoulder all the obligations of citizenship and therefore that they deserved political equality. They could also stiffen the spines of wavering male soldiers and raise morale behind the lines. Feminist leaders Maria Pokrovskaia and Anna Shabanova made these arguments in the spring of 1917, and by late May they had persuaded the Provisional Government to authorize the formation of all-female military units.

In the months that followed, women in at least fifteen cities from Petrograd to Odessa, Minsk to Ekaterinburg, as well as in Tashkent and Baku, set up organizations to recruit volunteers and raise the money to equip them. More than five thousand women answered their call. Most were Russians, though there were many Cossacks as well, probably because the Cossacks were a warrior people who prized valor among women as well as men. The volunteers were almost all young and single, and they came from all Russia's social ranks. Many had already done military service as nurses; a few were female infantry veterans who became NCOs in the women's units.

By late summer, sixteen companies—four infantry battalions, one naval unit, and eleven communications detachments—had been set up. The only one to see combat was the First Russian Women's Battalion of Death, so named because its members had sworn never to surrender. Sent into battle in Belarus in July, the three hundred or so women acquitted themselves honorably. So did the soldiers of the First Petrograd Women's Battalion, who were assigned to defend the ministers of the Provisional Government from arrest by the Bolsheviks in late October. The women stayed at their posts until a much larger contingent of Bolshevik troops arrived, then surrendered. Most of the male soldiers on duty with them had deserted ahead of time, which may speak to the valor of the women, or to their misreading of political reality.[42]

Women volunteered for the all-female units because they were patriots eager to defend Russia. Some were also seeking to prove their equality with men. They won the support of the soldiers they worked with, but were harassed, sometimes violently, by men from other units who were sick of war and angry that women had been sent to shame them into more killing and dying. Public opinion was mixed as well: some people were horrified, others inspired. Feminists hailed the young women as shining examples of women's involvement in the Revolution. Others, harkening back to older ideals, praised the female soldiers as martyrs willing to shed their "saintly blood" for Russia.[43]

The women's military movement ended in early fall, when army commanders canceled the experiment because they judged it a waste of time and resources. Bolshevik leaders agreed. In their view, which was widely shared, the women's units were a public-relations stunt, designed to drum up support for an unjust war. When they took power, they ordered the remaining battalions to disband and thereby alienated the most famous female soldier of 1917, Maria Bochkareva.

✦ ✦ ✦ MARIA BOCHKAREVA (1889–1920) ✦ ✦ ✦

Bochkareva was a Siberian peasant who married young to escape from a father who beat her, then ran away from her husband when he did the same. She next got involved with a thieving, drunken, abusive butcher. When the war began in 1914, Bochkareva decided to give up being a wife and enlist in the army. A bemused recruiting officer turned her down, but suggested that she petition the tsar. Nicholas was touched by Bochkareva's heartfelt expressions of patriotism, which had been written down for her by someone else, for she was illiterate. The tsar himself granted her request to join the infantry.

Bochkareva proved to be an able, courageous soldier. In combat in Belarus in February 1915, she repeatedly rushed, unbidden, onto the battlefield to rescue wounded comrades. Her heroism earned her the St. George's

A photograph probably taken on Maria Bochkareva's U.S. tour in 1918.
Prints and Photographs Division, Library of Congress.

MARIA BOCHKAREVA

In her memoir, Bochkareva recounted huddling in a trench at night, after her regiment's first battle, listening to the cries of the wounded.

"In the dark it seemed to me that I saw their faces, the familiar faces of Ivan and Peter and Sergei and Mitia, the good fellows who had taken such tender care of me. . . . They called me. I could see their hands outstretched in my direction, their wide-open eyes straining in the night in the hope of rescue, the deathly pallor of their faces. Could I remain indifferent to their cries? Was it not my bounden duty as a soldier, a duty as important as that of fighting, to render aid to stricken comrades?

I climbed out of the trench and crawled under our wire entanglements. There was comparative calm, interrupted only by occasional rifle shots, when I would lie down and remain motionless, as though I were a corpse. There were wounded within a few feet of our line. I carried them one by one to the edge of our trench where they were picked up and carried to the rear. The saving of one man encouraged me to continue my efforts till I reached the far side of the field. Here I had several narrow escapes. . . . When dawn broke in the East, putting an end to my expeditions through No Man's Land, I had saved about fifty lives."

SOURCE: MARIA BOTCHKAREVA, *YASHKA, MY LIFE AS A PEASANT, EXILE, AND SOLDIER*, AS SET DOWN BY ISAAC DON LEVINE (LONDON: CONSTABLE, 1919), 90–91.

Cross (Russia's highest military award), promotion to junior NCO, and three serious wounds. It also made her reputation among the men of her unit. They accepted her because she was brave, because she could perform as well as they, and because she had made herself into one of the boys. Bochkareva smoked, spat, swore, and beat up men who insulted her.

On a trip to Petrograd in May 1917, she became a convert to the idea of creating all-female units. Bochkareva was no feminist. She scorned women as weak creatures and referred to herself with masculine pronouns. She was, however, an enthusiastic and impressive advocate for the proposition that women could be soldiers. When the Provisional Government authorized the units in late May, Bochkareva was appointed commander of the Women's Battalion of Death. She trained her volunteers with an iron hand, driving many of them away in the process, and then led the troops to the front in July. They performed well.

That bloody campaign was the high point of Bochkareva's military career, but not of her fame. After the Bolsheviks disbanded her unit, she supported the anti-Bolshevik coalition known as the Whites. In 1918 she toured the United States and Britain to drum up support for the White armies. It was a highly publicized journey, during which Bochkareva met with President Woodrow Wilson and King George IV. She also told her life story to journalist Isaac Don Levine, who polished her recollections into prose and published them as *Yashka, My Life as Peasant, Officer, and Exile*. In 1919, her tour completed, Bochkareva returned to Russia and sought out the Whites. Before she could reach an army to enlist in, the Bolsheviks tracked her down. She was tried, found guilty of treason, and executed in May 1920.[44]

WOMEN IN THE SOCIALIST PARTIES

The socialist parties, the largest of which were the Socialist Revolutionaries and the two factions of Social Democrats—the Bolsheviks and Mensheviks—grew rapidly in 1917. Women, as in the past, were among the recruits. None of the parties kept good records in that tumultuous year, so it is impossible to determine how many such women there were. Probably they constituted 10 to 15 percent of party members. It is somewhat easier to reconstruct what women did. Among the Bolsheviks, they held a greater percentage of party offices than ever before or after, and the same may have been true of the Mensheviks and Socialist Revolutionaries.[45] Most of these women worked in the lower ranks, on neighborhood or city committees, where they spread their party's message through speeches, leaflets, and newspapers. Some, particularly Bolsheviks in Petrograd, reached out to women workers. A handful of women rose to the top leadership of their parties. Of these, the most prominent in 1917 were Maria Spiridonova and Alexandra Kollontai. Kollontai became a popular stump speaker and Spiridonova headed the Left Socialist Revolutionaries.

MARIA SPIRIDONOVA (1884–1941) AND ALEXANDRA KOLLONTAI (1872–1952)

Spiridonova was a fabled terrorist. Born into the lower-ranking nobility, she became a Socialist Revolutionary in her late teens. The Socialist Revolutionaries were socialists much influenced by Marxism but loyal as well to the populist mission of inspiring the peasants to revolt. They kept alive the populist tradition of assassinating brutal tsarist officials, and it was as an assassin that Spiridonova first became famous. In 1906 she gunned down a police commander in broad daylight. Spiridonova fit the profile of the female martyr-revolutionary: she was a pretty, young noblewoman who shot an evil man and then made no attempt to escape. Her case, including the fact that she had been severely beaten while under arrest, was widely publicized by her comrades and by the press. The publicity elicited an outpouring of sympathy for a frail girl who had killed a brute, and that sympathy in turn convinced the government to cut its public-relations losses by commuting her death sentence to life imprisonment in Siberia. As she headed east by train, crowds gathered at the stations through which she passed to greet her.

Freed in the spring of 1917, Spiridonova went to Petrograd to claim a place in the Socialist Revolutionary leadership. Prison had neither softened her radicalism nor weakened her self-confidence. After a few weeks in the capital, she decided that the Socialist Revolutionary leadership was too cautious and the Bolsheviks were right in calling for the overthrow of the Provisional Government. She did not become a Bolshevik, as did other socialists who agreed with their strategy. Rather she joined with like-minded Socialist Revolutionaries to set up a new organization, the Left Socialist Revolutionaries. They supported the Bolshevik seizure of power and worked in the new government for a few months afterward, but Spiridonova soon realized that the Bolshevik leaders had no intention of sharing power with her party. She was also repelled by the peace treaty Lenin signed with Germany in March 1918, because it ceded vast amounts of Russian territory to Germany. Spiridonova and her group broke with the Bolsheviks soon thereafter, and in the summer of 1918 she helped organize

Alexandra Kollontai in 1912.
Author's collection.

ALEXANDRA KOLLONTAI

In May 1917, Kollontai issued this call to arms in an article published in *Rabotnitsa,* the newly revived Bolshevik magazine for women.

"All our strength, all our hope lie in organizing!

Now our cry should be: comrade women workers. Don't stand alone! In isolation we are straw people that every boss can bend down. Organized, we are a great force that no one can crush.

We, women workers, in the first days of the Russian Revolution supported the Red Banner. We went to the streets first on Women's Day. We are hurrying now into the front ranks of the fighters for the workers' cause; we are joining trade unions, the Social Democratic Party, the Soviet of Workers' and Soldiers' Deputies!

By closing ranks, we will achieve the quickest end to the world war. We will fight against those who forgot the great call of the working people for unity, for the solidarity of workers of all countries.

Only in revolutionary struggle against the capitalists of all countries and only in unity with the female and male workers of the whole world will we establish a new, bright future—the socialist brotherhood of the workers."

SOURCE: A. M. KOLLONTAI, "NASHI ZADACHI," IN *IZBRANNYE STATI I RECHI* (MOSCOW: POLITIZDAT, 1972), 213. TRANSLATED BY BARBARA CLEMENTS.

the assassination of the German ambassador. The police arrested her, then released her. She refused to stop speaking out against the new government and in 1919 was arrested again. Spiridonova spent most the rest of her life in prison. She was executed in 1941.[46]

The other famous female radical of 1917, Kollontai, played on the winning side. A very popular speaker, she was elected to the Petrograd soviet as well as to the Bolsheviks' Central Committee. Kollontai was one of the Central Committee members who voted in early October for the party to overthrow the Provisional Government. After it did so, Lenin appointed her commissar of social welfare, and Kollontai set about enacting the reforms for women that she had long advocated. After a few months, she too fell out with Lenin, because she, like Spiridonova, believed the treaty with Germany was an unnecessary surrender to a capitalist power. In March 1918 Kollontai resigned her government position and went off to lick her political wounds.

Bochkareva, Kollontai, and Spiridonova were the most famous female activists of 1917. Like so many women in Russia's past, they became prominent because they were strong-willed, self-confident, talented people who seized the opportunities their times gave them. Those same qualities led them to oppose the new rulers, with disastrous consequences for Bochkareva and Spiridonova. Kollontai came out of her self-imposed exile later in 1918 and claimed a leading part in reforms for women, without recanting any of her criticism. A few years after that, she locked horns with Lenin again.

Women in the Civil War, 1918–21

THE BEGINNING OF SOVIET REFORMS FOR WOMEN

Both the Menshevik and the Bolshevik factions of the Social Democratic party endorsed the German Social Democrats' program for women's emancipation. In 1917 the Bolsheviks were its more energetic promoters, due to the presence within their ranks of hundreds of Bolshevik feminists. These women rejected the title "feminist" because they condemned feminists as propertied women interested only in their own class, but feminists they were, if by "feminists" we mean activists seeking women's emancipation. The Bolshevichki (the feminine plural form of "Bolshevik") also had much in common with self-identified feminists. Most came from the middling and upper social classes and had completed high school. Many were teachers, librarians, and doctors. About one-quarter were working-class women from the factories of the major cities. All these women were better educated than most women of their class and better educated as well than the majority of male members of the party. Education had empowered them, as it did the feminists and all the other activist women of the pre-revolutionary generation, enabling them to work outside the home and develop their social confidence and consciousness.[47]

After the Bolsheviks seized power, they moved quickly to enact their program of women's emancipation and thereby launched an assault on patriarchy. The Bolsheviks were, after all, revolutionaries. They sought to destroy all the old institutions—patriarchy, monarchy, church—and in their place construct a society in which the people as a whole owned and managed economic resources and shared the products of their labor. The economic equality of socialism would then make political equality possible, Bolsheviks believed, and would end prejudice, superstition, and all the other malign consequences of private property.

They began by issuing laws that established the principle of women's economic, educational, legal, and political equality with men, and by designing social services. In January 1918, Kollontai, the commissar of social welfare, drafted plans for providing publicly funded maternity care and stipends to new mothers. The same month, a government decree, "On the Socialization of the Land," asserted that women had equal rights with men to own and lease land. In the summer of 1918 the government issued a constitution that declared women's political equality with men. The Family Law Code of the fall of 1918 made marriage a civil procedure, thus removing it from the Church's jurisdiction, declared wives and husbands equal in the eyes of the law, legalized divorce, and granted children born out of wedlock the right to economic support by their parents. The Commissariat of Labor wrote regulations abolishing gender discrimination in hiring and mandating paid maternity leave. The Commissariat of Education reaffirmed the Provisional Government's decree of April 1917 that had declared all public education coeducational.

While Bolshevik officials were drafting the new laws, Russia fell into civil war. From 1918 to 1920, the Whites, a loose coalition of anti-Bolshevik generals leading rag-tag armies, battled the equally rag-tag Bolshevik-commanded Red Army across Siberia and into European Russia. The Reds won, because they were more unified and popular than the Whites. They emerged from this trial by fire determined to achieve their socialist objectives by using all the power they could amass. And so the revolutionaries who had overthrown tsarist dictatorship built one of their own. The Communist Party (the Bolsheviks adopted this name in 1918) and the Soviet government, consisting mostly of tsarist ministries now headed by communists, were formally independent of one another, but the party dominated. Organized into a hierarchy that extended from the Politburo and Central Committee down through regional and local committees and administrators, the party set policy and oversaw the functioning of government departments.

The Bolshevik feminists responded to the civil war by arguing that the party should cultivate the support of working-class and peasant women. They pointed to working women's activism since 1905 as evidence that they could be persuaded to support the Red side and to do volunteer work such as cleaning streets or assisting at hospitals. Party leaders agreed, and in 1919 authorized the creation of the Zhenotdel (Women's Department) within the party. Inessa Armand, a veteran Bolshevik and close friend of Lenin's, was its first head. When she died of cholera in the fall of 1920, Kollontai succeeded her. These women and the thousands who worked for them quickly built the Zhenotdel into an organization that publicized Marxist ideas of women's emancipation, cultivated the support of poor women, and advocated for women within the party.

WOMEN RESPOND TO THE COMMUNISTS

They had their work cut out for them. The Revolution had begun in anger, grief, and hope. While hope for a better future continued to inspire millions throughout the civil war, grief and anger remained their constant companions, for the civil war completed the ruin of the economy that World War I had begun. Armies rampaged through cities and countryside; transportation collapsed and food supplies dwindled further; cholera, dysentery, influenza, typhoid, and typhus carried off first the old and young, then malnourished people in their prime. Millions of peasant women were widowed. Some had to leave their villages when their neighbors, also struggling, would not help them. They took their children to the cities, where they begged for food in markets and churchyards. "We are dying," wailed desperate women in the streets of Ivanovo-Voznesensk in 1921. "The people are dying off."[48]

Many city folk passed the beggars by, for they too were hungry. Even in Moscow, the capital of Soviet Russia from the spring of 1918 onward, food and fuel were scarce. People watched when wraith-like cart horses came down their streets, hoping that the poor creatures would drop dead in the traces and provide meat for the neighborhood. There was no heat because there was no fuel to feed boilers. There was no running water because the pipes had burst in the unheated buildings. People fled back to their home villages, and so Moscow's population fell by more than 50 percent between 1918 and 1920, Petrograd's by 72 percent.[49] The returnees were mostly men because men were more likely than women to have close family in the countryside. Men also left the cities when they were drafted into the army.

For urban women of all classes, these developments were disastrous. It was difficult for an intact family to survive, and still more challenging for single women. The lucky ones were those working in the few factories that continued to operate. By 1918, women made up 45 percent of the much-shrunken industrial work force.[50] Others took jobs newly opened to women in the arts, clerical work, the court system, education, journalism, medicine, the police, and social services. Wages were low when they were paid at all, many merchants and nobles were denied food rations, and inflation devalued the currency. Childcare became increasingly problematic, because of the difficulty of keeping schools open and hungry children engaged in learning. Soon thousands of runaways, mostly boys, were living on the filthy streets, where they begged and stole to survive.

The hardship alienated many working women from politics and from the communists. At meetings in the fall of 1918, they angrily demanded that the party make good on its promise to improve their lives by bringing home their husbands and getting more food to the markets. Had the party been able to ease these difficulties, more peasants and workers might have listened to the communists' talk about women's emancipation. Had the government not requisitioned the peasants' crops, often without paying for them, peasant women might have been more welcoming. Instead many poor women in city and countryside came to believe that the people who had said they would make things better had only made them worse. So they rejected the communists' overtures and drove the party workers away.

Some women did answer the communists' calls. More than thirty thousand joined the Communist Party in the civil war years and thousands more participated in Zhenotdel conferences and programs. Sixty-five thousand women enlisted in the Red Army, making up 2 percent of that force and serving in a greater variety of jobs than ever before. They were clerks, couriers, drivers, nurses, spies, and political workers who propagandized the troops. A few women, following the precedent set in World War I, enlisted in combat units.[51]

The women who supported the communists believed that they were part of a righteous movement. Evdokia Poliakova, a factory worker who joined the party in 1917 at the age of seventeen, wrote in her memoirs, "In the Bolsheviks I saw people who had entered a decisive struggle with despotism and injustice, a struggle with a bright future for working people. I wanted to be with them and I was justly proud that they had taken me into their great, stern family."[52] Such women saw the Revolution as a liberation and the civil war as a struggle between good and evil, the future and the past. Less political women, the artists of the avant garde, for example, also were buoyed by the sense of limitless possibilities that the Revolution had fostered. When the civil war ended, these women hoped that a new world of peace and equality would be built on the ruins of tsarist Russia.

Women in the NEP Years, 1921–28

The New Economic Policy (NEP) was a series of measures adopted in the early 1920s that eased economic controls enacted during the civil war. A key provision ended the much-hated requisitioning of grain from the peasants. The government retained control of the large factories that it had seized from private owners, while permitting small businesses to operate. Eventually the term "NEP" came to refer not just to these less coercive economic policies but also more broadly to the years 1921–28, a time when the government allowed more economic, cultural, and social freedom than it would in the 1930s. NEP also saw the beginning of the creation of a much-revised social order in the newly declared Union of Soviet Socialist Republics. The nobility had lost its power, the Church was persecuted into impotence, and the Communist Party, staffed by recruits from the peasantry and the working class, became the new elite. As the party built the power of the central government, the peasants restored agriculture and workers, engineers, managers, civil servants, and professionals restored industry and public services. People from all walks of life also debated how to remake Russia and, as so often in the past, they put the woman question on the agenda.

Female activism continued under NEP, encouraged by the government, which expanded educational and employment opportunities and urged women to get involved in the public world. Tens of thousands enrolled in the wide array of adult education courses. Anna Matveeva, the servant who had been a marcher on Bloody Sunday, wrote happily in the 1920s, "I attend reading groups; I learn; my mind soaks up so much. I want so much to make up for lost time."[53] Some of these women moved on to white-collar jobs. Zhenotdel workers helped others set up daycare centers and cafeterias. Artists designed modernist clothes and wrote innovative film scripts. The new government also permitted a wide-ranging discussion of reform in family life.

FEMALE UNEMPLOYMENT AND PARTY CHOICES

The limits of the Communist Party's commitment to women's emancipation became apparent in the early 1920s, when its leaders tried to restore the shattered economy and integrate hundreds of thousands of former soldiers into the peacetime workforce. They ordered factory and office managers to run their operations more efficiently, which many interpreted as permission to replace female workers hired during the war with men returned from the army. At the same time, the government trimmed the civil service, putting still more women out of work, and cut funding for health care and other social services. Women who were laid off remained unemployed longer than men, because fewer of them had the job skills that were in high demand and also because managers preferred to hire men who, they believed, were more qualified and deserving. By 1923, women made up 70 percent of the unemployed in the Russian and Ukrainian republics of the Soviet Union; they remained the majority of those seeking work for the rest of the decade.[54]

Male workers replaced female ones across Europe after World War I and World War II as well, because women were seen as temporary employees who should yield their places to male breadwinners when the emergency passed. And yet, it seems odd that the Soviet government, which preached that women had to be in the paid-labor force in order to be emancipated, threw them out of work in the 1920s, then made their lives still more difficult by cutting benefits. This cruel inconsistency occurred because the country's destitution limited the government's options and because communists differed among themselves about how to achieve women's emancipation, and indeed about what emancipation entailed.

The party leaders believed that their primary objective was the creation of a modernized, socialized economy, one that was highly productive and fair in its distribution of goods and services. Emancipation of women, the elimination of religious and ethnic bigotry, communal living, and all the other communist projects of liberation were important and could be promoted by government laws and programs. Their achievement, however, depended on economic reconstruction. Social services would have to receive less attention if, in the judgment of the decision-makers, those programs took resources away from industrialization. So the government, committed to providing daycare for all children, then funded only a handful of centers.

The priorities set during the NEP years were also influenced by gender assumptions that party leaders were loath to acknowledge. These men believed, with good reason, that their political base lay among the men of the working class, and so they put a priority on hiring men. Behind this political decision was an assumption, rarely voiced but widely held, that men would be the leaders of the new society. Women could contribute and should be given opportunities. They deserved the emancipation promised them by an enlightened, benevolent male leadership. But they would have to be patient.

We should note that such attitudes were widespread among many liberationist groups in the twentieth century. Organizations as different from one another as the Chinese Communist Party and the nationalist Zambian United Independence Party encouraged women's participation in support roles under male leadership. Those parties that achieved ruling power did not recruit women to the top leadership, although many, especially the communist ones, promoted women's rights and expanded educational and employment opportunities. It was also common for women to hold higher offices in these organizations before the parties came to power than afterward. Being beleaguered, needing the help of everyone willing to lend a hand, seems to promote fidelity to principle and weakens gender norms. Having power has opposite effects.[55]

For all their shortcomings, Lenin, Trotsky, and other first-generation party leaders were far more committed to women's emancipation than many younger, lower-ranking communists. Throughout the NEP years and thereafter, the men who led the provincial and local levels of the party, government, and economy sabotaged policies designed to promote gender equality by employing the stalling techniques developed by peasants and bureaucrats alike under the tsarist system. When the central government issued orders not to lay off any more women, which it did repeatedly in the NEP years, factory managers ignored the directives. Trade unions declared their resolve to set up training programs for women, then did nothing. Moscow lacked the power and the will to enforce its instructions, and so the few attempts made to counter female unemployment in the 1920s withered on the vine.[56]

THE ZHENOTDEL

The party leadership did support the Zhenotdel. Kollontai, leader of the department from 1920 to 1922, refused to refrain from criticizing policies she disagreed with, and so was fired in the winter of 1922. Her successors were more circumspect and successful. By the mid-1920s they had built the department into a network of thousands of operatives, most of them young women from the middling and working classes. Through periodicals, internship programs, and a network of local, regional, and national meetings, the Zhenotdel communicated the party's message of women's emancipation to tens of thousands. In 1926–27, for example, 620,000 women attended Zhenotdel conferences.[57]

Zhenotdel workers served as advocates for women as well. They worked with staff from government agencies dealing with issues of particular concern to women, such as adult education, health care, and job training. They publicized the failures of local leaders to follow orders that would benefit women and the social evils that fell most heavily on women, such as unemployment, prostitution, alcoholism, and wife-beating. They conducted a wide-ranging discussion of gender norms that remains very current today. One typical series of articles in the Bolshevik magazine *Rabotnitsa* (Woman Worker) in 1926 asked the question, "Can a woman be a steelworker?" The answer was a resolute "Yes!" Zhenotdel spokespeople asserted that women should train for any job they were physically capable of doing. They also called for an ambitious program of affirmative action, arguing that issues of greatest consequence to working women would not be addressed until women served on trade union boards and in factory management, and until the government established training courses that would qualify women for the better-paying jobs. They discussed how women could manage their family responsibilities and their jobs. They considered ways to transform conjugal love, so that husbands would treat wives as equals.

ALEXANDRA ARTIUKHINA (1889–1969)

The Zhenotdel's most effective leader was Alexandra Artiukhina, a textile worker from central Russia. She grew up in a family of activists: her mother was a member of the textile workers' union; her uncle was a Socialist Revolutionary. Artiukhina herself joined the union in 1907 and the Social Democrats in 1910. She soon became a Bolshevik feminist, and in 1914 was an editor of *Rabotnitsa*. In 1917 she helped revive it, and in 1923, after working with her husband away from Moscow, she moved to the capital and joined the Zhenotdel. In 1925 she was appointed its head.

Under Artiukhina's leadership the department extended its operations across the Soviet Union. Artiukhina herself became a forceful spokesperson for Zhenotdel feminism. For example, she opposed the production of electrical appliances in 1930, because she thought such things would chain women to housework. "It is better," she declared, "to suffer now with the old dishrags, flat irons, and frying pans, in order to have the means and strength to throw into the construction of socialized institutions—cafeterias, nurseries, kindergartens, and laundries." Artiukhina also argued for affirmative action programs that would promote women to the leadership of the party, the economy, and academe.[58]

STRENGTHS AND WEAKNESSES OF
FEMALE ACTIVISM IN THE 1920s

Artiukhina was an extraordinary woman in charge of an extraordinary organization. For the first time in history, a ruling political party was sponsoring a thorough critique of patriarchy and encouraging women to challenge gender customs. The party leadership's commitment to women's emancipation, its shortcomings notwithstanding, was very progressive, particularly in the context of 1920s Europe. The women in northern, Protestant Europe had gained the vote by the early 1920s; those in Catholic countries and most of the Balkans were still waiting for it. Civic and legal inequality and discriminatory educational and employment policies persisted everywhere. Furthermore, Western feminist movements had shrunk, as their leaders cast around for new issues to focus on and a wave of political conservatism swept the continent.

Soviet Russia was at the forefront of women's emancipation in the 1920s because of the Communist Party leadership's willingness to implement the Social Democratic program drawn up in Germany in the 1890s. That willingness in turn was as much a product of Russian history as of communist ideology. The tsars had put changing women's situation on the reform agenda, the intelligentsia had kept it there, and female activists—professionals, feminists, and factory workers—had carved out spaces for women in the public world. During NEP, the intelligentsia continued to discuss the woman question. Architects, economists, educators, sociologists, and other professionals, many of them women, documented discrimination in the workplace and the hours women spent on housework, researched evolving sexual mores, considered ways to combat sexism in the classroom, and advocated policy-making that took women's needs into account. Female professionals worked on women's issues in the ministries in charge of education, health care, and social welfare. Women also continued to serve in the professions. Among these women were many feminists from the pre-revolutionary era, including the physicians Pokrovskaia, Shabanova, and Shishkina-Iavein.[59] The work of all these women had the support of the Communist Party leadership, because the men had imbibed intelligentsia ideas about the importance of women's emancipation before the Revolution and because there were female activists within the party and the intelligentsia lobbying them, doing the research, and creating many of the programs.

The weaknesses of both the Zhenotdel and the intelligentsia activists were rooted in Russia's past as well. They, like the feminists of the pre-revolutionary years, were dealing with an autocratic government, and they achieved what they did because they persuaded powerful men to back them. The most well-placed of these women were the communists, who were obligated to take orders from the leadership and propagate the party line. They could not accuse the leadership of making choices that hurt women. Instead, they criticized low-ranking officials for not carrying out orders or workers and peasants for being sexist. These charges, being generally true, did not ruffle the feathers of the Zhenotdel's bosses, but did remind them that the party's promises remained only partly fulfilled.

Zhenotdel leaders were particularly dependent on the men at the top because they had so little support lower down in the party. Communists in regional and local organizations thought the department was spreading feminist ideas and taking money out of their budgets that they could put to better uses. Some female communists agreed, arguing that women party members should work with male communists to develop socialism, which would emancipate women. Communists who felt this way refused to support Zhenotdel projects and transferred Zhenotdel workers to other assignments. Artiukhina and her colleagues, therefore, had to rely on the central party leaders just to keep the department alive.

Building support beyond party ranks was also difficult. Young people in the cities were receptive because the urban environment remained, as it had been before 1914, the place where traditions were weakest. The peasants were more resistant, and although the Zhenotdel had greater success with rural women in the 1920s than it had had during the civil war years, working in the countryside remained a daunting task. Many peasants, particularly male and female elders, were hostile not only to the Zhenotdel but to communists in general, whom they perceived as exploiters who seized grain without paying for it and dragooned men into the army. Such peasants took their antipathies out on the young Zhenotdel workers who ventured among them. Like the midwives who had gone to the countryside in the nineteenth century, the women of the Zhenotdel were often shunned, verbally abused, and driven from the villages.

✛ ✛ ✛   *THE UNVEILING CAMPAIGN*   ✛ ✛ ✛

The most violent confrontation between Zhenotdel workers and defenders of patriarchal traditions occurred in the Central Asian republic of Uzbekistan in the late 1920s. Zhenotdel leaders believed that the Muslim women of Central Asia—Kazakhstan, Kyrgyzstan, Tajikistan, Turkmenistan, and Uzbekistan—were the most oppressed women in the Soviet Union. The central party leadership agreed, and so, in the early 1920s, it authorized the Zhenotdel to reach out to Central Asian women by organizing clubs, literacy classes, manufacturing workshops, and cooperative stores staffed by and catering to women. It also outlawed such traditional practices as bride price, child marriage, marriage by capture (forcing a family to consent to a marriage by kidnapping the prospective bride), polygamy, and wife-beating. Soviet marriage law, which emphasized the independence and equality of bride and groom, was to take the place of these customs.

These were radical changes, made all the more unsettling to Central Asian people because the communists' tsarist predecessors had not meddled with local gender mores. Discussion of the woman question in the pre-revolutionary period had been confined to the very small Central Asian intelligentsia, and it had been cautious, concerned mostly with the importance of educating girls. When the communists began talking about new family laws and the Zhenotdel began its work among women, therefore, many Central Asians were first astonished, then outraged. In 1925–26, party leaders in Turkmenistan mollified the public by making divorce more difficult to obtain and overlooking the payment of bride price. In nearby Uzbekistan, communists took a more principled, more confrontational course. In 1927, they instructed the Zhenotdel to persuade Uzbek women to take off their veils and they ordered party members to have their female family members lead by example.[60]

By the time the Zhenotdel undertook its unveiling campaign, Europeans had a long history of attempting to change the family customs of the peoples they conquered. In the Americas, they had imposed their marriage laws on the natives. European women throughout the colonial world had instructed native women in the cult of domesticity and, after feminism developed, educated them and promoted their independence, as the Zhenotdel was trying to do in Central Asia. In the pre-revolutionary decades, as we have seen, Russian women had done such work in Siberia and the Caucasus. These were not minor endeavors, of interest only to the women involved; they were part of the imperial project of undermining local cultures and those patriarchal privileges that the Europeans considered uncivilized.

The communists shared with the imperialists they despised a conception of themselves as liberators, who had the welfare of the native people at heart. Perhaps it was this perception that led party leaders in Uzbekistan to gravely underestimate the possibility of serious resistance to unveiling. Why would women not welcome the chance to cast aside their full-length cotton robes, over which they wore horsehair veils that extended from the top of their heads to their waists? Since the veil had long been seen by Europeans and by Muslim reformers as the most visible sign of Muslim women's oppression, Zhenotdel workers and party leaders believed getting women to remove it would also have great symbolic importance. So did reformers in nearby Turkey, Afghanistan, and Iran, who were also sponsoring unveiling campaigns in the 1920s.

The veils and heavy robes played a more complex part in the lives of Muslim women than the critics recognized. Rabia khanum Sultan-Zade, an Azeri woman whose mother unveiled in the 1920s, summed up this complexity decades later when she said that the veil was "both a symbol of oppression and a symbol of protection, a tribute to custom and probably . . . a habit." Uzbeks believed that it was sinful for women to go outside their homes uncovered, and women who broke this prohibition risked loss of reputation and violent retribution. Rather than walking the streets uncovered, they were supposed to spend most of their lives within the family compound, doing the bidding of the senior members of the family. When they became senior members themselves, they could order around younger women. A family's honor depended on its women meeting these standards of female virtue. Encouraging women to unveil, therefore, was encouraging them to defy the authority of male and female elders and to shame the entire family. The communists knew this. Indeed, they were deliberately seeking to undermine the power of senior Uzbeks, particularly the propertied ones. They had already made major land reforms and were planning steps against the Muslim clergy when they launched the unveiling campaign.[61]

The campaign sparked a furious response from women as well as men. Matriarchs forbade their daughters to have anything to do with the Zhenotdel and ostracized families whose women had unveiled. Neighborhood women banded together to beat up offenders. Enraged Uzbek men, some of them lower-ranking communists, were still more violent, assaulting, raping, and murdering at least two thousand Uzbek women and Uzbek and

European Zhenotdel workers. Some of the corpses were mutilated. Clergy whipped up the frenzy by denouncing unveiled women as sinners, and people opposed to communist rule turned their fury on the defenseless. When it became clear that unveiling was very dangerous, most women who had unveiled covered up again.[62]

The party leadership responded by toughening criminal penalties for attacks on women and by sending out the police. Most perpetrators escaped prosecution because witnesses would not come forward for fear of retaliation and because some local officials supported, even participated in, the assaults. Marianne Kamp has argued that violence against women diminished only in 1929 when the party launched the collectivization of agriculture, and resistance against the communists turned its focus on the agents of those policies.[63]

THE END OF THE ZHENOTDEL

Despite its difficulties, the Zhenotdel played an important part in creating and institutionalizing the Soviet program of women's emancipation. The department took its message to millions of women across the nation and became a major voice in the discussion of the woman question in the 1920s. It mobilized people to set up daycare centers and factory lunchrooms that relieved women's domestic burdens. The Zhenotdel also was influential beyond the boundaries of the USSR, when communist parties elsewhere established women's departments of their own. One of the first was the Chinese Communist Party, which created a women's department within a few years of its founding in the 1920s. In the decades following World War II, communist women's departments in Africa, Asia, and Latin America scored many of the same successes and struggled with many of the same problems as the Zhenotdel.

Ironically, most of these organizations were set up after the Zhenotdel had been abolished. In 1930, over heartfelt protests from Artiukhina and Zhenotdel workers across the country, the department's work was transferred to Agitprop, the agitation and propaganda department of the Communist Party. The party leadership justified the closing of the Zhenotdel by declaring that women's emancipation was so advanced in the Soviet Union that the department was no longer necessary. The truth was that the leaders had finally accepted the argument that the Zhenotdel was a waste of resources. The country was now embroiled in the First Five-Year Plan, a massive effort to industrialize rapidly that had begun in 1928. Folding the Zhenotdel into Agitprop was one of several measures taken in 1930 to streamline the party's organization so that it could better manage the challenges ahead. The Agitprop officials to whom work with women was entrusted allowed it to languish.

Zhenotdel activists did not disappear, however. Many continued to lobby, in their new jobs, for attention to women's concerns. Artiukhina, who had once been a textile worker, became a national official of the textile workers' union and remained a staunch advocate for working women. She and other Zhenotdel veterans also passed their ideals on to younger women. The main Zhenotdel publications, *Krest'ianka* and *Rabotnitsa,* continued as well to propagate the principles of women's emancipation, Soviet style, and to publicize the difficulties in women's lives. Consequently the Zhenotdel's feminism remained alive throughout the Stalinist period.

PEASANT WOMEN DURING NEP

Peasant women passed the NEP years working to rebuild their families and villages. Many of the customs of rural life endured, as the peasants continued their long-standing practice of accepting those innovations from the cities that they found useful or attractive, and fending off those they did not. Male elders still ran the villages, and women stayed away from the organizations established by the communists. Very few voted in local soviet elections; fewer still served as elected officials.

The peasants' traditional notions about marriage and family endured as well. Parents and children worked the land together and shared ownership of family property. Most peasants, therefore, took a dim view of the Family Code of 1918 and the Land Code of 1922, which together legalized divorce and granted female family members the same property rights as their male relatives. Many saw these laws as an invitation to economic disaster, for dividing up poor people's meager possessions during a divorce would leave everyone poorer. There were other questions. Did the amount of property a wife was entitled to depend on how long she had been married? Did divorced women have claims on the property of their natal families? Women who were determined to leave their husbands and to receive the share of marital property that the law allowed now had the courts on their side and also got support from local communist activists. Most rural people struck to their long-established customs—that is, they stayed married.[64]

Communist values and city influences did promote more egalitarian arrangements and understandings. The power of the elders continued to wane, as more young people than ever asserted their right to choose their spouses and live in their own households. The Komsomol, the communist youth organization, recruited male and a few female peasants to its ranks, and they in turn propagated ideas about women's emancipation in the villages. A typical poem in the first issue of the Zhenotdel magazine *Krest'ianka* declared,

> The people's time has come.
> The old powers are no more.
> The women's share is freedom!
> The soviets are run by everyone![65]

These ideas also arrived in the newspapers available at reading rooms set up by the communists, and in movies, slide shows, and plays put on by itinerant propagandists.

The government tried to improve the lives of peasant women. Most importantly, it expanded primary education for children and established literacy classes for adult women. The Zhenotdel organized conferences at which peasant women were encouraged to discuss the difficulties of their lives, including their problems with abusive men, and it set up women's cooperatives, whose members farmed or manufactured handcrafts together and shared the profits. It also established summer daycare programs in the countryside. The cooperatives and the daycare centers were small pilot projects and peasant resistance to the Zhenotdel, as we have already seen, was considerable. Had the government chosen to do more, peasant women might have been more receptive.

THE *LISHENTSY*

One category of women, those labeled *lishentsy* or "former people," were persecuted by the new regime in the 1920s. The term suggests the nobles and the prosperous business owners, whom the Revolution and the communists had stripped of their political and economic power. These people were no threat in the 1920s. Huge numbers of them had emigrated from Russia, and the rest were struggling to adjust to the NEP world. But the communists, beset by the difficulty of governing an unruly, poverty-stricken country, worried that those they had overthrown were still working against them. Furthermore, they did not trust the peasants, or the clergy, or the Socialist Revolutionaries, or the Mensheviks, all of whom had resisted their control and in some cases had fought against them. So they continued their civil war practice of arresting people whom they suspected of seditious activity.

In the mid-1920s, the party undertook the first of many campaigns to root out lawbreakers or, far more ominously, potential lawbreakers.

The central government ordered school administrations, housing bureaus, soviet election commissions, tax collection agencies, and trade unions to identify people who had committed crimes such as illegal buying and selling or who belonged to groups under suspicion. Individuals identified as guilty—more than 4 million from 1926 to 1936—were labeled lishentsy. This stripped them of their right to vote, and, more importantly, of their eligibility for education, employment, health care, housing, and rationed goods.[66]

In its effects on women, this purge resembled those that would occur in the late 1920s and 1930s. The majority of the lishentsy were men, probably because officials assumed that men were more likely than women to actively oppose them. Most women were disfranchised not because of their own bad economic deeds, but because they were related to male offenders or were housewives who, by not working outside the home, were refusing to participate in building socialism. Wives of priests were particularly at risk, for they met both of these criteria. Nuns also came under suspicion. Officials who wanted to meet the required quotas of lishentsy to be identified without sacrificing their friends or disrupting the local economy targeted as well the disabled, elderly, and mentally ill, among whom there were many women.[67]

The "former people" could appeal, and many women did so. Golfo Alexopolous has found that women were particularly likely in their appeals to sing the ancient refrain that they were weak, ignorant unfortunates who deserved protection by the government. These cries for help often worked, particularly if the plaintiffs could make the case that they were hard-working, loyal citizens, married to hard-working men. Others who feared that their appeals would not be granted moved to new towns, got false identity papers, and started over again. The nation was too big and the government too inefficient to track all these migrants. We do not know how many women won pardons and how many managed to make new identities for themselves. Less successful female lishentsy swelled the ranks of the unemployed in the 1920s.[68]

URBAN WOMEN AND GENDER NORMS

Even while it was hunting for lishentsy and countenancing women's unemployment, the government opened up new opportunities in education and employment in the cities. Primary schooling and literacy programs expanded substantially. Women were also now eligible for jobs in the civil service, education, medicine, and sales that had been closed to them in the past. These improvements were particularly beneficial to young single women. Urban women, although less likely than urban men to join the Communist Party, vote, or serve as elected officials, were far more likely to do so than peasant women.

Life in the cities was hard. Everyone coped with food shortages, inadequate housing, and deficient social services; for single women, as in the past, the difficulties were often insuperable. Desperate ones took to prostitution or begging to survive; children who could not get enough to eat at home ran away to the streets. Many people were deeply troubled by these developments, for it seemed as though once again the most vulnerable were suffering the most. Furthermore, drunkenness, crime, overcrowded tenements, filth, and decrepitude seemed more prevalent than ever before, even while a fortunate few nouveaux riches flaunted the money they had made in the small businesses permitted by the government.

Soviet people were also concerned about the Revolution's effects on family life. Some young people were living in communes similar to those set up by the nihilists so many decades before, with the significant exception that the members of these communes took no vows of sexual abstinence. Instead they declared that the Revolution had destroyed all the old rules, so people could do as they pleased with their sex lives. Same-sex love, which the new government had decriminalized, was also being practiced more openly than ever before. The negative consequences of this experimentation drew a lot of attention. Young women complained in the press that young men were pressuring them into intimacy by claiming that it was old-fashioned to say no. Then they, the women, were left to cope with the resulting venereal infections or pregnancies on their own. Some resorted to abortion, which had been legalized in 1920. So did many married women. Studies done in 1926 revealed that one-third of urban women had had the procedure at least once and that the great majority of these women were not unmarried young people, as conventional wisdom might have assumed, but married women with children. And marriages were disintegrating. By 1926, the Soviet Union had the highest divorce rate in Europe, three times higher that of Germany or France. Most of these divorces were occurring in the cities among young people.[69]

Many communist leaders believed that men were the problem. They bemoaned the delinquency of homeless boys, the licentiousness of male students, the corruption of male party members by power, greed, and alcohol, and the irresponsibility of husbands who refused to support their wives and children. These criticisms had widespread public support, because there was a good deal of truth in them. For the party, they had the added attraction of permitting the leaders to blame individual men for problems that were caused in part by the party's economic policies.

In the mid-1920s, Lev Trotsky, then commander of the Red Army, Nikolai Semashko, the commissar of health, Anatoli Lunacharskii, the commissar of education, and a number of less prominent communists began to develop definitions of ideal masculinity for propagation to the party and the public. They perceived their endeavor as a response to men's bad behavior. It can also be seen as a basic task of any regime that seeks to transform a nation and believes that a prerequisite to such change is remaking the character of the men who will do the transforming. Peter the Great had tried to do it, as had Nicolas I.

There were surprisingly strong similarities between Peter's and Nicholas's definitions of the ideal man and those formulated by Trotsky, Semashko, and Lunacharskii. The communists wrote that the men of the Soviet Union needed to be diligent, skilled, and devoted to the building of a new social order. Such men were moral and abstemious; they did not drink to excess or frequent prostitutes or line their own pockets. They carried out the orders of their superiors. They supported the party. They treated all women with respect and consideration, were faithful to their wives, and provided for their children.

As this discussion developed in the mid-1920s, it became clear that most of the party's intellectuals advocated a reformed nuclear family based on monogamous heterosexuality, because they believed such a family would teach men responsibility and therefore help discipline them into being productive members of Soviet society. It was also the best way to bring up new citizens. "To rear children, to set them on their own feet, requires a minimum of fifteen years," Lunacharskii wrote in 1927. "That means marriage should be a long, companionate marriage."[70]

With a view to promoting this kind of marriage and protecting women from victimization, Soviet jurists in 1925 announced that they were going to revise the 1918 marriage law. The law had created no-fault divorce and decreed that husbands and wives had equal rights to marital property and to the custody of their children. The jurists already knew that peasants in the European areas of the Soviet Union and people in Central Asia rejected these provisions as unworkable and unsuitable. When they invited public comment in 1925, they heard from urban people that the law did not take into account women's unequal situation in Soviet Russia. Women earned much less than men, critics of the marriage law declared. They were more likely than men to lose their jobs and they bore the primary responsibility for children. Therefore the law's treatment of divorcing wives and husbands as equals needed to be reconsidered.

Thousands of women took part in the discussion of the marriage-law revisions. Kollontai, now a Soviet diplomat, urged the government to establish generous benefits for needy women, so that they would not be dependent on their ex-husbands. Other women favored a more conventional approach; they wanted men to pay child support. Julia Zaitseva, the wife of a factory worker, summed up the prevailing opinion: "In most cases a woman is more backward and has fewer skills, and therefore she is less independent than a man. For a woman marriage is often the only way 'to defend herself.' To get married, to have children, to become enslaved to the kitchen, and then to be thrown out by a man—it's very hard for a woman."[71]

Zaitseva and many others saw such women as victimized not just by their husbands, but also by the women who enticed those husbands into extramarital relationships. Women who slept with married men, they declared, were little better than prostitutes. The new law should not grant them any right to support from their lovers. Attentive to this heartfelt testimony, government officials issued a revised code in 1926 that legalized the payment of alimony and child support, and defined common-law marriage so as to clarify the obligations of people who had not legally registered their relationships. A common-law marriage existed, the law declared, when a couple had lived together, reared their children together, and presented themselves to others as married. Fifteen states in the United States, plus the District of Columbia, have very similar definitions of common-law marriage today.

The notion that extramarital sexual relationships, heterosexual as well as homosexual, were immoral and socially damaging had widespread support within the Communist Party and among the public. In the aftermath of the marriage-law discussion, party spokespeople began to stress the virtues of premarital abstinence and marital fidelity. It was time for young people to stop partying and get to work, they said. Socialism was about self-discipline, labor for the common good, and responsibility to kith and kin, not hedonism and self-indulgence. Many peasant and working-class women agreed. A female communist named Shurupova summed up their feelings during the marriage-law discussion: "He took two wives, each gave him a baby, so he must pay both of them. It's nobody else's fault. If you like tobogganing, you must like pulling your sledge uphill."[72]

The pronouncements on responsible masculinity, the revisions of the marriage law, and the condemnations of extramarital sex demonstrated widespread support among Soviet people, rulers and ruled alike, for the values of the contemporary nuclear family that were prevalent throughout urban Europe in the 1920s. Married women had more rights under Soviet law than did women elsewhere. They would continue throughout the Soviet period to limit their family size and to divorce at a record-setting pace. But by the end of the 1920s, the discussion of radical reconstruction of the family was over. And other sorts of experimentation—in lifestyle, in art, in women's emancipation—were also waning, as the revolutionary ferment subsided, the society stabilized, and a new party leadership, led by Joseph Stalin, pushed its way into power.

Conclusions

Between 1890 and 1930, female activists in Russia played a more important part in changing their society than did contemporary women in any other country. Before 1917, they propagated feminist values, expanded female education, gained admittance to most of the professions, and broke new ground in the arts and sciences. The Revolution empowered them to push for legal and political equality and left behind a structure of law that progressive women elsewhere saw as the gold standard of women's human rights. In the NEP years, female activists from the pre-revolutionary era led a new generation of women in a wide-ranging discussion of the woman question and in projects that affected more women from more of Russia's social groups than ever before. The patterns of women's participation in the public world established then would outlast the Soviet Union itself and would be spread by communist parties around the world.

The tsarist government failed to control the upsurge of female activism that began in the late nineteenth century, because it was too diverse to be contained. It included female doctors, feldshers, nurses, and teachers, whom the government relied on to deliver much-needed services; nuns who strengthened the church; artists and journalists who enriched cultural life; and revolutionaries who sought the government's destruction. So the tsars' administrators promoted women's participation in the paid-labor force and tolerated those activists who helped the poor, while refusing to accede to many of the feminists' demands and hunting down the revolutionaries.

The communists who supplanted the tsarist regime were more successful in harnessing female activism to their agenda. From the time they took power, the party's leaders encouraged women to be involved in the public world, because they genuinely wanted to abolish patriarchal abuses and because they thought women should join men in building socialism. To that end they rewrote the laws, provided greater access to education and employment, and, through the Zhenotdel, gave continuing prominence and support to the drive to equalize opportunities and promote respect for the nation's women. They also allowed female activists some leeway in discussing the woman question. As NEP drew to a close, the party leadership took a more regulatory course. It moved against the right and left wings of female activism, shutting down the convents in 1929 and the Zhenotdel less than a year later. This new autocracy intended to encourage female activism, while keeping it within approved boundaries.

6

TOIL, TERROR, AND TRIUMPHS

1930–53

Joseph Stalin was one of the most successful tyrants of the twentieth century. His government built the Soviet industrial base, defeated the Axis armies, and pushed the Soviet Union into the ranks of the superpowers. Women were crucial to all these endeavors. They made up the majority of workers entering the labor force in the 1930s. One million of them fought in World War II, and millions more kept manufacturing going behind the lines. After the war they worked in the rebuilding effort. Women also did most of the housework and childrearing.

These decades saw the Soviet program of women's emancipation reach the majority of Soviet women. Education grew rapidly, social services expanded, and the message that women were now men's equals was insistently broadcast. Women moved into occupations previously closed to them and moved up within the sectors in which they had been working since the nineteenth century. Women's activism—their participation in public institutions, particularly participation aimed at achieving social, political, or cultural change—continued, propelled by a new generation that took seriously the proclamations of women's equality. Assertive women pushed past gender prejudice to claim a place in pioneering ventures in construction, frontier settlement, and aviation. As in the past, however, most women made lower wages than men and very few were promoted into the top ranks of the professions or the government. They were missing entirely from the highest ranks of the leadership.

Official gender values solidified in the 1930s as well. The regime propagated ideals of femininity that combined Bolshevik feminism with an updated cult of domesticity. Women were to be free and equal participants in the society, supportive wives, and nurturing mothers who taught their children to be model Soviet citizens. Some women from the younger generation found this vision empowering. Others, especially the old, tried to preserve what they had long believed in.

For most Soviet women, the 1930s were an ordeal. Those who lived in the cities coped with the perennial difficulties of low wages, unsafe working conditions, inadequate social services, shortages of consumer goods, and crowded housing. In the countryside, peasant women suffered the assault of collectivization and struggled to rebuild agriculture in its aftermath. Women in city and countryside also fell victim to the depredations of Stalin's police. Then came the war. Men predominated among those killed by their own government and by the Axis powers, and the loss of so many of them intensified the hardship in women's lives. It also made women's work in the industrial construction of the 1930s, the maintenance of the economy during the war, and the reconstruction thereafter that much more crucial.

The Thirties

THE FIVE-YEAR PLANS

In 1928 the Communist Party launched the First Five-Year Plan, a blueprint for economic development that set growth targets and allocated resources. The plan emphasized the development of heavy industry—chemical production, defense industries, machine-building, mining, and steel-making. The government declared it a success in 1932 and immediately embarked on a second five-year plan that paid more attention to worker training, efficient use of resources, and production of consumer goods.

Initially the economists at Gosplan, the central planning agency, assumed that they could hire unemployed men to staff expanding industries, but they soon realized that there were not enough men available. Planners and party officials noticed that women, who made up 55 percent of the unemployed in 1930, were lining up to apply for the new jobs. So they once again ordered that training programs for women be established and that managers end discriminatory hiring practices. This time they enforced the decrees. They also encountered less local resistance than in the past, for many managers realized that they had to employ women if they were to meet the plan's demands. Women, especially young ones driven by necessity and hopeful of bettering their situations, flocked to the new jobs. The result was that the vast majority of workers joining the paid-labor force for the first time in the 1930s were women: 4 million were employed between

1929 and 1935, 1.7 million of them in industry. By 1940, women made up 39 percent of the paid-labor force in the Soviet Union, a higher percentage than anywhere else in the European world. In the United States, by contrast, 25 percent of paid workers in 1940 were female. The percentages for France, Germany, Italy, and Sweden in that year were 37, 30, 28, and 28 respectively.[1]

Soviet women entered fields that had been predominantly male, such as engineering and press operating; they took jobs in new industries such as light-bulb manufacturing; and they increased their participation in sectors already heavily female, such as textile production. They also moved into the professions in record numbers. By the late 1930s in the Russian republic of the Soviet Union, 63 percent of physicians, 42 percent of economists, and 36 percent of faculty at institutions of higher education were women. Twenty-three percent of all journalists, writers, and editors and 30 percent of all visual and performing artists were women. By contrast, American women held 14 percent of professional and technical jobs in the late 1930s. In much of the European world, hard hit by economic depression, women were being laid off, not hired.[2]

Patterns of gender difference in the workplace, although considerably weakened, were not eliminated. Peasants just arrived in the cities were still going to work as servants, now in the households of the new elite. Most female workers were employed in clerical work, education, food service, and textiles, which were paid less than male preserves such as metalworking. Occupations that were judged detrimental to women's reproductive health or beyond their physical strength, such as underground mining, were closed to them. Men harassed women entering previously male fields. The notions that men would lead and women would devote much of their time to family life remained powerful as well. Only 12 percent of the top jobs in the party and government of the Russian republic were held by women in 1939. In that year, women were 63 percent of physicians, but only 15 percent of the heads of medical institutions. Although the overwhelming majority of food-service workers, women led only 34 percent of food-service enterprises. To put this in perspective, it should be noted that similar gender patterns prevail worldwide today.[3]

COLLECTIVIZATION

As he set the First Five-Year Plan in motion, Stalin ordered the collectivization of agriculture. Marxists had long believed that private agriculture was a retrograde economic system that nurtured conservative values in rural people. In the early 1920s, the party had proposed to raise peasant consciousness and productivity by establishing collective farms. Villagers would own the means of production—tools, seed, and livestock—in common, but the land would be public property. Managers trained in modern farming methods would direct operations following plans made in Moscow. Party leaders knew that many peasants would not willingly give up the old ways, so they contented themselves with setting up demonstration collective farms until the late 1920s.

In 1929, Stalin ordered wholesale collectivization to begin, because he believed that it was essential to the success of the First Five-Year Plan that the government should manage agriculture as well as industry. Party workers recruited from the cities streamed into the countryside, where they seized control of crops, livestock, and equipment, rewarded those who cooperated with them, and punished those who resisted. Peasants branded "kulaks"—those with a bit more property than average, those who spoke up against communists, and those who were simply in the wrong place at the wrong time—were arrested and deported to "special settlements" in desolate areas far from their homes. Ksenia Dubovitskaia was ten years old when the collectivizers came to her family's house in a village in Tambov province. "These people started confiscating our property, which consisted of two sheep and one heifer, and all the linens like our bedding and other village things and they even took off me . . . a yellow dress that my older brother Grigory's wife had sewn for me out of my mother's skirt. They loaded it all up and took it away and we were left 'naked as the day we were born.' A day later my father was arrested . . . and two days after that we were thrown out of our house."[4]

The government expected that attacking the wealthier peasants would rally poorer ones to support collectivization. Instead, most peasants did as the Uzbeks had done during the unveiling campaign: they united against the outsiders. First they tried to avoid the collectivizers or put them off, and when that did not work, they turned to more direct measures—protesting, destroying property, and attacking government agents and their collaborators.

Soon police were reporting that the countryside was awash in *babi bunty,* a term that translates, very loosely, as "the grannies' revolt." Peasant women had turned on landlords and merchants in the past. Now they attacked the collectivizers. They broke up meetings held to cultivate their support by yelling out their complaints, a tactic working-class and peasant women had used against the Zhenotdel during the civil war. They refused to surrender their chickens, cows, and pigs. They marched on barns and tool sheds to take back what the collectivizers had seized. They prevented party operatives from arresting their neighbors. Sometimes they drove communists out of their villages and declared the collective farms dissolved. Many times they physically attacked the men they saw as persecutors. In Central Asia and Siberia, where resistance to collectivization was even more widespread than in the Slavic areas, women played a less prominent role, but there were some female-led uprisings there too. In volatile Uzbekistan in 1930, the leaders of a crowd of three hundred women tried to strangle several communist leaders, not an easy task when wearing robes and veils.[5]

Local party and police officials feared that sending armed police and soldiers against unarmed women would increase the unrest, and they shrank from using force on women, particularly older ones who reminded them of their mothers. They also thought that men, especially village elders and priests, were behind the protests, that they were sending the women out because they knew the police would be loath to move against them. There may have been some truth in this. When asked why the men were taking a back seat, one male peasant replied wryly, "They [the women] are equal now; as they decide, so we will agree."[6] The resistance built to a furious level, and in March 1930 Stalin published an article that condemned the collectivizers for abusing the peasants.

After a short pause, however, the government renewed the pressure, with disastrous results. The violent assault on the villages, coupled with massive disruptions caused by the cumbersome process of establishing new management, led to catastrophic declines in food production. The situation was exacerbated by continuing resistance: peasants across the Soviet Union, from the steppes of Ukraine to the forests of Siberia, preferred slaughtering their livestock and privately selling or consuming their crops to turning them over to the government. As grain supplies dwindled, still more animals had to be destroyed before they starved to death. The central government compounded the calamity by refusing to lower the amount of grain farmers were required to deliver to the authorities. By 1932, famine, this time created by Moscow's policies, ravaged the countryside. "So many laid [*sic*] dead in the streets around the cities, in yards and in houses," remembered Anastasia Serikova, a child when famine swept through her village in Krasnodar in the Caucasus. "A cart came around all the time with a white horse, took the dead to the cemetery and threw them in a ditch like dead dogs. They'd throw them in from up top and sprinkle some dirt on them."[7]

As conditions worsened, peasant women gave up their protests and turned to trying to survive. Once again hungry mothers took to the roads.

Maria Belskaia was eight when she set off with her mother Arina and five brothers and sisters to find food in 1933. Her father had been arrested and their neighbors, starving themselves, had driven the family from their village in the Altai region of Siberia. Belskaia later described their pilgrimage: "We knocked on people's windows and begged in Christ's name for a piece of bread or a potato. While we still had flour, Mother would mix it with cherry blossoms or hawthorn and boil it in our little pot. . . . But then the flour ran out, and we had to live on whatever good people could give us. In those hungry days, there were not many good people around."[8]

Belskaia's family survived; many others did not. Between 5 and 7 million people died tragically in the famine of 1932–33. More than 2 million kulaks were deported to Siberia and Central Asia; a hundred thousand more were imprisoned.[9] By 1933, the famished peasants had lost their battle with Soviet power. The government made some concessions; it granted villagers the right to own their houses and gardens and to keep cows and smaller animals. In city markets, they could sell their produce. Thereafter, the peasants' "private plots" became the main source of fruits and vegetables for townspeople.

RURAL WOMEN'S LIVES IN THE '30s

The Stalinists' subjugation of the countryside irrevocably altered the lives of the survivors. Millions of families were broken up by arrest or disease or out-migration. Among the migrants there were now many women: almost half the workers entering the urban paid-labor force in the 1930s were female peasants. The birthrate fell, as did the number of single women in the countryside. The power structure of the peasants' world also changed. By ruthlessly attacking uncooperative village elders and empowering government officials and the peasants who worked for them, the government destroyed the networks that had bound older and younger men together. A party-dominated system of clientage and patronage took the place of kinship and age as the method of distributing power in the countryside. The control of older women over younger weakened as well.

Peasant women preserved some traditional ideas and practices, while questioning others. Medical services in the countryside, although expanded, remained seriously inadequate, so village midwives still attended most births. Many women continued to be religious, despite the regime's propaganda against religion and attacks on religious leaders. They were more receptive than they had been in the 1920s to the criticism of patriarchy brought in by propagandists and periodicals. David Ransel has found that women who came of age in the 1930s believed that peasant custom gave too much power to men and oppressed women. Many girls demonstrated their rejection of the old ways by migrating to the cities. Those who remained in the countryside were more willing than older women to have abortions and to divorce.[10]

Women's discontents grew from the fact that men's power over women in the family and community was little changed by collectivization, despite the fact that women's work was more important than ever. Because men were still more likely to move away than women, women made up 60 percent of the rural labor force by the end of the decade. This did not change the patriarchal principle that men should lead. Seventy-five percent of farm managers were men in the Russian republic in the late 1930s; women held 67 percent of the least skilled jobs. As in the industrial sector, women were most likely to advance in those areas long considered their province, such as dairying.[11]

Collectivized agriculture did have its benefits. Some of the women who had worked on the farms in the 1930s remembered in their old age that the workload was lighter than under the old system, and that the new bosses were less demanding. They appreciated the fact that in 1935 the government granted them two months of maternity leave at half pay; in the past pregnant women had worked until they went into labor and returned to the fields soon after they gave birth. Women also praised the Soviet government for improving rural education. Between 1926 and 1939, the literacy rate among rural females aged 9–49 in the Russian republic increased from 39 percent to 80 percent. Fifty percent of the students enrolled in rural secondary schools in the Russian republic in 1939 were girls.[12]

These improvements were part of a government effort to cultivate support among peasant women. Policy makers recognized the importance of women's work to the building of Soviet agriculture, and so they improved benefits and funded services, albeit inadequately. They issued orders to promote women, which were derailed by the same resistance such orders encountered in the industrial sector. They instructed local officials to give highly publicized awards to particularly energetic female workers, hoping thereby to inspire other women and shame men into working harder.

The government also conducted campaigns to move women into better jobs, the most famous of which was the effort to sign them up as tractor drivers. Tractors were a potent symbol of the industrialization of Soviet agriculture, so teaching women to drive them, government officials believed, would expand the pool of qualified personnel and publicize the importance of women's emancipation. The first decrees to recruit female tractor drivers were issued in 1930, to little effect. Local managers ignored the orders and harassed the women who tried to sign up for training. The government then decided to establish courses exclusively for women, and party officials in Ukraine found a young peasant eager to lead such courses. Praskovia Angelina, better known by her nickname "Pasha," then became one of the most famous female activists of the 1930s.

PRASKOVIA ANGELINA (1912–59)

Angelina came from a family of ardent peasant communists. In 1930, when a male tractor driver moved out of her village, she volunteered to take his place. "At first people just laughed at me, but as . . . the tractor was sitting idle, I was allowed to give it a try," she wrote in her autobiography. Like most female activists, Angelina was persistent. She persuaded her brother, already a tractor driver, to teach her, and after she was trained, she talked her way onto an all-male team of drivers. Although her mates came to accept her when she proved that she could do the work, her achievements did not change their estimation of women's abilities. "Even my friends," she remembered, "say, 'Pasha may be doing okay because she's so spunky, but basically a woman doesn't belong on a tractor.' This means that my example is not enough. I need to organize an all-female tractor brigade." Local officials supported her, especially after Moscow sent out word to recruit more women. By 1933 Angelina had trained a group of female drivers, and they in turn were bringing in new recruits.[13]

Deeply committed to agricultural development and to women's participation in it, Angelina welcomed the opportunity to become an advocate for both. She joined the Communist Party in 1937, was given a variety of honorary appointments, and earned an advanced degree in agriculture in 1940. Everywhere she went, she sang the praises of the government and of Stalin. She also called for more daycare and medical services in the countryside and criticized the sexist prejudices that she and her colleagues were struggling to overcome. She did not have great success in persuading women to climb aboard the tractors, perhaps because of the sexism, perhaps also because operating the primitive machines was very hard work. In 1937, the peak year of female enlistment in the 1930s, they constituted only 6.8 percent of drivers.[14] Angelina did make it into the ranks of Soviet heroes, and her exploits were celebrated until the end of the Soviet period.

WOMEN IN THE CITIES

Throughout the 1930s, urban life was difficult. Food, housing, and public services had long been in short supply; now, with millions coming to the cities seeking work, the shortages worsened. No government could have

A photograph of Praskovia Angelina taken in the 1930s or 1940s.
http://en.wikipedia.org/wiki/File:Pasha_angelina.gif. Accessed June 27, 2011.

PRASKOVIA ANGELINA

In 1948, Angelina described a babi bunt against her brigade of female tractor drivers.

"Suddenly something terrifying occurred. At the entrance to the village we were met by a crowd of agitated women. They were standing in the middle of the road and shouting all together: 'Get out of here. We're not going to allow women's machines on our field! You'll ruin our crops!'

We Komsomol [Communist youth organization] members were used to kulak hatred and resistance, but these were our own women, our fellow collective farmers! Later we became friends, of course, but that first encounter was terrible.

You can imagine what a state we were in: we had been expecting a triumphant entry and now this. . . . My girls were on the brink of tears, and even I, normally quite feisty, didn't know what to do. The women surrounded us in a tight circle, yelling, 'One inch more, and we'll tear your hair out by the braids and kick you out of here!'

[After they fetched a local communist official, the crowd dispersed and they began plowing.]

The festive mood was gone, of course. The girls' faces were sweaty and angry. We felt like we were on a battlefield: one mistake and you're dead."

SOURCE: SHEILA FITZPATRICK AND YURI SLEZKINE, EDS., *IN THE SHADOW OF REVOLUTION: LIFE STORIES OF RUSSIAN WOMEN FROM 1917 TO THE SECOND WORLD WAR* (PRINCETON: PRINCETON UNIVERSITY PRESS, 2000), 313–14.

met the needs of all these newcomers, but Stalin's could have done more than it did, particularly during the First Five-Year Plan when it concentrated on building up heavy industry. So people crowded into already overcrowded apartments and dormitories, made do with limited running water, and ate plain food. Wendy Goldman has written that in 1932, "workers lived on dry rye bread and potatoes, a few seasonable vegetables (cabbage, onions, and carrots), and canned fish." Legal peasant markets and a black market in scarce goods filled some of the gaps, but at prices higher than many people could afford. Wages fell during the First Five-Year Plan; in 1937, they were still only 66 percent of the 1928 level. The standard of living improved somewhat in the mid-'30s, then worsened again in the late 1930s, when the government increased military spending.[15]

In the cities, as in the countryside, there were women who benefited from the Soviet system. Pasha Angelina had an urban counterpart in Valentina Bogdan, the daughter of a working-class family who traveled with friends to the city of Krasnodar in 1929 to take entrance examinations for the Institute of the Food Industry. Years later she remembered her feelings: "More than anything in the world, we wanted to enter [the institute] and join the elect. I said half-jokingly: 'Girls, let's pray to the institute, asking it to admit us.' We waited until nobody was around and then raised our arms and said loudly, in unison, 'Admit us within your walls. Admit us! Admit us!'"[16]

Bogdan was one of the millions of young, poor women who were admitted. By 1939, 56 percent of the students enrolled in secondary schools in the Russian republic of the Soviet Union were girls, as were 50 percent of the students in higher education.[17] These remarkable statistics would have delighted the pre-revolutionary feminists. Furthermore, the government constantly declared that workers and peasants were the favored classes in the Soviet Union, and backed up those declarations by giving preferential treatment to such people. It also proclaimed that Soviet women were men's equals and that they should improve themselves for their own sakes as well as for the public good. Lower-class women such as Bogdan and Angelina had reason to hope, therefore, that they could, through personal effort, earn better lives for themselves among the "elect."

The "elect" they sought to join was composed of families, most of them from the middling and lower ranks of pre-revolutionary society, whose adult members worked in the leadership of the party, government, industry, and the military. These people were allocated comfortable apartments, had access to better-staffed and equipped medical clinics, sent their children to the best schools, and rode around in government-issued cars.

They could afford to hire servants and buy the consumer goods that were available. Galina Shtange, the wife of an engineering professor, recorded in her diary in 1936 a glowing report on beautiful new stores in Moscow and concluded, "When you recall the first years after the revolution and the way things were back then, it's just exhilarating to think that all this has been achieved in just 20 years." Fruma Treivas, the wife of an editor at the party newspaper *Pravda,* wrote her memoirs years later, by which time she was more aware than Shtange of the differences between the elite and the rest of Soviet society in the 1930s. "We were so far removed from the lives of ordinary people that we thought this was the way it should be," she remembered. "The way I looked at it, Vasilkovsky [her husband] was killing himself working long hours at an important job, all for the glory of the motherland and Stalin."[18] Among the Stalinist elite, hard work and dedication legitimated privilege.

THE NEW SOVIET WOMAN

The 1930s saw the completion of the process, begun in the 1920s, of blending the revolutionary gender ideas espoused by the Bolshevik feminists with liberal contemporary notions and older ones inherited from Russia's past. The official results of this syncretism were the "New Soviet Man" and "New Soviet Woman," icons of masculinity and femininity that were rolled out in the arts and mass media throughout the decade.

As we have seen, the New Soviet Man first surfaced in the 1920s. He was a competent, diligent, responsible, and self-disciplined worker; a modest comrade who worked well with others; and a considerate, faithful husband who provided for his family and disciplined his children. He was "cultured," which meant that he dressed neatly, bathed regularly, appreciated the arts, read for pleasure, and did not swear, gamble, or get drunk with his pals every payday. The New Soviet Man strongly resembled both the respectable worker ideal of the pre-revolutionary era and still older paragons. He obeyed his superiors—a trait emphasized by Nicholas I, Peter I, and the author of *The Domostroi.* He was energetic and progressive, as Peter's ideal nobleman had been. These resemblances emerged from similar circumstances. Stalin was as dependent on loyal servitors as Peter and Nicholas, and he too wanted to make the people of his nation into model, modern Europeans.

The New Soviet Woman required more remodeling to serve the priorities of the 1930s. The party continued to praise women such as Pasha Angelina who devoted themselves to building socialism. They were held up as model workers, whom lesser women were supposed to emulate, and as living proof of the success of women's emancipation. Once women had been oppressed and backward; now they marched in the vanguard of the working class and, in so doing, freed themselves from the sexist traditions of the past and contributed to the building of a just society.[19]

The leadership also felt it necessary to address itself to the domestic side of women's lives, and so its spokespeople began encouraging wives to create cozy homes, teach socialist values to their children, and provide emotional support to their husbands. A. M. Poliakova, the wife of a blacksmith, declared in a speech in 1936, "Now if a wife welcomes her husband home with love and tenderness, if she respects him and talks to him, then the husband will go back to work in a good mood and will think only about his work. It's obvious that in this case his labor productivity will increase." Women could also help their husbands become New Soviet Men by teaching them the virtues of *kulturnost* ("culturedness"). Poliakova said proudly of her own spouse, "I've trained him to the point where he brings home books himself." She advised women to quiz their mates about movies they had just seen together, to make sure that the men had not nodded off during the show.[20]

The notion that women could teach men about the higher things in life had been around since medieval Europe. It was a theme in the cult of domesticity. Now in the 1930s, the age of the masses having arrived, Soviet communists taught that working-class wives could lead their menfolk toward kulturnost by supervising their drinking and making them stay awake in the movies. The accoutrements of domesticity enjoyed by the model wives featured in the press—the comfortable apartments, the good food, the movie tickets—testified to the accomplishments of their husbands, the New Soviet Men, who were making the money that bought such luxuries. Thus the idealized Soviet wife, like the bourgeois lady of the cult of domesticity, both nurtured and attested to male achievement.

The New Soviet Woman, indefatigable worker and civilizing wife, set standards and inspired emulation. She was no more out of touch with the reality of most women's lives than the long-suffering saint or the dainty bourgeois housewife. What she shared with those archetypes was a responsibility to realize her true nature by serving her family and her society. She was an updated affirmation of the very old ideal of female self-sacrifice—justified now by the promise that, through all her work, she emancipated herself even as she helped to build a better world and repaid the state for freeing her from patriarchal bondage. Her liberation, unlike that envisioned by feminists later in the twentieth century, was not sufficient unto itself. It served the greater good of building the world's first truly just and prosperous society.

VOLUNTEERING IN THE 1930s

The New Soviet Woman played a part in inspiring female volunteerism. The government had a prodigious need for people to help with a host of tasks, from cleaning streets to building dams, so it used every appeal it could fashion, including gendered ones. To reach women, it called out to both sides of the New Soviet Woman, the emancipated worker and the happy homemaker. Homemakers responded with the *obshchestvennitsa* movement.

Between 1934 and 1941, tens of thousands of unemployed wives of army officers, engineers, managers, and party officials became *obshchest-vennitsy*, which roughly translates as "socially engaged women." Organized into clubs, obshchestvennitsy donated supplies to workers' cafeterias, childcare centers, dormitories, and medical clinics; they spruced up work-places and neighborhoods; they planted flowers and hung curtains. Some obshchestvennitsy lectured workers, particularly female ones, on personal hygiene and housework and coached them on how to be supportive of their husbands. Others joined "control brigades" that inspected retail shops for cleanliness and good customer service, pitching in to dust the shelves when necessary.[21]

The obshchestvennitsy publicized the Soviet emancipation of women and organized projects for working-class women, as the Zhenotdel had done, but they possessed little of the Zhenotdel's feminism. They were more like the wives of nineteenth-century Russian governors who ran local charities. Empowered by their status as spouses of the new bosses, they saw themselves as bringing a woman's soothing, beautifying touch to the work-ers' world and setting an example of responsible citizenship, good taste, and good mothering to women less fortunate than they.[22]

The women who were most faithful to Bolshevik feminist ideals were the ones who answered the party's calls to pioneering work in the country-side, in the cities, and on the frontiers. Angelina was such a woman, and like so many others, when she became a model worker, she was a member of the Komsomol. The Komsomol was the Communist Party's youth orga-nization, open to people in their late teens and early twenties. In the 1930s it and the secondary schools from which it recruited new members were nurturing a generation of ambitious, idealistic women who were eager to participate in the building of socialism and to realize in their own lives the equality the party promised. Women were a minority in the Komsomol; perhaps the girls who joined were unusually assertive and independent. There is no question that many of them took seriously the proclamations of women's equality. They were often able to overcome male resistance because they were *Komsomoltsy,* that is, female Komsomol members, which gave them standing with party officials, and because they got support from managers eager to employ all the workers they could get. Once again, autocracy and need opened up possibilities that activist women were able to exploit.[23]

One of these women was Anna Egorova, a peasant who came from the countryside to Moscow in 1934 to work on the subway then under construction. The tall sixteen-year-old (she persuaded her employers that she was older) joined a unit of steel-fitters. When she heard that a flying club was seeking members, she eagerly signed up, and fell in love with planes and flying. Egorova ran into male hostility occasionally, but she managed to overcome it, and to build warm friendships with the other young men and women with whom she worked. She also found supportive male superiors, who encouraged her. As the great tunnels and stations of the metro came into being, as she learned to fly, as the government showered praise on the young volunteers, Egorova's self-esteem grew. "I began to acquire a certain confidence," she remembered in the 1990s, "a sense that I could do anything."[24]

The largest single example of Komsomoltsy volunteerism was the Khetagurovite campaign, which began in early 1937 when Valentina Khetagurova, a Komsomol activist who worked in the Siberian far east, published an article urging women to come east and help build that region's infrastructure. The response was overwhelming. In the next eight months, sixty-seven thousand women, most of them members of the Komsomol or of the party, wrote in to express interest. Elena Shulman has found that these people were idealistic patriots, drawn east by dreams of a pristine frontier where women were needed. Twenty thousand of them actually came in the next two years and found jobs as clerks, factory workers, medical personnel, party workers, prison-camp guards, teachers, and tractor drivers. Some Khetagurovites eventually moved back home; many made their peace with the rigors of the far east and remained.[25]

Among the Khetagurovites were women who spoke up against sexism. At conferences and in letters, they decried the refusal of managers to hire them, to pay them as much as men once they had hired them, and to assign them to skilled jobs. They also drew attention to sexual harassment. Pasha Angelina was making the same claim that gender barriers should not prevent women from taking equal parts in socialist construction. The willingness of all these women to protest against sexism spoke to the self-confidence they had learned as Komsomoltsy and pioneering workers, and portended the refusal of some of them, in 1941, to accept their exclusion from the military.[26]

THE FAMILY LAW OF 1936

To keep the economy developing and to maintain a strong military, the Soviet Union needed a growing population, so government officials were alarmed in the mid-1930s by the fact that the birthrate was falling. They responded with another revision of the marriage law, this one designed to encourage stable marriages and lots of childbearing. The Family Law of 1936 made it more expensive to obtain a divorce and required that both wife and husband attend a court hearing to dissolve their marriage. The law also increased child-support payments and imposed a two-year prison sentence on parents found guilty of non-payment. It raised state subsidies to new mothers, increased funding for maternity and childcare services, and established stipends for women who gave birth to seven children or more. These positive incentives to childbearing were paired with a penalty for avoiding it. The revised family law outlawed abortion except when the life or health of the mother was at risk or the fetus had a serious genetic disorder. Doctors could be sentenced to two years in prison for performing the procedure; women receiving it more than once could be fined.

As they had done in 1926, women of all classes welcomed the provisions in the revised law that were intended to tighten the bonds of marriage, but many, especially those from the European ethnic groups, opposed the outlawing of abortion. Working-class women did so because they said that they were too poor to support many children. Better-educated, more economically secure women argued that they should be permitted to limit their childbearing in order to work outside the home and thereby emancipate themselves. Such women were more likely than poorer ones to have had abortions.[27]

After the criminalization of abortion, the birthrate rose among Baltic, Jewish, and Slavic women for a year or so. (Women of the ethnic minorities of Central Asia, the Caucasus, and Siberia did not experience a similar rise because they had resorted to abortion far less.) Very soon, women of the European ethnic groups found ways to get abortions from medical personnel, from underground abortionists, or from their own self-applied methods. These resorts increased the number of women suffering complications that required hospital care or resulted in death. Nonetheless, women continued to terminate pregnancies. By 1940 the abortion rate across the Soviet Union was back to the level of 1935.

WOMEN IN THE CAUCASUS, CENTRAL ASIA, AND SIBERIA
THE CAUCASUS AND CENTRAL ASIA

After the upheavals in Central Asia in the late '20s, party leaders across that region and in the Caucasus proceeded cautiously with women's emancipation. Their construction of Stalinist political and economic systems cut the power of local elites, disrupted kinship networks, and undermined the customary authority of senior males over junior ones, and in so doing weakened the ability of traditional families to confine their women behind veils and walls. Education for girls and women expanded, women were enlisted to work alongside men on the collective farms, and the party continued to preach women's equality. Family law was brought formally in line with the Soviet code, but officials usually did not enforce prohibitions on customary practices such as bride price.

✦ ✦ ✦ *FIRUZA KERIMOVA (1906–?)* ✦ ✦ ✦

There were young women in the Caucasus who joined the Soviet emancipation project as enthusiastically as Pasha Angelina, Anna Egorova, and the Khetagurovites, in spite of their own fears and the resistance they encountered. Firuza Kerimova, an Azeri who lived near Baku in Azerbaijan, is an example. Like Angelina, she came from a family with radical views; her people, unlike Angelina's, were prosperous merchants. Before the revolution they had supported the revolutionary movement; afterward they were pro-communist. In the 1920s Kerimova ran a daycare center in her family's home in Balahani, a city in the Azeri oilfields. Insisting on marrying for love, she chose a young official in the Soviet government, Agahan Kerimov. As the couple moved from assignment to assignment, Kerimova spread the call to emancipation among local women.

When the Five-Year Plans began, Kerimova signed up to study engineering. In 1932, she graduated. "There are days that cannot be forgotten," she declared in a speech at the graduation ceremonies. "Today is such a day for me. Not very long ago I wore the chadrah [a veil], but today they call me the oil commander, an engineer-organizer." Her euphoria faded when she began her new job. The men who were supposed to work under her command harassed her, at one point pouring oil on her head. "At first she cried a lot," her daughter, Rabia khanum Sultan-zade, remembered. "The workers bluntly told her, 'This isn't a place for a woman. We used to get the

Firuza Kerimova at her daycare center in the 1920s.
http://www.gender-az.org/index.shtml?id_doc=2081.
Accessed December 1, 2010.

FIRUZA KERIMOVA

Rabia khanum Sultan-zade, Kerimova's daughter, wrote this account of her mother's first encounter with unveiling:

"Despite being quite young, my mother had been chosen a delegate to the First Non-Party Congress of Azerbaijani Women [in the early 1920s]. Standing at the podium making an important speech, she did not notice the rapt attention of S. Kirov, the first secretary of the Communist Party of Azerbaijan, who was sitting on the stage. The pretty, ardent girl with the burning turquoise eyes had wrapped herself in a chadrah [a veil]. Probably Kirov was trying to send a message when he came up to her during her speech and dramatically tore the chadrah off her and threw it into the audience, where the women tore it to pieces.

Scarlet with embarrassment and confusion, she stood on the stage, fingering her thick braids, and Anna Sultanova [a Zhenotdel leader], wise with experience, said, 'Such a beautiful face shouldn't be hidden under a chadrah.' The euphoria in the hall passed, the women went away, and Mama sat and cried, 'How can I go back to Balahani with-out the chadrah?' In those days one could not walk down the streets of Balahani without a chadrah. And then Kirov gave Firuza a scarlet silk scarf."

SOURCE: AZERBAIJAN GENDER INFORMATION CENTER (HTTP://WWW.GENDER-AZ.ORG/ INDEX.SHTML?ID_DOC=2081). TRANSLATED BY BARBARA CLEMENTS. REPRINTED BY PERMISSION.

oil out without you and we're going to keep doing it. You should stay home with your family.'"[28]

Kerimova managed to win over some of the men by refusing an appointment to a managerial position and instead doing manual labor alongside them. When she felt that she had proved herself, she moved into the ranks of the engineers, and within a few years had become the first woman to hold a top administrative position in the Baku oilfields. More than seventy years later, her daughter's proud story of her mother's struggles and triumphs was posted to the Azerbaijan Gender Information Center's website.

SIBERIA

In Siberia, the campaign to emancipate native women, which began in earnest in 1929, had the familiar components—outlawing bride price, dowry, and polygamy, publicizing the evils of traditional patriarchy, and encouraging women to exercise their new rights and take advantage of educational and employment opportunities. Because the native Siberians had a long history of negotiating with the Europeans and because their cultures were less patriarchal than those of Central Asia, reforms for women advanced rapidly.

Education expanded, as did women's participation in the political process. Women eagerly enrolled in the teachers' colleges set up to train Buryats, Koraks, Tatars, Yakuts, and others. Primary and secondary schooling for girls and women grew, as did literacy. Among Buryats, female literacy rates increased from 21 percent in 1926 to 66 percent in 1939. In that same year, girls made up 49 percent of Yakut elementary-school students. Women's involvement in politics expanded as well. By 1931 one-quarter of the delegates to soviets in the autonomous regions of Siberia were female. This percentage was far higher than the percentage of female delegates to Central Asian soviets and to some Russian ones. Probably the long-standing practice of Siberian women playing leading roles in their communities made politics less intimidating.[29]

Collectivization struck very hard in Siberia. In that land of nomads, the popular reaction was even more outraged than in the Russian heartland, for collectivization meant not only turning animals over to the government but settling down to become farmers. The Buryats, the Turkic peoples of the southwest, and the Koraks in the far east killed their livestock rather than surrender it to the government. The reindeer herders of the far north and east and the mountain people of the Altai region retreated into still more remote areas beyond the government's reach. After the worst excesses of collectivization receded in the mid-1930s, Soviet programs of improving health care and education made some headway, and supplies of food and manufactured goods increased.

Increasing also was the migration to Siberia of Europeans, for the Soviet government worked as assiduously as had the tsarist to entice settlers to move east. We have already noted the successful Khetagurovite campaign. The establishment of an "autonomous region" in Birobidzhan, set aside for Jews, also drew immigrants. Tens of thousands of other women came to Siberia involuntarily in the 1930s, for another tsarist practice that the Soviet government continued was the use of the east as a place of imprisonment.

THE TERROR

From the beginning of communist rule, the party filled the jails it had inherited from the tsars with people whom it labeled "enemies." It also sent such people into exile in remote areas or sentenced them to labor camps, as the tsars had done. The Soviet government under Stalin expanded the "enemies list" and hired many more police and jailers. The result was a police state comparable to Nazi Germany's, but longer lasting. Only Stalin's death in March 1953 brought this reign of terror to an end.

The Terror came in waves that swept up millions of people. They began in 1929 with collectivization, when unfortunates who had been branded kulaks were sent to the special settlements in the far north and Siberia. Local authorities then shipped more peasants accused of a variety of crimes off to labor camps throughout the 1930s. In 1934, the government criminalized workplace infractions such as lateness. Sodomy, which was not a crime in the early Soviet law codes, became one in 1933–34 and gay men (but rarely women) were arrested thereafter. In 1934, the police also began picking up communists who had criticized Stalin. The purge of the party grew into a full-fledged assault on Soviet officialdom that peaked in 1937 and subsided in 1939. Thereafter, Stalinist persecution rose and fell spasmodically, according to the dictator's whim. Anne Applebaum has estimated that as a consequence 18 million people served time in labor camps between 1929 and 1953.[30]

This brutal repression had multiple causes. Stalin and his inner circle ordered and directed it, because they believed that they had to root out opposition to their policies. The peasants had risen up against collectivization; workers struck from time to time; ordinary people grumbled about the hardships of everyday life. They also flouted the government's many rules, regulations, and directives. The black market flourished; factory managers falsified production data; orders issued by Moscow were ignored; party chairmen energetically feathered their own nests.

The leadership could not accept the fact that the system functioned only because people broke the rules. The five-year plans were poorly conceived and executed, which led to manifold foul-ups and privations. Without local officials filing bogus reports, without administrators burying demands from higher-ups under heaps of paperwork, without workers stealing from the factories, without a black market that supplied communists as well as ordinary citizens, Moscow's unrealistic directives and witless oppression would have driven the Soviet people to collapse or rebellion. Tragically, the fudging on the rules fed Kremlin paranoia. For it was easier for Stalin and his lieutenants to believe that disappointing economic figures and public discontent were the result of sabotage than to face the massive failures of their own leadership. They reasoned that arresting corrupt officials, malcontents, and scofflaws would remove real and potential "enemies" from the general population and frighten that population into compliance. As an added, and important, benefit, they could use the arrested people as a giant convict labor force. They did not care that the vast majority of those who fell into the net had done nothing to warrant imprisonment. Perhaps some of them even convinced themselves that there were millions of implacable foes out there working in secret to undermine them.

Gender ideas and practices affected Stalin's Terror, as they had the attacks on the lishentsy. The great majority of the police and party officials who carried out the persecutions were men, although there were a few women among the purgers. The most notorious of these was Rozalia Zemliachka, a veteran communist who had shown her lethal side as a political officer during the civil war. Then she had ordered soldiers executed for desertion and had participated in ferocious assaults on non-combatants in the Crimea. In the 1930s, she worked as an official of the government and party commissions that investigated accusations of wrongdoing. Zemliachka became notorious as a merciless inquisitor.[31]

Probably most of her victims were men. Eighty-nine percent of those prosecuted in the late 1930s were men, and men made up more than 90 percent of labor-camp inmates in the 1930s. In 1940, for example, there were 1,235,510 male prisoners in the camps and 108,898 female ones. The Terror targeted men because they held most of the leadership positions and because the authorities assumed that men, not women, threatened them. We have already seen such assumptions at work in the purge of the lishentsy and in police responses to the babi bunty. As in those operations, women were most likely to fall prey to Stalin's Terror when their husbands did. After the authorities crushed a strike in the textile town of Vichuga in 1932, for example, they arrested only those women who were related to male strikers, even though many women had participated in the unrest. The same male-centered selection process was at work when female peasants were exiled with their kulak husbands in 1930, and when the wives of arrested male communists were picked up in 1938.[32]

The government was able to maintain the Terror for more than two decades because it had learned valuable lessons from the peasant uprisings against collectivization. Thereafter the police avoided direct assaults on communities, preferring to pick off a few people at a time and striking without warning, for the most trivial of reasons. Women were hauled away for gleaning grain without permission, for making derogatory comments about communists when an informer was nearby, for being a few minutes late for work, for taking a pencil home from the office, or for walking by a police station when the men inside needed more victims to meet their monthly quota of arrests.

The government also took great pains to disguise the scale of the Terror. Radio broadcasts and newspapers talked a lot about how the party was keeping the country safe by rooting out evildoers, but they did not say how many people were falling into the net. Victims were taken away in the middle of the night and locked up incommunicado. Prisoners were transported in trucks disguised as delivery vans or in freight cars. The bodies of the executed were buried, late at night, in unmarked mass graves outside the cities. People learned to ask no questions about missing neighbors or upturned dirt in nearby forests. If they were lucky, they could believe the government's lies and go on with their lives.

When the NKVD, the agency charged with hunting down political enemies, turned its malignant attention to party members, those people proved to be as vulnerable as workers or peasants. Most took refuge in the official explanation that the police were hunting down enemies, and therefore that they, who had done nothing wrong, were safe. Inna Shikheeva-Gaister, the daughter of imprisoned communists, remembered years later, "We believed all the slogans. They screwed our heads on any way they wanted. I believed everything—completely and sincerely. . . . I believed everything I was supposed to about the enemies of the people and about all the arrests!"[33]

Fruma Treivas, who had once taken her status as the wife of a high-ranking communist for granted, found her faith crumbling in the summer of 1937. "From our balcony," she wrote years later, "we could see all the other balconies in the courtyard. If no one appeared for a while, and the balcony was sealed, it meant that those people had been taken away. What a state we were in! At night, when the vans [of the NKVD] would arrive, you would think, 'Oh, God, are they coming for us or someone else?' On the night of July 17, they came for us." Treivas's husband Grigori Vasilkovskii was executed in prison; she was sent to a camp for female relatives of arrested men.[34]

WOMEN IN THE GULAG

The first stop on the journey to the camps was a prison where the arrested were interrogated, tried, and sentenced. They had no legal rights and no defense attorneys. The purpose of interrogation was to persuade them to sign a confession composed by an NKVD interrogator, and to incriminate others. Those who refused to confess were tortured. The trials that followed were perfunctory exercises, the main purpose of which was to pass sentences that ran from a few years for petty theft to death for those convicted of being an enemy of the state. Statistics on the number and gender of the executed remain fragmentary; it is probable that far more men than women met that fate.

After sentencing, the prisoners were loaded onto trains and taken to labor camps, collectively known by the acronym "Gulag," that were spread across the Soviet Union.[35] Prisoners in the Gulag were required to work; indeed, they built some of the largest construction projects of the 1930s and they manufactured military equipment and consumer goods. Conditions in the camps varied. Those located in the western part of the Soviet Union were devoted to farming or light manufacturing. Prisoners there suffered from the chronic malnutrition that beset all Gulag inmates, but their work was less grueling and the climate easier than in Siberia or the far northwest. Women in the Siberian camps had heavier assignments. Hava Volovich, a Ukrainian journalist, later described her first attempts at cutting peat, which was used for fuel: "We were sent off into the bog to take off the top layer of vegetation. This layer was about eighteen inches thick and soggy with stagnant water. We had to slice it into pieces with our spades, then load it onto stretchers and, up to our ankles or knees in water, carry it forty or fifty yards off to the side."[36]

Female and male prisoners were usually separated in the Gulag. Women lived in separate camps or in their own section within larger complexes and worked with other women, under the supervision of male and female guards. They wore ragged clothing that did not keep out the cold or wet, worked with primitive equipment, lived in dirty, poorly heated barracks, and rarely got enough to eat. They also coped with abuse from guards and from inmates who were guilty of real crimes such as assault, murder, prostitution, and robbery. The so-called criminals operated much as do gangs in U.S. prisons today.

Female prisoners were most likely to survive the Gulag if they were young and healthy, and if they did indoor jobs such as clerical work, cooking, nursing, and sewing. Gulag veterans also remembered that friendships with other female prisoners were crucial, because friends shared food and clothes and gave one another emotional support. Some of these friendships were probably physically intimate as well. It is impossible to say how common lesbianism was, because same-sex love was so stigmatized in Soviet society that Gulag veterans discuss it only as deviant behavior engaged in by criminals.[37]

Prisoners learned to take pleasure in simple things. "Our favorite pastime was storytelling," wrote Vera Shulz, an actor from Moscow. "We would listen with bated breath, transported into another reality. . . . I heard stories by Chekhov, Gorky, Turgenev, Maupassant and others." Tamara Petkevich, an actor in Leningrad (formerly St. Petersburg), remembered taking breaks from work in a hemp-processing plant. "I shall never forget those moments. We lay surrounded by the fantastic moonlit night of Central Asia. It was as if we were floating in the clamorous sea of the steppe, which hummed with the rustling of sand and grass and the chirping of the cicadas. No one spoke."[38]

Survival required women to develop other skills common to concentration-camp inmates. They loafed on the job or faked illnesses to conserve their strength; they made small treasures, such as spoons; they stole needles and other necessities. Some women moved up in the Gulag hierarchy by becoming leaders of their work groups or qualifying for the more skilled, less physically taxing work. These "trustees" sometimes collaborated with the authorities by informing on fellow prisoners. Women also traded sexual favors for privileges. Some became camp prostitutes, servicing multiple partners among the criminals and the guards. Luckier women managed to establish long-term relationships with camp administrators. Some of the women who were sexually active became pregnant, a tragedy for them and their babies, most of whom died quickly in the camps' poorly supplied nurseries.

Veterans of the Gulag believed that women coped better than men with its hardships, because they formed stronger bonds with each other, had greater disease resistance, and could get by on less food. Until the statistics on mortality rates within the various camps have been analyzed, it is impossible to know whether these perceptions were true. We do know that women were more likely than men to be assigned to less physically demanding jobs and to camps located in the more moderate climate zones. These facts alone could account for more of them surviving.

Women also rebelled. Occasionally groups protested, and from time to time, individuals escaped. The most persistent resisters were the so-called "nuns," some of whom were Orthodox nuns who had been arrested after the government ordered all the monasteries dissolved, others of whom were devout Protestants. These religious women took time off from work to pray, and some refused to work on holy days. Veteran revolutionaries, particularly Socialist Revolutionaries, also defied the guards. Sometimes the nuns and the Socialist Revolutionaries got away with such infractions; usually they were severely punished. A few souls remained so adamant that they were executed, a fate some seem to have courted. Other women committed suicide in various ways, the most common being simply to stop struggling to live. In the Gulag, despair was often fatal.

There were free women who worked in the Gulag. Female guards patrolled women's camps, female administrators supervised the guards, and clerks and cooks ran offices and kitchens. In their background and training, these women were probably very similar to male Gulag employees, that is, they were from working-class or peasant families and had elementary-school educations.[39] Former inmates remember the female staffers as brutal, corrupt, and indifferent to the suffering around them. They often describe male guards and wardens in the same way, but it seemed particularly awful to them that women in authority could be as hard-hearted as men. The memoirists seem to have underestimated the capacity of a prison system, particularly one as cruel as the Soviet, to deform the characters of the people it employed.

The Gulag also threw its shadow over people who never came inside its barbed-wire fences. The NKVD rounded up children who had lost both parents to arrest. Liubov Stoliarova, the daughter of working-class people in Khabarovsk, in Siberia, met this fate in 1937. "They took me to a reception-distribution center in Kharkov [in Ukraine], where we lived for three months on starvation ration. . . . Since we were children of political 'enemies of the people,' they used to march us under guard with dogs."[40] The centers served as collection points, where the children were sorted by age (thereby separating brothers and sisters). Older teenagers were sent to the labor camps, younger children to miserable state orphanages. As the numbers of such children swelled, the government set up special orphanages to hold them. Oftentimes the authorities changed these children's names, with the result that relatives who came looking for them could not find them.

Adult relatives of arrested people endured the anguish of being separated from loved ones and not knowing whether they were alive or dead. They also labored under the stigma of being related to "enemies of the people." Former friends avoided them. They had trouble finding or keeping jobs. Anna Egorova, the construction worker on the Moscow metro and amateur pilot, was refused admission to an advanced pilot-training program in 1938 because her brother Vasili had been arrested. She did as many others did, and learned to lie about her personal history. She was fortunate in having valuable skills and a common name. So she managed to become an instructor at a flying club far from Moscow, where no one bothered to check her background.

Many wives, bereft of their husbands' support and ostracized by people who feared to be associated with an "enemy," endured enormous privation. The memoirs of survivors are full of stories of extraordinary pilgrimages over great distances to find food and avoid the authorities. Maria Novikova, whose parents were labeled kulaks during the collectivization in Belgorod, Ukraine, remembered, "How much suffering my mother endured all these years along with us! She dragged us through strangers' houses, naked, hungry. . . . Three of us children died during those years of wanderings. When one would die, my mother would take the corpse and make the sign of the Cross, saying 'Praise to You, O Lord, she's not suffering anymore.'" Moving from place to place, Novikova and her daughter Maria stayed alive.[41]

Survivors also tell of mothers who, despite the odds against them, managed to be reunited with their children after they were freed from their own imprisonment. One such woman was Evgenia Ginzburg, who came out of the Gulag determined to record what she had witnessed. In doing so, she produced one of the great prison-camp memoirs of the twentieth century.

÷ ÷ ÷   EVGENIA GINZBURG (1906–77)   ÷ ÷ ÷

The daughter of a Jewish pharmacist from Moscow, Ginzburg graduated from Kazan University in the early 1920s. After teaching in a school for workers, she became a journalist and Communist Party activist. When the NKVD came for her in 1937, she was married to the mayor of Kazan, Pavel Aksionov, had two sons, and was working for a local newspaper. She was sentenced to ten years' imprisonment for alleged contacts with "Trotskyites." After more than a year in prison, Ginzburg was sent to Kolyma, an enormous complex of labor camps in the far east. Released in 1949 but required to remain in the area, she and her partner Anton Walter, a doctor she had met in the Gulag, settled in the city of Magadan. Ginzburg found work as a kindergarten teacher, adopted an orphaned girl, and reunited with her son Vasili, who had survived internment in an orphanage. She learned that her older son had starved to death during World War II.

Ginzburg had long intended to write about the Gulag. "The collection of material for this book," she declared, "began from the moment when I first crossed the threshold of the NKVD's Inner Prison in Kazan." She described friends who helped orphaned children, and guards who were sometimes merciful, sometimes cruel. She told of reciting poetry in the freight cars that carried the prisoners east and of felling trees at fifty degrees below zero. She chronicled her "cruel journey of the soul" from "naïve young communist idealist into someone who had tasted . . . the fruits of the tree of the knowledge of good and evil." Ginzburg came through that journey able to affirm the possibility of good, even in the midst of consuming evil.[42]

Unfortunately, she did not live to see her memoirs published in her homeland. In the 1960s, she circulated them in typescript among the intelligentsia, to great acclaim, but no Soviet press would touch them. Ginzburg finally sent them abroad, where they appeared as two volumes, *Journey into the Whirlwind* (1967) and *Within the Whirlwind* (1979). She died in Moscow in 1977. Her masterpiece was published in the Soviet Union in 1989.

World War II

On June 22, 1941, Adolf Hitler launched an army of 4 million across the Soviet border. The nation that had been ravaged from within for decades now faced an enemy more formidable and merciless than any yet imagined in the murky depths of Stalin's paranoia. One-third of those who enlisted in the Soviet military, some 8.6 million people, would die. More than 20 million civilians would perish too, from warfare, malnutrition, disease, and Nazi oppression. By the end of the war, 25 million people were homeless and 2.75 million veterans were disabled.[43] One-third of the nation's material resources had been destroyed, and the western third of the USSR, an area equal in size to the entire United States, had been laid waste.

The low point of the war for the Soviets came in the first six months of 1942, when German forces swept through Ukraine, wiping out entire armies. In the summer, the leadership and the nation rallied. By then generals had learned how to manage their enormous armies, officers were formulating new strategies and tactics to counter German attacks, and enlisted men had become battle-hardened. Recognizing this rising competence, Stalin ordered that the political officers in the army be stripped of much of their power so that military commanders could lead more effectively. Meanwhile, the supply situation improved as Soviet factories, many of which had been dismantled and moved east beyond the reach of the invaders, churned out weapons and supplies. Aid from the United States in the form of aircraft, communications equipment, food, industrial raw materials, light trucks, and jeeps also began to arrive.

These improvements in organization, supply, strategy, and tactics were brought to bear in the fall of 1942 in the epic battle of Stalingrad. By January 1943, an Axis army of 290,000 men had been defeated. The next summer, the Soviet army scored a decisive victory in a huge tank battle at Kursk, in Ukraine west of Stalingrad. Although millions more Soviet and Axis troops and civilians would die before the Red Army received the German surrender in Berlin in May 1945, the tide of the war in the east had turned.

It was on the eastern front that German forces suffered their greatest defeats. This was an extraordinary achievement: the Soviet military, which had entered the war riddled with inefficiencies and reeling from Stalin's purges, had defeated one of the best armies in European history. It prevailed because the Soviet system rose to the occasion. Stalin's regime did not become gentler: the NKVD, though reined in, still went about its dirty work, and the recklessness of Soviet commanders produced far higher battlefield casualties than the Germans suffered. But Stalin's agencies relaxed their predatory supervision, administrators at the regional and local levels applied the survival skills acquired in the 1930s to cope with the disruptions of war, and the people resolved to follow their leaders. This resilience, born of desperate necessity, led to battlefield victories and to considerable achievements in military production. In 1943, for example, 24,000 tanks rumbled out of Soviet factories; Germany produced only 17,000 that year. The disparities in 1944 were still greater. John Barber and Mark Harrison report that during the four years of the war, Soviet workers manufactured "100,000 tanks, 130,000 aircraft, 800,000 field guns and mortars and up to half a billion artillery shells, 1.4 million machine guns, 6 million machine pistols and 12 million rifles." This output was roughly equal to that of Great Britain and was half that of the United States, which began the war with a more developed economy than the Soviets and experienced no enemy invasion.[44]

Perhaps German arms production could not keep up with the Soviet because the Germans did not have as skilled a female labor force, for it was mostly women who built the Soviet tanks. They also kept the farms going and served as support troops in the military. In no other combatant nation did women play such a significant part in the war effort, so the most important contribution of Stalinist industrialization to the Soviet victory in World War II may well have been its preliminary mobilization and training of female workers.

WOMEN IN THE ARMED FORCES

More than 1 million women served in the Soviet military during World War II. At their greatest participation in 1943, they were 800,000 to 1,000,000 strong, 8 percent of the regular army. This was by far the largest enlistment of women by any of the combatant nations. By contrast, the U.S. and German militaries contained 400,000 women each and the British 450,000.[45]

Before the war, the government had not intended to recruit women. In the late 1930s, planners decided that, should war come, women would remain on the home front, where they would fill in for men who had been drafted. Women would also participate in civil defense. To that end, the government encouraged them to take courses in first aid, marksmanship, demolitions, and radio communications and invited them to learn to fly at aviation clubs. Immediately after the German invasion, the government called on female doctors and nurses, communications and demolition experts, truck drivers, paratroopers, and engineers to join the army. It turned away tens of thousands of other women who volunteered for service. Some of these then found their way into the service by talking low-ranking officers into accepting them or joining the "people's corps," hastily assembled to defend the major cities.[46]

A few female aviators also refused to take no for an answer. Chief among them was Marina Raskova, who had made a series of record-setting long-distance flights in the 1930s and had afterward received a commission in the Soviet army. In the late summer of 1941, Raskova began working her connections to party bosses, perhaps including Stalin himself. In the fall she received permission to recruit women for three all-female air-corps regiments. Anna Krylova argues that the top leadership saw the women's regiments as a worthwhile experiment; they were proved correct. By the spring of 1942, the graduates were flying combat missions.[47]

As the several hundred female pilots trained, huge losses at the front and women's continuing efforts to join the military were forcing the Soviet government to reconsider its decision to limit women's service. In the spring of 1942, it ordered the Komsomol to recruit female volunteers. Recruitment drives continued periodically through 1944.

The majority of the women in the Soviet army were unmarried, Slavic, and young, as were the men. The women, many of them Komsomol members, were also better educated than rank-and-file infantrymen, most of whom had been conscripted from the peasantry. The women's motives for volunteering were very similar to those of the female soldiers of World War I: they wanted to avenge loved ones killed by the Germans; their friends were going; they thought of war as a great adventure. Above all, female veterans later remembered that they went because they felt they had the same obligation as men to defend their country. Vera Malakhova was a medical student who enlisted with some of her classmates right after the German invasion. "What was there to talk about?" she remembered years later. "We had graduated, they had given us our diplomas. Naturally, it was our duty to go to the front."[48]

The Soviet high command did not assign women to a separate army corps, as did the British and U.S. militaries. Soviet women served in all-female units within the larger command structure or in units that were gender-integrated. They received the same pay as men of their rank and were equally eligible for promotion and benefits. Most female soldiers worked in support services, as they had done during the civil war. That is, they were medical personnel, truck drivers, translators, communications operators, clerks, and cooks. Women constituted about 70 percent of the personnel in some communications and transport units. By 1945, some anti-aircraft regiments were entirely composed of women. They were 41 percent of physicians and 43 percent of feldshers at the front. Women also served as political officers. Officially these were non-combat assignments, but those stationed close to the front often came under fire.[49]

Women also made up 5 to 10 percent of the partisan forces operating behind enemy lines in Belarus and Ukraine. Some fought alongside men, sabotaging communications, sniping at German patrols, carrying messages, and collecting intelligence. Others were double agents, working for the German occupiers while reporting to the anti-German underground. Most partisan women did housekeeping chores, that is, cooking, cleaning, and taking care of children. Some protested against this state of affairs, as did some male officers, and the central command of the partisan forces, headquartered in Moscow, periodically issued orders to involve women as men's equals in operations. The orders and the complaints were usually disregarded. Local commanders, operating far from Moscow, could not be forced to take women on dangerous missions. This arrangement was probably fine with many women, who had fled with their children to the partisans' forest camps to escape from the occupiers, not to fight them.[50]

One hundred and twenty thousand women served in combat units in the regular army. They were armorers, artillery and anti-aircraft personnel, machine and mortar gunners, pilots, and snipers. The 1,885 graduates of the Women's Sniper Training School proved particularly skilled at the cruel arts of their trade. In the summer of 1942, two snipers, Maria Polivanova and Natalia Kovshova, Komsomol members and fast friends, received the Order of the Red Star, the highest Soviet military medal, for killing more than three hundred enemy soldiers. Soon afterward, their platoon was surrounded. Although wounded, Polivanova and Kovshova kept firing until they ran out of ammunition. When German troops closed in, they blew up themselves and some of their captors with hand grenades. Posthumously they were declared Heroes of the Soviet Union, an award equivalent to the U.S. Congressional Medal of Honor. Many other women in the Soviet military performed heroically; by the end of the war, more than a hundred thousand had received medals.[51]

THE FLYERS

The most famous women's units in the Soviet military were the three air-force regiments—the 46th Guards Night Bomber, the 125th Guards Bomber, and the 586th Fighter—founded as a result of Raskova's lobbying in 1941. The female pilots in the British and American armies during World War II flew transport missions; only the Soviet army sent women into air combat. Furthermore, almost all the personnel of the three combat regiments, from the ground crews that kept the planes flying to the officers, were women. The 125th and 586th had male commanders during some of their service; the 46th was led by Lieutenant-Colonel Evdokia Bershanskaia throughout the war. The regiments received no special treatment; they were assigned the same types of aircraft as male units, flew the same missions, and dealt with the same anguish and danger. Polina Gelman, a pilot in the 46th, remembered "a night when I flew with tears on my face. We were pushed back from the Ukraine to the Caucasus. We were bombing the advancing columns of German tanks. They were advancing so fast that we had no time to change bases. We didn't even have maps. It was August and September, we could not harvest grain, so they burned it. And so I was crying. Because it was my country and it was burning."[52]

Much has been written about the 46th Night Bomber Regiment, perhaps because its equipment was antiquated and its missions so dangerous. Its plane was the Po-2, a plywood and fabric biplane that carried the pilot in the forward cockpit and the navigator-bombardier in the rear. Pilots affectionately nicknamed the Po-2 "little farmer," because it could land in small fields and was very maneuverable, able to fly low and dodge away from fighter fire. The women of the 46th flew it at night, navigating with maps when they had them and the aid of whatever landmarks they could see. When they were near their targets, the pilots cut the engines and swooped in low. The navigators released the bombs, the pilots fired up the engines and the Po-2 climbed as fast as it could away from enemy fire and shrapnel rocketing up from the blasts. Crews routinely flew five to ten of these missions per night. The Germans called them "the Night Witches," which the women took as a compliment. By the end of the war, thirty-one of these flyers, 27 percent of flight-crew members in the regiment, had died. Given the conditions in which they fought, it is surprising that casualties were not higher.[53]

The women of the three air regiments, eager to prove their competence, pushed themselves, as did other women assigned to combat units. By 1945, the 46th had flown 24,000 missions and the 125th had dropped 980,000 tons of bombs; each received the honorific "guards regiment" in recognition of their achievements. The pilots of the 586th Fighter Regiment also went beyond the call of duty. Their most celebrated member was Lilia Litviiak, who was reassigned to a male regiment during the battle of Stalingrad. Litviiak was a small, pretty blonde who wore polka-dot scarves over her leather flight jacket, dyed her hair blonde, and painted flowers on her plane. She scored eleven solo kills in sixty-eight combat flights in eleven months, a record that earned her a series of promotions. In June 1943, Litviiak became a flight commander and on August 1, leading her fourth mission of the day, she was shot down. Her remains were not found until 1979.[54]

✣ ✣ ✣   *ANNA TIMOFEEVA-EGOROVA (1918–)*   ✣ ✣ ✣

One of the most accomplished fighter pilots who flew in a male unit was Anna Egorova, the young woman who had worked as a steel-fitter on the Moscow metro, learned to fly at a flying club, and then been refused further training in 1938 because her brother was in the Gulag. When she got that news, Egorova endured a few weeks of despair and a long, aimless train ride. Then she pulled herself together, got off the train at Smolensk, and found a sympathetic local Komsomol head, who signed her up to teach at a flying club. He also advised her, she remembered, "If they ask you to write a resume, don't waste too much paper on brothers. Got it?"[55] With talent, determination, and the support of male mentors, Egorova taught novices and improved her own flying skills. When the war began, she and three friends volunteered for the military, but were turned down.

Refusing to take no for an answer, Egorova went to Moscow. She talked a colonel into assigning her to a flying club in Ukraine, then made the long, dangerous journey south. Once there, she found an air-corps major who was willing to take her as a replacement for pilots lost at the front. She began her military career flying communications and reconnaissance missions in Po-2s and later moved on to the Ilushin-2 fighter-bomber, which provided air support to troops at the front. In 1944 Egorova was promoted to the position of chief navigator of the 805th Attack Aviation Regiment. By then she had flown hundreds of missions through heavy enemy fire, had been wounded often, and had crashed several times. Once she enlisted a Cossack and his horse to pull her battered Po-2 to safety. In August of 1944, Egorova's luck ran out. Leading an attack on German forces near Warsaw, she was shot down, captured, and, close to death, was taken to a prisoner-of-war camp.

Egorova survived, due to the ministrations of the prison doctors, themselves prisoners, and the tender care given her by other inmates. When Soviet troops entered the camp in 1945, she came into the custody of SMERSH, the police agency charged with investigating returned prisoners of war, all of whom Stalin had condemned as traitors for having allowed themselves to be captured. She was freed after ten days, because her friends from the camp had written letters on her behalf attesting to the fact that she had been shot down, rather than surrendering voluntarily. Still recuperating from her injuries, Egorova went back to Moscow.

Soon thereafter, she retired from the military with the rank of lieutenant and a pocket full of honors, including the For Bravery medal and two Order of the Red Banner medals. She accepted the marriage proposal of the commander of her former division, Colonel Viacheslav Timofeev, and settled down to a quiet life raising two sons. Her brother survived the Gulag; other brothers and nephews died in the war.

The stain of having been a POW hung over Egorova. "There's always some vigilant flunky politician," she wrote in the early 1990s, "who feels the need to remind you that you are 'marked,' and you'd better keep a low profile." She refused to submit, fighting instead to have her reputation restored. She prevailed in the 1960s when the government began to acknowledge the injustices done to POWs. In 1965, she was awarded the Soviet Union's highest award, the title Hero of the Soviet Union. When she received the news, Egorova, like many veterans so honored, thought of those who had perished. "As I read the words of this solemn document," she remembered, "I saw the faces of my regimental comrades, who had ascended into the flaming heights, never to return. I heard the formations of Shturmoviks [Il-2s], roaring evermore into the troubled skies of my youth."[56]

GENDER RELATIONS

Soviet soldiers lived with boredom, terror, injuries, death, disease, and dirt. They slept in tents, huts, or dugouts in the earth, went for weeks with little food and sleep, and were dirty most of the time. To keep down the lice, they shaved their heads and picked the bugs out of the seams in their clothes. Women learned to make do with uniforms and boots that were sized for men. They fashioned menstrual cloths from old clothing and adjusted to dropping out of the line of march to relieve themselves. Some women tried to keep in touch with their feminine side by decorating tents with flowers or pictures cut from magazines. Some decorated themselves as well: Lilia Litviiak wore a polka-dot scarf, Anna Egorova a blue one.

Many male soldiers did not want women at the front. They believed the age-old ideas that women could not handle the stresses of war, that they disrupted the camaraderie of the men, and that they brought bad luck. Women in command positions were a still greater affront. These convictions coexisted with shame born of the equally ancient notion that men should protect women from war, not send them into it. "We men had a guilty feeling about girls having to fight; and that feeling is still with me," declared Nikolai Borisovich, the commander of an engineering battalion. Years later he was still haunted by the memory of a female medic lying dead by the side of the road. "A lovely girl with a long braid; she was all covered with mud. The girl's presence among us and her death amidst all that horror, mud, and chaos, it was all so unnatural."[57]

Female veterans wrote in their memoirs that male soldiers accepted them once they proved their competence, that feelings of comradeship developed, and that some of the men, in Egorova's words, "protected" and "helped" the women. This had also been the experience of female soldiers in World War I, the Revolution, and the civil war. In all these wars, working together knit bonds of trust and comradeship. Lelia Novikova, a medic, told journalist Vasili Grossmann in 1942 that before her unit was moved forward into the battle of Stalingrad, the female medics and male soldiers had argued a lot, but once they went into combat, the friction disappeared. "And now the soldiers are saying, 'We are very grateful to our girls,'" Novikova told Grossmann. "We have gone on the attack with our platoon, and crawled side by side with them. We have fed soldiers, given them water, bandaged them under fire. We turned out to be more resilient than the soldiers; we even used to urge them on." The women's courage engendered respect, as did the very significant facts that they were volunteers who had chosen to subject themselves to the horrors of the front and who were there with the support of the authorities.[58]

Although military regulations prohibited sexual relations between male and female soldiers, people found a way. "I was young," remembered Lidia Kravits, a partisan in Belarus, "and like many young women I thirsted for love." Death was ever-present and pleasures were few, making sex that much more appealing. Some of the couples that met at the front stayed together after the war, and veterans remembered such marriages as particularly close, enduring ones.[59]

Sex in the military was also sometimes predatory. In their memoirs, female veterans report incidents of sexual harassment, most of which they say they successfully rebuffed. Rape, which undoubtedly occurred, is not discussed in the sources. Veterans did talk about "front marriages" between officers, particularly commanders, and women assigned to their units. Military regulations outlawed such liaisons, but many officers declined to enforce the rules. As a result, commanders often took "field wives," much to the disgust of lower-ranking soldiers, female as well as male. Women resented the fact that the "wives" got better rations and lighter work loads than women not so well connected, and they denounced them as little better than prostitutes. This criticism was not always justified, for some of the wives had been coerced into living with their commanding officers. Others, no doubt, had not.

WOMEN ON THE HOME FRONT

The great majority of Soviet women contributed to the war effort on the home front. There they worked alongside men in civil defense, maintaining barrage balloons, watching for enemy aircraft, and operating searchlights and anti-aircraft batteries during bombing raids. Anna Ostroumova-Lebedeva, a Leningrad artist, wrote in her diary in August 1941, "In our building an around-the-clock watch has been organized. . . . Each person keeps watch two hours on the stairs leading to the attic. It's light there, and one can sew, darn and read." Meanwhile, 150,000 women in Moscow were digging a labyrinth of anti-tank trenches around the city.[60] After the German bombers flew away, women and men fought fires and removed unexploded munitions. They also searched for survivors in the rubble. Most of these workers were volunteers serving during time off from their regular jobs.

In those regular jobs, women were more important to the Soviet economy than ever before, because so many men had been sent to the military and because women who had not been employed before joined the paid-labor force during the war. Such women were not all volunteers; beginning in February 1942, the government drafted unemployed women aged sixteen to fifty into jobs in agriculture, construction, manufacturing, and transportation. The feminization of the workforce that followed was substantial. The percentage of women among non-agricultural workers climbed from 39 percent in 1940 to 57 percent in 1943. In the same period, the percentage of women in the American paid-labor force increased from 25 to 37 percent. There were still more women working in certain geographic regions and economic sectors. In Moscow, women had been 46.6 percent of the labor force in 1939; they were 63 percent in 1945. In Leningrad in December 1942, 80 percent of all factory workers were women. Occupations and manufacturing sectors with predominantly female workforces before the war became even more feminized: by 1945, 80 to 90 percent of the workers in light industry were women. Women were 52 percent of collective farmers in 1941, 80 percent in 1945. Even in occupations in which men had previously been in great majority, the numbers of women grew. By 1943, the majority of tractor drivers were female; by 1944, 41 percent of coal miners in the Donets Basin of southern Ukraine were women.[61]

Female workers moved from one type of employment to another to meet war needs. Clerks became lathe operators and teachers learned to drive trolleys. Women also moved geographically, fleeing the front in the first years of the war for towns in the rear to which factories were relocated, and then returning to the liberated west as the Soviet army drove the Germans out. Women moved upward in the labor force as well, into skilled blue-collar jobs and managerial positions vacated by men. This was especially true on the collective farms, where women in large numbers became mechanics and brigade leaders.

Promotions into positions once held by men brought higher wages, but no raise in pay could compensate for the enormous hardships of life during the war. Like the soldatki of World War I, Soviet wives suffered financially because they lost the support of their husbands' incomes when the men were drafted. As in the past, the government promised to help; as in the past, the allotments were lower than most husbands' peacetime pay and were often late in coming. The government also cruelly removed from the rolls of military dependents the wives of the millions of Soviet POWs held by the Germans.

Women coped with worsening working conditions as well. Insistent on maximizing production, the government suspended health and safety regulations and increased penalties for absenteeism. Women worked ten- to twelve-hour days for weeks on end. They also took physically taxing jobs once reserved for men, such as lumbering, steel-making, and manufacturing heavy equipment. Valentina Bushueva remembered loading logs onto trains bound for Leningrad: "You lift the log on your shoulders and carry it along the ladder to the cars. And don't even dream of looking around! The commander of our group would be watching. . . . We worked that way for twelve hours at a stretch. Fifty minutes work, ten minutes rest. One month—day shift; the next—night shift. We lived in a dugout; inside there were communal bunk beds that slept sixty people. . . . No holidays, no days off, nothing of the sort, no let up."[62]

Peasant women endured equally grueling conditions because so many male peasants were drafted into the army and the industrial labor force. Between 1941 and 1944 the number of able-bodied men working on the collective farms dropped from 16.9 million to 3.6 million.[63] Women, older men, and children took their places; those too old or young to work in the sprawling grain and potato fields tended family gardens. In Siberia, native women cared for the reindeer herds and took the fishing boats out to sea. All this work was made more taxing by the fact that the army had requisitioned trucks, tractors, and horses. Growing shortages of spare parts and fuel then made it difficult to keep the equipment that was left running.

The women least affected by the war were the wives of top party officials and generals, many of whom were evacuated to places far from the invaders where they received the best housing and consumer goods available. The millions of less privileged women mended again oft-mended clothes, got by with little soap and water, coped with power outages, and heated their homes with firewood they gathered themselves. Peasant women made difficult journeys to the towns to sell or trade their produce for manufactured goods. Still more challenging was the crisis in the food supply.

Because the war was fought on the best Soviet farmland, because so many peasants were drafted and so many farm machines sat idle for lack of spare parts, and because the government gave first priority to feeding the troops, food supplies for civilians dwindled. Most urban women subsisted on bread; rural women lived on potatoes. City dwellers turned vacant lots into kitchen gardens and traded food with people from the countryside. These efforts and the government's rationing system beat back starvation in most of the Soviet Union, but they could not prevent chronic malnutrition and the diseases that accompanied it—influenza, malaria, pneumonia, scurvy, typhus, and tuberculosis. Nor could they save the most vulnerable—children, the infirm, and the old—who died by the millions.

Women closest to the front suffered the most. In Leningrad, under siege from the summer of 1941 to the summer of 1944, 3 million people perished from the bombardment and from starvation. Millions died in areas under German occupation as well. In the Baltics, Belarus, and Ukraine, the invaders rounded up millions of Jews for immediate execution or shipment to the death camps. Included were children plucked from the orphanages. They also raided the orphanages for teenagers who could be sent, along with millions of adults, to be slave laborers in Germany. Most of the deported women became factory workers, but Hitler also wanted to help out German housewives, so in 1942 he ordered his commissars to deport half a million Ukrainian women, aged eighteen to thirty-five, to work as servants in German homes.[64]

Those people they did not execute or deport, the occupiers terrorized. They seized peasants' crops and animals, kept rations at starvation levels, and, in reprisal for partisan attacks, destroyed entire villages. In the time-honored tradition of armies, they raped captive women and forced some to become their lovers. Karel Berkhoff has found that the Germans and their allies fathered ten thousand children in Ukraine alone. Some of these babies were born of consensual relationships, for local women, desperate for food and willing to make the best deal available to them, became collaborators. In retaliation for the depredations visited on their people, Soviet soldiers driving toward Berlin in the last months of the war gang-raped German and Polish women.[65]

THE EFFECTS OF THE WAR ON THE FAMILY AND GENDER IDEAS

As the front ebbed and flowed across the western landscape, many died, many fled, and in the chaos, families became separated. By 1943, almost seven hundred thousand homeless children were living in orphanages.[66] Women who managed to keep their loved ones nearby found that the double shift had become far more burdensome because their hours at work were so much longer. Childcare became a struggle as daycare centers and schools closed intermittently because of air raids, power outages, and shortages of teachers. Moscow's entire school system shut down for the academic year 1941–42. Many of the teenagers released from school found work: the legal minimum age for employment was fourteen, but children as young as twelve were often hired, and their income made a crucial contribution to their families' survival. Other youngsters roamed the streets, adding to the crime wave that swept through Soviet cities during the war. For mothers, therefore, the burdens of endless work were exacerbated by fears about their children.

Those who were married coped with long separations. Soldiers at the front worried about how their wives were managing without them and whether they were being faithful. Soldiers in all the armies of World War II had these worries, in part because they knew that people were taking a more relaxed attitude toward marital fidelity during the crisis. Given the shortage of men on the Soviet home front, and the manifold difficulties women faced providing for themselves and their children, it seems unlikely that many wives had the time or the opportunity to have love affairs. Instead, they lived in constant fear of joining the ranks of war widows. Millions did.

Soviet authorities worried about the war's effects on the family. People married in great numbers in the summer of 1941, before the draft carried the men away, but thereafter the rates of marriages and births fell precipitously and remained low until 1944. When men began to return in that year, the birthrate rose, as did the number of divorces, for the years of separation and the post-traumatic stress that men and women experienced made the readjustment to living together very difficult for many.

Wishing to encourage marriage and childbearing, the government took a familiar course: it revised the marriage law yet again. The Family Law of 1944 attempted to discourage divorce by raising the fees charged for it and extending the period of time required to complete the process. Realizing that the immense losses of young men in the war meant that many women would never marry, and wanting to encourage them to have children anyway, the lawmakers promised government-funded benefits to single mothers. The law also lengthened pregnancy leave to seventy-seven days, raised the food rations allotted to pregnant and nursing mothers, and cut the fees charged by daycare centers to families with more than two children. The new marriage law also reaffirmed an income tax, first instituted in 1941, on people of childbearing age who did not have children. To prevent single mothers from breaking up marriages by claiming child support from the fathers of their children, the drafters of the code prohibited such claims.

It was also in 1944 that the Soviet government launched the much-publicized "mother-heroine" campaigns. Women who bore more than two children received cash bonuses on the birth of each additional child. The award rose to the substantial sum of five thousand rubles when the tenth baby arrived. Women with seven or more children also received medals and were written up in the Soviet press. The heroine-mother awards continued on after the war, becoming the source of many Soviet jokes while having little impact on the birthrate.

The authorities need not have feared that the war had caused permanent changes in Soviet family values. For most people, it had made family seem more precious than ever. Virtually all the surviving female soldiers, who had lived the most unconventional lives during the war, did as Egorova did, that is, they left the army as soon as they could and tried to build a peacetime life. "When the war was over," remembered Zinaida Korzh, a medic from Minsk, "I wanted to forget about it as quickly as possible." Her comrade, Tamara Umniagina, agreed. "We'd had enough of it, the girls who served at the front." Zinaida's sister Olga, also a medic, remembered that on Victory Day, May 8, 1945, "I felt then as if I had wakened from a terrible dream. . . . Suddenly we all began to talk about the future. We talked about love. We all wanted to love. And although we had lived through a grim war, nevertheless we all managed to give birth to beautiful children. That's the most important thing."[67]

Reconstruction and Late Stalinism, 1945–53

The period between the end of World War II and Stalin's death in March 1953 began in victory celebrations across the Soviet Union. The joy soon dissipated in the struggle to mourn the dead, heal the wounded, and rebuild the country. The war had ravaged a generation: three-quarters of the military dead were men aged nineteen to thirty-five; 90 percent of the draftees born in 1921 were killed. Severe shortages of food, consumer goods, and housing continued for years. The people of southern Russia and Ukraine knew famine again in 1946–47, because of drought and government mismanagement. But by the early 1950s, most of the country's economic infrastructure had been restored. Social reconstruction also proceeded rapidly. People got back in touch with their kin, married, and bore their "beautiful children," as Olga Korzh put it. Among those new mothers were 1,700,000 single women who registered for government benefits between 1945 and 1950.[68]

It is a tragic irony that the process of restoration included recriminations against the women who had served in the military. Some people said that the female veterans had become lesbians. Others spread rumors about heterosexual liaisons at the front. "Who have you got married to?" wailed Tamara Umniagina's new mother-in-law to her soldier son in 1945. "An army girl. Why, you have two younger sisters. Who will marry them now?" Similar aspersions had been cast on the members of the women's battalions in 1917 and on civil war veterans. Some returning World War II veterans also bore the disgrace of having been captured. Anna Egorova wrote bitterly, "I hadn't returned from the war like a victorious knight on his horse, but amid shame and accusations." Most women learned to keep their military service a secret. The large-scale enlistment of women in the military ended, never to be renewed.[69]

Beginning in 1943, the government, realizing that peace was coming, began to stress once again the importance of women attending to their domestic tasks. This theme reverberated through the post-war years, but it was not accompanied by the massive layoffs of working women that happened in the United States and Britain. The Soviet government and people alike believed that women had to play a crucial role in the economy.[70] There was no choice, for the deaths of so many made the need for female labor even greater than in the past. The war also strengthened the leadership's conviction that the military, and the heavy industrial sector on which it depended, should receive a substantial proportion of future resources. Women's double shift—working outside the home and doing most of the housework—would continue.

Some women yielded their jobs to returning men. This was particularly true in the countryside, where men reclaimed leadership positions on the collective farms and climbed aboard the tractors again. The percentage of women among heavy machine operators fell from a high of 55 percent in 1943 to a mere 5 percent in 1949. For years after the war, women's advancement in the paid-labor force was also negatively affected by the policy of giving male veterans preferential treatment in education, employment, and recruitment into the party. Women did keep some of the gains that they had made in the professions, in industrial management, and the middle ranks of government bureaucracies.[71]

In 1945, many Soviet citizens hoped that the easing of the dictatorship that had occurred during the war would continue, and that the government would reward the people for the supreme achievement of defeating the Nazis by granting them more liberty. They were soon disappointed. In 1945, when victory was certain, the Politburo tightened the reins again. Returning POWs were executed or shipped off to the Gulag. Ethnic groups from Ukraine and the Caucasus—Balkars, Chechens, Crimean Tatars, Ingush, Kalmyks, Karachais, Kemshils, Kurds, Meshketian Turks, and Volga Germans—were deported from their homelands on charges that they had collaborated with the enemy. Later in the 1940s, intellectuals, particularly Jewish ones, were arrested on bogus accusations of treason. This continuing persecution made the last years of Stalin's rule a time of high anxiety and deep disappointment in the Soviet Union.

Conclusions

Stalin died on March 5, 1953. Evgenia Ginzburg was in Magadan when she heard the news. "I collapsed on the table, sobbing loudly. My body shook. It was my unwinding, not only for these last months spent awaiting my third arrest; I was also weeping for two lost decades. In the space of a minute the whole procession of events swept before my eyes. All the tortures and all the prison cells. All the long files of those who had suffered the final penalty, and the countless legions of those who had been made to suffer. And my own life destroyed by his diabolical will. And my boy, my dead son."[72]

Women who had been spared Stalin's assaults mourned his death for very different reasons. Many of them believed that he had been a stern but benevolent leader who had looked after his people and led them in their greatest achievement, the defeat of Hitler. Pasha Angelina spoke for these women when, in her 1948 autobiography, she described Stalin as "the man who raised my whole generation, a man who is associated with everything that is good in your lives and mine, with all our hopes for the future."[73] Ginzburg understood that it would take generations to count the dead and weigh their suffering against the achievements of the Soviet Union under Stalin's rule. This painful moral calculus is still ongoing today.

The Stalin regime institutionalized Bolshevik feminism in a fashion that suited its purposes, and in so doing propagated the ideals of emancipation broadly and changed public attitudes profoundly. Education and women's participation in the paid-labor force expanded quickly in the 1930s. This enabled women to make crucial contributions to the construction of heavy industry, social services, and government bureaucracy during that decade, even while doing most of the housework and childcare. When war came, the majority of the workers who produced the weapons the soldiers fought with and the food they ate were women. After the war, they labored on to rebuild the nation.

Individual women's experiences of these years ran the gamut from Ginzburg to Angelina. Many suffered from overwork and government persecution. Many became the first in their families to get an education or hold a white-collar job. Many took up projects that had engaged earlier generations of female activists, such as building daycare centers and teaching in adult literacy programs. Others volunteered for service in new industries and on the frontiers. By so doing they greatly expanded women's participation in the public world. Soviet women could feel tremendous pride in what they had accomplished during the Stalin years. With the dictator dead, they could also dare to hope that better times were coming.

7

MAKING BETTER LIVES

1953–91

The communist leaders who succeeded Stalin ran the Soviet system without the Terror. They maintained the dictatorship, but reined in the police and sought to build public support by raising the standard of living. They also pursued an ambitious agenda of controlling client states in Eastern Europe and competing with the United States for influence around the world. In the 1970s, the Soviet economy faltered under the strain of this expensive foreign policy and of inefficiencies caused by centralization and bureaucratization. A new leadership, committed to wholesale reform, came to power in 1985. By 1991, these men had stumbled into dismantling the Soviet Union itself.

Life improved for millions of Soviet women after 1953. The programs and gender ideas established in the 1930s continued, with better funding for social services and education. Although gender norms that had weakened during the war strengthened and political leadership remained a male preserve, many women rose to middle management in government and the economy, and still more worked in the professions. Wages increased, and across the Soviet Union there were more consumer goods and greatly improved housing, communications, and transportation. The regime had long sung the praises of women who kept cozy homes. Finally that ideal came within reach of millions of Soviet people.

From the late 1950s onward, professional women—academics, journalists, physicians—maintained a government-sponsored critique of the remaining hardships in women's lives. Central to their complaints was the persistence of the double shift. Decades after the government had pledged to lighten the burdens of housework and childcare, social services remained inadequate. Publicly these critics had to forswear talking about the gender assumptions that affected policy-making and thereby contributed to inequities in employment and promotion. Privately, some of them did just that. So when, in the late 1980s, reform began, there were women ready to launch a feminist critique of the Soviet system and to begin a new phase of independent activism.

Khrushchev and the Woman Question, 1955–64

Reforms came quickly after Stalin died. In 1953 and 1954, the new leaders reduced the power of the police and began releasing prisoners from the Gulag. They also eased press censorship and promised to provide more consumer goods and lighten the load on the peasants. By 1955, Nikita Khrushchev had maneuvered his way into the top position, first secretary of the Communist Party. He set out to mobilize the population to work diligently and enthusiastically to fulfill the government's plans for economic growth.

Although Khrushchev never made the woman question a high priority, his administration did institute important changes. In 1955 it legalized abortion, on the grounds that backstreet procedures were harming women's health. In the late 1950s it lowered the fees charged for divorce and increased paid maternity leave from 77 to 112 days. The government also instituted stricter enforcement of protective labor laws, which benefited some women while excluding others from better-paid jobs.

Accompanying these improvements was the most unfettered consideration of the woman question since the 1920s. *Rabotnitsa* and *Krest'ianka,* the national women's magazines, had bemoaned the burdens of the double shift throughout the Stalinist period. Now, with Khrushchev's encouragement, magazines such as *Literaturnaia gazeta* (Literary Gazette) and *Trud* (Labor) joined the women's press in calling for expanded social services. They also wrote about the dismal working conditions some women endured and lamented the fact that women on average earned less than men. Some writers declared that husbands should stop bossing their wives around and do more housework and childcare.[1]

The first secretary himself joined in, charging that sexism pervaded the Soviet system. Women suffered from the double shift, Khrushchev charged, because the Soviet Union had been too poor in the past to provide adequate services and labor-saving household appliances, and also because men discriminated against women. The result of the prejudice, he asserted, was that very few women occupied leadership positions. This was an extraordinary charge for a member of Stalin's leadership to make; on the handful of earlier occasions when the men of the Politburo had talked about the woman question, they had congratulated themselves on all they had done for Soviet women. Khrushchev may have been sensitized to sexist behavior by his wife Nina, a Bolshevik who had served in the Zhenotdel during the civil war. Perhaps he also discussed discrimination with Elena Furtseva, an official in the Moscow party organization who was one of his political allies. Furtseva served on the party Presidium (i.e., the Politburo), the first woman ever to do so. She was also minister of culture in the early 1960s.

To set a better example, Khrushchev ordered more women appointed to government committees and regional soviets. He approved the creation of a training program for female cosmonauts and personally selected Valentina Tereshkova, a textile worker, to be the first woman to orbit the Earth. Khrushchev also authorized the establishment of "women's soviets" (*zhensovety*) to involve women in improving their communities.

Enthusiastic promoters of the zhensovety hailed them as reincarnations of the Zhenotdel. There were similarities. The Zhenotdel and the zhensovety consisted of networks of committees led by female communists. Both enrolled tens of thousands of women in community-service projects. Both advised women on getting the social services they needed. They suffered from similar weaknesses, too. The zhensovety's relationship to the party was even more vaguely defined than the Zhenotdel's had been. It was not clear whether they were party organizations or a revival of the *obshchestvennitsy* movement, with a membership no longer confined to the wives of elite men. Furthermore, no zhensovety were established in Moscow or Leningrad, on the grounds that women's consciousness was already sufficiently high there. Rather, they were concentrated in rural areas, smaller cities, and non-European republics, far from the centers of power, where their members had to address their complaints and suggestions to local leaders with limited authority and resources.[2]

NINA KHRUSHCHEVA (1900–84) AND VALENTINA TERESHKOVA (b. 1937)

The two Soviet women best known in the West during Khrushchev's rule were the leader's wife and the woman he sent into space. American journalists built their coverage of them on Cold War stereotypes. They made fun of Khrushcheva's matronly figure and unfashionable clothing and trivialized Tereshkova's flight as a propaganda stunt. Soviet women, reporters suggested, were either frumpy peasants or party puppets. Had they done their homework, these people might have understood that Khrushcheva and Tereshkova exemplified Soviet gender ideals that valorized both homemaking and breaking down gender barriers. This was a complexity then unknown in the dominant gender regimes of the United States and Western Europe.

Khrushcheva was the daughter of Ukrainian peasants. She graduated from secondary school in 1919, joined the Communist Party in 1920, and for a short time headed the Zhenotdel in western Ukraine. She met Khrushchev in 1922, they married, and when his career blossomed, she retired from party work to rear their three children. Khrushcheva remained true to communism's egalitarian principles after her husband became a party boss. Her son Sergei remembered, "She tried to bring us up so that we didn't go around thinking we were the children of powerful people and could do whatever we wanted." Khrushcheva also hired tutors to teach her children English and music, filled their home with books, and took the family to the opera and ballet. In short she was an exemplary Soviet first lady, a well-educated, culturally sophisticated, strong-willed communist who devoted herself to her family.[3]

Tereshkova was also a lower-class woman who rose to prominence. Like Pasha Angelina, she became a highly publicized pioneer in a field dominated by men. She was a textile worker in the Iaroslavl area, a member of the Komsomol, and an amateur parachute jumper at a local flying club when, on April 12, 1961, Yuri Gagarin became the first person to fly beyond Earth's atmosphere. Tereshkova and many other young women, who had grown up idealizing the female pilots of the past, were fascinated by these new heroes of aviation. "Everything fell into place . . . when I read that Gagarin was a student of an aerospace club, just like I was," Tereshkova remembered. "And then I decided. I'll be a cosmonaut."[4] Her parachuting experience was an important qualification, because cosmonauts ejected from their spacecraft on re-entry and parachuted to earth.

When letters from women requesting admission to cosmonaut training began flooding in, the administrators of the spaceflight program decided to admit a few in order to score points against the United States in the space race. A small group, Tereshkova among them, trained with the men, under the tutelage of and with the support of experienced cosmonauts. "In general they accepted me into their 'cosmic family,'" Tereshkova remembered, "without even a shadow of coldness or special accommodation to the 'weaker sex.'"[5] Khrushchev then chose Tereshkova from among the four women who had performed best during training, because she had charmed him and because she was from the working class.

A photograph of Valentina Tereshkova widely circulated after her flight.
Prints and Photographs Division, Library of Congress.

VALENTINA TERESHKOVA

In a 1964 memoir, Tereshkova remembered the first minutes of her flight:

"The titanic force of the boiling gases [the exhaust of the rocket carrying her up] tears away the Earth's gravitation. I feel like the weight [of g-forces] reached its limit, but it still grows. How much time has passed since the start? A minute? An hour? A day? I cannot collect my thoughts; I know I have to, but I cannot.

'Chaika, Chaika [her call name, meaning "seagull"], everything is excellent, the machine is working great.'

I shake with surprise. The voice of Yury Gagarin sounds so near, as if he's sitting next to me, as an instructor in the right seat of the plane. I don't answer at once; maybe because of the cheering words of my friend, maybe because the flight to orbit is over, and the pressure has disappeared, as it melted under the warm wave spreading in my body. Breathing becomes easy.

I open my eyes and look out of the illuminator. (The illuminator is the porthole.) In a loud voice, I comment about what I see. 'I am Chaika. I see the horizon. There is a blue stripe. This is the Earth. How beautiful it is! Everything is going well.'

Hello universe!"

SOURCE: VALENTINA TERESHKOVA, "THE 'FIRST LADY OF SPACE' REMEMBERS: EXCERPTS FROM VALENTINA TERESHKOVA'S MEMOIRS *STARS ARE CALLING*, MOSCOW 1964," *QUEST: THE HISTORY OF SPACEFLIGHT QUARTERLY* 10, NO. 2 (2003): 19. THE TRANSLATION HAS BEEN SLIGHTLY EDITED HERE BY BARBARA CLEMENTS. REPRINTED BY PERMISSION.

On June 16, 1963, Vostok 6 took her up. By the time she bounced back to earth on the 19th, she had flown 70 hours and 40 minutes, longer than all the American astronauts to date combined. The Soviet press hailed her mission as a demonstration of gender equality in the USSR. In fact, most of the men in the Soviet and U.S. space programs believed that women were emotionally and physically unsuited for space flight, so twenty more years would elapse before another woman, the American Sally Ride, went into orbit. "They forbade me from flying, despite all my protests and arguments," Tereshkova remembered. "After once being in space, I was desperately keen to go back there. But it didn't happen." She spent the rest of the 1960s on publicity tours at home and abroad. She also continued her military training, graduating from Zhukovskii Aviation Academy in 1969. Thereafter, Tereshkova became a high-profile Soviet representative, praising her country's progressive programs for women at international meetings and pressing the case for similar social services everywhere.[6]

Brezhnev and the Woman Question, 1964–82

By October 1964, Communist Party leaders had tired of Khrushchev's bombast, his poorly planned reforms, his misadventures in foreign policy, and his increasingly autocratic behavior. They forced him to resign and replaced him with a coalition led by Leonid Brezhnev. Under Brezhnev the Politburo continued to experiment with reform, but it prized restraint and careful planning, as Khrushchev had not. The new leadership greatly increased spending on the military and invested more in agriculture. Wages improved, as did social services. Consumer goods remained in short supply, so to meet pent-up demand the government permitted a black market in imported clothing and electronics. It also brought in foreign investment to pump up the economy and it permitted Soviet students to study abroad. Contacts with the world outside the Eastern Bloc countries of Bulgaria, Czechoslovakia, East Germany, Hungary, Poland, and Romania, first encouraged by Khrushchev, expanded.

Brezhnev and his colleagues understood, as Soviet leaders had since the 1920s, that the double shift limited women's productivity in the workplace and caused them to keep their families small. They considered both outcomes undesirable. The Soviet Union, they believed, required increasing labor productivity and robust population growth to raise the standard of living and keep up in the Cold War's arms race. The leaders of the Brezhnev era also saw that Stalin's coercive measures—outlawing abortion and making divorce more difficult to obtain—had not remedied the situation. Most urban women were still having no more than two children and were also working fewer hours than men because of their domestic duties.

The government, following Khrushchev's example, attempted to replace the sticks with carrots. To alleviate the double shift, it improved social services. By 1970, 50 percent of urban children were enrolled in daycare, and the numbers continued to climb thereafter. Subsidies paid during maternity and family leave were raised, and welfare payments for children in low-income families were instituted. In the early 1980s the government extended fully paid maternity leave to eight weeks before the baby's birth and eight weeks after. Women could take an additional ten months off without loss of seniority at work. The government also increased pensions paid to retirees, the great majority of whom were women. These improvements mitigated the long-standing problem of women, by virtue of their lower wages, being financially dependent on their husbands, and they provided support for the millions of single women of all ages. They were equivalent to or superior to those provided by most Western European countries and far superior to the minimal benefits available to American women.[7]

The government also eased the restrictions on divorce. It issued new laws in 1965 and 1968 that simplified divorce procedures and reduced fees. The 1968 code also legalized community property and instituted no-fault divorce, waiving the requirement for a court appearance for couples with no children. Courts were still to oversee the divorce and custody arrangements of parents with minor children. These revisions kept the Soviet Union at the forefront of European nations in the permissiveness of its divorce laws, a position it had held since the Revolution.

These improvements in benefits were accompanied by a propaganda campaign in the arts and the electronic and print media, which restated the Stalinist credo on the importance of family life. Now the government put more stress on mothering, rather less on women's civilizing of their husbands. Women were told that kindness and care-giving came more naturally to them than to men, and were more important to them emotionally. So, although it was important for women to work in the wider world and to develop their own interests, being a mother would be the most fulfilling part of their lives. These ideas required very little selling, for they were widely believed by Soviet people and, indeed, by people across the European world.

There was a crucial difference between the Soviet and the Western European or American rhapsodies on domesticity, however: the Soviet ones also sang the praises of women's work outside the home. That work was seen by the regime and by many in the nation as crucial to women's sense of self and to their equality in the larger world. The goal of public policy and social services, therefore, should be to assist women to enjoy fulfilling work and family lives. In a short history entitled *Woman in the Development of Socialist Society*, Z. E. Novikova wrote that "the improvement of the social position of women and their development as individuals demands purposeful and objective work, so that they receive new, always more beneficial possibilities for successfully combining their professional and social activities with maternity, family, and everyday life."[8]

To assist in the attainment of all this, the Brezhnev government sponsored academic study of women's problems. The result was the largest collection of scholarly studies on women's work and family lives, as well as of public opinion on gender issues, produced since the 1920s. Differences of opinion quickly surfaced. Specialists in education, many of them men, declared that women should concentrate on their families. Sociologists, many of them women, disagreed. They argued that there should be more equality between spouses, that men should do their share of housework, that women needed to work outside the home in order to realize themselves as individuals, and that being involved in the larger world would make them better mothers. Some academics even criticized Marxist economic theory for not valuing the contribution that domestic labor made to the national economy.

The revival of feminism to the west affected the academic study of the woman question in the Brezhnev era. This so-called "second-wave feminism" emerged in the United States in the 1960s and quickly grew into an international movement that broadened feminist theory, expanded educational and employment opportunities, overturned discriminatory laws, and propagated more egalitarian norms of family life. Its theoreticians paid a great deal of attention to the Marxist critique of "bourgeois feminism" and to the Soviet program of women's emancipation, much of which they admired. They also pointed out its shortcomings, particularly its subordination of women's emancipation to other government priorities and its inattention to lingering sexism in the family and the larger society. Brezhnev's government responded by encouraging journalists and scholars to publicize the many Soviet accomplishments. To support research into Western feminist thought, a few libraries established special collections, accessible only to approved people, and in short order, studies confirming the righteousness of the Soviet system began appearing.

Even as they followed the party line, some of those permitted to read the germinal works of second-wave feminism found them very persuasive. More than half the feminist activists from Moscow interviewed by Valerie Sperling in the 1990s reported that research into Western feminism in the Brezhnev years had awakened them to the pervasiveness of sexism in the Soviet Union. Some read as well the histories of women in Russia being written in the West and were inspired by the pre-revolutionary feminists, who had been demonized in Soviet historiography. Gradually and surreptitiously, the intelligentsia's connection to international feminist thought, so strong in Russia before 1917, was being revived.[9]

Urban Women's Lives, 1953–85

EDUCATION AND PARTICIPATION IN THE PAID-LABOR FORCE

The post-war decades saw many significant improvements in Soviet women's lives. Among the most important were those in education. There were differences from region to region and between various ethnic groups, but by the 1970s the majority of Soviet women had at least a high-school education, and females made up half of all students in higher education.[10] This was a substantial accomplishment in a society where, sixty years earlier, most women had been unable to sign their names.

Women's work in these decades changed as well. By the 1960s, the majority of Soviet people were living in urban areas, in part because of a huge migration of peasant women out of the countryside. Most of these women went to work in blue-collar jobs, replacing urban women who moved into white-collar jobs. By the mid-1960s, women were 75 percent of employees in the civil service, educational, medical, and retail sectors, and 45 percent of industrial workers. Women all over the European world in the second half of the twentieth century were making the same choice, because white-collar work, although often as poorly paid as blue-collar, was less grueling, brought higher status, and was easier to combine with family responsibilities. Factory work for Soviet women was made still more difficult by the fact that, as in the Stalin period, automation came first to industries with a predominantly male work force and to jobs held mostly by men.[11]

Women's presence in managerial and administrative positions and in the professions increased steadily, putting the Soviet Union far ahead of Western European and North American nations. In 1974, for example, 70 percent of Soviet physicians were women, compared to 7 percent of

American ones.[12] Thousands of Soviet women worked as architects, judges, lawyers, scientists, and university professors. Similar advances were made by women in the Eastern Bloc and in China, the communist governments of which had imported the Soviet program of women's emancipation. The disparity between the capitalist democracies and the socialist nations began to diminish in the late 1970s as second-wave feminism broke down discriminatory practices and inspired young women to enter the professions, but it did not disappear.

The gender hierarchy of the Soviet workforce established in the Stalin years persisted. It too was adopted by the Eastern European client states, and so women across the region, who enjoyed such a significant edge over Western women in gaining access to the professions, still bumped up against a "glass ceiling." Male engineers and architects headed the big construction projects while female ones made the blueprints. The majority of judges were women, while the more prestigious position of prosecutor went to men. Women dominated sectors of the economy—the arts, education, food processing and sales, medicine, textile and clothing manufacture— that were poorly funded and therefore poorly paid. Furthermore, the demands of the double shift meant that married women in the Eastern Bloc did not have time to upgrade their job qualifications by taking training programs or correspondence courses. They also chose jobs that would be less demanding of their time; such jobs, as in the West, were lower-ranking and lower-paying. As a consequence, in the 1960s and 1970s, Soviet women earned 60 to 70 percent of what men earned, a disparity little changed since the 1920s. It should be noted that the same gender gap in wages prevailed in the West in these decades. In the United States in 1965, women were earning 59 percent of men's wages.[13]

The glass ceiling was still lower in the ruling communist parties of Eastern Europe. Female membership in the Soviet party stood at 26.5 percent (4.5 million women) in 1981. Most of these women worked in local committees running community outreach activities, a role similar to that played by female members of political parties in the Western democracies. Such work had been assigned to communist women for so long that it carried the stigma of being women's work and was therefore a professional dead end. Between 2 and 4 percent of the members of the party's Central Committee, which consisted of the most important national and provincial leaders, were female in the post-war decades. Most of these women were tokens appointed to demonstrate the party's bona fides on women's issues.[14] Elena Furtseva, who had worked her way up in the Moscow party organization, was one of very few exceptions.

DAILY LIFE IN THE CITIES

THE BURGEONING ELITE

As in the past, those benefiting most from the rising standard of living in the 1960s and 1970s were the highest-ranking people in the party, government, and professions and their families. The regime prided itself on its egalitarianism, so its leaders did not parade their wealth, as did the capitalist barons of the West. They received modest salaries, which were supplemented by access to the best housing, transportation, consumer goods, and medical care. Their children went to the best schools. Beneath the leadership in the hierarchy of privilege was an expanding group of professionals and middle managers, and below them the working class. This class structure was very similar to that prevailing elsewhere in the European world, particularly in those countries where ancient ruling classes had been destroyed (the Eastern Bloc) or had never existed (the United States). The economic growth and expanding opportunities of the 1950s and 1960s meant that many Soviet people could hope to climb the social ladder themselves, or provide for their children to do so. Statistics on women's education and their movement into the white-collar labor force document this mobility.

The rising standard of living also meant that increasing numbers of people could afford more than the bare necessities. By the late 1960s, the privileged young in the big cities were wearing jeans and listening to Jimi Hendrix. Women who could sew (many could) copied the dresses they saw in foreign fashion magazines. They and their menfolk scoured the shops for housewares and furniture and cosmetics. And of course they measured themselves against one another according to how much they and those others could afford to buy.

"Consumerism" is a modern word for an ancient human practice, the amassing of goods for the delight and comfort of having them and also to show off one's status. The rich had played this game for millennia; by the second half of the twentieth century, a hugely expanded middle class was at the table as well. Everywhere, wives were central players, for they chose many of the things with which their families were clothed and their homes decorated. The ideals of twentieth-century consumerism—that women should be the builders of tastefully adorned homes, that by so doing they would demonstrate their own competence and impart *kulturnost* to their children and husbands—had been around in Russia since the nineteenth century, as we have seen. What changed in the second half of the twentieth century, in the Soviet Union and elsewhere, was the number of women who could aspire to realize those ideals.

THE ARTS

Expanding incomes meant more money to spend on the mass media, and the providers of those media responded accordingly. Soviet movie companies produced hundreds of films, shown in a huge network of theaters. Radio flourished, as did short-wave broadcasts from abroad. Newsstands offered newspapers and glossy magazines; bookstores sprang up in the first floors of new apartment blocks. People reading on the subways, their books protected by homemade covers, became a common sight. Theaters were full, as were the sports stadiums and ice hockey rinks. Dozens of circuses toured the country.

Women figured prominently in the arts, as they had done for a century. There were celebrated film and stage actors, singers of popular songs and opera, and ballerinas. Among the last, perhaps the most famous was Natalia Marakova of Leningrad's Kirov Ballet, who became an international star in the 1960s. Now people also followed the exploits of female athletes. Among these was Liudmila Belousova, who, with her partner Oleg Protopopov, dominated pairs figure skating for several Olympics.

Less well known were the thousands of female poets and writers, many of whom explored women's family lives. One of the most famous of these was Natalia Baranskaia, who published an insightful portrait of a woman coping with the double shift in 1967. In the same decade, the banned works of Evgenia Ginzburg and poet Anna Akhmatova were becoming important in the re-emergence of the critical intelligentsia in the Soviet Union. More will be said of these writers later in this chapter.

THE KOMMUNALKA

Elite Soviet women of the 1960s and 1970s could afford the furniture, appliances, and clothes for sale at the nicer shops and available through back-channel deals at black-market prices. The great majority of urban women contented themselves with a standard of living that was comparable to that of poor people elsewhere in Europe. They bought the cheap goods sold in state stores and ate cheap foods, such as macaroni and canned fish.

Perhaps the most vivid indicator of status differences in the post-war era was urban housing. The government alleviated the chronic shortages by rehabbing older buildings and constructing new concrete-block apartment towers. By the late 1960s, battleship-grey high-rises surrounded the bigger cities across the Soviet Union and the Eastern Bloc. Compared to the single-family homes then filling up British and American suburbs, the two- or three-room Soviet apartments were small and spartan. For Soviet city folk, many of whom lived in much tighter quarters, the new housing was a huge improvement. The waiting lists to get a flat in the towers were long. It helped to have connections to people who could influence the selection process.

A large majority of people lived in communal flats, the *kommunalki* (the singular is *kommunalka*), which were one of the most reviled institutions of post-war Soviet life. Many of these were in buildings that had been constructed for the prosperous before the Revolution. After 1917 the government took ownership and carved the formerly luxurious spaces into small (100–200 square feet) one-room flats, with one communal kitchen, bathroom, and toilet to serve the residents of each floor. (In keeping with the custom across Eastern Europe, toilets were in separate rooms from baths.) By the 1960s these buildings were run like public housing projects elsewhere in the European world. The rules for the occupants were set by the administration and policed by a resident supervisor. Disputes were taken to a court, made up of neighbors and representatives of the housing authority, and decisions of that body could be appealed to the district court. The housing authority also organized inexpensive excursions for the residents, maintained clubs with activities for children and adults, and employed repairmen to do routine maintenance. Residents were required to clean their own flats and share in cleaning the indoor and outdoor common areas.

The social center of the kommunalka was the kitchen. Ilia Kabakov, a veteran of the kommunalki, later wrote of the kitchen, "Everything finds its place in it—the base and the great, the everyday and the romantic, love and battles over a broken glass, unconditional generosity and petty arguments over the payment for light, the treating to a just-baked pie and the problem of taking out the garbage."[15] Ranging in size from two to four hundred square feet, the kitchens contained two or three stoves and a couple of sinks. Food was prepared on tables, one per household, lined up against the walls, with shelves mounted on the wall above them and clotheslines hung from the ceiling. The tables and cooking utensils belonged to individual families. Women cooked in the kitchens; families ate meals in their rooms.

Because women ran the kitchens and because the kitchens were the places where neighbors had the most contact with one another, women played a central role in the social life of the kommunalka. Kabakov observed that "men feel like outsiders and almost never go into the kitchen, and they don't look out into the corridor often either. All contact is carried out by women, and the atmosphere here depends primarily on them." Women shared food and recipes, looked after one another's children, and offered support in times of trouble. They also celebrated together. V. D. Baranov, a Muscovite who kept a diary of his life in a kommunalka in the 1960s, recorded one such party: "Finally, for Nikitichna, the oldest one in the kitchen, there's a big holiday. She had a birthday and all of the residents chipped in and bought her a new coffeepot, white with red flowers. She was very happy. And she threw the old one in the garbage."[16] Consumerism for Nikitichna was receiving a flowered coffeepot from her neighbors.

The kitchens were also sites of epic enmities. Anyone who has lived in a college dorm will recognize the causes: people refused to clean up after themselves, they stole other people's things, they spread nasty stories about their neighbors, they bossed one another, or they encroached on other people's space. Sometimes these feuds came to blows. More often an offended party complained to the offender, and if she did not stop her annoying behavior, the complainant took her case to a gathering of the residents in the kitchen. As the animosity grew, some women found inventive ways to get their point across. "This morning," Baranov reports, "Stepanova hung her pants [to dry] over Valya Prokofieva's table and [Valya] took them down and intentionally put them in front of the door to the apartment so that people could wipe their feet on them. And she said that water was dripping from them onto her table."[17] He does not record Stepanova's response. She had broken the rules by hanging her wet laundry on someone else's line.

Sharing bathrooms and toilets also required patience and cooperation. Residents made up schedules for washing themselves and their clothes in the bathroom. They were asked to leave the baths clean and to share the work of giving them a weekly cleaning. The same was true of the toilets. In many kommunalki, residents had their own toilet seats, which they hung on the wall of the toilet room or carried with them to the room, along with toilet paper. When light bulbs were in short supply, they brought them along as well. Kabakov remembered that in his apartment people lined up in the mornings outside the bathroom, but not outside the toilet. "The tenants simply stand inside their rooms, by the door," he wrote, "waiting to tell by the sound and footsteps that the toilet is free so that they can dash into it." It is little wonder that the bulletin boards of communal apartments featured long lists of rules for using the toilet, including the admonition not to stand on it.[18]

THE DOUBLE SHIFT

The kommunalki became a woman's domain because women did most of the housework. They cooked, washed, and cleaned; men repaired things. This division of labor, an adaptation of ancient ways to city life, prevailed throughout the European world. Soviet studies in the 1960s and '70s found that husbands spent fifteen to twenty hours a week on domestic chores, wives twice that. Single women—of whom there were many in the post-war decades, because of the huge losses of men in the war and also because women were living longer than men—spent less time on housework than married women did; they did not have husbands to care for.

It should be noted that in the 1950s and '60s, Soviet men were doing more housework than their counterparts in Western Europe and North America, who averaged ten hours a week. Perhaps this was because far more of the Western wives were homemakers. As increasing numbers of these women joined the paid-labor force (the numbers of working wives jumped in Britain from 32 percent of all married women in 1960 to 59 percent in 1990; in France the increase was from 31 to 53 percent), they too began working the double shift, even though their husbands increased their contribution to housework. By the 1980s, women in the industrialized countries of Western Europe, like their Soviet counterparts, were devoting thirty to forty hours a week to housework, and men ten to twenty.[19]

One important difference between housework in West and East was the amount of physical labor required. In prosperous countries such as France, for example, there were affordable, nearby public laundries and reliable hot water in the flats, so most urban dwellers did not have to heat water in huge pots in the kitchen and then lug the pots down the hall to the bathtub in order to wash their clothes, as Soviet women did. Western women also more often spent part of their lives as housewives, rather than working the double shift throughout their childbearing years. It should be noted that not all the women of Western Europe were so fortunate. There were many in poorer countries, such as Spain and Greece, or in poorer parts of prosperous countries, such as southern Italy, who led lives as demanding as those lived by most Soviet women. There were also differences within the Soviet Union itself. Life was easier in the big cities of the European republics, harder in urban areas of Central Asia, the Caucasus, and Siberia, and harder in rural areas everywhere.

The Soviet government did not produce enough housing, plumbing, and consumer goods to make everyone's life easier, because it spent so much on the military, because it failed to overcome inefficiencies in the centralized system, and because it deliberately kept the prices of necessities low and thereby kept low as well the revenue from consumer purchases that could have been used to develop the consumer sector. Exacerbating the difficulties was the grinding poverty inherited from Russia's past and exacerbated by Stalinist excesses and the war. That the economy grew as well as it did in the 1950s and 1960s was a tribute to the society's ability to overcome enormous obstacles.

Shortages of services and consumer goods remained, even as people's wages and aspirations rose, and so few women left for work without stuffing their shopping bags into their purses. Many bought bread and other perishables every day or so. And they might see something scarce—toilet paper, children's clothes, light bulbs—in the shops. Soviet people shared their finds with one another; if someone spotted newly arrived canned fish, she or he (husbands shared shopping with their wives) would buy more than the family needed and trade the extras with friends, co-workers, and neighbors for scarce goods they had stocked up on. People who worked in the shops, most of whom were women, were important players in these networks, and so being a retail clerk was a far more lucrative position in the Soviet Union than it was in the West.[20]

Shopping also took a lot of time because Soviet retailing was antiquated. Women went to groceries for canned goods and staples, butcher shops for meat or fish, bakeries for bread, and milk stores for dairy products. (This was true across Europe, but elsewhere the time-saving supermarket was beginning to appear.) Once in a shop, people endured a ridiculously time-consuming sales process. Merchandise was kept behind counters rather than on open shelves, so customers had to find a salesperson to bring out things for them to examine. Salespeople also measured and packaged bulk foods such as flour. When a customer made her choice, she got a hand-written note from the salesperson, identifying the item and its price. She took the note to a cashier, whom she paid and from whom she received a receipt. She then took the receipt back to the salesperson and picked up her purchase. At each stage of this old-fashioned ritual, which dated back to the nineteenth century, women stood in line. If they found that a shop had sold out of what they wanted, they walked to another. They carried their purchases from store to store and then home on crowded trams, buses, or metros, along concrete sidewalks to their apartments, and then up flights of stairs. Very few Soviet people owned cars, and few apartment buildings had elevators.

Bosses helped by looking the other way when their employees nipped out in mid-afternoon to shop. This eased the burden, as did the sharing of goods through informal networks. People also relied on their parents and in-laws, particularly the female ones, to help with shopping and child-care. But none of the coping strategies made the daily grind of the double shift go away. Like the housewives of 1917, Soviet women let their frustrations show on the streets. They grumbled to one another while standing in line and yelled at surly clerks. They pushed and shoved to get into stores. To friends and family they complained about the shortages and the lines. They complained about always being tired, and they complained about their husbands. Lida, a thirty-one-year-old chambermaid and single mother from Moscow interviewed in the 1970s, was typical: "At home a woman usually does everything. When the husband comes home he reads his paper and watches t.v., contrary to what the newspapers say. They show men on March 8 [Women's Day] cooking and cleaning and shopping and scrubbing floors. But it's really the women who do everything."[21]

By the end of the 1960s, many women in Soviet cities were feeling overworked and angry. It did not mollify them when the government pointed out that they were better off than their grandmothers had been, for they were no longer content to measure their lives by that miserable standard. For decades the government had asked women to work hard and promised to provide the social services and consumer goods that would make their lives easier. They had worked, they were working, and still the shops were often empty, still there were not enough laundries, and still women were ending the day exhausted. In 1969, a museum worker brought all these frustrations to life in a short story that became a sensation.

❖ ❖ ❖ *NATALIA BARANSKAIA (1908–2004)* ❖ ❖ ❖

Natalia Baranskaia was sixty-one years old when she published "A Week like Any Other Week" in the literary magazine *Novyi mir* (New World). Her heroine was Olga, a research scientist, wife, and mother. Olga loves her children, her husband, and her job, but the stress of coping with the double shift drives her to despair. Asked how she spends her leisure time, Olga thinks, "Personally, my sport is running. Running here, running there. A shopping bag in each hand and . . . up, down: trolleybus, autobus; into the metro, out of the metro."[22] Her husband Dima helps with their two young children, while Olga does the cooking, washing, and shopping. Sometimes she just wants to be alone. "Suddenly I am overwhelmed by the longing to walk unencumbered, without a load, without a goal," she muses one night on her way home (679). When her husband proposes that she quit her job, Olga fires back, "What you are suggesting would just . . . destroy me. And my five years of study? My degree? My professional standing? My dissertation subject? How easy it is for you to throw it all out—whisk! And it's finished! And what would I be like, staying home? Angry as the devil: I'd growl at you all the time" (701).

Olga cannot figure out how to lighten her load. "Did I choose this?" she asks herself as she rushes off to work. "No, of course I didn't. Do I regret it? No, never" (674). It does not occur to her to ask her husband to do more of the housework or to explain to her boss that she is sometimes late because the trams were running behind schedule. Feeling helpless, she blames herself. "Am I really such a good mother, is it right to praise me as a worker, and what exactly does the concept of 'a Soviet woman' entail?!" she asks herself (666). The "week like any other" ends with Olga lying in bed, sleepless, wondering, "Then, what is disturbing me?" (703).

Baranskaia herself had lived Olga's story, even though she was a generation older than her heroine. She had graduated from Moscow University in 1929 and spent most of her career working in museums. Her husband died in World War II, so she reared her two children on her own. Baranskaia started writing in her fifties and produced a considerable body of fiction, including a well-regarded novel about women caught up in World War II, *Remembrance Day* (1989). "A Week like Any Other Week" remains her most widely read work because it speaks to and for women everywhere who are working the double shift.

Rural Women's Lives, 1953–85

In the mid-1960s, the women of the villages of the Baltics, Belarus, Russia, and Ukraine still followed the rhythms of nature's year, rising before winter dawns to tend the cows, shepherding the ewes and lambs through the hesitant spring, spending summer and fall planting and harvesting. The work was hard and the amenities few because the Soviet government, like its tsarist predecessors, put the peasants last in its priorities. In the 1970s most country folk still did not have central heating or indoor toilets, their stores were poorly stocked, their schools were short of books, and few of their children were in daycare. Progressive change was occurring. Medical care and maternity leave improved, as did wages and pensions. The gulf between city and village continued to narrow, as improved transportation and communication brought the city closer than ever before. Now many women could travel to the larger world or bring it to their villages by turning on the radio. The result was the largest migration of women out of the countryside in Russian history and continuing changes in the attitudes of those who remained in the villages.

EDUCATION AND PARTICIPATION IN THE
PAID-LABOR FORCE

Schooling for rural girls expanded in the countryside after World War II. In 1959, only 23 percent of village women had attended secondary school. By 1979, 44 percent of them, and well over 90 percent of those younger than thirty, had. Sixteen percent had studied at an institution of higher education. For the first time in Russian history, many wives in the rural population of the European USSR were better educated than their husbands.[23]

Better education did not lead to better jobs. The percentages of women among heavy-equipment operators fell in the post-war period despite the government's continuing efforts to enlist female tractor drivers. There were more female agronomists, biologists, doctors, journalists, and teachers in rural areas than ever before, but women made up a smaller percentage of white-collar workers in the country than in the cities. They never regained the presence in collective-farm leadership that they had achieved during World War II. By 1960 they held 6 percent of top management jobs, a figure that did not change thereafter. Khrushchev sharply summed up the situation at an agricultural conference in Kiev in 1961: "It turns out that it's the men who do the managing and the women who do the work."[24]

Women who were not willing to accept this situation left the countryside for the cities in the post-war years, and by so doing reversed the historic pattern of men migrating and women staying behind. According to the 1970 census, the rural population aged fifteen to thirty in the Russian republic of the Soviet Union was 52 percent male and 48 percent female, at a time when women made up 54 percent of the total Soviet population. Most of the migrants were young, for they had the best job prospects. They did not go because the villages had thrown them out, as did widows in the late nineteenth century. Nor were most of them following men who had already left. Instead they went on their own or with girlfriends, and many apparently went with the blessings of their parents. "Her father and I have spent our whole lives in muck and filth," declared the mother of one of these young women. "Let Zina do some other work." Once in the cities the youngest and least well educated peasants found jobs as live-in babysitters, the post-war equivalent of domestic servants. Those with more skills took blue- or white-collar jobs.[25]

FAMILY LIFE IN THE COUNTRYSIDE

In the post-war years, many traditional beliefs and practices died away. Public opinion surveys in the 1960s reported that most peasants believed that people should marry for love and companionship, not economic security. They were also willing to countenance abortion, so by the 1970s there was very little difference in family size between urban and rural people of the European ethnic groups. Because peasants now believed that mothers should devote considerable time to looking after their children and because mechanization had lightened the workload, peasants no longer turned toddlers over to eight-year-old nannies. Nor did they give birth at home, attended by peasant midwives. By 1970 most rural women in the European regions of the Soviet Union delivered their children in medical facilities and maternal and child mortality had declined significantly.[26]

Patriarchy's influence was waning too. Rural women of the European nationalities reported to interviewers in the 1960s and 1970s that they enjoyed a greater voice in family decision-making and more respect from their husbands than their mothers had, an improvement they attributed to their being better educated. Another sign of their growing confidence and independence was the fact that they were far more willing to leave bad marriages than their mothers' generation. The rural divorce rate doubled among the European nationalities in the 1970s, and the majority of those suing for divorce were women. It was still difficult to be a single woman in the countryside, and only one-quarter of peasant marriages ended in divorce, as compared to half of urban ones.[27] This disparity notwithstanding, the increase in divorces in the countryside indicated that more women than ever before believed that they no longer had to remain in unhappy marriages.

Women in the Caucasus, Central Asia, and Siberia

In the decades following World War II, the government maintained its careful approach to challenging patriarchy in the Caucasus and Central Asia. Local people were offered education and jobs in the cities, and once there they imbibed Soviet gender values. The influence of those values was strengthened by the continuing in-migration of Soviet citizens from the European areas. This assimilative process brought about the transformation the government wanted, especially within the urban elite of professionals, managers, party officials, and their families. By the 1970s, most women in Baku, Tbilisi, Alma Ata, and Tashkent were educated, were working in the same sorts of jobs as women elsewhere in the Soviet Union, were having fewer children than their mothers' generation—though more than Soviet women of European ethnicity—and were living healthier lives than their mothers had. They were also professing many of the same ideas about family life and women's role in society as other Soviet women. These were substantial changes, particularly when compared to the much less advanced process of gender reform in nearby, culturally similar countries such as Afghanistan, Iran, and Turkey. Russian autocracy had once again demonstrated its ability to accelerate reforms for women.[28]

In Siberia, government policies were less accommodating of local customs. The largest, most urban, and most prosperous peoples—the Buryats and Yakuts—managed the transition to Soviet values and practices most easily. Among the smaller tribes, Soviet officials pursued policies of forced assimilation that were much like those that the Canadian and U.S. governments had adopted toward indigenous people in the decades before World War II. They denigrated local cultures, forced nomads to become farmers, and took children away to boarding schools. Sexual contacts between native women and non-native men also weakened native cultures; by the late Brezhnev years, more than 50 percent of the children in some Eskimo villages were the offspring of European fathers with whom they had no contact. The native Siberians were unable to mount effective resistance to these policies, because there were few places left to retreat to and more Europeans than ever to deal with. In 1979, native people constituted a mere 11 percent of the Siberian population, despite the fact that better health care had lowered childhood mortality rates among them. The results were similar to those in North America—rising levels of education and migration to cities, some economic success among collective farmers and herders, and among others high rates of alcoholism, alienation, and unemployment.[29]

The peoples of the Caucasus, Central Asia, and Siberia preserved some traditional customs, including patriarchal ones. Clan and extended family connections remained strong, providing support and entailing obligations. Muslim elders in the Caucasus and Central Asia enforced their remaining prerogatives, so that practices such as wife-beating and arranged marriage continued, even though they were illegal and were occasionally prosecuted by Soviet authorities. The power of senior women persisted as well. In Turkmenistan, the most conservative of the Central Asian republics, Turkmen women continued to believe that bride price and dowry were important to cementing the relationship between the families of the bride and groom, and also to affirming the importance of parents, who made the payments and negotiated the marriage contracts. Once married, young Turkmen women moved in with their husbands' families, and for the first year of their married lives they were forbidden to leave the house alone, eat with the family, or speak directly to their mothers-in-law or fathers-in-law.[30] Elsewhere in Central Asia women still wore veils in public and divided their homes into male-only and female-only spaces.

Caucasian, Central Asian, and Siberian women preserved other traditions as well. Older women among the Yakuts cherished the belief that their cows understood everything humans said to them, and so they talked to them as they milked and explained to them what was happening when the calves started to be born.[31] Uzbek women cooked in clay ovens built into the floors of their city houses. Armenians embroidered centuries-old designs onto table linens. They and the women of many other ethnic groups also taught their children the history of their families, passed on the proverbs and folk tales of their ancestors, and kept their people's religions alive. In the Caucasus, most of the congregants of Georgian and Armenian Christian churches were female. Among Islamic peoples, mothers and grandmothers instructed their children in the Qur'an. Female shamans on the Pacific coast chanted the ancient invocations to ancestral spirits for healing; Buryat women taught their children about the Buddha.

Many observers believed that women played the key role in keeping native cultures alive, for cultural traditions could be practiced in the home, a place less subject to government inspection than the public world. "Women were expected to be the main identity markers, the primary repositories of 'authenticity . . . ,' tradition, ethnic codes, and customs," wrote Nayereh Tohidi of Azeri women.[32] We saw this idea among Polish nationalists in Russia in the nineteenth century. It was an important theme in nationalism from the ideology's inception in the eighteenth century and it is widespread today across Africa and Asia, as people adapt to the onslaught of foreign power and influence.

Gender Discontents and Feminist Whispers

The Khrushchev and Brezhnev regimes tinkered with Stalinist gender values. The basic paradigm remained the same—women and men were to be hard-working, honest, patriotic, public-spirited citizens, and women were also to be nurturing wives and mothers, men considerate, civilized husbands. In the post-war world, the government paid more attention to motherhood, as we have seen, and to fatherhood too. The New Soviet Men of the 1930s had been praised for providing for their families. In the 1950s and 1960s, they were also urged to pay attention to their children. "A good father," Deborah Field has written, "helped his children with homework, took them on interesting excursions, and taught them hobbies." Popular magazines such as *Sovetskii sport* (Soviet Sport) urged men to instruct their sons in the masculine virtues of diligence, self-control, sobriety, patriotism, and athleticism. The women's magazines *Rabotnitsa* and *Krest'ianka* urged them to help with housework.[33]

These officially approved definitions of masculinity were adapted by men of different social ranks and ethnicities, as hegemonic values always are. Working-class and peasant men put more stock in physical strength and manual competence than did white-collar workers. They also cherished those rowdy pleasures—competitive cursing, heavy drinking with male friends, brawling in bars and at soccer matches, seducing women— that the regime had long tried to stamp out, and they continued, as their peasant ancestors had, to admire clever men from the lower classes who figured out how to beat the system. Peoples of the Caucasus and Central Asia insisted more than did the Europeans on dutifulness to parents and family loyalty from both genders. They also believed that defense of one's family and of one's personal honor were essential male responsibilities.[34]

Soviet women made their own adaptations of the post-war variant of the New Soviet Woman. Like Baranskaia's fictional "Olga," younger women of the Brezhnev years were proud of being more emancipated and better off than earlier generations had been. Many of them, like Olga, considered their work outside the home very important to their sense of self-worth and they valued family life as well, but many complained, as we have seen, about the domestic division of labor. Some came to see themselves as "brave victims," to use the terminology of Polish sociologists Mira Marody and Ann Giza-Poleszczuk. They were laboring endlessly to meet the demands of their families and of a system that did not keep its promises. The "brave victim" was yet another variant of the ancient theme of women as suffering servants. It valorized the self-sacrifice, endurance, patience, kindness, and resourcefulness of wives and mothers. It also deprecated men, for the Soviet "Knights of the Sofa" were loafers compared to their endlessly laboring wives.[35]

The complaints about husbands arose from real grievances over the double shift and also from what some observers have described as a "crisis of masculinity" in the late decades of the Soviet period. By the 1970s it was harder for poor people to climb the social ladder because the stagnating economy was generating fewer new jobs and because the elites were keeping the best educations and jobs for themselves and their children. It now all too often took connections as well as hard work to get into good schools or to move up the waiting lists for telephones and apartments. As gaps between the privileged and the poor widened, the promises made by the government became harder to trust. At the same time, women were less economically dependent on their husbands than in the past, because they had their own incomes and could rely more on public services. The decreased social mobility of the Brezhnev years and the perception that women were more independent made some men feel diminished.[36]

In the midst of these discontents, independent feminist thought resurfaced from within a much repressed but persistent dissident movement. The dissidents were a loosely organized collection of writers, scientists, and other intellectuals who began in the 1960s to criticize the regime's dictatorial habits, to document the evils of Stalinism, and to urge democratization and improved relations with the West. Within their ranks were Jewish dissidents who pressed for the right to emigrate to Israel to escape anti-Semitism. The dissidents could not publish their work legally, so they circulated newsletters, manifestos, poems, and novels in typescript copies. Women's participation in the dissident movement was very similar to that of their predecessors in the nineteenth-century intelligentsia and also to that of women in the rising opposition movements in Eastern Europe, particularly Poland. They made copies of the dissidents' writings; they hosted meetings at their apartments; they helped friends undergoing persecution. "Our movement had no leaders," wrote Liudmila Alexeeva, a Moscow teacher. "They weren't needed. Each of us decided what he wanted to do and acted only on his own behalf."[37] Elena Bonner, a physician whose communist father had died in the purges, was perhaps the most prominent female dissident. She became a spokesperson for her husband Andrei Sakharov, a nuclear physicist and human-rights advocate who was a leading dissident.

Important among the writings that the dissidents circulated in typescript were the works of three women. Anna Akhmatova's poetry collection *Requiem* (1940) recorded the anguish of women who waited for news of their arrested loved ones. Evgenia Ginzburg's memoirs told the story of the camps. Nadezhda Mandelshtam, the widow of poet Osip Mandelshtam, who died in the Gulag in 1938, testified in *Hope against Hope* and *Hope Abandoned* (published abroad in 1970 and 1974) to the anguish and struggles of wives who had lost their husbands to the Terror. Akhmatova, Ginzburg, and Mandelshtam did not participate directly in the dissident movement, but their work played an important part in the building criticism of the Soviet system. The quality of their writing also placed the three among the major authors of twentieth-century Russian literature.

Until the late 1970s, the dissident movement paid little attention to the situation of women in the Soviet Union, because most dissidents, female as well as male, considered the woman question a less pressing issue than the absence of democracy. In 1979, a small group of Leningrad women began to argue that there was a connection between the autocratic government and women's difficulties. Tatiana Goricheva (a philosopher) and Tatiana Mamonova and Julia Voznesenskaia (both writers of poetry and prose) published an underground magazine, *Almanac: Woman and Russia,* which contained articles by professional women and blue-collar workers documenting in touching detail the hardships of Soviet women's lives. Contributors blamed those hardships on the sexism pervading Soviet society, a sexism, they argued, that was promoted by the very regime that claimed to have liberated women from sexism. "Equality between Soviet men and women is observed primarily on paper," declared Ekaterina Alexandrova, a professional from Leningrad, "and . . . the assertion that women have the same opportunities as men for any type of work is pure nonsense." Once again, as in the 1850s, feminists were arguing that the system itself was patriarchal, and they were implying that women could only be emancipated by thoroughgoing political change. They implied as well that women's emancipation should be a priority for those seeking to change the Soviet system.[38]

The publication of *Almanac* marked the re-emergence of feminism within the critical intelligentsia. Very soon after the magazine began to circulate in typescript, the police came calling on its editors. They were expelled from the Soviet Union in 1980.

The Gorbachev Years, 1985–91

GLASNOST AND PERESTROIKA

Brezhnev died in 1982, and was succeeded by Yuri Andropov, the head of the KGB, the powerful successor to the NKVD. Andropov succumbed to kidney failure in February 1984; the new head of the party was another member of the old guard, Konstantin Chernenko, who died a year later. In 1985 the younger generation of communists could no longer be put off; they elected fifty-four-year-old Mikhail Gorbachev first secretary of the party. Gorbachev and his colleagues in the new leadership believed that fundamental change in domestic and foreign policy was long overdue.

Many of these people had come of age under Khrushchev and they sought, as he had, to make Soviet socialism succeed by reforming it. They began that process, as Alexander II had, by loosening controls on intellectuals and the communications media in order to encourage criticism of the status quo and thereby build support for reform. They called this process *glasnost* (openness). They also undertook a program of economic restructuring (*perestroika*) that included decentralization of economic management, experimentation with private ownership of small businesses, and encouragement of foreign investment.

There was resistance to reform from the very beginning, openly from conservative party leaders, more covertly from factory and collective farm managers, directors of scientific institutes, and many others whose encrusted power and privileges were threatened. Gorbachev headed a shifting coalition of party leaders; as they encountered resistance, they pushed for more democratization in hopes that mobilizing public support would increase the pressure on entrenched interests. Demonstrations and strikes were permitted. New political parties began to form. A fairly representative legislature, the Congress of People's Deputies, was elected in 1989.

At the same time, the government was pursuing a radically altered foreign policy. Gorbachev and foreign minister Edvard Shevardnadze negotiated disarmament treaties with the United States. In 1986 they began withdrawing Soviet troops from Afghanistan, ending a bloody war that had begun when the Soviet Union invaded the country in 1979. Three years later, as political ferment spread in Eastern Europe, Soviet leaders made it clear to the unpopular communist governments of Czechoslovakia, East Germany, and Poland that they were not going to deploy Soviet troops to prop them up. Poland was the first country to establish democratic government in 1989, the other Eastern Bloc countries quickly followed, and these developments emboldened independence movements within the Soviet Union itself. In March 1990 a newly elected legislature in Lithuania declared that republic's independence. Kazimiera Prunskiene, the female prime minister of the breakaway government, wryly observed in May 1990, "Freedom, like a genie that's been let out of the bottle, doesn't necessarily want to listen to the dictates of the person who uncorked the bottle."[39] Early the next year there were bloody confrontations between protesters and army troops in Vilnius and Riga.

Perhaps Gorbachev and his allies could have survived the upwelling public discontent had they improved the economy. They had been more cautious with economic changes than with political reforms and foreign policy, because they wanted to preserve socialist structures and because they feared the disruptions that would come from dismantling the centralized system. Their indecision made things worse. By the end of the 1980s shortages were growing and the gross national product was falling. For women, for all Soviet people, this meant ever longer lines, ever more hardship, and ever greater discontent with the politicians.

By 1991 the Kremlin leadership was split between those who thought they could manage the swelling pressures for change and those who wanted to curtail, if not reverse, the reforms already granted. This conflict built to a crisis in August, when a small group of conservatives in the Politburo ordered military units in Moscow to arrest the reformers. Most of the generals, reluctant to get involved in a coup, hesitated, and as they stalled, the parliament of the Russian republic, led by its popular president, Boris Yeltsin, forced the conspirators to back down. Gorbachev, who had been held captive in his vacation home in the Crimea, returned to Moscow, weakened by his association with the fallen conservatives. Less than a month later a new leadership, headed by Yeltsin, ordered the Communist Party to suspend operations and seized control of the party's property. The leaders of the republics then rushed to declare independence. The process was completed in December 1991, when the presidents of the Russian, Belarusian, and Ukrainian republics announced the abolition of the Soviet Union and its replacement by a loose confederation of independent states.

The difficulties of women's lives were on Gorbachev's agenda. He reaffirmed the importance of women's domestic duties, and, like Khrushchev before him, criticized the double shift and pledged to improve social services. The new leadership also authorized the creation of still more social-science study groups to consider women's problems. It charged the Soviet Women's Committee, an organization that represented the Soviet Union at international women's meetings, to take over leadership of the zhensovety and discuss the woman question. Gorbachev also appointed a female party official, Alexandra Biriukova, to the Politburo, and he sought the advice of a female economist and sociologist, Tatiana Zaslavskaia.

TATIANA ZASLAVSKAIA (b. 1927)

Zaslavskaia had earned her doctorate in economics in Moscow in the 1950s and, from the 1960s onward, had worked in a research institute in Novosibirsk, Siberia, which was home to a group of reformist economists. In 1982, asked to brief Gorbachev, then a Politburo member specializing in agricultural policy, Zaslavskaia delivered a frank report on the hardships of peasant life and the failures of government policy. It was soon leaked to the press, and Zaslavskaia and her colleagues were reprimanded by the administrators of their institute. For his part, Gorbachev had been impressed, not offended, by the Novosibirsk economists' critique, so when he became party secretary, he brought them to Moscow to design reforms.[40]

Zaslavskaia quickly became a prominent advocate for democratizing the Soviet system. "It is not only impossible for top people to regulate everything from above but stupid of them to have insisted that they could," she declared in 1987. She publicized perestroika at home and abroad through interviews, articles, and a book, *The Second Soviet Revolution* (1990). As the political struggle intensified, Zaslavskaia's criticism sharpened. By 1991 she was denouncing the Communist Party for oppressing the working class.[41]

Zaslavskaia also argued passionately for the freeing of sociologists from ideological controls. To govern effectively, she argued, officials needed to understand how people felt and how society functioned, which they could only do if they consulted sociologists and pollsters who were free to tell them what they did not want to hear. To promote the development of such information, Gorbachev authorized the creation of the first national polling organization, the All-Union Institute for the Study of Public Opinion, in 1987 and appointed Zaslavskaia its head. Conservatives pushed back with articles attacking her, but she managed to get the institute up and running. Soon public-opinion polling was being done, for the first time in Soviet history.

After the Soviet Union ended, Zaslavskaia decided to go back to academe. "I am convinced that the personal qualities of a scientist and of a politician are diametrically opposite," she said in 2005. "Politicians must be sly, dodgy, today say one thing and tomorrow contradict it. A scientist, on the contrary, must be straight, critical . . . but he will never succeed in politics, this is for sure." She continued to call for reform in the years that followed and to defend her discipline from politicization.[42]

WOMEN IN POLITICS

Zaslavskaia was one of a handful of professional women who rose to political prominence in the late 1980s. Another was Kazimiera Prunskiene, an economist and prime minister of Lithuania's secessionist government. In Azerbaijan, Elmira Gafarova, a philologist, chaired that republic's parliament. Zaslavskaia, Prunskiene, and Gafarova were the exceptions. As usual in women's history, the personal successes of a few individuals did not weaken male control over politics. Sixteen percent of the people elected to the national Congress of People's Deputies in 1989 were women, because the Communist Party leadership, true to its commitment to encourage women to speak up, had allotted some of the seats to women. Far smaller percentages of women served in the more democratically elected legislatures in the Soviet republics.[43]

Women did participate in political life in the late 1980s, even though, as in 1917, most did not join political parties. They voted in large numbers for reform candidates; Boris Yeltsin, for example, claimed to have drawn much of his support from the women of Moscow. Women joined men in petitioning, demonstrating, and striking, as they had in 1917, and were active in the resistance to the coup attempted in August 1991.

WOMEN DISCUSS THE WOMAN QUESTION

Women also spoke out about the hardships of their lives in interviews and letters to the press. At first most repeated publicly the complaints that they had been making privately, that men were lazy and party leaders did not keep their promises. "In general in this country we have so many problems," said Olya, a seventeen-year-old vocational student interviewed in 1989. "Men don't want to face them, and they can't resolve them, and the women take everything on themselves." Many bemoaned the dismal economy. E. Frolova, A. Govorukhina, and N. Borisova, three women from the provincial city of Morshansk, wrote to the magazine *Ogonok* in 1987, "People who have been to Paris are ecstatic over the women there. They look so young and elegant. In our opinion, the point is not the women themselves. How are you supposed to be young-looking when you're prematurely gray and there's no hair dye available to give your hair the right color?"[44]

As public criticism of the Soviet regime intensified, a handful of professional women began to publish the feminist critique of Soviet-style emancipation that had been circulating quietly for years. The much-vaunted programs had not freed them, they declared; they had exploited and controlled them. Larisa Kuznetsova, a philologist, wrote in 1989, "Women have been manipulated through most of our history. Put on tractors or on steam engines, or dropped out of planes with parachutes. . . . Spiritual food and values have always been offered from without. From ready-made recipes . . . We won't have any women's movement until women have the chance to stop this race, to concentrate on themselves, to understand and hear their own voices."[45]

Kuznetsova and others argued that it was time for men to share power with women in the Kremlin and in the family, a change that would only happen if a new woman's movement arose. Journalist Nina Belaeva sketched out this feminist plan for social regeneration in 1989, in terms that would have pleased both Kollontai and the Russian feminists Kollontai had so often criticized: "Though there are still no signs of a mass movement, the first women's associations have appeared. They will foster leaders, public figures, and politicians with a female face. Then women shall have a place in the social hierarchy worthy of our intellect, experience, education, and creativity. Women will occupy this place not by 'battling their way' into it, but by naturally imparting their womanhood to society. Maybe then society will also understand that whenever women flourish, the nation stands to gain."[46]

Belaeva's feminism, unlike Kollontai's, was not Marxist; it did not attribute women's subordination to economic forces, but rather to the persistence of patriarchal values. Belaeva and many other women who spoke up in the 1980s also subscribed to what the Federation of Women Writers labeled "the woman principle." That is, they believed that women were naturally more sympathetic, generous, and loving than men. Belaeva saw this as a reason for women to be involved in the public world, where they would bring their natural virtues to bear on social problems. These traditional ideas about women—present in feminism since its inception—were being stressed in the 1980s by cultural feminists in the West as well, but Soviet feminists were not much influenced by Westerners, with whom they had little contact. Rather, they were staying true to the core principles of Soviet-style women's emancipation—women should be free and equal citizens and they were, by nature, more moral than men—but joining them to calls for more democracy, which would enable women to work to reform patriarchy.

ACTIVISM ON THE WOMAN QUESTION

The rapid emergence of this feminist discussion suggests that feminist ideas had won widespread acceptance among elite women before glasnost began. So did the development of organizations dedicated to reforms for women. The largest was the Soviet Women's Committee (SWC), which held a national meeting of representatives of the zhensovety in 1987. Valentina Tereshkova, the head of the SWC, who had spent decades singing the praises of Soviet women's emancipation at international conferences, delivered an attack on sexism in Soviet society that repeated many of the officially approved themes. Delegates listened and then, in an effort to revitalize the SWC, replaced the cosmonaut with Zoia Pukhova, a regional party official. Pukhova soon drafted a proposal to extend paid maternity leave to two years and advocated the abolition of fees charged for daycare and abortions. In 1989 the SWC was awarded a block of seats in the Congress of People's Deputies, and for the next two years Pukhova and her successor Alevtina Fedulova worked to promote attention to women's problems.[47]

There were many female activists, most of them professionals, who scorned the SWC as a tool of the regime. They created a variety of independent organizations in the larger cities, some of these small associations of friends who shared ideas and support, others larger groups dedicated to propagating feminist ideas and developing feminist scholarship. In 1989, Anastasia Posadskaia, Natalia Rimashevskaia, Natalia Zakharova, and Valentina Konstantinova, all academics in Moscow, formed the League for the Emancipation from Sexual Stereotypes. The following year, they won government approval for the establishment of the Moscow Center for Gender Studies in the Institute of Socioeconomic Population Problems. That year also saw the launching of other feminist groups, among them the Independent Women's Democratic Initiative (its Russian acronym is NeZhDI, which means "Don't wait") and the Free Association of Feminist Organizations (SAFO). In 1991, NeZhDi, SAFO, and others held a conference at Dubna, near Moscow, that brought together two hundred delegates from forty-eight women's organizations. The authorities stationed police at the meetings, as the tsarist police had done at the 1908 Women's Congress, but they could not dampen the enthusiasm of the delegates or prevent lively discussions and networking.

OTHER ACTIVISM

Women's activism in the late 1980s extended beyond the ranks of the feminists to become almost as wide-ranging as the activism of the late nineteenth century. Once again women mounted a religious revival. An easing of government regulation permitted the number of convents to grow from a dozen in the mid-1980s to more than one hundred in the early 1990s. Most remained small, for Orthodox authorities were as reluctant as their nineteenth-century predecessors to admit large numbers of women to religious orders. They did welcome the laywomen who held Bible-study classes and helped maintain church property. The restore-the-church movement was also strong in the Baltics, Ukraine, and Georgia, where religious faith (Lutheranism and Catholicism in the Baltics, Ukrainian Orthodoxy and the Uniate Church in the Ukraine, and Georgian Orthodoxy in Georgia) was bolstered by a nationalist belief that the churches were repositories of ethnic identity. In Siberia as well, religious practices that had been performed in secret began to come out into the open. For decades Yakut women had hung *salamas,* decorated ropes that solicited the good will of the spirits, in their cow sheds, only to take them down when outsiders came around. Now newly braided salamas went up in late winter, when the cows were due to calve, and stayed there for the rest of the year.[48]

Less religious women also felt the pull of ethnic and national loyalties. Evdokia Gayer, a member of the Nanai tribe of northern Siberia, was one of the organizers of the Association of Small Peoples of the North, which advocated the improvement of living conditions for native peoples and the ending of environmentally destructive development on their ancestral lands. Two of the largest of the independence movements, Rukh in Ukraine and Sajudis in Lithuania, recruited female members. In Baku, the Association in Defense of Azerbaijan Women's Rights worked as a women's auxiliary of the Popular Front of Azerbaijan. In Tatarstan, three women's organizations, Apa, Ak Aky, and Ak Kalfak, demonstrated for national independence. Like the revolutionaries and nationalists of the nineteenth century, these women denigrated feminism as self-interested and declared themselves dedicated to the emancipation of all their people. Many repeated the widespread belief that women had a special role to play in preserving native cultures and thus that they should leave the paid-labor force to concentrate on their families.

Activists also worked in many other volunteer organizations, some of them exclusively female. The smaller groups were usually confined to a single city, where they pursued all sorts of projects, from philanthropy and historic preservation to handcrafts. There were also larger organizations, such as the Committee of Soldiers' Mothers, that lobbied in Moscow for increased veterans' benefits and better treatment of soldiers. Similar groups in Ukraine and Georgia demonstrated against young men's being sent to military service outside their home republics. Within the professions, academics and writers formed all-female organizations to promote contacts with Western Europe and North America, as well as to press claims for funding. Memorial, an organization that publicized the atrocities of the Stalin era and encouraged Gulag survivors to write down their stories, had many female members. All this volunteerism added up to the highest levels of independent organizing by women since the Revolution.

Conclusions

The last decades of Soviet history were far easier than the earlier ones had been. The terror diminished to police surveillance and occasional brutality. Differences between classes and ethnicities eased. Conveniences were few, but the basics were within the reach of many. The government, attentive to domestic needs and international opinion, improved women's marital and reproductive options and encouraged analysis of the difficulties in their lives. Then, as the economy slowed and the leadership proved unable to rise to the challenge, women's grumbling about the double shift became one of the major themes in a subdued but pervasive chorus of complaint about the shortcomings of the Soviet system.

When real reform began, most women soldiered on with their everyday lives, as they had done through good and bad times in the past. A few revived the independent social activism of the pre-revolutionary era. The Soviet Women's Committee asserted itself, while feminists, nationalists, religious women, soldiers' mothers, and women concerned about the plight of their neighbors organized their own independent groups. Meanwhile the economy faltered, the borderlands broke away, and then, on a December day in 1991, the leaders of the Russian, Ukrainian, and Belarusian Republics dissolved the Soviet Union. The empire that most had thought unshakeable had collapsed, taking with it the hard-won stability of the post-war era.

8

GAINS AND LOSSES

1991–2010

In the 1990s, the peoples of the fifteen nations that emerged from the collapse of the Soviet Union—Armenia, Azerbaijan, Belarus, Estonia, Georgia, Kazakhstan, Kyrgyzstan, Latvia, Lithuania, Moldova, Russia, Tajikistan, Turkmenistan, Ukraine, and Uzbekistan—set about remaking their political and economic systems. The largest and most populous of these successor states was Russia, presided over for eight years by President Boris Yeltsin. A courageous, boisterous, undisciplined man, Yeltsin seemed to embody the chaos of the 1990s. In 1999 he handed power to his hand-picked successor, a former intelligence agent named Vladimir Putin. Putin rebuilt the power of the center, repressed critics, and pursued an assertive foreign policy. In 2008, at the end of the two terms permitted to the president by the new Russian constitution, he became prime minister and was succeeded as president by an ally, Dmitri Medvedev.

Some of the governments of the other republics were more democratic than Russia's, some less. In Belarus and Central Asia, Soviet-era leaders and renamed communist parties remained in power into the early twenty-first century. Ukraine and the states of the Baltic and Caucasus developed more democratic regimes. All these governments instituted similar economic reforms: they shut down inefficient factories, privatized some state-owned enterprises, encouraged the creation of privately owned farms and businesses, and cut funding for social services and benefits programs.

These developments had similar consequences for women across the former Soviet Union (FSU). Many, particularly the elderly, felt that much had been lost with the passing of a system that was a source of security and pride for those who had worked so hard to build it. These feelings of loss were fed by severe economic problems. Unemployment rose, especially for women, as did the cost of living; social services declined. Gender values and practices were not much affected, and so the double shift became still more laborious.

The post-Soviet period did bring more freedom of information and expression, particularly in the European republics and the Caucasus. Relaxation of censorship made it possible to read a much greater variety of books and periodicals, more people could travel abroad, and many had access to the internet. Property rights were extended with the legalization of private business and farming. The easing of controls that occurred in some republics enabled women to set up thousands of voluntary organizations. Greater religious freedom permitted still more Christian women to join convents, Muslim ones to teach the faith in girls' schools, and Siberian shamans to practice their healing arts openly. These new liberties resulted in still more social activism among women and the most unfettered consideration of gender arrangements since the revolutionary era.

Women's Work in the Post-Soviet World

For the great majority of women, the post-Soviet period began with great hardship. When antiquated factories were closed and government ministries downsized, some managers responded as they had in the NEP years, that is, they laid women off and refused to hire new ones because they judged women more expensive employees than men. Government figures suggest that roughly the same percentages of women and men lost their jobs in Russia; in Ukraine, in the Caucasus, and among some native people in Siberia, more women than men became unemployed. Most people remained officially employed, but received no wages for months or were paid only with goods from the enterprise or produce from the collective farms. They stayed on the job because there were so few others available and because they hoped thereby to remain vested in government pension programs.[1]

Making the situation worse was the fact that the cost of living rose, wiping out savings and reducing the value of already meager incomes. This occurred because governments had pegged local currencies to international standards, because expensive imports flooded in and domestic manufacturing dropped, and because the resulting economic depression cut government revenues, causing funding for social services to fall and the price of those services to the public to rise. The poverty was worst in the places that had always been poorest—the countryside, small towns, Central Asia, native settlements in Siberia—and among the most vulnerable—children, the disabled, the elderly, and single mothers. Single older women, who made up the great majority of those living on pensions, were particularly hard hit. Hundreds of them begged outside subway stations and churches in the mid-1990s.

More fortunate people worked harder and relied on family and friends. In the cities, women put in overtime at their regular jobs or took additional part-time jobs. "Everyone around, degree or no degree, seemed to be looking for work that could bring quick cash: this could be a translating job, as well as babysitting for an affluent family or going into retail business," remembered Elena Gapova, a history graduate student in Minsk in the early 1990s. "No one knew where opportunities were and who would win, in the end. People tried what they could." Teachers became cleaning women after hours; professors tutored high-school students; doctors took on private patients. Friends and family loaned one another money and traded goods. It had long been common for urban people to grow some of their own food in community gardens near the cities or at rural cottages (dachas); now they grew more. Grandmothers pitched in, putting up the food grown at the dachas and taking care of children when daycare centers closed or became too expensive.[2]

In the countryside, the peasants doubled or even tripled the output of their kitchen gardens so as to have more to sell at local markets. Women did much of this additional work, because the private plots had long been their responsibility, but men in Russia, Kazakhstan, and Siberia helped out more than in the past. Among the Sakha (formerly the Yakuts), men left unemployed by the closing of collective farms looked after the children while their wives planted and weeded and the old women tended the cows. By 2003, the private plots, the source of much of Soviet produce since Stalin's time, were growing 93 percent of Russia's potatoes and 80 percent of other vegetables.[3]

Millions of people coped with the hard times by leaving home. One million ethnic Russians living in Central Asia and Siberia moved to European Russia in 1994 alone. Some returned to their hometowns or to places where relatives lived. Those who lacked such connections settled in the smaller cities, where residency permits were easier to obtain. Even though building a new life was not easy, families moved in hopes that their children would have more opportunities in predominantly Russian areas than they had as minorities in the other successor states.[4]

Many others went on the road to find permanent or temporary jobs. A million Armenians journeyed to work in the Slavic republics in the 1990s.

For some citizens of the FSU, this migration took on epic proportions. In the early 2000s, Mikhail Sondak, a mechanic, and his wife Ekaterina, a retired feldsher, drove every six weeks or so from Pinsk, Belarus, to the White Sea port of Murmansk, 1500 miles to the northeast. In that frigid city, Mikhail could earn higher wages than at home. Periodically, the couple would drive back to Pinsk to check on their teenaged daughter, Irina. Tens of thousands of other people from the FSU found work in Western and Central Europe and in North America. Between 1995 and 2000, 400,000 women left Ukraine for the West. They were part of the largest migration out of Eastern Europe since World War II.[5]

Some of the women who stayed home found work in the new economy. Female entrepreneurs set up beauty salons, cosmetics distributorships, groceries, and laundries. Others became small traders, selling food, consumer goods, and handcrafts in hometown markets. In the Caucasus and Central Asia, such women created burgeoning family businesses. By the mid-1990s, many had become importers, traveling abroad to buy clothes, packaged foods, and other portable consumer goods for resale at home. Ekaterina and Mikhail Sondak made the reverse choice: in the early 2000s they opened a clothing store in Murmansk. Hiring an accountant and a salesperson to conduct daily business, the couple continued to make the three-thousand-mile round-trip to Pinsk to buy inventory produced in new Belarusian factories.[6]

Female entrepreneurs were most likely to succeed in small businesses with low start-up costs and female clienteles, such as beauty parlors and clothing stores. Even these ventures were risky, and women struggled against gender beliefs as well. Many people considered it disreputable to be a merchant, an opinion that had been around since long before the Revolution and was strengthened in the post-Soviet period by the rampant corruption. The common wisdom held that women should not sully themselves by getting involved in such things. Nor were women welcome in the higher levels of the new economy, which was run, as the Soviet economy had been, by networks of men. Gender and age discrimination were common, even in fields such as banking that had employed many female managers during the Soviet period. To provide support for one another, businesswomen set up clubs in large and small cities.[7]

Some women resorted to making a living in the sex trade. Law enforcement had kept prostitution and pornography underground throughout the Soviet period. After 1991, that enforcement languished and they came out in the open, particularly in the European republics of the FSU. Pornography was sold at neighborhood newsstands. Well-dressed call girls frequented hotel lobbies in the big cities. Hundreds of websites aimed at foreign men featured gorgeous young women available for on-line chat or marriage. When interviewed, many of these women gave economic necessity as their motive for being sex workers or for seeking foreign husbands. Liuda, a teenager in the small city of Efremov, Russia, confided to documentary filmmaker Josef Pasternak in 2002 that she had become a stripper in order to save enough money to go to acting school in Moscow.[8]

The press publicized the criminal side of the sex trade, particularly incidents of women being recruited for jobs abroad, only to discover when they got to Germany or the United States, that they were virtual slaves to pimps who forced them into prostitution. Such stories horrified many people, who came to see the legal and the illegal trafficking in sex to be a product of post-Soviet decadence, created by a corrupt new elite and the influx of Western influences. This decadence, like other malign developments of the 1990s, seemed to be disproportionately affecting women.[9]

Discussing Gender

As so often during periods of rapid change in Russian history, there was a widespread perception in the post-Soviet years that gender required discussion. When that discussion began in the early 1990s, it centered on the perception that women's burdens, considerable in Soviet times, had increased. They were being laid off in record numbers, the social services they relied on to ease the double shift had been slashed, and they were openly discriminated against in the new economy. The family seemed imperiled as well. The birthrate fell, along with male life expectancy, and by the late 1990s the populations of all the successor states save those in Central Asia were declining. Alarming statistics documented widespread domestic violence in families stressed by the hard times. Bride capture was reportedly on the rise in Kazakhstan. Because so many people believed that survival of the family depended primarily on women, the question of how they were to live in the new societies took on critical importance. The result was a broadening and deepening of the discussion begun under Gorbachev into the liveliest public consideration of gender matters since NEP.[10]

Most participants agreed that the Soviet system had exploited women. Historian Liudmila Popkova summed up a widespread attitude when she wrote, "The Soviet state institutionalized a distinctive order in which the roles of men and women were defined according to the needs of the communist state." Galina Starovoitova, an ethnographer, declared sardonically that women had "enjoyed the privilege of heavy manual labor, work in foundries and metallurgical plants, and could sit in the make-believe parliament of a dictatorial regime; it was not real equality." Opinion on how to rectify that situation quickly divided into two schools of thought, the "feminist" and the "maternalist."[11]

The feminists developed the arguments they had begun making under Gorbachev. They declared that women should be men's equals in the new society and that they should not suffer disproportionately from the economic collapse. To remedy the situation, feminists made the argument made so long ago by Zhenotdel leaders: political parties should encourage women to move into leadership positions. Governments should enforce equal access to new economic, political, and cultural opportunities and increase funding for health care, daycare, and maternity leave. Furthermore, society's awareness of the pervasiveness of sexism had to be increased. Men should do more housework; benefits programs should be conceptualized as assisting families rather than enabling women to work the double shift. "We advocate harmony in the development of society, healthy families, partnership between men and women in making decisions regarding the government, society, the economy, and daily life. But unfortunately, patriarchal traditions are still strong in our society, asserting the priority of male strength, intelligence, and power," wrote Liudmila Iacheistova, a member of the zhensovet of Vologda, northeast of Moscow. If those traditions could be overcome, feminists argued, women could enjoy equality of rights and opportunities. They could make their own choices, wrote philosopher Olga Lipovskaia, "to create, to earn money, to sit at home with the children, or go on a business trip."[12]

Feminists believed that the transformation had to begin with individuals shaking off the shackles of Soviet-era thinking. This was a common belief in the 1990s, as people across the FSU struggled to orient themselves to the new world. Anastasia Posadskaia, a founding member of feminist organizations during perestroika, declared, "I believe that women should understand that no one ever has liberated us and no one ever will liberate us, unless we do it ourselves. We must free ourselves from our silence, stereotypes and political manipulation. Only a revolution of morals and ideology can transform women from the objects of a policy formulated by others into the driving force of social change."[13] That revolution must begin, Posadskaia and other feminists believed, with women joining together with like-minded others, as feminists in the West had done during the early stages of second-wave feminism.

The maternalists agreed with the feminists that women had been exploited by the Soviet system. They proposed very different remedies for this exploitation, however. Rather than become even more engaged in the public world, women should leave the paid-labor force, maternalists argued. Childrearing was women's primary social duty and most rewarding undertaking, but too many had been unable to be good mothers in the past because the state had made them work outside the home. If they became homemakers, they could nourish their own well-being and restore the family, which had been battered by Soviet policies. The state, the maternalists declared, had taught children that it was the authority on morality, and had thereby usurped the role of parents and undermined their authority. By paying benefits to mothers, it had weakened the standing of men within their families. "What emerged was a situation in which women relied increasingly on the state as the omnipresent, reliable father and husband," wrote historian Sergei Khukhterin, "while men were effectively marginalized, their domestic power curtailed, along with their ultimate responsibility to and for their families."[14] The consequences were high divorce rates, domestic violence, alcoholism and drug abuse, the alienation of young people, and the early death of dispirited men. To get society on the right track, maternalists wanted women to have more children, create happy homes, and support the authority of their husbands.

Nationalists added that if women stayed home, they could better preserve native cultures and nurture the next generation. This venerable argument was very popular in all the successor states, where people and governments were attempting to define their national identities. As part of this effort, nationalists across the FSU coupled their praise of real mothers with veneration of folklore heroines. The most spectacular example of this unearthing of earth mothers was the gigantic winged statue of Oranta-Berehynia erected in Kyiv's (Kiev's) Independence Square in 2001. Critics charged that this purported goddess of the ancient Slavs was an especially gaudy and expensive example of myths manufactured by maternalist nationalists.[15]

The leaders of the predominantly Muslim republics of the Caucasus and Central Asia were seeking to build national identity and cohesion too. To that end, they endorsed Islam as the faith of their people. They did not, however, adopt the conservative Islamic prescriptions about women popular in neighboring Iran and Afghanistan. Indeed, they held Islamism at arm's length and sometimes arrested its proponents. Governments and social commentators in Azerbaijan and Central Asia also endorsed women's legal and civil equality and their right to education and employment. The authoritarian politics of the Soviet era lived on in these countries, and so did the principles of women's emancipation.[16]

Soviet ideas, and older feminist ones, were at the heart of the discussions of gender in the post-Soviet world. The maternalists' core notion—that a woman's most gratifying experience and greatest social service was motherhood—had been a constant theme of the Brezhnev years. It was widely accepted by women as well as men. Although the feminists asserted the importance of gender equality and women's participation in the world beyond the family, many of them agreed with the maternalists that women were innately more nurturing and moral than men. Some used this claim of women's superiority, a legacy of the cult of domesticity, to justify civic engagement, as women had from the earliest days of feminism. What was new after 1991 was the principle, stressed by both sides, that women should be free to make their own choices, rather than being marshaled to tasks set for them by the state. Feminists and maternalists added the promise that women would make choices that promoted social welfare, and in this pledge too they were echoing the reassurances issued by feminists since the nineteenth century.[17]

Discussions of masculinity also continued the themes of the Brezhnev years; they focused on male weakness and decline. Social commentators and ordinary folk alike feared that men, who had been demoralized by the Soviet system, were now collapsing under the strain of the crisis, leaving their wives to keep families going. "The women take absolutely everything on themselves," a peasant woman told historian Susan Bridger. "The men are all alcoholics, they won't do anything." Tatiana Khainovskaia, a Belarusian university student, complained in 2007 that the biggest problems in women's lives were "lack of real men and lack of money."[18]

These laments were reinforced by dismal statistics. Between 1992 and 2000, male life expectancy fell from 62 years to 59 in Russia; female life expectancy in 2000 was 72 years. The most horrifying examples of displaced men were the veterans of the wars in Afghanistan and Chechnya, many of whom had returned to civilian life suffering from post-traumatic stress disorder, but had received little treatment or social support. Less stricken men worried about how to define themselves. A nineteen-year-old Siberian interviewed by Sergei Oushakine in the late 1990s expressed a common feeling when he declared, "Masculinity has lost its former essence, and no new definitions have popped up on the surface yet. I cannot even tell what the contemporary meaning of such a notion as masculinity consists of." Similar laments were heard in the Caucasus.[19]

There were tales of men who were thriving. Websites and magazines glowed with images of stylish, handsome "New Ukrainians" and "New Georgians" who had become rich in private business. These men were successful, press coverage suggested, because they had the energy, courage, and will to reinvent themselves. In the summer of 2007, Vladimir Putin laid claim to being such a man by circulating photographs of himself fishing, bare-chested, in a Siberian river and captaining a sailboat, with his beautiful family alongside. In December 2010 Putin, now prime minister, added cosmopolitan coolness to his resume. He took the stage at a gala fund-raiser in St. Petersburg to sing, badly and sheepishly, the rock-and-roll classic "Blueberry Hill."[20]

Putin's elevation to a paragon of post-Soviet masculinity did not mean that his government had the power to lay down hegemonic masculine ideals, as its predecessors had. In the age of the internet and a flourishing commercial press at home, it could not control the dissemination of masculine ideals, and indeed, it did not try to do so. It also faced a public that did not admire the "New Men." Ordinary people viewed most of them as nouveau-riche thieves in league with corrupt politicians.

Politics in the Successor States

The new rulers were mostly men from the Soviet elite. "While women were waiting on line for food," feminist Maria Arbatova observed tartly, "men carved up the country into pieces." The successor governments did not continue the Soviet practice of setting quotas for female representation in their legislatures and bureaucracies, with the result that the numbers of women in those institutions fell. In 1993, 14 percent of the delegates to the Russian Duma, the national legislature, were women; by 2003 that proportion had dipped below 10 percent. There were more women in regional legislatures and city councils; 26 percent of the members of the Tver municipal Duma in 2005 were female. The public seemed to consider this continuance of male dominance in politics unexceptional. Women did not have the temperament to serve in elected office, many believed. They meant this as a compliment; politics, like business, corrupted everyone who participated in it. Women should devote their talents to the higher callings of education, health care, and childrearing.[21]

PUBLIC POLICY

In the 1990s, the governments of the successor states passed constitutions and other laws that affirmed women's rights to civil, educational, employment, legal, and political equality with men. They continued Soviet benefits programs, but, on the advice of such foreign lenders as the World Bank, they shifted much of the responsibility for funding public services to local governments. Because those administrations were even more strapped for revenues than the national ones, the results were disastrous. Thousands of daycare centers closed; others raised their fees. Maternity and child-support benefits went unpaid. The sick had to bear more of the cost of treatment, even while conditions in the hospitals deteriorated. The implementation of all these changes was made still worse by poor planning and local foot-dragging, the same difficulties that had plagued many Soviet projects.

Abortion rights in the Western successor states were also imperiled. Nationalist conservatives and the Orthodox and Catholic Churches advocated restricting abortion, citing declining populations as a rationale. The Russian and Ukrainian governments made some unpublicized, minor changes in the regulations in 2003–2004, but widespread public support for the availability of the procedure dissuaded them from going further. Perhaps they were influenced as well by the fact that women were having fewer abortions. Between 1991 and 2001, there was a 50 percent drop in the abortion rate in Russia and Ukraine because public-health workers and volunteer organizations, supported by international agencies and foundations, expanded family-planning counseling and increased supplies of affordable contraceptives.

Women in Central Asia and the Caucasus had less access to contraceptives and underwent fewer abortions. They continued to prefer having large families. In 2007, the Uzbek government, worried about overpopulation, ordered physicians to promote surgical sterilizations; the birthrate dropped in consequence, even as complaints about women being forced to have the procedures increased.[22]

WOMEN IN POLITICS

The most important women in the governments of the FSU were those who kept social services functioning. In cities and towns, many of the civil servants who staffed the schools, hospitals, and social-service agencies were women; some of these people worked hard to preserve programs benefiting women and to create new ones, staffed by volunteers, that could help people deal with the economic crisis. In Uzbekistan, this collaboration resulted in a network of women's committees extending from the national to the neighborhood level. Neighborhood committee members served as volunteer social workers, passing out poor relief, advising women on family matters, and teaching Islam. Many people across the FSU, especially poor women, believed that women did such jobs better than men, because they were more sympathetic to the plight of the disadvantaged. The general disgust with politicians did not extend, therefore, to those civil servants who helped women get through the hard times.[23]

The political parties that sprang up after 1991 were predominantly male organizations, with a couple of fleeting exceptions. The largest and most successful of these was the Women of Russia party (WOR), formed in 1993 by the Union of Women of Russia, an alliance of three women's groups: the Soviet Women's Committee, the Association of Women Entrepreneurs of Russia, and the Women of the Naval Fleet. WOR ran on a platform that criticized other parties for not paying attention to women's plight, praised female legislators as more effective than male ones, and advocated increased spending on services beneficial to women. The campaign succeeded; WOR won twenty-one seats. The party's delegates to the Duma concentrated on funding social services, such as family planning, and on writing laws that affirmed gender equality.[24]

WOR's successes were short-lived. In elections in 1995, their delegation shrank to three representatives. Political inexperience, which plagued all the new parties, contributed to this decline, as did WOR's own particular weaknesses. Its leaders quarreled with one another and with other female activists. Feminist groups denounced WOR for its association with the Soviet Women's Committee and charged that its delegates were mere tokens who did as men told them. The fact that WOR became more assertively feminist during its two years in the Duma did not allay the suspicions. There was still greater diversity of political opinion among the masses of female voters, huge majorities of whom did not vote for WOR.[25]

Women participated in other parties much as they had done in the Soviet communist party—that is, they remained in the lower ranks, where they did clerical and organizational work. In the Caucasus and Central Asia, women ran female auxiliaries derived from the Soviet Women's Committees. Male party leaders reported that they valued their female comrades as dependable, reliable functionaries who were more compliant and less ambitious than male politicians.[26] Perhaps the ambitious ones learned to content themselves with whatever they could achieve.

A handful of women did rise to positions of regional and national leadership across the FSU. There were probably several thousand such women in the period under consideration here, of whom two, Kazimiera Prunskiene of Lithuania and Yulia Tymoshenko of Ukraine, reached the highest offices in their nations.

KAZIMIERA PRUNSKIENE (b. 1943), AND
YULIA TYMOSHENKO (b. 1960)

Prunskiene and Tymoshenko were Ph.D. economists who, like Tatiana Zaslavskaia, entered politics during the Gorbachev years, but who, unlike Zaslavskaia, stayed in the game after 1991. Prunskiene was the sort of politician that Zaslavskaia scorned as "sly, dodgy." Her admirers praised her pragmatism and flexibility. A specialist in agricultural development, Prunskiene was one of the founders of the independence movement Sajudis. In 1990 she became prime minister, then resigned a year later because of policy differences with parliamentary leaders. She set up a consulting firm and returned to academics, publishing studies of economic development in post-socialist Eastern Europe.

Soon Prunskiene's ambitions drew her back into the political fray. First she tried to build a base among women. Following the example of WOR, she founded the Women's Party of Lithuania in 1995 and criticized the continuing economic and political inequality of women as well as conservative Catholic influences. When the Women's Party failed to win popular support, Prunskiene renamed it the New Democracy Party and arranged a merger with the larger Farmers' Party. Now she became an advocate for the peasants, supporting the development of private enterprise in rural areas, declaring her allegiance to "conservative values (family, local communities, Christian morality)," and speaking fondly of her own childhood in the countryside. She served as a delegate to the national legislature, the Seimas, from 1996 onward, and managed to build up her own popularity, if not that of her party. In 2004 the Farmers and New Democracy Party won 6.6 percent of the popular vote in parliamentary elections, while Prunskiene, running for president that same year, lost by only 3 percent of the vote. Thereafter she became minister of agriculture. Her adaptation to democratic politics had succeeded.[27]

Yulia Tymoshenko exercised her political skills in Ukraine's more turbulent political world. She had worked in the Komsomol during graduate school. When perestroika came, she built a successful chain of video-rental stores. In the 1990s, she moved to the more lucrative field of managing privatized energy companies and made a fortune. Politics then began to interest her again, and she decided to run for election to Ukraine's national legislature, the Verkhovna Rada. Eloquent and beautiful, Tymoshenko received huge majorities from her constituents.

In the late 1990s, she began to criticize the corruption of the new elite, of which she herself was such a successful member. Appointed deputy

A photograph of Kazimiera Prunskiene in the 2000s.
http://en.wikipedia.org/wiki/File:Kazimiera_Prunskiene.2008-05-23.jpg. Accessed June 27, 2011.

KAZIMIERA PRUNSKIENE

In 1990, after Lithuania had declared its independence, Prunskiene came to Washington, D.C. The visit put the U.S. political establishment, then supporting Mikhail Gorbachev, in a difficult position. According to Maureen Dowd of the *New York Times,* Prunskiene rose to the occasion.

"At a dinner tonight, with journalists at the house of Christopher Matthews, a columnist for *The San Francisco Examiner,* Mrs. Prunskiene was asked why Lithuania had not waited a year to declare its independence.

She smiled and said, 'We felt we had to do it quickly, like a karate chop, if it was to work.'

Mrs. Prunskiene, a 47-year-old economist and former Communist Party official, had a small entourage, no security guards and she rode in a dark-blue sedan paid for by a private person in the Lithuanian-American community. As a translator, she used the head of a Lithuanian-American organization based in Washington.

Even so, she showed a natural aptitude for American politics. When the Prime Minister settled in her room at the Embassy Row hotel here on Wednesday night, her friends and advisers gathered around to counsel her on how to handle the American politicians she would be meeting.

They told her that each politician would think he was more important than the last.

'And my job,' she said, smiling knowingly, 'is to confirm that.'"

Yulia Tymoshenko speaking to the press on December 2, 2010.
http://www.tymoshenko.ua/. Accessed December 2, 2010.

YULIA TYMOSHENKO

In July 2010, on her husband's birthday, Tymoshenko wrote this about him on her blog:

"There are people (very few, unfortunately) who you can always rely on in the most difficult moments. You know that they'll never betray you, they'll never turn away, they'll never judge. Such is my Oleksandr. And not because he's my husband, but because he's a real man—120%.

We were once in the same detention facility in Lukianivka. It was clear that they threw my husband behind bars only because he was my husband. Back then this was a 'crime.' One night he and I were both being taken for questioning and we saw each other for just a moment, for just one breath. But for me this was enough. This gave me such a boost of energy, faith and courage that I felt I could endure and survive everything. It seems the prison administrators also sensed this because the next day Sasha was transferred to a prison in the Zhytomyr oblast. He handed me a note directly into the cell on which he wrote: 'Don't give up.' . . .

Why am I writing all this? Just because. I'm grateful to my husband for simply being. I'm grateful that I have someone I can rely on. I'm grateful that in all these years he has never said a word about the fact that I haven't dedicated myself entirely to my family. . . .

I hope that you always have lots of people you can rely on. "

SOURCE: YULIA TYMOSHENKO, HTTP://BLOG.TYMOSHENKO.UA/EN/ARTICLE/ACNONAA4.
THE TRANSLATION HAS BEEN SLIGHTLY EDITED HERE BY BARBARA CLEMENTS

prime minister for the fuel and energy sector by Prime Minister Victor Yushchenko in 1999, Tymoshenko set about closing tax loopholes that were benefiting many of her former colleagues. They retaliated by having President Leonid Kuchma fire her in January 2001, and then arrest her on corruption charges. Tymoshenko emerged from a month in jail more critical of the government than ever. She organized her own political party, the Yulia Tymoshenko Bloc, and began holding public protests. She was targeted for assassination in 2003, but survived a suspicious auto crash.

Tymoshenko came to international attention during Ukraine's Orange Revolution of December 2004, when hundreds of thousands of demonstrators gathered in downtown Kyiv to protest Kuchma's clumsy attempts to falsify the results of a presidential election in favor of his candidate, Victor Yanukovich. Her long blond hair now braided and curled around her head in a hairdo once favored by Ukraine's peasant women, Tymoshenko became the voice of the protestors, speaking often before them and to the international press. Kuchma soon backed down and a coalition of reform parties chose Tymoshenko as prime minister in January 2005.

When the coalition fell apart nine months later, Yushchenko fired Tymoshenko. She returned to building her reputation and her party. She vowed to end corruption, reform the economy, and assert Ukraine's independence from Russia. She also promised to make life better for peasant women. Tymoshenko continued to cultivate foreign elites, publishing articles in such prestigious journals as *Foreign Affairs* and traveling often to Western Europe. By the fall of 2007 she was heading two political parties, the Yulia Tymoshenko Bloc and the All Union Fatherland Party. In elections that summer, her Bloc received one-third of the vote. In December, she once again became prime minister. In February 2010, she lost a bid for the presidency to a resurgent Yanukovich, and thereafter resigned from the premiership and became the leader of the coalition of opposition parties in the parliament. The vicious jockeying for power that had bedeviled Ukraine's politics for more than a decade continued thereafter.[28]

Tymoshenko and Prunskiene were intelligent, ambitious, determined, adroit, and assertive. In their political skills, they resembled Catherine the Great. Like Catherine, they were elite women who reached for power to which the patriarchal rules of the game did not entitle them. Like Catherine, they built alliances with powerful men and tailored their advocacy to the public mood. They also created reassuringly feminine images, as Catherine had done. Prunskiene dressed the part of a matronly professional and embraced family values. Tymoshenko wore designer clothes that showed off her figure, publicized her church-going, and kept her bright hair in that peasant braid. The clothes and the smiles cloaked the reality that these women, like Catherine, were hard-nosed political infighters. Prunskiene and Tymoshenko may have been even more skilled at the dark arts of politics than Catherine, for Catherine was sustained at least in part by her courtiers' deference to her royal rank. The other two made their way in the free-for-all of post-Soviet politics.

WOMEN IN THE MEDIA

There were many women among the journalists who worked to build an independent press in the successor states. It was a risky business, for the autocratic regimes in Belarus and Central Asia arrested their critics, while in Ukraine President Kuchma arranged automobile accidents or poisonings for his. In Russia, Yeltsin was fairly tolerant of the electronic and print media; Putin was not. He closed offending television networks, arrested critics on trumped-up charges, and approved assassinations. Estimates of the number of journalists murdered in Russia between 1991 and 2010 range from several dozen to more than three hundred. Despite the intimidation and the increasingly strict regulation of the media, a few outspoken women remained. Of these, two of the best known were Maria Arbatova and Anna Politkovskaia.

MARIA ARBATOVA (b. 1957) AND
ANNA POLITKOVSKAIA (1958–2006)

Maria Arbatova was a sardonic, self-promoting playwright, poet, novelist, talk-show host, radio broadcaster, actor, and blogger who became famous in the 1990s as "Russia's first feminist." She was not the first, but she, unlike the academic feminists, had a national audience. Arbatova was a Muscovite who began publishing stories on women's lives in the 1980s and embraced feminism during the Gorbachev years. In the 1990s she organized women's groups, became an adviser to Yeltsin, and wrote still more on feminist themes. She became famous as host of the television show *I Myself.* Her co-host, also a woman, sang the praises of motherhood as woman's highest calling; Arbatova championed feminism. In an effort to break down feminism's negative connotations for her audience, Arbatova dressed well, talked lovingly about her twin sons, bemoaned the double shift, and asserted women's rights to independence and equality. The show became a hit, particularly with working-class women, and Arbatova became a star.[29]

After *I Myself* went off the air, Arbatova remained Russia's foremost celebrity feminist. Broadening her criticism in the Putin years to include human-rights issues, she larded her public pronouncements with humor. Her novel, *How I Tried to Get into the Duma Honestly* (2007), mocked political corruption. In 2007 she drew international attention when she proposed that since Russian men were drinking and smoking themselves to death, the government should import Indian men for Russian women to marry. She had married one herself. Arbatova hosted a radio program, *The Right to Be Yourself,* and maintained a lively website and a Facebook page.[30]

Anna Politkovskaia was a muckraking journalist of exceptional courage and determination. She came to prominence by publishing reports on atrocities committed by the Russian army during the war with separatists in the province of Chechnya. Soon she turned her attention to passionate exposés of corrupt politicians, judges, and businessmen. Politkovskaia was unsparing in her condemnation of Putin. "I dislike him for a matter-of-factness worse than felony," she wrote in 2004, "for his cynicism, for his racism, for his lies . . . , for the massacre of the innocents that went on throughout his first term as president."[31] When Chechen terrorists seized a school in the city of Beslan in 2004, Politkovskaia flew south to help mediate the confrontation. En route, she became seriously ill, probably because she had been poisoned. Undeterred, she continued to write her scathing articles. On October 7, 2006, Putin's birthday, gunmen lying in wait in the elevator of her apartment building in Moscow assassinated her.

The fact that she was publishing her criticism abroad and thereby publicizing the regime's brutality to the world, even as it was trying to present itself as humane and democratic, may have sealed her fate. Officially, the government denied any involvement in her death, then launched an investigation that proceeded according to well-established precedents. Police found the gunmen, but not those who had hired them. In 2009, the three men tried for her murder were acquitted, the acquittal was overturned on appeal, and a new trial was ordered. The same year, five people who had worked with Politkovskaia to expose human-rights abuses in Chechnya were killed.[32]

FEMALE TERRORISTS

The atrocities in Chechnya also called forth a terrorist campaign against the Russians in which a handful of women participated.

The most lethal attacks were the occupation of the Dubrovka Theater in Moscow in the fall of 2002 and of a school in the southern city of Beslan in 2004. In both cases the terrorists included a few heavily armed women. In both cases hundreds of people died when police tried to free the hostages. The women called themselves *shakhidki,* a Russification of the Arabic word for martyr. Dressed in black headscarves or veiled from head to foot, shakhidki also conducted most of the group's suicide bombings. In August 2004, two of them blew up two passenger jets in flight, killing ninety people. A few weeks later a single shakhidka destroyed herself and nine others in a Moscow subway station. In March 2010, two women, one of them identified as Dzhanet Abdurakhmanova, the seventeen-year-old widow of a Chechen militant leader, killed forty people and wounded more than ninety in a suicide attack on the Moscow subway.[33]

Veiled women assaulting defenseless civilians seemed to confirm the long-standing Russian belief that the male Chechen terrorists were savages and female terrorists their benighted dupes. Most Russians had not read Politkovskaia's articles. They did not know that their army had committed war crimes against the Chechens, including the rape of children, which went unpunished. The shakhidki, inspired by the militant Islamism preached among Chechen guerillas and by the suicide bombers of the Palestinian Intifada, sought through terrorism to avenge their dead and draw attention to the crimes perpetrated against their people. Vengeance seemed the stronger of their motives, for the mass killing of civilians did nothing to inform Russians about the depredations of their own government.[34]

The New Activism

Some women responded to the freedoms and stresses of post-Soviet times by joining a wide variety of volunteer groups, the so-called "civic organizations." In the early 2000s, 2 to 2.5 million people, the majority of them women, belonged to these groups in Russia alone. They joined for a variety of reasons. Some were attempting to help themselves by helping others. This was the case with the women who established an organization, Our House, to give aid to large families in Kyiv. Others, such as the midwives who did home-birthing in St. Petersburg, were applying their professional skills to volunteer work. Still others were continuing the projects begun during the Soviet period by the zhensovety. Many members of civic organizations believed that their work fostered the development of democratic politics; feminists also saw them as a way to organize women to achieve their emancipation. Activists and the public believed that civic organizations were suited to women because they were philanthropic and because they were independent of the government. Julie Hemment has written, "The market and formal politics were regarded as dirty, but also as masculine domains. . . . The non-governmental . . . sphere was seen to be decent, moral, and in this way peculiarly feminine."[35]

WOMEN-CENTERED CIVIC ORGANIZATIONS

Soviet women began organizing civic organizations to address issues of particular concern to women in the late 1980s, as we have seen. To establish connections between groups, hundreds of these activists met at Dubna, outside Moscow, in 1991 and again in 1992. Their networking led to the creation in 1994 of the Moscow Information Center of the Independent Women's Forum, an umbrella organization that maintained communications between groups, distributed information, provided grants, and sponsored regional and national conferences. Meanwhile, in Ukraine, the Baltics, Armenia, and Azerbaijan, members of the women's auxiliaries of the pre-1991 independence movements were creating civic organizations. They too coordinated their activities through national committees.[36]

Most of the women-centered civic organizations were small local groups set up to help women, including the volunteers themselves. The Ivanovo Committee of Single-Parent Families, led by single mothers, lobbied that city's government to fund programs and organized support groups. In Kiev, For Life worked with pensioners. In Armenia, women's civic organizations helped families of men killed in the war with Azerbaijan in the early 1990s.[37]

The number of professional organizations grew as well. Businesswomen in many cities, most in the European republics, set up clubs to share information about entrepreneurship. In Moscow, *Tvorchestvo* (Creative Work) did fund-raising, held job-training classes for unemployed artists, and, in a poignant echo of the 1860s, organized sewing workshops. Societies established by female academics sponsored conferences, published scholarly proceedings, and assisted their members in obtaining funding for research. Particularly influential was the Moscow Center for Gender Studies, organized in 1990 with the goal of "using the results of our own and foreign scholarship to overcome discrimination against women." It and centers at universities in Kharkov, Minsk, St. Petersburg, Tver, and elsewhere promoted the development of gender studies and a lively critique of gender inequality.[38]

This activism was not confined to the European successor states. In the Caucasus, Baku once again became a center of female activism. Women there established civic organizations to support female entrepreneurs and assist the poor and victims of domestic violence. In 2002, female academics set up the Azerbaijan Gender Information Center to serve as "the first informational, analytical, bibliographical, and documentary center of the women's movement in the territory of the South Caucasus." The organization's website published articles on international activism and on the history of Azeri women. It publicized conferences, government programs, and sources of information on legal and psychological counseling and medical care.

Some women-centered civic organizations undertook public advocacy. Many lobbied local, regional, and national governments for supportive legislation and increases in benefits. Sappho-Petersburg published a newsletter for lesbians and held educational meetings to counter homophobia. *Sestri* (Sisters) ran a domestic-violence hotline and held workshops on sexual violence for the general public as well as for safety forces. In the late 1990s its leaders worked with female attorneys and counselors across Russia to establish the Russian Association of Crisis Centers for Women, which acted as an informational clearinghouse for people helping victims of rape and domestic violence.[39]

OTHER CIVIC ORGANIZATIONS

Women worked as well in civic organizations advocating for environmental conservation and human rights. Of the latter groups, one of the largest was the Union of Committees of Soldiers' Mothers; it was also the largest women's civic organization. Founded in 1989 to protest the brutal treatment of draftees in the Soviet army, it grew into a network of committees spread across Russia and Ukraine and coordinated by a national board headquartered in Moscow. "They [the local committees] were born of maternal love," the committee declared on its website, "of a refusal to accept violence, and of a strong sense of civic responsibility." The soldiers' mothers lobbied the government for army reforms, advised parents of draftees on their legal rights, and even, on occasion, sheltered AWOL soldiers. They set up a website that published investigations of beatings and other abuse. The committees protested the war in Chechnya and publicized the war's horrors. They helped the mothers of soldiers who were imprisoned in Chechnya to travel to the area to plead for their sons' release. All this activism earned the committees widespread public support in Russia and Ukraine and inspired the formation of other groups, including the Mothers of Beslan, which sought to uncover the truth about the botched attempt to free the hostages taken by Chechen terrorists in the school siege of September 2004.[40]

LIUDMILA ALEXEEVA (b. 1927)

Most human-rights organizations were led by men, but there was one important exception: Helsinki Watch Moscow, set up by dissidents in the 1970s. In 1996, it invited Liudmila Alexeeva, one of its founders, to become its head. Two years later she was elected president of the International Helsinki Federation on Human Rights. Famous among the intelligentsia as a "legendary dissident and human-rights defender," Alexeeva proved to be a forceful critic of the government. She spoke up against the repression and the brutality of the Chechen war. She scorned Yeltsin as "Bloody Boris," and was just as critical of Putin. At a demonstration on the first anniversary of Anna Politkovskaia's assassination, Alexeeva declared, "They murdered her because she was fearless. She was fighting against lawlessness, against violence, and against lies." The octogenarian scoffed at the dangers of being so blunt. "If I were to be killed, no one would say, 'Oh, what a tragedy, she was cut down so young,'" she told an interviewer in 2007. "But I also think it's better to go [on] doing what you want."[41]

Alexeeva happily took part in annual rallies held on New Year's Eve to dramatize the government's refusal to honor the constitutional guarantee of freedom of assembly. On December 31, 2009, she showed up dressed as the mythic snow maiden, in a sparkling blue gown and white muff. She was quickly arrested and almost as quickly released, because the government wanted to avoid martyring an old woman with an international reputation. It did not escape embarrassment. The U.S. government and the European Parliament promptly condemned the arrest, and a picture of Alexeeva being manhandled by police ran in newspapers across Europe. "If it serves as a lesson to them," Alexeeva told a *New York Times* reporter, "I wouldn't call it a victory, but it would be useful. Whether it will serve as a lesson I can't say, because they study very badly."[42]

ACHIEVEMENTS AND DIFFICULTIES

There were parallels between post-Soviet activism and that of the pre-revolutionary era. The post-Soviet activists, many of them professionals, were a tiny minority of women, as their predecessors had been. They struggled to sustain the morale, staffing, and funding of their organizations and they coped with government intransigence and sometimes with oppression. As in the past, women with connections to the political leadership had the greatest success. Unlike the pre-revolutionary generations, some of the activists of the post-Soviet world enjoyed support from international sources and access to modern communications that facilitated organizing. Their endeavors were made easier by nearly universal literacy and widespread acceptance, thanks to progress in the Soviet era, of the notion that women should be involved in public life.

Self-identified feminists were a tiny minority among the women in civic organizations. Maternalist ideas, especially the notion that activists were applying their nurturing skills to helping mothers and children, were far more common, especially in the early 1990s. As time passed, awareness of the systemic nature of gender inequities grew among the activists, because they found themselves struggling against them and because contacts with feminists from abroad proliferated. Particularly important for the women of the Baltics, the Caucasus, and Central Asia was the United Nations Women's Conference of 1995. The governments of the successor states, eager to be accepted into the international community, sent female delegates to the meeting in Beijing, and there they met thousands of female activists from around the world.[43]

The contact with foreigners, particularly international aid agencies and foundations, was a mixed blessing. Their grants buoyed the fortunes of many civic organizations. For example, the Ford Foundation and the Canadian Fund for Gender Equality supported the Tver Center for Women's History and Gender Studies. The U.S. Agency for International Development gave grants to battered women's shelters, and the League of Women Voters sponsored travel by female politicians from Russia and Ukraine to the United States. Foundations from Europe and the United States underwrote research projects and scholarly publications. But the relationship between the foreigners and the activists could be problematic. Many of the outsiders took a patronizing attitude toward the people of the FSU, and their assumption of the superiority of their own perspectives affected which projects received funding. Battered women's shelters were a favorite in the late 1990s, while organizations that espoused maternalism were not. The funding priorities of the international agencies also shifted over time, and grants were usually short-term, leaving civic organizations to redirect their activities or find other sources of support when the money ran out. This situation also plagued women's groups elsewhere in Eastern Europe.[44]

Another frustration arose from frictions between the civic organizations and national, regional, and local governments. In smaller cities, particularly in the European republics, many workers in civic organizations maintained good relations with the authorities. The activists gained access thereby to office space in publicly owned buildings and funding for their projects from officials glad to have the volunteers' help in providing services. In Ivanovo, Russia, for example, the leaders of the local chapter of the Union of Women of Russia, the successor to the Soviet Women's Committee, collaborated with the bureaucracy in the late 1990s in establishing programs to help poor families. Civic organizations in the major cities were more suspicious of involvement with government, and government officials often viewed the larger and more feminist groups as troublemakers. The most autocratic regimes, such as that of President Alexander Lukashenko of Belarus, permitted only politically compliant philanthropic organizations to operate. The Russian government under Yeltsin was more tolerant, under Putin less so. It issued regulations in 2004 and 2005 tightening oversight, particularly over the public-advocacy civic organizations and foreign funders. Perhaps following the Russian example, Lukashenko then began harassing with regulations even such resolutely apolitical groups as the American-based Children of Chernobyl, which brought Belarusian children to the United States in the summer for vacations and medical care. By the mid-2000s, governments in the autocratic successor states were still letting volunteers help out with problems caused by the drastic cuts in social services, especially if those volunteers would fund their projects themselves, but they were keeping a close eye on them. Here was yet another carryover of Soviet practices, and of tsarist ones as well.[45]

The women of the civic organizations trained millions of women in social activism, helped millions more cope with hardship, and disseminated reformist ideas. But their immediate impact on the great majority of women in the FSU was limited. A 2002 poll of women in Russia found that 70 percent of respondents did not know whether civic organizations were active in their regions. Still worse, more than half of those who were aware of them doubted that they themselves might benefit from their operations, and, when asked whether women were better than men at defending women's interests, only 62 percent answered in the affirmative. Better-educated women were more likely to have heard about and participated in civic organizations, a finding that reflected the organizations' base among such women.[46]

This weakness plagued all civic organizations. Across the FSU, people were far less likely to participate in volunteer groups than were citizens of the Western democracies.[47] This was a legacy of Soviet times, when volunteerism had been required and controlled by the regime and people had avoided it when possible. There was little motivation to change that habit after 1991, with survival demanding so much and volunteerism giving back so little. Once again, as in the past, female social activists worked assiduously to improve their own situation, preserve their organizations, cultivate government support, and reach out to poorer women. The poor concentrated on getting by and relied on family, friends, and help from local governments.

Satisfactions and Concerns

In the second decade after the end of the Soviet Union, women across the FSU voiced many of the same satisfactions and concerns about their personal lives and their societies. The hardships and disappointments of the period had provoked widespread feelings that the new world was less secure and less fair than the old. Remembering Soviet times, Ekaterina Sondak, the feldsher from Pinsk who became a businesswoman, commented, "There were many good things. In spite of everything, life was very calm and people were sure that tomorrow would be like today. In 1991, all people were in the same material position. They had the same possibilities; everybody had the same clothes, the same food. There was no range of production in shops. Everyone was equal, with equal salaries and wages." Elena Khainovskaia, a Belarusian physician, agreed: "There were many really good things [in the Soviet period]. Free education, free health care; for different work credits, you could get a car or a flat or something else. There were some bad things, but as the time passes I forget them."[48]

The old world had not been as egalitarian as Sondak and Khainovskaia remembered; the elite then too enjoyed a far higher standard of living than did less fortunate folk. Much had been lost, though. The Soviet guarantees—employment for high-school and university graduates, job security once hired, cheap public services, and low prices for the goods that were available—were either gone or greatly weakened. Now money and connections mattered more than ever, income disparities grew, and professionals, who had enjoyed high status as members of the intelligentsia in the Soviet system, struggled to get by on wages that did not keep up with rising prices. Tatiana Khainovskaia, Elena's daughter, summed up the situation eloquently in 2010: "So the people who have some of the most important jobs (doctors save people's lives and teachers sometimes save students' souls) earn the same amount of money (if not less) than someone working in a clothing store."[49]

For the great majority of women, life was harder. Eighty-five percent of respondents to a 2002 poll of women in Russia said childrearing had become more difficult since 1991. Substantial percentages of these women also reported that they now had more trouble finding employment (79 percent), getting a good education (64.8 percent), having a rewarding private life (53 percent), and doing their housework (47 percent).[50]

No strangers to hardship, many of these women said that they were learning to cope with the new challenges. Sixty-three percent of the respondents described their personal situations as "satisfactory," and 25 percent said that theirs were "good." The majority rated as adequate the availability of consumer goods and food, and said the same of their housing. Naturally enough, poorer women reported greater discontents, while those who held good jobs and lived in big cities were the most satisfied. Strong majorities of rural and urban women in Russia reported in other polls that they considered their husbands loving, hard-working, supportive, and attentive to the children. Perhaps this was because, even as public opinion bemoaned the crisis in masculinity, most men were successfully adjusting to the new reality.[51]

Women speaking to pollsters and the press took a much more critical view of the world beyond their families, and they worried about that world's impact on their children. In the Soviet system, education had been a pathway to good jobs, economic security, and social mobility. After 1991 the cost of education, particularly higher education, rose, so poorer women feared that their children would be unable to better themselves by studying hard. As always, the peasants were the most disadvantaged and the most pessimistic. In rural areas of Central Asia and the Caucasus by the mid-1990s, some parents had to keep their daughters out of school because they could only afford to pay tuition for their sons.[52]

Women across the FSU also worried about the difficulties of teaching children morality in a society that seemed to have lost its moral compass. Most felt that they themselves could resist the temptations of the new times. Ninety-one percent of the women questioned in the 2002 Russian poll affirmed that they could "live an honest life" even in a society that they regarded as more corrupt than the one they had lost. The children were another matter. When asked in 2007 to name the greatest changes since 1991, Liudmila Buloichik, an English teacher in Minsk, pointed to rising rudeness and materialism among young people, brought on by exposure to Western consumer culture and by a lack of discipline at home and in the schools. A group calling itself "Vologda Mothers for the Morality of Children" expressed the same concerns in a 2004 letter to President Putin: "The reasons for our anxiety and pain are not only local conflicts and wars, the lingering economic and political crises, poverty and unemployment. No less terrible fears arise from the loss of faith and hope, from apathy and depression, from the immorality overwhelming our society, from the ever more rampant deficiencies of alcoholism and drug addiction, sexual dissipation and prostitution, permissiveness and lawlessness."[53]

Few women agreed with the maternalist argument that they should leave the paid-labor force. Work, for most of them, was an economic necessity, and the majority told pollsters that their jobs gave them a sense of personal fulfillment and a community of colleagues and friends. Furthermore, their jobs were less boring than housework and provided a break from the pressures of family life. Many women, particularly in the European republics, still resented the double shift, and their criticism of it echoed those Soviet women had made for decades. "Nowadays, though women and men are considered to be equal, women remain hearth-keepers," lamented Irina, a university student and daughter of the businesswoman Ekaterina Sondak, in 2007. "So her duty is not only to earn money, but to be a good mother, to cook, to keep the house, clean, etc. Not a lot of men help women with these duties because they believe it's not masculine work." Opinion polls in the 1990s reported that two-thirds of wives and husbands thought that the refusal of men to do housework was a major cause of strife between spouses. This statistic seems particularly unfortunate in view of the fact that, as a consequence of the cutbacks in social services, women's chores, particularly childcare, had become more time-consuming. "Leisure for the majority of our contemporaries," wrote the authors of the 2002 Russian poll, "for the most part is reduced to breaks between paid work and housework, during which they pay some attention to the children and watch t.v." Many women complained, as they had done during the Brezhnev years, that the double shift prevented them from upgrading their credentials in order to qualify for better jobs.[54]

Many women perceived as well that continuing gender inequities were affecting their economic opportunities. When asked in 2007 whether women and men were equals in Belarus, Tatiana Khainovskaia, the university student, replied, "Theoretically yes, but practically, men in Belarus seem to have more rights than women." Respondents to the 2002 Russian poll reported that men were more able than women to pursue political careers and become entrepreneurs. They earned higher wages and had greater job mobility. When explaining these inequities, women often attributed them not to gender discrimination, but to natural differences between the sexes. "We know from the Holy Bible that all the people are equal," declared Liudmila Yushko, a student at the Belarusian State University in Minsk in 2007. "But, of course, there are a lot of differences in their psychologies. First of all, we have different values. So, for a woman the most important thing is her family, her children. For a man, it is his career." The 2002 poll of women in Russia found that poorer women were more sensitive to gender discrimination than more privileged ones, probably because they experienced it more frequently.[55]

Polls also found that many women were optimistic about their personal prospects. In the 2002 poll, 75 percent of respondents said that they believed that they would be able to "find real love," "create a happy family," "raise good children," and "have good friends and interesting work." In 2007, the Belarusians Ekaterina Sondak, the businesswoman, and Elena Khainovskaia, the physician, shared this optimism. Despite the hardships and disruptions they had lived through, despite the political repression and poverty of Belarus, they had managed well. The Sondaks' clothing store in Murmansk was a going concern, their son Andrei was an accountant, and their daughter Irina was a student at the best university in Minsk. The Khainovskiis had done well too. Elena's husband Sergei worked in a bank, where he earned a decent salary, and she kept up her medical practice. Her daughter Tatiana and son Andrei were successful students. Both mothers hoped for still more for their daughters. Asked "Do you think Irina will have a better life than you did because of the changes since 1991?" Sondak replied, "I'm sure of that. She is getting a perfect education. And now if she wants to have success in her life, she will have more opportunities than I did in our times." Khainovskaia was less certain. "I think so," she said, "because our society develops and changes and I think that it will give Tania an opportunity to have a better life."[56]

In 2007, the daughters, Irina and Tatiana, aspired to have good jobs and happy families, as their mothers had, but to enjoy more comforts and freedoms than the older generation had known. Tatiana, always enthusiastic and optimistic, declared, "I want to have three children and enough money to provide perfect lives for them, my brother, my parents, and my grandparents, and to work in the tourism business." Irina, a steelier personality, had a less rosy vision: "When I was younger I wanted to become a businesswoman. But now I realize that this is very hard. And being a female is one of the hardships. That's why I want to have a more or less well-paid job with the possibility of promotion. I want to get married, have children, and do everything possible to make their lives easier. I hope that in the future my children will be able not only to dream about a perfect job but to have it." Her limited hopes were widely shared by women across the FSU.[57]

Tatiana Khainovskaia in 2010.
Author's collection.

TATIANA KHAINOVSKAIA

In 2008–2009, Tatiana studied tourism at Central Washington University. A year later, asked about her hopes for the future, she wrote:

"I don't want to leave my country. I was born here. I want to see it develop and flourish. I don't want to have to explain to people from different countries what Belarus is and where it is situated. I want people to know my country. I don't want tourists who are planning their European tour to miss my country. I want them to come here and to see what we have to show and to feel what we have to give them. We are young. We are only 20 years old. It takes time for any country to develop, to grow, to bloom. Rome wasn't built in one day either.

I want to work in the tourism business, because to my mind it's the easiest way of peaceful and beneficial communication between people from all over the world. Ideally, tourism is about creating, not about destroying, but in reality it's not always true. So it's our job, young peoples' job, to create. I want to create an image of my country so that people will want to know about it. I want them not to be afraid of the mythical dangers that await them on the streets of our cities (many still believe that there are bears walking along the streets in Minsk).

I'm proud of my country and I want other people to understand why I'm proud of it. And when I say 'country,' I don't mean the government or the economy . . . I mean the people and nature and everything around us that we see every day."

SOURCE: TATIANA KHAINOVSKAIA, LETTER, NOVEMBER 23, 2010.

Conclusions

The first twenty years of the post-Soviet period were a mélange of gains and losses. By lowering the standard of living, increasing unemployment, and intensifying gender patterns that disadvantaged women, these decades made women's lives more difficult. By weakening the remaining autocratic governments and giving birth to more democratic ones, they expanded civil liberties and contacts with the outside world. Activists grabbed the new opportunities, as they had done before in Russian history. A handful became leaders. Some confronted the authorities. Women in all the successor states launched independent organizations that addressed social problems. Feminism once again flourished within the intelligentsia.

While the activists organized, ordinary folk devoted themselves to adjusting to the new realities. By the early 2000s, women in some of the European republics were telling pollsters that although life was still hard, they had hope for the future. Elena Khainovskaia and Ekaterina Sondak were typical. No one had asked them if they wanted the Soviet Union to end. The country's leaders had simply ended it, and expected them to deal with the wreckage. They had done that well.

Their daughters, Tatiana and Irina, were among the lucky children of the new world, for they had loving, hard-working parents who nurtured their talents. They were middle-class people, not rich by the standards of their country, but able to afford stylish clothes and automobiles. The girls surfed the web, watched pirated foreign movies on the social networking site *V kontakte,* and devoured the Harry Potter novels. They text-messaged. They were critical of the autocratic behavior of the Lukashenko regime. These liberties and possibilities, taken for granted by them, had been unimaginable when their mothers were their age. Their mothers, although wistful about what had been lost, rarely talked to their daughters about the way things had been before.

By the end of the first decade of the twenty-first century, the nations that had been born from the dismantling of the Soviet Union were settling into revised political and economic arrangements and new social consensuses that preserved many Soviet values. With that stability came increasingly authoritarian governments that sought to rein in independent groups and independent voices. Foreign funding receded, regulations on civic organizations increased, and the difficulties of maintaining voluntary organizations overwhelmed many activists. Perhaps their movement would be seen, from the distance of several decades, as an efflorescence born of the instability of the immediate post-Soviet period.

Or perhaps the situation was very different now, because the world was very different—more mobile, more connected—so that emancipatory ideas flowed as freely across borders as the embroidered jeans and girly magazines. Irina and Tatiana were far freer to express themselves and explore the world than their mothers had been. They also had very different points of reference and expectations. In 2010, Tatiana and her classmates at the Belarusian State University publicly criticized one of their teachers for being "totalitarian," because she discouraged classroom discussion. These students did not long for the old ways, which they associated with "totalitarianism." They thought teachers should listen to them, not simply talk at them. Perhaps small rebellions such as theirs portended greater changes when they and the other millions of young women across the FSU became adults. Perhaps some of them would join the ranks of all those women in Russian history who demanded better than the status quo, and made history in the process.

CONCLUSIONS

Several unifying themes have emerged from this study of the history of women in Russia from the tenth century to the twenty-first. One of the most important is the proposition that that history is closely linked to that of women in other European nations. For most of the women in Russia's past, the gender values and norms, the social hierarchy, the division of labor, the religions, and the myriad of customs that structured daily life were very similar to those that prevailed elsewhere on the continent. Those similarities were reinforced by the ebb and flow of contacts and therefore of influences across the continent. Consequently, during the Kievan and Appanage periods, elite, merchant, artisan, and peasant women lived lives very like those of their contemporaries in Tuscany or Burgundy. When industrialization and urbanization came, they had many of the same consequences for women in Russia as elsewhere. Russia's imperial ventures were also markedly like those of other European colonial powers in their effects on conquering and conquered women. In Russia, as elsewhere, periods of instability weakened gender norms and enabled women to move outside patriarchal controls. The return of social stability saw the reassertion of the rules. Revolution had the power to hasten rule revision; usually gender values changed slowly.

The particularities of the history of women in Russia arose from the geography and environment of the region, from the customs of the peoples, and from the way in which changes in gender norms and practices, ongoing across the continent, played out in the Russian context. The demanding physical environment made agriculture more uncertain in its outcomes than it was in more salubrious areas of Europe, thereby contributing to the impoverishment of the peasantry. The remoteness kept the Rus and the Muscovites out of touch with transformative political, economic, and intellectual developments ongoing to the west. Content in their isolation, Muscovite rulers created a centralized monarchy, legalized serfdom, and eventually realized to their chagrin that other Europeans had surpassed them in technology and prosperity. Peter the Great and his successors tried to close the gap and opened Russia up to an influx of influences and processes of development that they could not control.

The results for women have been the subject of this history. From Kiev to Muscovy, their lives closely resembled those of other European women. Peasant women grew the food, merchant women sold the goods, and noble women managed their households and played politics. Because they were not serfs in the earlier centuries, peasants were less under the control of the elite than were women elsewhere. When serfdom did come, it proved to be as oppressive as its earlier Western variants. The government that legalized it also played a more powerful role in women's history than did other European governments. Peter and his successors put gender change on the agenda and promoted the importation of gender ideas from Western and Central Europe. They also fostered the development of an intelligentsia that took discussions of the woman question further than the regime wanted. Noblewomen responded by improving their education and amassing property. A few joined the intelligentsia and became feminists and revolutionaries.

By the end of the nineteenth century these women had launched a period of female activism that, in its scope and consequences, was one of the most progressive and consequential in the European world. Initially most of the activists were noblewomen, because Russia's middle class was far smaller and more politically and culturally conservative than the middle class in Western Europe and because its poor women were fully occupied with making ends meet. As the tsarist era drew to a close, increasing numbers of working-class women were becoming politically conscious, joining unions, and protesting against the abuses of the government.

After the Revolution, the pace of change in women's lives accelerated, because the uprising legitimated the questioning of ancient truths and because it brought to power a party committed on paper to emancipating women. Female Bolsheviks then persuaded male party leaders to make good on those promises, and communist and non-communist activists from the pre-revolutionary generation turned those promises into concrete programs and policies that affected women of all the ethnic groups of the nation. The Stalinist regime reined in independent female activism, while continuing many of the programs, enlisting women in the paid-labor force, and taking a directive role in the lives of the women under its rule. An eager few from the younger generation pushed the regime further than it had imagined going, and so became pioneering workers in economic construction and the military. After World War II, the Soviet government required Eastern Bloc client states to adopt its principles of gender equity and its policies. Now Russia was exporting rather than importing gender ideas.

The deep cultural connections between Russia and the rest of Europe continued to shape gender values and norms throughout the Soviet period and thereafter. The government lauded notions about women's roles in family life that were virtually identical to those being preached in Chicago and Brussels, even as they marshaled women into the factories. Patriarchy persisted in setting limits on women's participation in the public world, limits that, it should be noted, were more capacious than those that prevailed to the west. After the Soviet Union was dissolved, the flow of gender influences from the West increased, bringing in the ideas of second-wave feminism and the sexualized, commercialized notions of femininity propagated by popular culture.

Persisting as well through the Soviet and post-Soviet periods was the poverty that had plagued the lives of most women throughout Russian history. It was compounded by the brutal mismanagement of the Stalin regime, the catastrophe of World War II, and the economic instability that followed the end of the Soviet Union. That poverty inhibited the development of education for women and girls and the provision of social services and it increased the burden of their domestic work.

The image of the horribly oppressed Russian woman is an old one. It appears in the tales told by foreign merchants of their travels in Muscovy. They had only been allowed to see elite women doing embroidery, so they concluded that embroidery was all those poor, walled-in creatures did. To dramatize the evils of tsarist rule, nineteenth-century Russian intellectuals portrayed the peasant woman as a pathetic victim, toiling, ignorant, bedraggled, and downtrodden. This notion persisted among foreigners throughout the Cold War. In the 1980s, television advertisements for an American hamburger chain featured a Soviet fashion show. "Day wear," an unseen announcer intoned, as a stocky middle-aged woman in a faded print dress strutted proudly down a shabby runway. "Night wear," he declared in the next scene, as she appeared in the same dress, now flourishing an enormous flashlight.

The laments about the dolorous lot of women in Russian history are justified. The words "cope" and "struggle" recur in this book. But they do not tell the whole story. There has also been much in these pages about women's engagement with their world and about the contribution of all of them to the history of their peoples. The mundane character of the lives of most women must not lead us to undervalue them, as historians in the past so often did. Their work was crucial to the survival of their families, their communities, and their country. Their adjustments to change shaped that history, as did the extraordinary few women who rose to leadership. This finding was to be expected; this is what women have done in all cultures, throughout history.

NOTES

INTRODUCTION

1. Armitage, "Through Women's Eyes," 11.
2. Engel, *Women in Russia;* Pushkareva, *Women.*

A SKETCH OF THE HISTORIOGRAPHY

1. Mikhnevich, "Russkaia zhenshchina"; Kollontai, *Sotsial'nye osnovy.*
2. Kudelli, *Rabotnitsa;* Igumnova, *Zhenshchiny Moskvy.*
3. Stites, *Women's Liberation Movement;* Engel, *Mothers and Daughters.*
4. Worobec, *Peasant Russia;* Glickman, *Russian Factory Women;* Clements, Engel, and Worobec, *Russia's Women;* Marrese, *A Woman's Kingdom;* Jaworski and Pietrow-Ennker, *Women;* Forsyth, *A History.*
5. Website of the Moskovskii tsentr gendernykh issledovani; Gapova, *Zhenshchiny;* Pushkareva, *Gendernaia teoriia;* Uspenskaia, *Aleksandra Kollontai.*

1. THE WOMEN OF THE RUS, 900–1462

1. Martin, *Medieval Russia,* 61.
2. Pushkareva, *Women,* 53–60.
3. Cross and Sherbowitz-Wetzor, *The Russian Primary Chronicle,* 191, 193.
4. Ibid., 191–92.
5. Butler, "A Woman," 781–87; Butler, "Ol'ga's Conversion," 238–40.
6. Cross and Sherbowitz-Wetzor, *The Russian Primary Chronicle,* 84.
7. Heppell, *The Paterik,* 117.
8. Levin, *Sex,* 80.
9. Veder, *The Edificatory Prose,* 51.
10. Ibid., 51, 71.
11. Roesdahl, *The Vikings,* 60–61; Weickhardt, "Legal Rights," 4–7; Shahar, *The Fourth Estate,* 176–79.
12. R. Frank, "Marriage," 477–84.
13. Shahar, *The Fourth Estate,* 82, 94.
14. Zenkovsky, *Medieval Russia's Epics,* 247.
15. Kollmann, *Kinship,* 29.

16. Martin, *Medieval Russia*, 201; Langer, "The Black Death," 53–67.
17. Levin, "The Role," 7, 70, 72.
18. Kaiser and Marker, *Reinterpreting*, 87, 90.
19. Kollmann, *Kinship*, 131–35; Thyrêt, *Between God and Tsar*, 19, 20; Wood-worth, "Sophia," 190–96.
20. Woodworth, "Sophia," 197.
21. Levin, "The Role," 10–42; Weickhardt, "Legal Rights," 10; Kleimola, "'In Accordance,'" 206–14; Kaiser and Marker, *Reinterpreting*, 89.
22. Levin, "The Role," 82.
23. Russian family names are gendered, that is, women's names end in "a," men's in "i" or "v." Marfa Boretskaia's husband and her sons, therefore, were named Boretskii.
24. Kaiser and Marker, *Reinterpreting*, 91.
25. Lenhoff and Martin, "Marfa Boretskaia," 343–68.

2. THE AGE OF *THE DOMOSTROI*, 1462–1695

1. Crummey, *The Formation*, 87; Blum, *Lord*, 120.
2. Kollmann, *Kinship*, 5.
3. The Cossacks were the descendants of runaway peasants. In the sixteenth century, they established independent communities in southern Russia and Ukraine and supported themselves through farming and mercenary soldiering.
4. All the proverbs quoted here come from Watson, *Russian Proverbs*.
5. Hellie, *Slavery*, 15.
6. Hellie, "Women," 15, 213.
7. One data set lists 71 percent of slave women as married and living with their husbands; another set gives a figure of 87 percent. These numbers are suggestive, but only that, because they do not distinguish between women who married before becoming slaves and those who married after. (Hellie, *Slavery*, 414, 459.)
8. Ibid., 108–14; Hellie, "Women," 218.
9. Hellie, *Slavery*, 442–59.
10. The definitive edition in English is Pouncy, *"The Domostroi."* The title of the book literally means "house-building." What follows here relies heavily on Pouncy's analysis in her introduction, 1–53.
11. Shahar, *The Fourth Estate*, 98–106.
12. Houlbrooke, *The English Family*, 30–31.
13. "Medieval Sourcebook"; Kollmann, "The Seclusion," 176.
14. Dmytryshyn, *Medieval Russia*, 411.
15. Levin, *Sex*, 245–46; Kaiser, "'He Said,'" 197–216; Kollmann, "Self," 366.
16. Thyrêt, *Between God and Tsar*, 50; Thyrêt, "Women," 166.
17. Thyrêt, *Between God and Tsar*, 81.

18. Kremlins were heavily fortified compounds first built by the princes in the Appanage period. The Moscow Kremlin contained palaces, churches, gardens, and service buildings.

19. Thyrêt, *Between God and Tsar,* 122–23.

20. Kleimola, "'In Accordance,'" 215–16.

21. Weickhardt, "The Pre-Petrine Law," 672–73.

22. Kleimola, "'In Accordance,'" 227–29; Kivelson, "The Effects," 207–11; McVay, *Envisioning,* 57–59; Anderson and Zinsser, *A History,* 2:33.

23. Hellie, *Slavery,* 611; Kollmann, "Self," 361.

24. Zenkovsky, *Medieval Russia's Epics,* 395.

25. Thomas, "Muscovite Convents," 232.

26. Kivelson, "Through the Prism," 75, 83.

27. Kivelson, "Sexuality."

28. The above paragraphs are based on Kivelson, "Through the Prism," 74–94; Zguta, "Witchcraft Trials," 1187–1207; Kivelson, "Political Sorcery," 270–71; Kivelson, "Male Witches," 607–608, 618–21; Kivelson, "Patrolling," 312–23.

29. Worobec, *Possessed;* Kivelson, "Through the Prism," 91–93. Katerinka's story is told by Kivelson in "Patrolling," 309–16.

30. Kivelson, "Patrolling," 310.

31. Kivelson, "Coerced Confessions." Many thanks to the author for sharing this article and her thoughts on Katerinka's case with me.

32. Forsyth, *A History,* 75, 10.

33. Ibid., 67.

34. Woodworth-Ney, *Women,* 144.

35. Zenkovsky, *Medieval Russia's Epics,* 364; Pushkareva, *Women,* 82–83; Avrich, *Russian Rebels,* 92.

36. Massa, *A Short History,* 111.

37. Ibid., 150, 160.

38. See also Thyrêt, *Between God and Tsar,* 108–16.

39. Michels, "Muscovite Elite Women," 428, 448.

40. Ziolkowski, *Tale,* 6; Michels, "Muscovite Elite Women," 432.

41. Ziolkowski, *Tale,* 52. Italics in the original.

42. Ibid., 59, 53.

43. Michels, "Muscovite Elite Women," 440.

44. Ziolkowski, *Tale,* 79, 82.

45. Levin, "The Christian Sources," 131–40, 132.

46. Michels, "Muscovite Elite Women," 433.

47. These are the six that survived to adulthood. Two others did not.

48. Thyrêt, *Between God and Tsar,* 134–35.

49. Hughes, *Sophia,* 37, 40.

50. Ibid., 116–94.

51. Ibid., 224.

3. EMPRESSES AND SERFS, 1695–1855

1. Kollmann, "'What's Love,'" 15–32.
2. Hughes, *Russia*, 191, 190.
3. Ibid., 193.
4. Peter took the title "emperor" in 1721, relegating "tsar" to a secondary position among his titles. His successors followed his precedent.
5. Cruse and Hoogenboom, *Memoirs*, 15–18.
6. Ibid., 13.
7. Ibid., 152.
8. Wortman, *Scenarios*, 1:110–46.
9. Madariaga, *Russia*, 498.
10. Kuxhausen, "Ideal Citizens."
11. Black, *Citizens*, 262.
12. Kuxhausen, "Ideal Citizens," 32–33; Nash, "Educating."
13. Dashkova, *The Memoirs*, 34, 36. The titles *tsaritsa* and *tsarevna* had fallen out of use in the eighteenth century, having been replaced by empress, *velikii kniaz* (son of an emperor), and *velikaia kniagina* (wife of a *velikii kniaz* or daughter of an emperor). These terms are anglicized as "grand duke" and "grand duchess."
14. Ibid., 124, 14.
15. Glagoleva, *Dream*, 36–66.
16. This discussion of property rights is based on Marrese, *A Woman's Kingdom*.
17. *Blackstone's Commentaries*, book 1, chapter 15.
18. Marrese, *A Woman's Kingdom*, 113, 116; Marrese, "From Maintenance," 209–26.
19. Marrese, *A Woman's Kingdom*, 5.
20. Dolgorukaia, "Svoeruchnye zapiski," 271, 261.
21. Glagoleva, *Dream*, 16–17; Cavender, "Kind Angel," 391.
22. Dolgorukaia, "Svoeruchnye zapiski," 259, 278–79.
23. Labzina, *Days*, 16.
24. Dolgorukaia, "Svoeruchnaia zapiski," 266; Labzina, *Days*, 48–49, 99.
25. Kaiser and Marker, *Reinterpreting*, 295.
26. Cruse and Hoogenboom, *Memoirs*, 15, 30–31.
27. Wortman, *Scenarios*, 1:264; Lincoln, *Nicholas I*, 157. The portraits described here are those done by Scottish artist Christina Robertson in 1840–41.
28. Wortman, *Scenarios*, 1:253–69, 333–78.
29. Cavender, "Kind Angel," 393, 404; Schrader, "Unruly Felons," 240.
30. Bisha et al., *Russian Women*, 28.
31. Davidoff and Hall, *Family Fortunes*, 357–96.
32. Friedman, *Masculinity*, 2–4, 28–36.
33. Wagner, *Marriage*, 62, 64.

34. Ibid., 62.
35. Freeze, "Bringing Order," 711–12.
36. The preceding section is based on Wagner, *Marriage,* 62–81.
37. Bisha et al., *Russian Women,* 163, 181.
38. Clyman and Vowles, *Russia,* 78.
39. Ibid., 49.
40. Lindenmeyr, *Poverty,* 116.
41. Bisha et al., *Russian Women,* 30.
42. Heldt, *Terrible Perfection,* 62.
43. Kelly, *A History,* 105.
44. Moon, *The Russian Peasantry,* 20–21; Blum, *Lord and Peasant,* 420. That other category of bondage in Russia, slavery, was abolished in 1723.
45. Until 1762–64, the church also owned serfs; thereafter the church serfs became state peasants.
46. Mikhnevich, "Russkaia zhenshchina," 236; Marrese, *A Woman's Kingdom,* 191; Turgenev, *The Hunting Sketches,* 157–75.
47. Worobec, "Masculinity," 76–93.
48. Bohac, "Widows," 109.
49. Bisha et al., *Russian Women,* 266.
50. Kaiser and Marker, *Reinterpreting,* 293.
51. Moon, *The Russian Peasantry,* 165.
52. Labzina, *Days,* 7–26; Clyman and Vowles, *Russia,* 244–46, 282–310. Many thanks to Steven Grant for his comments on this paragraph.
53. Ryan, *The Bathhouse,* 177.
54. Kaiser, "The Poor," 138–42.
55. Bisha et al., *Russian Women,* 33–34, 35.

4. INDUSTRIALIZATION AND URBANIZATION, 1855–1914

1. R. Johnson, *Peasant,* 28, 31; Wirtschafter, *Social Identity,* 135.
2. Bisha et al., *Russian Women,* 42.
3. Turgenev, *On the Eve,* 69.
4. Lebedev and Solodovnikov, *Vladimir Vasil'evich,* 12.
5. Johanson, *Women's Struggle,* 29.
6. Ibid., 32; Anderson and Zinsser, *A History,* 1:186, 188.
7. Johanson, *Women's Struggle,* 72.
8. Ibid., 69.
9. Anderson and Zinsser, *A History,* 1:188.
10. Johanson, *Women's Struggle,* 5.
11. Clyman and Vowles, *Russia,* 167.
12. Ibid., 184.
13. McVay, *Envisioning,* 128; Bolt, *Feminist Ferment,* 77–78.
14. Engel and Rosenthal, *Five Sisters,* 15–16.

15. McNeal, "Women," 144.

16. Stites, *Women's Liberation Movement*, 142.

17. Engel, *Mothers and Daughters;* Engel and Rosenthal, *Five Sisters,* 69.

18. Subtelny, *Ukraine,* 265.

19. Worobec, *Peasant Russia,* 62–70.

20. Ibid., 69–70; Farnsworth, "The Litigious Daughter-in-Law," 91, 94–98; Freeze, "Profane Narratives," 149.

21. Farnsworth, "The Litigious Daughter-in-Law," 91; Wagner, *Marriage,* 61; Semyonova Tian-Shanskaia, *Village Life,* 163.

22. Eklof, *Russian Peasant Schools,* 279, 312.

23. Ramer, "Childbirth," 107–15; Ransel, "Infant-Care Cultures," 117–18, 123–31.

24. Ramer, "Childbirth," 107.

25. Pallot, "Women's Domestic Industries," 179; McDermid and Hillyar, *Women,* 61–67.

26. Ransel, *Mothers of Misery,* 3.

27. The foregoing paragraphs are based on Ransel, *Mothers of Misery.*

28. Blobaum, "The 'Woman Question'"; McDermid and Hillyar, *Women,* 37.

29. Pallot, "Women's Domestic Industries," 168.

30. Eklof, *Russian Peasant Schools,* 379.

31. Calculated from data in Engel, *Between the Fields and the City,* 67. Warsaw statistics from Nietyksza, "The Vocational Activities," 145.

32. Glickman, *Russian Factory Women,* 60; Ransel, *Mothers of Misery,* 164; McDermid and Hillyar, *Women,* 91.

33. Lapteva, "Domashnaia rabotnitsa," 43.

34. S. Frank, "Narratives," 560; Ransel, *Mothers of Misery,* 167–71.

35. Glickman, *Russian Factory Women,* 74–75, 76, 80, 83; Kessler-Harris, *Out to Work,* 152; Franzoi, *At the Very Least,* 22; McDermid and Hillyar, *Women,* 86.

36. Glickman, *Russian Factory Women,* 86–87; Wirtschafter, *Social Identity,* 143.

37. Glickman, *Russian Factory Women,* 145.

38. Ibid., 70.

39. Kessler-Harris, *Out to Work,* 152.

40. Seamstresses did finishing work; dressmakers made entire garments; tailors catered mostly to men.

41. Glickman, *Russian Factory Women,* 66–67, 115.

42. P. Novikova, "Tri sestry," 43–44.

43. Engel, *Between the Fields and the City,* 203.

44. Ibid., 211, 222; Glickman, *Russian Factory Women,* 121, 90.

45. Engel, *Between the Fields and the City,* 227; Gorky, *Autobiography,* 68.

46. S. Frank, "Narratives," 541–66.

47. Il'iukhov, *Prostitutsiia,* 552. This paragraph and those that follow summarize the findings of Bernstein in *Sonia's Daughters.*

48. Il'iukhov, *Prostitutsiia*, 550.
49. Tsentral'noe statisticheskoe upravlenie, *Zhenshchiny*, 55; Eklof, *Russian Peasant Schools*, 311.
50. Ruane, *The Empire's New Clothes*, 131–32.
51. Bradley, *Muzhik*, appendix A; Nietyksza, "The Vocational Activities," 159; Kelly, "Teacups," 55–77; Newman, "The Gals," 6.
52. Johanson, *Women's Struggle*, 100.
53. Eklof, *Russian Peasant Schools*, 183, 186; Bradley, *Muzhik*, appendix A.
54. Ruane, *Gender*, 192, 117, 204.
55. Johanson, *Women's Struggle*, 100; Frieden, *Russian Physicians*, tables 9.7 and 9.8; Ramer, "Childbirth," 108.
56. Calculated from figures in Bradley, *Muzhik*, appendix A; Ramer, "Childbirth," 108, 112; Frieden, *Russian Physicians*, table IV.B.1.
57. Calculated from figures in Bradley, *Muzhik*, appendix A.
58. Ibid.
59. Ibid.
60. Clyman and Vowles, *Russia*, 226.
61. Ibid., 225.
62. Ruane, *The Empire's New Clothes*, 87–113, 134–38; Von Geldern and McReynolds, *Entertaining*, 98.
63. S. Smith, "Masculinity," 94–112.
64. Engel, *Breaking*, 6; Wagner, *Marriage*, 96; Freeze, "Profane Narratives," 149; Crews, "Empire," 76.
65. Freeze, "Profane Narratives," 168, 160, 158–62; Engel, *Breaking*, 171–78, 6–7.
66. Iashchenko, "Zametky," 89–104.
67. Hyman, *Gender*, 51–80.
68. Nietyksza, "The Vocational Activities," 152; Abrams, *The Making*, 61.
69. Kebalo, "Exploring Continuities," 41–44; Bohachevsky-Chomiak, *Feminists*.
70. Forsyth, *A History*, 192; Dolidovich and Fedorova, *Zhenshchiny*, 58, 196; Goncharov, "Zhenshchiny frontira," 326, 339.
71. Dolidovich and Fedorova, *Zhenshchiny*, 184–89.

5. ACTIVIST WOMEN AND REVOLUTIONARY CHANGE, 1890–1930

1. Meehan-Waters, "To Save Oneself," 121–33; Wagner, "The Transformation," 806–10, 824–25; Wagner, "Paradoxes of Piety," 211, 215, 217–19, 222, 236; Wagner, "'Orthodox Domesticity,'" 134, 136. Many thanks to William Wagner for sharing his work with me.
2. Wagner, "The Transformation," 806–807, 813–18.

3. Meehan-Waters, "To Save Oneself," 121–33; Wagner, "The Transformation," 808–10, 824–25; Wagner, "Paradoxes of Piety," 215, 217–19, 222; Wagner, "'Orthodox Domesticity,'" 134, 136.

4. Blobaum, "The 'Woman Question.'"

5. Lindenmeyr, *Poverty,* 142–226.

6. Bisha et al., *Russian Women,* 366; Steinberg, *Proletarian Imagination,* 40.

7. Lindenmeyr, "The Elusive Life." Many thanks to Adele Lindenmeyr for sharing this paper with me.

8. Norton and Gheith, *An Improper Profession,* 283–310.

9. McReynolds, "'The Incomparable,'" 273–94.

10. Schuler, "Actresses," 107–21.

11. Bek, *The Life,* 93; Dolidovich and Fedorova, *Zhenshchiny,* 167–79.

12. Koblitz, *A Convergence,* 113–268.

13. Matveeva, "V 1905," 33, 35.

14. Glickman, *Russian Factory Women,* 189–95; Kudelli, "Rabotnitsy," 11–13; Clements, *Bolshevik Women,* 102.

15. Ruthchild, "Soiuz ravnopraviia," 79; Ruthchild, "Women's Suffrage," 8.

16. Ruthchild, "Soiuz ravnopraviia," 38.

17. Ruthchild, *Equality,* 71.

18. Tyrrell, *Woman's World,* 63.

19. Herlihy, *The Alcoholic Empire,* 8, 98–107.

20. Ibid, 98–107.

21. Ruthchild, *Equality,* 126–35.

22. Kollontai, *Sotsial'nye osnovy.*

23. Clements, *Bolshevik Women,* 30; Edmondson, *Feminism,* 133–34.

24. Offen, *European Feminisms,* 216.

25. Ruthchild, *Equality,* 83–87.

26. Karciauskaite, "For Women's Rights," 131–37; Edmondson, *Feminism,* 84; Henriksson, "Minority Nationalism."

27. Blobaum, "The 'Woman Question.'"

28. Rorlich, "Intersecting Discourses," 154. Molla Nasreddin was a legendary trickster.

29. Suyumbike was the queen of Kazan when it fell to Ivan IV in 1552. The foregoing is based on ibid., 143–61; and Tohidi, "Gender," 249–92.

30. Ruthchild, *Equality,* 193.

31. Glickman, *Russian Factory Women,* 195–215; Clements, *Bolshevik Women,* 32.

32. Glickman, *Russian Factory Women,* 213.

33. Clements, *Daughters,* 29; Stoff, *They Fought,* 25–26.

34. Stoff, *They Fought,* 23–52; Stockdale, "'My Death,'" 85; Timofeyeva-Yegorova, *Red Sky,* xiii–xiv.

35. MacKenzie and Curran, *A History,* 521.

36. Engel, "Not by Bread," 706.

37. Ibid., 710–17.

38. St. Petersburg was renamed Petrograd in 1915 because that name was more Russian than the Germanic "Petersburg."

39. Igumnova, *Zhenshchiny Moskvy,* 11.

40. Ruthchild, *Equality,* 226–30. The Constituent Assembly met in January 1918 and was immediately prorogued by the Bolshevik government.

41. The phrase is Stoff's, from *They Fought,* 90–91.

42. The preceding paragraphs are based on ibid., 53–162; Stockdale, "'My Death,'" 88–116.

43. Stoff, *They Fought,* 163–95. The phrase "saintly blood" is from a newspaper article in *Sinii zhurnal,* quoted in ibid., 169.

44. Ibid., 69–89, 211–13; Stockdale, "'My Death,'" 113.

45. Clements, *Bolshevik Women,* 134–35.

46. Boniece, "The Spiridonova Case," 586–606; Rabinowitch, "Spiridonova," 182–83.

47. Clements, *Bolshevik Women,* 32, 44–45.

48. *Kommunistka,* no. 1 (1922): 13.

49. Koenker, "Urbanization and Deurbanization," 81.

50. Goldman, *Women at the Gates,* 1.

51. Clements, "Working-Class and Peasant Women," 225; Clements, *Daughters,* 47; Clements, *Bolshevik Women,* 162.

52. *Kaluzhskie bol'shevichki,* 141.

53. Matveeva, "V 1905," 37.

54. Wood, *The Baba,* 209; Goldman, *Women at the Gates,* 111.

55. Wolf, *Revolution,* 15–21; Geisler, *Women,* 24; Clements, "Communism."

56. The Bolsheviks moved the capital from Petrograd to Moscow in 1918.

57. Rizel', "Sostav," 27.

58. Clements, *Bolshevik Women,* 267–71.

59. Ruthchild, *Equality,* 252–53.

60. Edgar, "Emancipation," 145–47; Northrop, *Veiled Empire,* 131.

61. Sultan-Zade, "Oil Commander"; Kamp, *The New Woman,* 186–88.

62. Northrop, *Veiled Empire,* 83–101.

63. Kamp, *The New Woman,* 212–14, 220–22; Edgar, "Bolshevism," 266–67.

64. Farnsworth, "Rural Women," 167–88.

65. *Krest'ianka,* nos. 1–2 (1922).

66. Alexopoulos, *Stalin's Outcasts,* 3, 20–31, 49–51.

67. Ibid., 27, 62–69.

68. Ibid., 37–39, 99, 118–22, 130–35, 141.

69. Goldman, *Women, the State, and Revolution,* 270–75, 107; Clements, "The Effects," 115.

70. Lunacharskii, *O byte,* 202.

71. *Rabotnitsa,* no. 15 (1926): 16.

72. Clements, "The Birth," 231.

6. TOIL, TERROR, AND TRIUMPHS, 1930–53

1. Goldman, *Women at the Gates*, 1, 26–27; Tsentral'noe statisticheskoe upravlenie, *Zhenshchiny*, 35; Weiner, *From Working Girl*, 4; Boxer and Quataert, *Connecting Spheres*, 222.

2. Rossiiskii gosudarstvennyi arkhiv, *Vsesoiuznaia perepis'*, 177–79; Goldman, *Women at the Gates*, 26–27; Opdycke, *Routledge Atlas*, 90.

3. Rossiiskii gosudarstvennyi arkhiv, *Vsesoiuznaia perepis'*, 163–96.

4. Hoffman, *The Littlest Enemies*, 37–38.

5. Viola, "*Bab'i Bunty*," 189–205; Olcott, *The Kazaks*, 181; Forsyth, *A History*, 291–93; Northrop, *Veiled Empire*, 320.

6. Viola, "*Bab'i Bunty*," 199.

7. Hoffman, *The Littlest Enemies*, 47.

8. Fitzpatrick and Slezkine, *In the Shadow*, 229–30.

9. Viola, *The Unknown Gulag*, 32; Applebaum, *Gulag*, 47.

10. Ransel, *Village Mothers*, 108–109, 88.

11. Manning, "Women," 211; Rossiiskii gosudarstvennyi arkhiv, *Vsesoiuznaia perepis'*, 163–64.

12. Ransel, *Village Mothers*, 236; Manning, "Women," 236; Rossiiskii gosudarstvennyi arkhiv, *Vsesoiuznaia perepis'*, 82, 135.

13. Fitzpatrick and Slezkine, *In the Shadow*, 308, 312.

14. Ilic, "*Traktoristka*," 114.

15. Goldman, *Women at the Gates*, 80, 104–105.

16. Fitzpatrick and Slezkine, *In the Shadow*, 253.

17. Rossiiskii gosudarstvennyi arkhiv, *Vsesoiuznaia perepis'*, 135.

18. Garros, Korenevskaya, and Lahusen, *Intimacy*, 209; Fitzpatrick and Slezkine, *In the Shadow*, 326.

19. Chatterjee, "Soviet Heroines," 52; Krylova, *Soviet Women*, 41–43.

20. Fitzpatrick and Slezkine, *In the Shadow*, 362, 363.

21. Randall, *Soviet Dream World*, 124; Buckley, *Mobilizing*, 275–78.

22. Neary, "Mothering"; Schrand, "Soviet 'Civic-Minded' Women," 127.

23. Krylova, *Soviet Women*, 41–43, 49–51.

24. Timofeyeva-Yegorova, *Red Sky*, 47; Krylova, *Soviet Women*, 14, 41–43.

25. Shulman, *Stalinism*, 119–48.

26. Ibid., 187–221.

27. Davies, *Popular Opinion*, 67; Goldman, *Women at the Gates*, 292–93; Krylova, *Soviet Women*, 72–73.

28. Sultan-Zade, "Oil Commander."

29. Rossiiskii gosudarstvennyi arkhiv, *Vsesoiuznaia perepis'*, 88–89, 152; Forsyth, *A History*, 287.

30. Getty and Naumov, *The Road*, 588; Applebaum, *Gulag*, 580.

31. Clements, *Bolshevik Women*, 286–87.

32. Getty, Rittersporn, and Zemskov, "Victims," 1025; Mason, "Women," 132; Applebaum, *Gulag*, 311; Rossman, "A Workers' Strike," 78; Clements, *Bolshevik Women*, 279–80.

33. Fitzpatrick and Slezkine, *In the Shadow*, 390.

34. Ibid., 327–30.

35. "Gulag" stands for Glavnoe upravlenie ispravitel'no-trudovikh lagerei I kolonii: in English, Main Administration of Corrective Labor Camps and Colonies.

36. Vilensky, *Till My Tale*, 255.

37. Healey, "Lesbian Lives."

38. Vilensky, *Till My Tale*, 157, 225.

39. Applebaum, *Gulag*, 260.

40. Hoffman, *The Littlest Enemies*, 109.

41. Timofeyeva-Yegorova, *Red Sky*, 49–55; Hoffman, *The Littlest Enemies*, 110, 52–71, 153–55, 167, 180–81, 185.

42. Ginzburg, *Within the Whirlwind*, 417–18, 423.

43. Overy, *Russia's War*, 288; Merridale, *Ivan's War*, 363.

44. Overy, *Russia's War*, 193; Barber and Harrison, *The Soviet Home Front*, 180.

45. Opdycke, *Routledge Atlas*, 101; Krylova, *Soviet Women*, 3, 115–16.

46. Krylova, *Soviet Women*, 89, 94–97.

47. Pennington, *Wings*, 22; Krylova, *Soviet Women*, 124.

48. Krylova, *Soviet Women*, 40; Engel and Posadskaya-Vanderbeck, *A Revolution*, 189.

49. Clements, *Daughters*, 82–83; Krylova, *Soviet Women*, 10, 155.

50. Slepyan, *Stalin's Guerrillas*, 197–206.

51. Krylova, *Soviet Women*, 40–41, 90, 163; Cottam, *Women*, 197–201.

52. Pennington, *Wings*, 79.

53. Ibid., 72–89; Timofeyeva-Yegorova, *Red Sky*, 71.

54. Pennington, *Wings*, 72, 90, 136–40; Krylova, *Soviet Women*, 247–49.

55. Timofeyeva-Yegorova, *Red Sky*, 55.

56. Ibid., 210, 212. The foregoing is based on the memoir.

57. Alexiyevich, *War's Unwomanly Face*, 63. The author does not provide this man's last name, only his first name and patronymic. See also Krylova, *Soviet Women*, 189, 194–96.

58. Timofeyeva-Yegorova, *Red Sky*, 105; Beevor and Vinogradova, *A Writer*, 184; Krylova, *Soviet Women*, 233.

59. Tek, "U partisan," 183; Pennington, *Wings*, 98; Alexiyevich, *War's Unwomanly Face*, 79.

60. Simmons and Perlina, *Writing*, 29; G. Smith, "The Impact," 79.

61. Bridger, "The Heirs," 200; G. Smith, "The Impact," 73, 77; Harrison and Barber, *The Soviet Home Front*, 216–17.

62. Simmons and Perlina, *Writing*, 137–38.

63. Barber and Harrison, *The Soviet Home Front*, 217.

64. Overy, *Russia's War*, 134; Hoffman, *The Littlest Enemies*, 167, 157.

65. Simmons and Perlina, *Writing*, ix; Berkhoff, *Harvest*, 182; Overy, *Russia's War*, 134; Merridale, *Ivan's War*, 305–28.

66. Barber and Harrison, *The Soviet Home Front*, 226.

67. Alexiyevich, *War's Unwomanly Face*, 122, 245, 123–24.

68. Ibid., 123–24, 122, 245; Merridale, *Ivan's War*, 337–38; G. Smith, "The Impact," 282.

69. Alexiyevich, *War's Unwomanly Face*, 244; Stoff, *They Fought*, 170–71; Timofeyeva-Yegorova, *Red Sky*, 208.

70. Bucher, *Women*, 65.

71. Bridger, "The Heirs," 200; Bucher, *Women*, 65–71.

72. Ginzburg, *Within the Whirlwind*, 356.

73. Fitzpatrick and Slezkine, *In the Shadow*, 316.

7. MAKING BETTER LIVES, 1953–91

1. Ilic, "Women," 12–17; Attwood, "Celebrating," 165.

2. Browning, *Women*.

3. Taubman, *Khrushchev*, 60, 59–61.

4. Tereshkova, "The 'First Lady,'" 13.

5. Ibid., 16.

6. Clements, "Tereshkova."

7. Tsentral'noe statisticheskoe upravlenie, *Zhenshchiny*, 62–63; Katz, *Gender*, 104.

8. Z. Novikova, *Zhenshchina*, 144.

9. Kharchev, *Brak*, 222; Lapidus, *Women*, 174; Clements, "Communism"; Sperling, *Organizing Women*, 223–24; Hemment, *Empowering*, 29–30; Valentina Uspenskaia, personal communication.

10. Tsentral'noe statisticheskoe upravlenie, *Zhenshchiny*, 61–62.

11. Filtzer, *Soviet Workers*, 180, 185, 192.

12. Clements, *Daughters*, 99–100.

13. Katz, *Gender*, 74, 110–11; Chapman, "Equal Pay," 225–26; Opdycke, *Routledge Atlas*, 113.

14. Clements, *Daughters*, 100–101.

15. Kabakov, *Na kommunal'noi kukhne*, 28.

16. Ibid., 40, 110.

17. Ibid., 107.

18. Ibid., 38, 177.

19. The statistics in the last two paragraphs derive from Tsentral'noe statisticheskoe upravlenie, *Zhenshchiny*, 68–69; UN Department of International and Social Affairs, *The World's Women*, 82; Seager and Olson, *Women*, chart 13; Boxer and Quataert, *Connecting Spheres*, 253.

20. Katz, *Gender*, 78.

21. Hansson and Linden, *Moscow Women*, 110.

22. Baranskaya, "A Week," 661.
23. Clements, *Daughters,* 106.
24. Bridger, *Women,* 78, 81.
25. Wegren, *Land Reform,* 23; Katz, *Gender,* 99; Bridger, *Women,* 211.
26. Bridger, *Women,* 140–53; Ransel, *Village Mothers,* 116–18, 146–47.
27. Clements, *Daughters,* 110.
28. Moghadam, "Gender," 30.
29. Forsyth, *A History,* 361, xv, 402; Vitebsky, "Withdrawing," 182–83.
30. Bastug and Hostacsu, "The Price," 128–35.
31. Crate, "Walking," 119.
32. Tohidi, "Gender," 249.
33. Field, "Mothers," 102; Gilmour and Clements, "'If You Want,'" 210–22; Attwood, "Celebrating," 167–68.
34. Friedman and Healey, "Conclusions," 232–33.
35. Marody and Giza-Poleszczuk, "Changing Images," 163; Ries, *Russian Talk,* 73–75.
36. Ries, *Russian Talk,* 74–75; Kay, *Men,* 11–14.
37. Alexeyeva and Goldberg, *The Thaw Generation,* 246; Penn, *Solidarity's Secret.*
38. Mamonova, *Women,* 32.
39. Dowd, "Evolution."
40. Rosenthal, "A Soviet Voice."
41. S. White, *Gorbachev,* 53, 79, 143; Dzieciolowski, "Tatyana Zaslavskaya's Moment"; Stankovic, "Soviet Academician"; Zaslavskaya, "Correlation."
42. Zaslavskaya, "Correlation"; Zaslavskaya, *The Second Socialist Revolution;* Dzieciolowski, "Tatyana Zaslavskaya's Moment."
43. Clements, *Daughters,* 132–33.
44. Adelman, *The Children,* 74; Cerf and Albee, *Small Fires,* 115.
45. Belayeva, "Feminism," 18.
46. Ibid., 19.
47. Sperling, *Organizing Women,* 108–11.
48. Kononenko, "Folk Orthodoxy," 47–49; Davis, *A Long Walk,* 154–58; Crate, "Walking," 122.

8. GAINS AND LOSSES, 1991–2010

1. Ashwin and Bowers, "Do Russian Women," 23–25; A. White, *Small-Town Russia,* 82; Phillips, *Women's Social Activism,* 47.
2. Shevchenko, *Crisis,* 11, 173; A. White, *Small-Town Russia,* 111–16; Bridger, "Rural Women," 42, 52; Crate, "The Gendered Nature," 132, 141; Gapova, "On 'Writing.'"
3. Werner, "Feminizing," 111–12; Crate, "Walking," 118; U.S. Department of Agriculture, "Russia."

4. Pilkington, "'For the Sake,'" 127–30.

5. Irina Sondak, interview; A. White, *Small-Town Russia*, 18; Taraban, "Birthday Girls," 107.

6. Irina Sondak, interview.

7. Bridger, "Rural Women," 39; Bruno, "Women," 57.

8. Website of "Russian Women"; Oushakine, "The Fatal Splitting," 6; Pasternak, *Chto vizhu;* Taraban, "Birthday Girls," 105–27.

9. Il'iukhov, *Prostitutsiia,* 5–6.

10. Rivkin-Fish, *Women's Health,* 1; UN Department of Economic and Social Affairs, *World Abortion Policies 2007.*

11. Popkova, "Women's Political Activism," 173; Starovoitova, "Being." Many women avoided the term "feminist," which had pejorative connotations. I will use it in the same sense as earlier, to refer to social activists who work for women's emancipation from patriarchal institutions and customs.

12. Iacheistova, *Zhenshchiny,* 25; Sperling, *Organizing Women,* 87.

13. Posadskaya, "Women," 11.

14. Kukhterin, "Fathers," 78.

15. Tohidi, "Gender," 284; Zhurzhenko, "Strong Women," 28.

16. Harris, "The Changing Identity," 213–14; Tohidi, "Gender," 250; Abramson, "Engendering," 72–77.

17. Kay, "Meeting," 244.

18. Bridger, "Rural Women," 51; Tatiana Khainovskaia, interview.

19. Oushakine, "The Fatal Splitting," 11; Bridger, "Rural Women," 51; A. White, *Small-Town Russia,* 41; Kay, *Men,* 5–28; Tohidi, "Gender," 257.

20. Website of Vladimir Putin; "Singing PM," http://www.youtube.com/watch?v=1V4IjHz2yIo.

21. Salmenniemi, *Democratization,* 85; Mereu, "What Women Want"; Gorshkov and Tikhonova, *Zhenshchina,* 88; Shevchenko, *Crisis,* 152–61, 165–71.

22. N. White, "Women in Changing Societies," 207–208; Philipov et al., "Induced Abortion," 95–117; UN Department of Economic and Social Affairs, "Ukraine"; UN Department of Economic and Social Affairs, *World Abortion Policies 2007;* Mirovalev, "Uzbek Women."

23. Saktanber and Ozatas-Baykal, "Homeland," 234–35; Buckley, "Adaptation," 161; N. White, "Women in Changing Societies," 209; Gorshkov and Tikhonova, *Zhenshchina,* 88; A. White, *Small-Town Russia,* 149.

24. Sperling, *Organizing Women,* 121; Buckley, "Adaptation," 167–70.

25. Nechemias, "The Women of Russia," 356–59; Sperling, *Organizing Women,* 119, 124.

26. Saktanber and Ozatas-Baykal, "Homeland," 234–39; Popkova, "Women's Political Activism," 182; A. White, *Small-Town Russia,* 183.

27. Website of Kazimiera Prunskiene; website of the Lietuvos valstieciu liaudininku sajunga; Girdzijauskas, "Special Lithuanian Presidential Election"; D. Smith et al., *The Baltic States,* 121–22.

28. The foregoing paragraphs are based on Wolczuk and Wolczuk, "Julia Tymoshenko"; "Profile: Yulia Tymoshenko"; website of Yulia Tymoshenko.

29. Website of Mariia Arbatova; Rotkirch, "Arbatova," 202–204.

30. "Marry Indian."

31. Politkovskaya, *Putin's Russia,* 242.

32. Holley, "Russian Journalist."

33. Baker and Glasser, *Kremlin,* 19, 22, 161, 177; "Teen Widow."

34. "Teen Widow."

35. Salmenniemi, *Democratization,* 33, 40, 57; Sperling, *Organizing Women,* 34–37; Buckley, "Adaptation," 166; Rivkin-Fish, *Women's Health,* 221; Ishkanian, "Working," 269; Hemment, *Empowering,* 54.

36. Sperling, *Organizing Women,* 19, 135; Rivkin-Fish, *Women's Health,* 221; Pavlychko, "Feminism," 308; Kebalo, "Exploring Continuities," 52–54; N. White, "Women in Changing Societies," 210–11; Dudwick, "Out of the Kitchen," 244–45.

37. Pavlychko, "Progress," 230; Hemment, *Empowering,* 30; Phillips, *Women's Social Activism,* 33; Dudwick, "Out of the Kitchen," 245.

38. Website of the Moskovskii tsentr gendernykh issledovani; website of Informatsionnyi portal; Sperling, *Organizing Women,* 26–27; website of Tverskaia tsentr; website of Universitetskaia set'; Uspenskaia, *Aleksandra Kollontai;* Pushkareva, *Gendernaia teoriia.*

39. J. Johnson, "Sisterhood," 221–24.

40. Caiazza, "Committees," 218–20; website of Soiuz komitetov; "'Materi Beslana.'"

41. Azhgikhina, *Kto zashchishchaet,* 3; Holley, "Russian Journalist"; Danilova, "Lyudmila Alexeyeva"; Feifer, "Russia's New Dissidents."

42. Barry, "Russian Dissident's Passion."

43. Sperling, *Organizing Women,* 55–57, 220; N. White, "Women in Changing Societies," 211–12.

44. Rivkin-Fish, *Women's Health,* 35–65; Sperling, *Organizing Women,* 232–39; Hemment, *Empowering,* 49–54; J. Johnson, *Gender Violence,* 2–3; Phillips, *Women's Social Activism,* 80; Funk, "Fifteen Years," 212.

45. Pavlychko, "Progress," 229; Sperling, *Organizing Women,* 134–35, 202–203; Kuehnast and Nechemias, "Introduction," 2, 13; Tohidi, "Women," 167; Popkova, "Women's Political Activism," 189.

46. Gorshkov and Tikhonova, *Zhenshchina,* 94–99; Hemment, *Empowering,* 5; Salmenniemi, *Democratization,* 223.

47. Salmenniemi, *Democratization,* 5.

48. Ekaterina Sondak and Elena Khainovskaia, interviews; Shevchenko, *Crisis,* 40.

49. Shevchenko, *Crisis,* 41–43; Tatiana Khainovskaia, interview.

50. Gorshkov and Tikhonova, *Zhenshchina,* 102.

51. Ibid., 102, 114; Malysheva et al., *Marriages,* 86; Kay, *Men;* A. White, *Small-Town Russia,* 125–26.

52. Malysheva et al., *Marriages,* 114–15; A. White, *Small-Town Russia,* 142; Gorshkov and Tikhonova, *Zhenshchina,* 102–104, 33, 40; Akiner, "Between Tradition and Modernity," 289; Harris, "The Changing Identity," 217; Shevchenko, *Crisis,* 47.

53. Liudmila Buloichik, interview; Iacheistova, *Zhenshchiny,* 31.

54. Irina Sondak, interview; Gorshkov and Tikhonova, *Zhenshchina,* 13, 116, 29, 75–76; Malysheva et al., *Marriages,* 55, 79; A. White, *Small-Town Russia,* 133; Lyon, "Housewife Fantasies," 31–32.

55. Gorshkov and Tikhonova, *Zhenshchina,* 100, 104; Liudmila Yushko, interview.

56. Gorshkov and Tikhonova, *Zhenshchina,* 102; Ekaterina Sondak and Elena Khainovskaia, interviews.

57. Tatiana Khainovskaia and Irina Sondak, interviews.

BIBLIOGRAPHY

PRIMARY SOURCES

Alexeyeva, Ludmilla, and Paul Goldberg. *The Thaw Generation: Coming of Age in the Post-Stalin Era.* Boston: Little, Brown, 1990.

Azhgikhina, N. *Kto zashchishchaet zhenshchin.* Moscow: Aslan, 1996.

Baranskaya, Natalya. "A Week like Any Other Week." Translated by Emily Lehrman. *The Massachusetts Review* (Autumn 1974): 657–703.

Bek, Anna. *The Life of a Russian Woman Doctor: A Siberian Memoir, 1869–1954.* Translated and edited by Anne D. Rassweiler; foreword and additional notes by Adele M. Lindenmeyr. Bloomington: Indiana University Press, 2004.

Belayeva, Nina. "Feminism in the U.S.S.R." In "Soviet Women," special issue of *Canadian Woman Studies/Le Cahiers de la Femme* 10, no. 9 (Winter 1989): 17–20.

Bisha, Robin, Jehanne M. Gheith, Christine Holden, and William G. Wagner, compilers. *Russian Women, 1698–1917: Experience and Expression.* Bloomington: Indiana University Press, 2002.

Blackstone's Commentaries on the Laws of England. The Avalon Project at Yale Law School. http://www.yale.edu/lawweb/Avalon/"Blackstone." Accessed May 4, 2005. (Now at http://avalon.law.yale.edu/subject_menus/blackstone .asp.)

Botchkareva, Maria. *Yashka, My Life as a Peasant, Exile, and Soldier.* As set down by Isaac Don Levine. London: Constable, 1919.

Cerf, Christopher, and Marina Albee, editors. *Small Fires: Letters from the Soviet People to Ogonyok Magazine, 1987–1990.* New York: Summit, 1990.

Chernyshevsky, Nikolai. *What Is to Be Done.* Translated by Michael R. Katz. Annotated by William G. Wagner. With an introduction by Michael R. Katz and William G. Wagner. Ithaca, N.Y.: Cornell University Press, 1989.

Clyman, Toby W., and Judith Vowles, editors. *Russia through Women's Eyes: Autobiographies from Tsarist Russia.* New Haven: Yale University Press, 1996.

Cross, Samuel Hazard, and Olgerd P. Sherbowitz-Wetzor, translators and editors. *The Russian Primary Chronicle, Laurentian Text.* Cambridge, Mass.: Mediaeval Academy of America, 1973.

Cruse, Mark, and Hilde Hoogenboom. *The Memoirs of Catherine the Great.* New York: Modern Library, 2006.

Dashkova, E. R. *The Memoirs of Princess Dashkova.* Translated and edited by Kyril Fitzlyon. Introduction by Jehanne M. Gheith. Durham, N.C.: Duke University Press, 1995.

Dmytryshyn, Basil, editor. *Medieval Russia: A Source Book, 850–1700.* Third edition. Fort Worth, Tex.: Harcourt Brace Jovanovich, 1991.

Dolgorukaia, Natal'ia. "Svoeruchnye zapiski kniagini Natal'i Borisovny Dolgorukoi, docheri r. fel'dmarshala grafa Borisa Petrovicha Sheremeteva." In *Tainy istorii, bezvremen'e i vremenshchiki, vospominania ob "epokhe dvortsovykh perevorotov" (1720–1760e gody).* Moscow: Terra, 1996.

Engel, Barbara Alpern, and Anastasia Posadskaya-Vanderbeck, editors. *A Revolution of Their Own: Voices of Women in Soviet History.* Translated by Sona Hoisington. Boulder, Colo.: Westview, 1998.

Engel, Barbara Alpern, and Clifford N. Rosenthal, editors. *Five Sisters: Women against the Tsar.* New York: Knopf, 1975.

Fitzpatrick, Sheila, and Yuri Slezkine, editors. *In the Shadow of Revolution: Life Stories of Russian Women from 1917 to the Second World War.* Princeton: Princeton University Press, 2000.

Gapova, Elena. "On 'Writing Women's and Gender History in Countries in Transition,' and What We Saw There." Paper presented at the Russian and East European Institute, Indiana University, 2005. http://www.indiana .edu/~reeiweb/events/2005. Accessed October 16, 2007.

Garros, Véronique, Natalia Korenevskaya, and Thomas Lahusen, editors. *Intimacy and Terror: Soviet Diaries of the 1930s.* Translated by Carol A. Flath. New York: New Press, 1995.

Ginzburg, Eugenia. *Within the Whirlwind.* Translated by Ian Boland. Introduction by Heinrich Böll. New York: Harcourt Brace Jovanovich, 1981.

Gorky, Maxim. *The Autobiography of Maxim Gorky.* New York: Collier, 1962.

Hansson, Carola, and Karin Linden. *Moscow Women.* Translated by Gerry Bothmer, George Blecher, and Lone Blecher. New York: Pantheon, 1983.

Heppell, Muriel, translator and editor. *The Paterik of the Kievan Caves Monastery.* Cambridge, Mass.: Harvard University Press, 1989.

Herzen, Alexander, editor. *Memoirs of Catherine the Great.* New York: Appleton, 1859.

Hoffman, Deborah, translator and editor. *The Littlest Enemies: Children in the Shadow of the Gulag.* Bloomington, Ind.: Slavica, 2009.

Iacheistova, L. G. *Zhenshchiny zemli Vologodskoi.* Vologda, Russia: n.p., 2004.

Kabakov, I. *Na kommunal'noi kukhne.* Paris: Galerie Dina Vierny, 1993.

Kaiser, Daniel H., and Gary Marker, editors. *Reinterpreting Russian History: Readings, 860–1860s.* New York: Oxford University Press, 1994.

Kharchev, A. G. *Brak i sem'ia v SSSR.* Second edition. Moscow: Mysl, 1979.

Kollontai, A. M. "Nashi zadachi." In *Izbrannye stat'i i rechi.* Moscow: Politizdat, 1972.

———. *Sotsial'nye osnovy zhenskogo voprosa.* St. Petersburg: Znanie, 1909.

Kudelli, P. F., editor. *Rabotnitsa v 1905 g. v S-Peterburge: Sbornik statei i vospominanii.* Leningrad: Priboi, 1926.

———. "Rabotnitsy v 1905 gody." In *Rabotnitsa v 1905 g. v S-Peterburge: Sbornik statei i vospominanii,* edited by P. F. Kudelli. Leningrad: Priboi, 1926.

Kukhterin, Sergei. "Fathers and Patriarchs in Communist and Post-Communist Russia." In *Gender, State and Society in Soviet and Post-Soviet Russia,* edited by Sarah Ashwin. London: Routledge, 2002.

Labzina, Anna. *Days of a Russian Noblewoman: The Memories of Anna Labzina.* Translated and edited by Gary Marker and Rachel May. DeKalb: Northern Illinois University Press, 2001.

Lapidus, Gail Warshofsky, editor. *Women, Work, and Family in the Soviet Union.* Armonk, N.Y.: Sharpe, 1982.

Lapteva, P. "Domashnaia rabotnitsa v 1905 godu." In *Rabotnitsa v 1905 g. v S.-Peterburge: Sbornik statei i vospominanii,* edited by P. F. Kudelli. Leningrad: Priboi, 1926.

Lebedev, A. K., and A. V. Solodovnikov, editors. *Vladimir Vasil'evich Stasov: Zhizn' i tvorchestvo.* Moscow: Mysl', 1976.

Lunacharskii, V. *O byte.* Moscow and Leningrad: n.p., 1927.

Mamonova, Tatyana, editor. *Women and Russia: Feminist Writings from the Soviet Union.* Boston: Beacon, 1984.

Massa, Isaac. *A Short History of the Beginnings and Origins of These Present Wars in Moscow under the Reign of Various Sovereigns down to the Year 1610.* Translated with an introduction by G. Edward Orchard. Toronto, Ont.: University of Toronto Press, 1982.

"'Materi Beslana' prishli v iarost'." NTV, May 29, 2007. http://news.ntv.ru/news/ NewsPrint.jsp?nid+110319. Accessed August 5, 2007.

Matveeva, Anna. "V 1905 gody." In *Rabotnitsa v 1905 g. v S-Peteburge: Sbornik statei i vospominanii,* edited by P. F. Kudelli. Leningrad: Priboi, 1926.

"Medieval Sourcebook: The Goodman of Paris, 1392/4." Part of the Internet Medieval Sourcebook at the Fordham University Center for Medieval Studies. http://www.fordham.edu/halsall/source/goodman.html. Accessed April 12, 2009.

Novikova, P. A. "Tri sestry." In *Bez nikh my ne pobedili by.* Moscow: Politizdat, 1975.

Novikova, Z. E. *Zhenshchina v razvitom sotsialisticheskogo obshchestve.* Moscow: Mysl, 1985.

Pasternak, Josef, director. *Chto vizhu, to poterli.* Arte France/Rodu Productions, 2004.

Politkovskaya, Anna. *Putin's Russia: Life in a Failing Democracy.* Translated by Arch Tait. New York: Henry Holt, 2007.

Posadskaya, Anastasia. "Women as the Objects and Motive Force of Change in Our Time." In *Women in Russia: A New Era in Russian Feminism,* edited by Anastasia Posadskaya and others at the Moscow Gender Center, and translated by Kate Clark. London: Verso, 1994.

Pouncy, Carolyn Johnston, editor and translator. *"The Domostroi": Rules for Russian Households in the Time of Ivan the Terrible.* Ithaca, N.Y.: Cornell University Press, 1994.

Riha, Thomas, editor. *Readings in Russian Civilization.* Second edition. Volume 1. Chicago: University of Chicago Press, 1969.

Rizel', F. "Sostav delegatskikh sobranii sozyva 1926/27 g." *Kommunistka,* no. 9 (September 1927): 26–27.

Rossiiskii gosudarstvennyi arkhiv ekonomiki. *Vsesoiuznaia perepis' naseleniia 1939 goda. Osnovnye itogi, Rossiia.* Sankt-Peterburg: Russko-baltiiskii informatsionnyi tsentr BLITS, 1999.

Semyonova Tian-Shanskaia, Olga. *Village Life in Late Tsarist Russia.* Edited by David L. Ransel. Bloomington: Indiana University Press, 1993.

Simmons, Cynthia, and Nina Perlina, editors. *Writing the Siege of Leningrad: Women's Diaries, Memoirs, and Documentary Prose.* Pittsburgh, Penn.: University of Pittsburgh Press, 2002.

"Singing PM: 'Fats' Putin over the Top of 'Blueberry Hill' with Piano Solo." YouTube video. Uploaded by RussiaToday on December 11, 2010. http://www.youtube.com/watch?v=IV4IjHz2yIo. Accessed January 12, 2011.

Starovoitova, Galina V. "Being a Woman Politician in Today's Russia." Transregional Center for Democratic Studies *Bulletin* 31 (1999). http://www.newschool.edu/centers/cds/bu1031.htm#vvu13102. Accessed September 17, 2007. (Now at http://www.newschool.edu/tcds/bul031.htm.)

Sultan-zade, Rabia khanum. "Oil Commander." Website of the Azerbaijan Gender Information Center, http://www.gender-az.org. Accessed November 12, 2010.

Tereshkova, Valentina. "The 'First Lady of Space' Remembers: Excerpts from Valentina Tereshkova's Memoirs *Stars Are Calling,* Moscow 1964." *Quest: The History of Spaceflight Quarterly* 10, no. 2 (2003): 6–21.

Timofeyeva-Yegorova, Anna. *Red Sky, Black Death: A Soviet Woman Pilot's Memoir of the Eastern Front.* Translated by Margarita Ponomaryova and Kim Green. Edited by Kim Green. Bloomington, Ind.: Slavica, 2009.

Tsentral'noe statisticheskoe upravlenie pri Sovete Ministrov SSSR. *Zhenshchiny v SSSR: Statisticheskii sbornik.* Moscow: Statistika, 1975.

Turgenev, I. S. *The Hunting Sketches.* Translated by Bernard Guilbert Guerney. New York: New American Library, 1962.

———. *On the Eve.* In *The Vintage Turgenev,* volume 2. Translated by Harry Stevens. New York: Vintage, 1960.

Veder, William R., translator. *The Edificatory Prose of Kievan Rus'.* Cambridge, Mass.: Harvard University Press, 1994.

Vilensky, Simeon, editor. *Till My Tale Is Told: Women's Memoirs of the Gulag.* Bloomington: Indiana University Press, 1999.

Von Geldern, James, and Louise McReynolds, editors. *Entertaining Tsarist Russia: Tales, Songs, Plays, Movies, Jokes, Ads and Images from Russian Urban Life, 1779–1917.* Bloomington: Indiana University Press, 1998.

Watson, Aldren, editor and translator. *Russian Proverbs.* Mt. Vernon, N.Y.: Peter Pauper, 1960.

Zaslavskaya, Tatyana. *The Second Socialist Revolution: An Alternative Social Strategy.* Bloomington: Indiana University Press, 1990.

Zenkovsky, Serge A., editor. *Medieval Russia's Epics, Chronicles, and Tales.* Revised edition. New York: Dutton, 1974.

Ziolkowski, Margaret, editor. *Tale of Boiarynia Morozova: A Seventeenth-Century Religious Life.* Lanham, Mass.: Lexington, 2000.

INTERVIEWS AND LETTERS

Buloichik, Liudmila. August 4, 2007.

Khainovskaia, Elena. July 16, 2007.

Khainovskaia, Tatiana. July 16, 2007; November 23, 2010.

Sondak, Ekaterina (pseud.). August 10, 2007; November 11, 2007.

Sondak, Irina (pseud.). August 10, 2007; November 11, 2007.

Yushko, Liudmila. August 15, 2007.

NEWSPAPERS

Kommunistka, 1920s.

Krest'ianka, 1922.

Rabotnitsa, 1920s.

WEBSITES

Arbatova, Mariia. http://www.arbatova.ru. Accessed October 16, 2007.

Association for Women in Slavic Studies. http://www.awss.org.

Azerbaijan Gender Information Center. http://www.gender-az.org. Accessed October 15, 2007, and November 10, 2010.

Informatsionnyi portal—zhenshchina i obshchestvo. http://www.owl.ru. Accessed October 15, 2007.

Lietuvos valstieciu liaudininku sajunga. http://www.lvls.lt. Accessed October 13, 2007.

Moskovskii tsentr gendernykh issledovani. http://www.gender.ru. Accessed October 15, 2007, and May 14, 2010.

Prunskiene, Kazimiera. http://www.prunskiene.lt. Accessed October 13, 2007.

Putin, Vladimir. http://www.kremlin.ru. Accessed October 16, 2007.

Russian Women, Girls, Russian Women, Russian Brides. http://www.russian-women.net. Accessed September 29, 2007.

Soiuz komitetov soldatskikh materei Rossii. http://www.ucsmr.ru. Accessed August 5, 2007.

Tverskaia tsentr zhenskoi istorii I gendernykh issledovanii. http://www .tvergenderstudies.ru. Accessed October 15, 2007.

Tymoshenko, Yulia. http://www.tymoshenko.ua. Accessed October 15, 2007, and December 12, 2010.

Universitetskaia set' gendernym issledovaniiam dlia stran byvshego SSSR. http://www.gender.univer.kharkov.ua. Accessed October 15, 2007.

SECONDARY SOURCES

Abrams, Lynn. *The Making of Modern Woman: Europe, 1789–1918*. London: Longman, 2002.

Abramson, David. "Engendering Citizenship in Postcommunist Uzbekistan." In *Post-Soviet Women Encountering Transition: Nation Building, Economic Survival, and Civic Activism,* edited by Kathleen Kuehnast and Carol Nechemias. Washington, D.C.: Woodrow Wilson Center Press, 2004.

Adelman, Deborah. *The Children of Perestroika: Moscow Teenagers Talk about Their Lives and the Future*. Armonk, N.Y.: Sharpe, 1992.

Akiner, Shirin. "Between Tradition and Modernity: The Dilemma Facing Contemporary Central-Asian Women." In *Post-Soviet Women: From the Baltic to Central Asia,* edited by Mary Buckley. Cambridge: Cambridge University Press, 1997.

Alexiyevich, S. *War's Unwomanly Face*. Translated from the Russian by Keith Hammond and Lyudmila Lezhneva. Moscow: Progress, 1985.

Alexopoulos, Golfo. *Stalin's Outcasts: Aliens, Citizens, and the Soviet State, 1926–1936*. Ithaca, N.Y.: Cornell University Press, 2003.

Anderson, Bonnie S., and Judith P. Zinsser. *A History of Their Own: Women in Europe from Prehistory to the Present*. 2 vols. Revised edition. Oxford: Oxford University Press, 2000.

Applebaum, Anne. *Gulag: A History*. New York: Anchor, 2003.

Armitage, Susan. "Through Women's Eyes: A New View of the West." In *The Women's West,* edited by Susan Armitage and Elizabeth Jameson. Norman: University of Oklahoma Press, 1987.

Ashwin, Sarah, and Elain Bowers. "Do Russian Women Want to Work?" In *Post-Soviet Women: From the Baltic to Central Asia,* edited by Mary Buckley. Cambridge: Cambridge University Press, 1997.

Attwood, Lynne. "Celebrating the 'Frail-Figured Welder': Gender Confusion in Women's Magazines of the Khrushchev Era." *Slavonica* 8, no. 2 (2002): 159–77.

Avrich, Paul. *Russian Rebels, 1600–1800*. New York: Norton, 1972.

Baker, Peter, and Susan Glasser. *Kremlin Rising: Vladimir Putin's Russia and the End of Revolution*. New York: Scribner, 2005.

Barber, John, and Mark Harrison. *The Soviet Home Front, 1941–1945: A Social and Economic History of the USSR in World War II.* London: Longman, 1991.

Barry, Ellen. "Russian Dissident's Passion Endures Despite Tests." *New York Times,* January 12, 2010.

Bastug, Sharon, and Nuran Hostacsu. "The Price of Value: Kinship, Marriage, and Meta-narratives of Gender in Turkmenistan." In *Gender and Identity Construction: Women of Central Asia, the Caucasus, and Turkey,* edited by Feride Acar and Ayse Günes-Ayata. Leiden: Brill, 2000.

Beevor, Anthony, and Luba Vinogradova. *A Writer at War: Vasily Grossman with the Red Army, 1941–1945.* New York: Pantheon, 2005.

Berkhoff, Karel C. *Harvest of Despair: Life and Death in Ukraine under Nazi Rule.* Cambridge, Mass.: Belknap, 2004.

Bernstein, Laurie. *Sonia's Daughters: Prostitutes and Their Regulation in Imperial Russia.* Berkeley: University of California Press, 1995.

Black, J. L. *Citizens for the Fatherland: Education, Educators, and Pedagogical Ideas in Eighteenth-Century Russia.* New York: East European Monographs, 1979.

Blobaum, Robert E. "The 'Woman Question' in Russian Poland." *Journal of Social History* 35, no. 4 (2002). Accessed February 18, 2005, on http://www .questia.com.

Blum, Jerome. *Lord and Peasant in Russia from the Ninth to the Nineteenth Century.* Princeton: Princeton University Press, 1961.

Bohac, Rodney. "Widows and the Russian Serf Community." *Russia's Women: Accommodation, Resistance, Transformation,* edited by Barbara Evans Clements, Barbara Alpern Engel, and Christine D. Worobec. Berkeley: University of California Press, 1991.

Bohachevsky-Chomiak, Martha. *Feminists Despite Themselves: Women in Ukrainian Community Life, 1884–1939.* Toronto, Ont.: Canadian Institute of Ukrainian Study, 1988.

Bolt, Christine. *Feminist Ferment: "The Woman Question" in the U.S.A. and England, 1870–1940.* London: Routledge, 1995.

Boniece, Sally A. "The Spiridonova Case, 1906: Terror, Myth, and Martyrdom." *Kritika* 4, no. 3 (Summer 2003): 571–606.

Boxer, Marilyn J., and Jean H. Quataert, editors. *Connecting Spheres: European Women in a Globalizing World, 1500 to the Present.* Second edition. Oxford: Oxford University Press, 2000.

Bradley, Joseph. *Muzhik and Muscovite: Urbanization in Late Imperial Russia.* Berkeley: University of California Press, 1985.

Bridger, Susan. "The Heirs of Pasha: The Rise and Fall of the Soviet Woman Tractor Driver." In *Gender in Russian History and Culture,* edited by Linda Edmondson. Houndmills, UK: Palgrave, 2001.

———. "Rural Women and the Impact of Economic Change." In *Post-Soviet Women: From the Baltic to Central Asia,* edited by Mary Buckley. Cambridge: Cambridge University Press, 1997.

———. *Women in the Soviet Countryside: Women's Roles in Rural Development in the Soviet Union.* Cambridge: Cambridge University Press, 1987.

Brower, Daniel R. *The Russian City between Tradition and Modernity, 1850–1900.* Berkeley: University of California Press, 1990.

Browning, Genia K. *Women and Politics in the USSR: Consciousness Raising and Soviet Women's Groups.* New York: St. Martin's, 1987.

Bruno, Marta O. "Women and the Culture of Entrepreneurship." In *Post-Soviet Women: From the Baltic to Central Asia,* edited by Mary Buckley. Cambridge: Cambridge University Press, 1997.

Bucher, Greta. *Women, the Bureaucracy, and Daily Life in Postwar Moscow, 1945–1953.* New York: Columbia, 2006.

Buckley, Mary. "Adaptation of the Soviet Women's Committee: Deputies' Voices from 'Women of Russia.'" In *Post-Soviet Women: From the Baltic to Central Asia,* edited by Mary Buckley. Cambridge: Cambridge University Press, 1997.

———. *Mobilizing Soviet Peasants: Heroines and Heroes of Stalin's Fields.* Lanham, Md.: Rowman and Littlefield, 2006.

Butler, Francis. "Ol'ga's Conversion and the Construction of Chronicle Narrative." *The Russian Review* 67, no. 2 (April 2008): 230–42.

———. "A Woman of Words: Pagan Ol'ga in the Mirror of Germanic Europe." *Slavic Review* 63, no. 4 (Winter 2004): 771–93.

Caiazza, Amy. "Committee of Soldiers' Mothers of Russia (Komitet soldatskikh materei Rossii) (1989–)." In *Encyclopedia of Russian Women's Movements,* edited by Norma Corigliano Noonan and Carol Nechemias. Westport, Conn.: Greenwood, 2001.

Cavender, Mary Wells. "'Kind Angel of the Soul and Heart': Domesticity and Family Correspondence among the Pre-emancipation Russian Gentry." *The Russian Review* 61, no. 3 (July 2002): 391–408.

Chapman, Janet G. "Equal Pay for Equal Work?" In *Women in Russia,* edited by Dorothy Atkinson, Alexander Dallin, and Gail Warshofsky Lapidus. Stanford, Calif.: Stanford University Press, 1977.

Chatterjee, Choi. "Soviet Heroines and the Language of Modernity, 1930–39." In *Women in the Stalin Era,* edited by Melanie Ilic. Houndmills, UK: Palgrave, 2001.

Clements, Barbara Evans. "The Birth of the New Soviet Woman." In *Bolshevik Culture: Experiment and Order in the Russian Revolution,* edited by Abbott Gleason, Peter Kenez, and Richard Stites. Bloomington: Indiana University Press, 1985.

———. *Bolshevik Women.* Cambridge: Cambridge University Press, 1997.

————. "Communism: Comparative History." In *The Oxford Encyclopedia of Women in World History,* edited by Bonnie G. Smith. Oxford: Oxford University Press, 2008. E-book edition, http://rave.ohiolink.edu/ebooks/ebc/ t247. Accessed May 13, 2010.

————. *Daughters of Revolution: A History of Women in the U.S.S.R.* Arlington Heights, Ill.: Harlan Davidson, 1994.

————. "The Effects of the Civil War on Women and Family Relations." In *Party, State, and Society in the Russian Civil War,* edited by Diane P. Koenker, William G. Rosenberg, and Ronald Grigor Suny. Bloomington: Indiana University Press, 1989.

————. "Tereshkova, Valentina." In *The Oxford Encyclopedia of Women in World History,* edited by Bonnie G. Smith. Oxford: Oxford University Press, 2008. E-book edition, http://rave.ohiolink.edu/ebooks/ebc/t247. Accessed May 13, 2010.

————. "Working-Class and Peasant Women in the Russian Revolution, 1917–23." *Signs* 8, no. 2 (1982): 215–35.

————. See also Newman, Barbara Evans.

Clements, Barbara Evans, Barbara Alpern Engel, and Christine D. Worobec. *Russia's Women: Accommodation, Resistance, Transformation.* Berkeley: University of California Press, 1991.

Cottam, Kazimiera J. *Women in War and Resistance: Selected Biographies of Soviet Women Soldiers.* Nepean, Canada: New Military Publishing, 1998.

Crate, Susan A. "The Gendered Nature of Viliui Sakha Post-Soviet Adaptation." In *Post-Soviet Women Encountering Transition: Nation Building, Economic Survival, and Civic Activism,* edited by Kathleen Kuehnast and Carol Nechemias. Washington, D.C.: Woodrow Wilson Center Press, 2004.

————. "Walking behind the Old Women: Sacred Sakha Cow Knowledge in the 21st Century." *Human Ecology Review* 15, no. 2 (2008): 115–29.

Crews, Robert. "Empire and the Confessional State: Islam and Religious Politics in Nineteenth-Century Russia." *American Historical Review* 108, no. 1 (February 2003): 50–83.

Crummey, Robert O. *The Formation of Muscovy, 1304–1613.* London: Longman, 1987.

Danilova, Maria. "Lyudmila Alexeyeva Speaks Her Mind." *St. Petersburg Times,* June 15, 2004. http://www.sptimes.ru/index.php?action_id=2&story_ id=771. Accessed October 15, 2007.

Davidoff, Leonore, and Catherine Hall. *Family Fortunes: Men and Women of the English Middle Class, 1780–1850.* Chicago: University of Chicago Press, 1987.

Davies, Sarah. *Popular Opinion in Stalin's Russia: Terror, Propaganda, and Dissent, 1934–1941.* Cambridge: Cambridge University Press, 1997.

Davis, Nathaniel. *A Long Walk to Church: A Contemporary History of Russian Orthodoxy.* Boulder, Colo.: Westview, 1995.

Dolidovich, O. M., and V. I. Fedorova. *Zhenshchiny Sibiri: Vo vtoroi polovine XIX–nachale XX veka (Demograficheskii, sotsia'nyi, professional'nyi aspekty).* Krasnoiarsk: Krasnoiarskii gosudarstvennyi pedagogicheskii universitet im. V. P. Astaf'eva, 2008.

Dowd, Maureen. "Evolution in Europe: Lithuania Premier Sees Bush, but There's No Red Carpet." *New York Times,* May 4, 1990, http://www .nytimes.com. Accessed October 10, 2007.

Dudwick, Nora. "Out of the Kitchen into the Crossfire: Women in Independent Armenia." In *Post-Soviet Women: From the Baltic to Central Asia,* edited by Mary Buckley. Cambridge: Cambridge University Press, 1997.

Dzieciolowski, Zygmunt. "Tatyana Zaslavskaya's Moment." Open Democracy, http://www.opendemocracy.net/article/tatyana_zaslavskaya_s_moment. Accessed October 10, 2007.

Edgar, Adrienne. "Bolshevism, Patriarchy, and the Nation: The Soviet 'Emancipation' of Muslim Women in Pan-Islamic Perspective." *Slavic Review* 65, no. 2 (Summer 2006): 253–72.

———. "Emancipation of the Unveiled: Turkmen Women under Soviet Rule, 1924–29." *The Russian Review* 62, no. 1 (January 2003): 132–49.

Edmondson, Linda. *Feminism in Russia, 1900–1917.* Stanford, Calif.: Stanford University Press, 1984.

Eklof, Ben. *Russian Peasant Schools: Officialdom, Village Culture, and Popular Pedagogy, 1861–1914.* Berkeley: University of California Press, 1986.

Engel, Barbara Alpern. *Between the Fields and the City: Women, Work, and Family in Russia, 1861–1914.* Cambridge: Cambridge University Press, 1994.

———. *Breaking the Ties That Bound: The Politics of Marital Strife in Late Imperial Russia.* Ithaca, N.Y.: Cornell University Press, 2011.

———. *Mothers and Daughters: Women of the Intelligentsia in Nineteenth-Century Russia.* Cambridge: Cambridge University Press, 1983.

———. "Not by Bread Alone: Subsistence Riots in Russia during World War I." *Journal of Modern History* 69, no. 4 (December 1997): 696–721.

———. *Women in Russia, 1700–2000.* Cambridge: Cambridge University Press, 2004.

Farnsworth, Beatrice. "The Litigious Daughter-in-Law: Family Relations in Rural Russia in the Second Half of the Nineteenth Century." In *Russian Peasant Women,* edited by Beatrice Farnsworth and Lynne Viola. New York: Oxford University Press, 1992.

———. "Rural Women and the Law: Divorce and Property Rights in the 1920s." In *Russian Peasant Women,* edited by Beatrice Farnsworth and Lynne Viola. New York: Oxford University Press, 1992.

Feifer, Gregory. "Russia's New Dissidents Defend Human Rights." *All Things Considered,* National Public Radio, March 7, 2007. http://www.npr.org. Accessed October 13, 2007.

Field, Deborah A. "Mothers and Fathers and the Problem of Selfishness in the Khrushchev Era." In *Women in the Khrushchev Era,* edited by Melanie Ilic, Susan E. Reid, and Lynne Attwood. Houndmills, UK: Palgrave, 2004.

Filtzer, Donald. *Soviet Workers and De-Stalinization: The Consolidation of the Modern System of Soviet Production Relations, 1953–1964.* Cambridge: Cambridge University Press, 1992.

Forsyth, James. *A History of the Peoples of Siberia: Russia's North Asian Colony, 1581–1990.* Cambridge: Cambridge University Press, 1992.

Frank, Roberta. "Marriage in Twelfth- and Thirteenth-Century Iceland." *Viator* 4 (1973): 477–84.

Frank, Stephen P. "Narratives within Numbers: Women, Crime, and Judicial Statistics in Imperial Russia, 1834–1913." *The Russian Review* 55, no. 4 (October 1996): 541–66.

Franzoi, Barbara. *At the Very Least She Pays the Rent: Women and German Industrialization, 1871–1914.* Westport, Conn.: Greenwood, 1985.

Freeze, Gregory L. "Bringing Order to the Russian Family: Marriage and Divorce in Imperial Russia, 1760–1860." *Journal of Modern History* 62, no. 4 (December 1990): 709–46.

———. "Profane Narratives about a Holy Sacrament: Marriage and Divorce in Late Imperial Russia." In *Sacred Stories: Religion and Spirituality in Modern Russia,* edited by Mark D. Steinberg and Heather J. Coleman. Bloomington: Indiana University Press, 2007.

Frieden, Nancy Mandelker. *Russian Physicians in an Era of Reform and Revolution, 1856–1905.* Princeton: Princeton University Press, 1981.

Friedman, Rebecca. *Masculinity, Autocracy, and the Russian University, 1804–1863.* Houndmills, UK: Palgrave, 2005.

Friedman, Rebecca, and Dan Healy. "Conclusions." In *Russian Masculinities in History and Culture,* edited by Barbara Evans Clements, Rebecca Friedman, and Dan Healey. Houndmills, UK: Palgrave, 2002.

Funk, Nanette. "Fifteen Years of the East-West Women's Dialogue." In *Living Gender after Communism,* edited by Janet Elise Johnson and Jean C. Robinson. Bloomington: Indiana University Press, 2007.

Gapova, Elena, ed. *Zhenshchiny na kraiu Evropy.* Minsk: Evropeiskii Gumanitarnyi Universitet, 2003.

Geisler, Gisela. *Women and the Remaking of Politics in Southern Africa: Negotiating Autonomy, Incorporation and Representation.* Stockholm: Nordic African Institute, 2004.

Getty, J. Arch, and Oleg Naumov, editors. *The Road to Terror: Stalin and the Self-Destruction of the Bolsheviks, 1932–1939.* Translated by Benjamin Sher. New Haven: Yale University Press, 1999.

Getty, J. Arch, T. Rittersporn, and Viktor N. Zemskov. "Victims of the Soviet Penal System in the Pre-War Years: A First Approach on the Basis of Archival Evidence." *American Historical Review* 98, no. 4 (October 1993): 1017–49.

Gilmour, Julie, and Barbara Evans Clements. "'If You Want to Be like Me, Train!': The Contradictions of Soviet Masculinity." In *Russian Masculinities in History and Culture,* edited by Barbara Evans Clements, Rebecca Friedman, and Dan Healey. Houndmills, UK: Palgrave, 2002.

Girdzijauskas, Simonas. "Special Lithuanian Presidential Election—Adamkus Elected President." Joint Baltic American National Committee, July 12, 2004. http://www.jbanc.org/ltback.html. Accessed October 13, 2007.

Glagoleva, Olga. *Dream and Reality of Russian Provincial Young Ladies, 1700–1850.* Carl Beck Papers in Russian and East European Studies, no. 1405. Pittsburgh, Penn.: Center for Russian and East European Studies, 2000.

Glickman, Rose L. *Russian Factory Women: Workplace and Society, 1880–1914.* Berkeley: University of California Press, 1984.

Goldman, Wendy Z. *Women at the Gates: Gender, Politics, and Planning in Soviet Industrialization.* Cambridge: Cambridge University Press, 2002.

———. *Women, the State, and Revolution: Soviet Family Policy and Social Life, 1917–1936.* Cambridge: Cambridge University Press, 1993.

Goncharov, Iu. M. "Zhenshchiny frontira: Sibiriachki v regional'nym sotsiume serediny XIX–nachala XIX vv." In *Sostial'naia istoriia: Ezhegodnik 2003: Zhenskaia i gendernaia istoriia.* Moscow: Rosspen, 2003.

Gorshkov, M. K., and N. E. Tikhonova, editors. *Zhenshchina novoi Rossii: Kakaia ona? Kak zhivet? K chemy stremitsia?* Moscow: Rosspen, 2002.

Harris, Colette. "The Changing Identity of Women in Tajikistan in the Post-Soviet Period." In *Gender and Identity Construction: Women of Central Asia, the Caucasus, and Turkey,* edited by Feride Acar and Ayse Günes-Ayata. Leiden: Brill, 2000.

Healey, Dan. "Lesbian Lives Observed in the Gulag: Memoirs and the Memory of Same-Sex Love in Forced Labor Camps." Paper presented at the annual meeting of the American Association for the Advancement of Slavic Studies, Boston, 2009.

Heldt, Barbara. *Terrible Perfection: Women and Russian Literature.* Bloomington: Indiana University Press, 1987.

Hellie, Richard. *Slavery in Russia, 1450–1725.* Chicago: University of Chicago Press, 1982.

———. "Women and Slavery in Moscow." *Russian History* 10, pt. 2 (1983): 213–29.

Hemment, Julie. *Empowering Women in Russia: Activism, Aid, and NGOs.* Bloomington: Indiana University Press, 2007.

Henriksson, Anders. "Minority Nationalism and the Politics of Gender: Baltic German Women in the Late Imperial Era." *Journal of Baltic Studies* 27, no. 3 (1996): 213–28.

Herlihy, Patricia. *The Alcoholic Empire: Vodka & Politics in Late Imperial Russia.* Oxford: Oxford University Press, 2002.

Holley, David. "Russian Journalist Remembered on Anniversary of Slaying." *Los Angeles Times,* October 8, 2007. http://www.latimes.com. Accessed October 10, 2008.

Houlbrooke, Ralph A. *The English Family, 1450–1700.* London: Longman, 1984.

Hughes, Lindsey. *Sophia, Regent of Russia, 1657–1704.* New Haven: Yale University Press, 1990.

Hyman, Paula E. *Gender and Assimilation in Modern Jewish History: The Roles and Representation of Women.* Seattle: University of Washington Press, 1995.

Iashchenko, Oksana. "Zametky k etnographii gorodskoi zhizni: Povsednevnost' gomel'chanok v nachale xx. v." In *Zhenshchiny na kraiu Evropy,* edited by Elena Gapova. Minsk: Evropeiskii Gumanitarnyi Universitet, 2003.

Igumnova, Z. P. *Zhenshchiny Moskvy v gody grazhdanskoi voiny.* Moscow: Moskovskii rabochii, 1958.

Ilic, Melanie. "*Traktoristka:* Representations and Realities." In *Women in the Stalin Era,* edited by Melanie Ilic. Houndmills, UK: Palgrave, 2001.

———. "Women in the Khrushchev Era: An Overview." In *Women in the Khrushchev Era,* edited by Melanie Ilic, Susan E. Reid, and Lynne Attwood. Houndmills, UK: Palgrave, 2004.

Il'iukhov, A. A. *Prostitutsiia v Rossii: S XVII veka do 1917 goda.* Moscow: Novyi khronograf, 2008.

Ishkanian, Armine. "Working at the Local-Global Intersection: The Challenges Facing Women in Armenia's Nongovernmental Organization Sector." In *Post-Soviet Women Encountering Transition: Nation Building, Economic Survival, and Civic Activism,* edited by Kathleen Kuehnast and Carol Nechemias. Washington, D.C.: Woodrow Wilson Center Press, 2004.

Jaworski, Rudolf, and Bianka Pietrow-Ennker, editors. *Women in Polish Society.* Boulder, Colo.: East European Monographs, 1992.

Johanson, Christine. *Women's Struggle for Higher Education in Russia, 1855–1900.* Montreal: McGill-Queen's University Press, 1987.

Johnson, Janet Elise. *Gender Violence in Russia: The Politics of Feminist Intervention.* Bloomington: Indiana University Press, 2009.

———. "Sisterhood versus the 'Moral' Russian State: The Postcommunist Politics of Rape." In *Post-Soviet Women Encountering Transition: Nation Building, Economic Survival, and Civic Activism,* edited by Kathleen Kuehnast and Carol Nechemias. Washington, D.C.: Woodrow Wilson Center Press, 2004.

Johnson, Robert Eugene. *Peasant and Proletarian: The Working Class of Moscow in the Late Nineteenth Century.* New Brunswick, N.J.: Rutgers, 1979.

Kaiser, Daniel H. "'He Said, She Said': Rape and Gender Discourse in Early Modern Russia." *Kritika* 3, no. 2 (Spring 2002): 197–216.

———. "The Poor and Disabled in Early Eighteenth-Century Russian Towns." *Journal of Social History* 32, no. 1 (1998): 125–55.

Kaluzhskie bol'shevichki. Kaluga: n.p., 1960.

Kamp, Marianne. *The New Woman in Uzbekistan: Islam, Modernity, and Unveiling under Communism*. Seattle: University of Washington Press, 2006.

Karciauskaite, Indre. "For Women's Rights, Church, and Fatherland: The Lithuanian Catholic Women's Organization, 1908–1940." *Aspasia* 1 (2007): 128–52.

Katz, Katarina. *Gender, Work, and Wages in the Soviet Union: A Legacy of Discrimination*. Houndmills, UK: Palgrave, 2001.

Kay, Rebecca. "Meeting the Challenge Together? Russian Grassroots Women's Organizations and the Shortcomings of Western Aid." In *Post-Soviet Women Encountering Transition: Nation Building, Economic Survival, and Civic Activism,* edited by Kathleen Kuehnast and Carol Nechemias. Washington, D.C.: Woodrow Wilson Center Press, 2004.

———. *Men in Contemporary Russia: The Fallen Heroes of Post-Soviet Change?* Aldershot, UK: Ashgate, 2006.

Kebalo, Martha Kichorowska. "Exploring Continuities and Reconciling Ruptures: Nationalism, Feminism, and the Ukrainian Women's Movement." *Aspasia* 1 (2007): 36–60.

Kelly, Catriona. *A History of Russian Women's Writing, 1820–1992*. Oxford: Clarendon Press, 1994.

———. "Teacups and Coffins: The Culture of Russian Merchant Women, 1850–1917." In *Women in Russia and Ukraine,* edited by Rosalind Marsh. Cambridge: Cambridge University Press, 1996.

Kessler-Harris, Alice. *Out to Work: A History of Wage-Earning Women in the United States*. Oxford: Oxford University Press, 1982.

Kivelson, Valerie A. "Coerced Confessions, or if Tituba Had Been Enslaved in Muscovy." In *The New Muscovite Cultural History: A Collection in Honor of Daniel B. Rowland,* edited by Valerie A. Kivelson, Karen Petrone, Nancy Shields Kollmann, and Michael S. Flier. Bloomington, Ind.: Slavica, 2009.

———. "The Effects of Partible Inheritance: Gentry Families and the State in Muscovy." *The Russian Review* 53, no. 2 (April 1994): 197–212.

———. "Male Witches and Gendered Categories in Seventeenth-Century Russia." *Comparative Studies in Society and History* 45, no. 3 (2003): 606–31.

———. "Patrolling the Boundaries: Witchcraft Accusations and Household Strife in Seventeenth-Century Muscovy." *Harvard Ukrainian Studies* 19, edited by Nancy Shields Kollmann, Donald Ostrowski, Andrei Pliguzov, and Daniel Rowland, 302–23. Cambridge, Mass.: Harvard University Press, 1995.

———. "Political Sorcery in Sixteenth-Century Muscovy." In *Culture and Identity in Muscovy, 1359–1584,* edited by A. M. Kleimola and G. D. Lenhoff. Moscow: ITZ-Garant, 1997.

———. "Sexuality and Gender in Early Modern Russian Orthodoxy: Sin and Virtue in Cultural Context." In *Letters from Heaven: Popular Religion in*

Russia and Ukraine, edited by John-Paul Himka and Andriy Zayarnyuk. Toronto, Ont.: University of Toronto Press, 2006.

———. "Through the Prism of Witchcraft: Gender and Social Change in Seventeenth-Century Muscovy." In *Russia's Women: Accommodation, Resistance, Transformation,* edited by Barbara Evans Clements, Barbara Alpern Engel, and Christine D. Worobec. Berkeley: University of California Press, 1991.

Kleimola, Ann M. "'In Accordance with the Canons of the Holy Apostles': Muscovite Dowries and Women's Property Rights." *The Russian Review* 51, no. 2 (April 1992): 204–29.

Koblitz, Ann Hibner. *A Convergence of Lives: Sofia Kovalevskaia, Scientist, Writer, Revolutionary.* Boston: Birkhäuser, 1983.

Koenker, Diane P. "Urbanization and Deurbanization in the Russian Revolution and the Civil War." In *Party, State, and Society in the Russian Civil War,* edited by Diane P. Koenker, William G. Rosenberg, and Ronald Grigor Suny. Bloomington: Indiana University Press, 1989.

Kollmann, Nancy Shields. *Kinship and Politics: The Making of the Muscovite Political System, 1345–1547.* Stanford, Calif.: Stanford University Press, 1987.

———. "The Seclusion of Elite Muscovite Women." *Russian History* 10, part 2 (1983): 170–87.

———. "Self, Society, and Gender in Early Modern Russia and Eastern Europe." In *A Companion to Gender History,* edited by Teresa A. Meade and Merry E. Wiesner-Hanks. Malden, Mass.: Blackwell, 2004.

———. "'What's Love Got to Do with It?' Changing Models of Masculinity in Muscovite and Petrine Russia." In *Russian Masculinities in History and Culture,* edited by Barbara Evans Clements, Rebecca Friedman, and Dan Healey. Houndmills, UK: Palgrave, 2002.

Kononenko, Natalie. "Folk Orthodoxy: Popular Religion in Contemporary Ukraine." In *Letters from Heaven: Popular Religion in Russia and Ukraine,* edited by John-Paul Himka and Andriy Zayarnyuk. Toronto, Ont.: University of Toronto Press, 2006.

Krylova, Anna. *Soviet Women in Combat: A History of Violence on the Eastern Front.* Cambridge: Cambridge University Press, 2010.

Kuehnast, Kathleen, and Carol Nechemias. "Introduction: Women Navigating Change in Post-Soviet Currents." In *Post-Soviet Women Encountering Transition: Nation Building, Economic Survival, and Civic Activism,* edited by Kathleen Kuehnast and Carol Nechemias. Washington, D.C.: Woodrow Wilson Center Press, 2004.

Kuxhausen, Anna. "Ideal Citizens/Ideal Mothers: Discourse and Experience at Smolnyi Institute, 1764–1783." Paper presented at the Midwest Russian History Colloquium, DeKalb, Ill., October 2001.

Langer, Lawrence N. "The Black Death in Russia: Its Effects upon Urban Labor." *Russian History* 2, nos. 1–2 (1975): 53–67.

Lenhoff, Gail, and Janet Martin. "Marfa Boretskaia, *Posadnitsa* of Novgorod: A Reconsideration of Her Legend and Her Life." *Slavic Review* 59, no. 2 (Summer 2000): 343–68.

Levin, Eve. "The Christian Sources of the Cult of St. Paraskeva." In *Letters from Heaven: Popular Religion in Russia and Ukraine,* edited by John-Paul Himka and Andriy Zayarnyuk. Toronto, Ont.: University of Toronto Press, 2006.

———. "The Role and Status of Women in Medieval Novgorod." Ph.D. dissertation. Indiana University, 1983.

———. *Sex and Society in the World of the Orthodox Slavs.* Ithaca, N.Y.: Cornell University Press, 1989.

Lincoln, W. Bruce. *Nicholas I, Emperor and Autocrat of All the Russias.* Bloomington: Indiana University Press, 1978.

Lindenmeyr, Adele. "The Elusive Life of Countess Sofia V. Panina, 1871–1956." Paper presented at the annual meeting of the American Association for the Advancement of Slavic Studies, December 2004.

———. *Poverty Is Not a Vice: Charity, Society, and the State in Imperial Russia.* Princeton: Princeton University Press, 1996.

Livezeanu, Irina, June Pachuta Farris, Mary Zirin, and Christine Worobec, editors. *Women and Gender in Central and Eastern Europe, Russia, and Eurasia.* 2 vols. Armonk, N.Y.: Sharpe, 2007.

Lyon, Tania Rands. "Housewife Fantasies, Family Realities in the New Russia." In *Living Gender after Communism,* edited by Janet Elise Johnson and Jean C. Robinson. Bloomington: Indiana University Press, 2007.

MacKenzie, David and Michael W. Curran. *A History of Russia, the Soviet Union, and Beyond.* Fourth edition. Belmont, Calif.: Wadsworth, 1993.

Madariaga, Isabel de. *Russia in the Age of Catherine the Great.* New Haven: Yale University Press, 1981.

Malysheva, Marina, Marina Pisklakova, Natalia Rimashevskaya, and Dana Vannoy. *Marriages in Russia: Couples during the Economic Transition.* New York: Praeger, 1999.

Manning, Roberta. "Women in the Soviet Countryside on the Eve of World War II, 1935–1940." In *Russian Peasant Women,* edited by Beatrice Farnsworth and Lynne Viola. New York: Oxford University Press, 1992.

Marody, Mira, and Anna Giza-Poleszczuk. "Changing Images of Identity in Poland: From the Self-Sacrificing to the Self-Investing Woman?" In *Reproducing Gender: Politics, Publics, and Everyday Life after Socialism,* edited by Susan Gal and Gail Kligman. Princeton: Princeton University Press, 2000.

Marrese, Michelle Lamarche. "From Maintenance to Entitlement: Defining the Dowry in 18th-Century Russia." In *Women and Gender in 18th-Century Russia,* edited by Wendy Rosslyn. Aldershot, UK: Ashgate, 2003.

———. *A Woman's Kingdom: Noblewomen and the Control of Property in Russia, 1700–1861.* Ithaca, N.Y.: Cornell University Press, 2002.

"Marry Indian, Save Russia." RIA Novosti, September 12, 2007, as published in *Hindustan Times.* http://www.hindustantimes.com. Accessed October 16, 2007.

Martin, Janet. *Medieval Russia, 980–1584.* Cambridge: Cambridge University Press, 1995.

Mason, Emma. "Women in the Gulag in the 1930s." In *Women in the Stalin Era,* edited by Melanie Ilic. Houndmills, UK: Palgrave, 2001.

McDermid, Jane, and Anna Hillyar. *Women and Work in Russia, 1880–1930: A Study in Continuity through Change.* London: Longman, 1998.

McNeal, Robert H. "Women in the Russian Radical Movement." *Journal of Social History* 2, no. 5 (Winter 1971–72): 143–63.

McReynolds, Louise. "'The Incomparable' Anastasiia Vial'tseva and the Culture of Personality." In *Russia, Women, Culture,* edited by Helena Goscilo and Beth Holmgren. Bloomington: Indiana University Press, 1996.

McVay, Pamela. *Envisioning Women in World History, 1500–Present.* 2 vols. Boston: McGraw Hill, 2008.

Meehan-Waters, Brenda. "To Save Oneself: Russian Peasant Women and the Development of Women's Religious Communities in Prerevolutionary Russia." In *Russian Peasant Women,* edited by Beatrice Farnsworth and Lynne Viola. New York: Oxford University Press, 1992.

Mereu, Francesca. "What Women Want: A Seat in the Duma." *Moscow Times,* September 17, 2003. Yabloko website, http://www.eng.yabloko.ru. Accessed September 20, 2007.

Merridale, Catherine. *Ivan's War: Life and Death in the Red Army, 1939–1945.* New York: Metropolitan, 2006.

Michels, Georg. "Muscovite Elite Women and Old Belief." *Harvard Ukrainian Studies* 19, edited by Nancy Shields Kollmann, Donald Ostrowski, Andrei Pliguzov, and Daniel Rowland, 428–50. Cambridge, Mass.: Harvard University Press, 1995.

Mikhnevich, V. "Russkaia zhenshchina XVIII stoletiia." In *Russkaia zhenshchina,* edited by V. Tret'iakova. Moscow: Terra, 1997.

Mirovalev, Mansur. "Uzbek Women Accuse State of Mass Sterilizations." MSNBC.com. http://www.msnbc.msn.com/id/38293092/ns/world_news-south_and_central_asia/. Accessed January 10, 2011.

Moghadam, Valentine M. "Gender and Economic Reforms: A Framework for Analysis and Evidence from Central Asia, the Caucasus, and Turkey." In *Gender and Identity Construction: Women of Central Asia, the Caucasus, and Turkey,* edited by Feride Acar and Ayse Günes-Ayata. Leiden: Brill, 2000.

Moon, David. *The Russian Peasantry, 1600–1930: The World the Peasants Made.* London: Longman, 1999.

Nash, Carol. "Educating New Mothers: Women and the Enlightenment in Russia." *History of Education Quarterly* 21, no. 3 (Fall 1981): 301–16.

Neary, Rebecca Balmas. "Mothering Socialist Society: The Wife-Activists' Movement and the Soviet Culture of Daily Life, 1934–41." *The Russian Review* 58, no. 3 (July 1999): 396–412.

Nechemias, Carol. "The Women of Russia Political Movement *(Politicheskoe dvizhenie Zhenshchiny Rossii),* or WOR (1993–)." In *Encyclopedia of Russian Women's Movements,* edited by Norma Corigliano Noonan and Carol Nechemias. Westport, Conn.: Greenwood, 2001.

Newman, Barbara Evans. "The Gals of Kittitas County, 1890–1920." Paper read at the Local-History Lecture Series, Kittitas County Historical Museum, Ellensburg, Wash., March 16, 2007.

———. See also Clements, Barbara Evans.

Nietyksza, Maria. "The Vocational Activities of Women in Warsaw at the Turn of the Nineteenth Century." In *Women in Polish Society,* edited by Rudolf Jaworski and Bianka Pietrow-Ennker. Boulder, Colo.: East European Monographs, 1992.

Northrop, Douglas. *Veiled Empire: Gender and Power in Stalinist Central Asia.* Ithaca, N.Y.: Cornell University Press, 2004.

Norton, Barbara T., and Jehanne M. Gheith, editors. *An Improper Profession: Women, Gender and Journalism in Late Imperial Russia.* Durham, N.C.: Duke, 2001.

Offen, Karen. *European Feminisms, 1700–1950: A Political History.* Stanford, Calif.: Stanford University Press, 2000.

Olcott, Martha Brill. *The Kazaks.* Second edition. Stanford, Calif.: Hoover, 1995.

Opdycke, Sandra. *The Routledge Historical Atlas of Women in America.* New York: Routledge, 2000.

Oushakine, Serguei Alex. "The Fatal Splitting: Symbolizing Anxiety in Post-Soviet Russia." *Ethnos* 66, no. 3 (2001): 1–30.

Overy, Richard. *Russia's War.* New York: Penguin, 1998.

Pallot, Judith. "Women's Domestic Industries in Moscow Province, 1880–1900." In *Russia's Women: Accommodation, Resistance, Transformation,* edited by Barbara Evans Clements, Barbara Alpern Engel, and Christine D. Worobec. Berkeley: University of California Press, 1991.

Pavlychko, Solomea. "Feminism in Post-Communist Ukrainian Society." In *Women in Ukraine and Russia,* edited by Rosalind Marsh. Cambridge: Cambridge University Press, 1996.

———. "Progress on Hold: The Conservative Faces of Women in Ukraine." In *Post-Soviet Women: From the Baltic to Central Asia,* edited by Mary Buckley. Cambridge: Cambridge University Press, 1997.

Penn, Shana. *Solidarity's Secret: The Women Who Defeated Communism in Poland.* Ann Arbor: University of Michigan Press, 2005.

Pennington, Reina. *Wings, Women, and War: Soviet Airwomen in World War II Combat.* Lawrence: University Press of Kansas, 2001.

Philipov, Dimitrer, Evgueni Andreev, Tatyana Kharkova, and Vladimir M. Shkolnikov. "Induced Abortion in Russia: Recent Trends and Underreporting in Surveys." *European Journal of Population* 20, no. 2 (2004): 95–117.

Phillips, Sarah D. *Women's Social Activism in the New Ukraine: Development and the Politics of Differentiation.* Bloomington: Indiana University Press, 2008.

Pilkington, Hilary. "'For the Sake of the Children': Gender and Migration in the Former Soviet Union." In *Post-Soviet Women: From the Baltic to Central Asia,* edited by Mary Buckley. Cambridge: Cambridge University Press, 1997.

Popkova, Ludmila. "Women's Political Activism in Russia: The Case of Samara." In *Post-Soviet Women Encountering Transition: Nation Building, Economic Survival, and Civic Activism,* edited by Kathleen Kuehnast and Carol Nechemias. Washington, D.C.: Woodrow Wilson Center Press, 2004.

"Profile: Yulia Tymoshenko." BBC News. March 27, 2006. http://news.bbc .co.uk. Accessed October 15, 2007.

Pushkareva, Natalia. *Gendernaia teoriia i istoricheskoe znanie.* Sankt-Peterburg: Aleteiia, 2007.

———. *Women in Russian History from the Tenth to the Twentieth Century,* edited and translated by Eve Levin. Armonk, N.Y.: Sharpe, 1997.

Rabinowitch, Alexander. "Spiridonova." In *Critical Companion to the Russian Revolution,* edited by Edward Acton, Vladimir Iu. Cherniaev, and William Rosenberg. London: Arnold, 1997.

Ramer, Samuel C. "Childbirth and Culture: Midwifery in the Nineteenth-Century Russian Countryside." In *Russian Peasant Women,* edited by Beatrice Farnsworth and Lynne Viola. New York: Oxford University Press, 1992.

Randall, Amy. *The Soviet Dream World of Retail Trade and Consumption in the 1930s.* Houndmills, UK: Palgrave, 2008.

Ransel, David L. "Infant-Care Cultures in the Russian Empire." In *Russia's Women: Accommodation, Resistance, Transformation,* edited by Barbara Evans Clements, Barbara Alpern Engel, and Christine D. Worobec. Berkeley: University of California Press, 1991.

———. *Mothers of Misery: Child Abandonment in Russia.* Princeton: Princeton University Press, 1988.

———. *Village Mothers: Three Generations of Change in Russia and Tartaria.* Bloomington: Indiana University Press, 2000.

Ries, Nancy. *Russian Talk: Culture and Conversation during Perestroika.* Ithaca, N.Y.: Cornell University Press, 1997.

Rivkin-Fish, Michele. *Women's Health in Post-Soviet Russia: The Politics of Intervention.* Bloomington: Indiana University Press, 2005.

Roesdahl, Else. *The Vikings.* Revised edition. Translated by Susan M. Margeson and Kirsten Williams. London: Penguin, 1998.

Rorlich, Azade Ayse. "Intersecting Discourses in the Press of the Muslims of the Crimea, Middle Volga, and Caucasus: The Woman Question and the

Nation." In *Gender and Identity Construction: Women of Central Asia, the Caucasus, and Turkey,* edited by Feride Acar and Ayse Günes-Ayata. Leiden: Brill, 2000.

Rosenthal, Andrew. "A Soviet Voice of Innovation Comes to Force." *New York Times,* August 28, 1987. http://www.nytimes.com. Accessed October 13, 2007.

Rossman, Jeffrey J. "A Workers' Strike in Stalin's Russia: The Vichuga Uprising of April 1932." In *Contending with Stalinism: Soviet Power and Popular Resistance in the 1930s,* edited by Lynne Viola. Ithaca, N.Y.: Cornell University Press, 2002.

Rotkirch, Anna. "Arbatova, Mariia Ivanovna (1957–)." In *Encyclopedia of Russian Women's Movements,* edited by Norma Corigliano Noonan and Carol Nechemias. Westport, Conn.: Greenwood, 2001.

Ruane, Christine. *The Empire's New Clothes: A History of the Russian Fashion Industry, 1700–1917.* New Haven: Yale University Press, 2009.

———. *Gender, Class, and the Professionalization of Russian City Teachers, 1860–1914.* Pittsburgh, Penn.: University of Pittsburgh Press, 1994.

Ruthchild, Rochelle Goldberg. *Equality and Revolution: Women's Rights in the Russian Empire, 1905–1917.* Pittsburgh, Penn.: University of Pittsburgh Press, 2010.

———. "Soiuz ravnopraviia zhenshchin (Women's Equal Rights Union) (1905–1908)." In *Encyclopedia of Russian Women's Movements,* edited by Norma Corigliano Noonan and Carol Nechemias. Westport, Conn.: Greenwood, 2001.

———. "Women's Suffrage and Revolution in the Russian Empire, 1905–1917." *Aspasia* 1 (2007): 1–35.

Ryan, W. F. *The Bathhouse at Midnight: An Historical Survey of Magic and Divination in Russia.* University Park: Pennsylvania State University Press, 1999.

Saktanber, Ayse, and Asli Ozatas-Baykal. "Homeland within Homeland: Women and the Formation of Uzbek National Identity." In *Gender and Identity Construction: Women of Central Asia, the Caucasus, and Turkey,* edited by Feride Acar and Ayse Günes-Ayata. Leiden: Brill, 2000.

Salmenniemi, Suvi. *Democratization and Gender in Contemporary Russia.* New York: Routledge, 2008.

Schrader, Abby M. "Unruly Felons and Civilizing Wives: Cultivating Marriage in the Siberian Exile System, 1822–1860." *Slavic Review* 66, no. 2 (Summer 2007): 230–56.

Schrand, Thomas G. "Soviet 'Civic-Minded' Women in the 1930's: Class, Gender, and Industrialization in a Socialist Society." *Journal of Women's History* 11, no. 3 (1999): 126–50.

Schuler, Catherine. "Actresses, Audience, and Fashion in the Silver Age: A Crisis of Costume." In *Women and Russian Culture: Projections and Self-Perceptions,* edited by Rosalind Marsh. Oxford: Berghahn, 1998.

Seager, Joni, and Ann Olson. *Women in the World: An International Atlas*. New York: Touchstone, 1986.

Shahar, Shulamith. *The Fourth Estate: A History of Women in the Middle Ages*. Translated by Chaya Galai. Revised edition. London: Routledge, 2003.

Shevchenko, Olga. *Crisis and the Everyday in Postsocialist Moscow*. Bloomington: Indiana University Press, 2009.

Shulman, Elena. *Stalinism on the Frontier of Empire: Women and State Formation in the Soviet Far East*. Cambridge: Cambridge University Press, 2008.

Slepyan, Kenneth. *Stalin's Guerrillas: Soviet Partisans in World War II*. Lawrence: University Press of Kansas, 2006.

Smith, David J., Artis Pabriks, Aldis Purs, and Thomas Lane. *The Baltic States: Estonia, Latvia, and Lithuania*. London: Routledge, 2002.

Smith, Gregory Malloy. "The Impact of World War II on Women, Family Life, and Mores in Moscow, 1941–1945." Doctoral dissertation. Stanford University, 1989.

Smith, S. A. "Masculinity in Transition: Peasant Migrants to Late-Imperial St. Petersburg." In *Russian Masculinities in History and Culture*, edited by Barbara Evans Clements, Rebecca Friedman, and Dan Healey. Houndmills, UK: Palgrave, 2002.

Sperling, Valerie. *Organizing Women in Contemporary Russia: Engendering Transition*. Cambridge: Cambridge University Press, 1999.

Stankovic, Slobodan. "Soviet Academician: Gorbachev Should 'Free People from Their Chains.'" *1 Danas* (Zagreb). http://files.osa.ceu.hu. Accessed October 13, 2007.

Steinberg, Mark D. *Proletarian Imagination: Self, Modernity, and the Sacred in Russia, 1910–1925*. Ithaca, N.Y.: Cornell University Press, 2002.

Stites, Richard. *The Women's Liberation Movement in Russia: Feminism, Nihilism, and Bolshevism, 1860–1930*. Princeton: Princeton University Press, 1978.

Stockdale, Melissa K. "'My Death for the Motherland Is Happiness': Women, Patriotism, and Soldiering in Russia's Great War, 1914–1917." *American Historical Review* 109, no. 1 (February 2004): 78–116.

Stoff, Laurie S. *They Fought for the Motherland: Russia's Women Soldiers in World War I and the Revolution*. Lawrence: University Press of Kansas, 2006.

Subtelny, Orest. *Ukraine, a History*. Third edition. Toronto, Ont.: University of Toronto Press, 2000.

Taraban, Svitlana. "Birthday Girls, Russian Dolls, and Others: Internet Bride as the Emerging Global Identity of Post-Soviet Women." In *Living Gender after Communism*, edited by Janet Elise Johnson and Jean C. Robinson. Bloomington: Indiana University Press, 2007.

Taubman, William. *Khrushchev: The Man and His Era*. New York: Norton, 2003.

"Teen Widow ID'd as One of Moscow Bombers." *Arizona Daily Star*, April 3, 2010, A16.

Tek, Nekhama. "U partisan i sud'ba zhenshchin." In *Zhenshchiny na kraiu Evropy,* edited by Elena Gapova. Minsk: Evropeiskii Gumanotarnyi Universitet, 2003.

Thomas, Marie A. "Muscovite Convents in the Seventeenth Century." *Russian History* 10, part 2 (1983): 230–42.

Thyrêt, Isolde. *Between God and Tsar: Religious Symbolism and the Royal Women of Muscovite Russia.* DeKalb: Northern Illinois University Press, 2001.

———. "Women and the Orthodox Faith in Muscovite Russia: Spiritual Experience and Practice." In *Orthodox Russia: Belief and Practice under the Tsars,* edited by Valerie A. Kivelson and Robert H. Greene. University Park: Pennsylvania State University Press, 2003.

Tohidi, Nayereh. "Gender and National Identity in Post-Soviet Azerbaijan: A Regional Perspective." In *Gender and Identity Construction: Women of Central Asia, the Caucasus, and Turkey,* edited by Feride Acar and Ayse Günes-Ayata. Leiden: Brill, 2000.

———. "Women, Building Civil Society, and Democratization in Post-Soviet Azerbaijan." In *Post-Soviet Women Encountering Transition: Nation Building, Economic Survival, and Civic Activism,* edited by Kathleen Kuehnast and Carol Nechemias. Washington, D.C.: Woodrow Wilson Center Press, 2004.

Tyrrell, Ian. *Woman's World/Woman's Empire: The Woman's Christian Temperance Union in International Perspective, 1880–1930.* Chapel Hill: University of North Carolina Press, 1991.

UN Department of Economic and Social Affairs, Population Division. "Ukraine." *World Abortion Policies 2007.* http://www.un.org/esa/population/publications/abortion/doc/ukraine.doc. Accessed October 2, 2007.

———. *World Abortion Policies 2007.* http://www.un.org/esa/population/publications/2007. Accessed October 2, 2007. (Now at http://www.un.org/esa/population/publications/2007_Abortion_Policies_Chart/2007AbortionPolicies_wallchart.htm.)

———. Department of International Economic and Social Affairs. Statistical Office. *The World's Women, 1970–1990: Trends and Statistics.* New York: United Nations, 1991.

U.S. Department of Agriculture, Foreign Agricultural Service. "Russia: Agricultural Overview." http://www.fas.usda.gov/pecad2/highlights/2005/03// Russia_Ag/index. Accessed November 6, 2007.

Uspenskaia, V. I., editor. *Aleksandra Kollontai: Teoriia zhenskoi emancipatsii v kontekste rossiiskoi gendernoi politiki.* Tver: Zolotaia bukva, 2003.

Viola, Lynne. "*Bab'i Bunty* and Peasant Women's Protest during Collectivization." In *Russian Peasant Women,* edited by Beatrice Farnsworth and Lynne Viola. New York: Oxford University Press, 1992.

———. *The Unknown Gulag: The Lost World of Stalin's Special Settlements.* Oxford: Oxford University Press, 2007.

Vitebsky, Piers. "Withdrawing from the Land: Social and Spiritual Crisis in the Indigenous Russian Arctic." In *Postsocialism: Ideals, Ideologies, and Practices in Eurasia,* edited by C. M. Hann. London: Routledge, 2002.

Wagner, William G. *Marriage, Property, and Law in Late Imperial Russia.* Oxford: Clarendon, 1994.

———. "'Orthodox Domesticity': Creating a Social Role for Women." In *Sacred Stories: Religion and Spirituality in Modern Russia,* edited by Mark D. Steinberg and Heather J. Coleman. Bloomington: Indiana University Press, 2007.

———. "Paradoxes of Piety: The Nizhenovgorod Convent of the Exaltation of the Cross, 1807–1935." In *Orthodox Russia: Belief and Practice under the Tsars,* edited by Valerie A. Kivelson and Robert H. Greene. University Park: Pennsylvania State University Press, 2003.

———. "The Transformation of Female Orthodox Monasticism in Nizhii Novgorod Diocese, 1764–1929, in Comparative Perspective." *Journal of Modern History* 78, no. 4 (December 2006): 793–845.

Wegren, Stephen K. *Land Reform in the Former Soviet Union and Eastern Europe.* London: Routledge, 1998.

Weickhardt, George G. "Legal Rights of Women in Russia, 1100–1750." *Slavic Review* 55, no. 1 (Spring 1996): 1–23.

———. "The Pre-Petrine Law of Property." *Slavic Review* 52, no. 4 (Winter 1993): 663–79.

Weiner, Lynn Y. *From Working Girl to Working Mother: The Female Labor Force in the United States, 1870–1980.* Chapel Hill: University of North Carolina Press, 1985.

Werner, Cynthia. "Feminizing the New Silk Road: Women Traders in Rural Kazakhstan." In *Post-Soviet Women Encountering Transition: Nation Building, Economic Survival, and Civic Activism,* edited by Kathleen Kuehnast and Carol Nechemias. Washington, D.C.: Woodrow Wilson Center Press, 2004.

White, Anne. *Small-Town Russia: Postcommunist Livelihoods and Identities.* London: Routledge, 2004.

White, Nijole. "Women in Changing Societies: Latvia and Lithuania." In *Post-Soviet Women: From the Baltic to Central Asia,* edited by Mary Buckley. Cambridge: Cambridge University Press, 1997.

White, Stephen. *Gorbachev and After.* Cambridge: Cambridge University Press, 1992.

Wirtschafter, Elise Kimerling. *Social Identity in Imperial Russia.* DeKalb: Northern Illinois University Press, 1997.

Wolf, Margery. *Revolution Postponed: Women in Contemporary China.* Stanford, Calif.: Stanford University Press, 1985.

Wolczuk, Kataryna, and Roman Wolczuk. "Julia Tymoshenko: The Iron Princess." *Independent,* November 4, 2007. http://news.independent.co.uk/people/profiles/articles3096925.ece. Accessed November 5, 2007.

Wood, Elizabeth A. *The Baba and the Comrade: Gender and Politics in Revolutionary Russia.* Bloomington: Indiana University Press, 1997.

Woodworth, C. K. "Sophia and the Golden Belt: What Caused Moscow's Civil Wars of 1425–50." *The Russian Review* 68, no. 2 (April 2009): 187–98.

Woodworth-Ney, Laura E. *Women in the American West.* Santa Barbara, Calif.: ABC CLIO, 2008.

Worobec, Christine. "Masculinity in Late-Imperial Russian Peasant Society." In *Russian Masculinities in History and Culture,* edited by Barbara Evans Clements, Rebecca Friedman, and Dan Healey. Houndmills, UK: Palgrave, 2002.

———. *Peasant Russia: Family and Community in the Post-Emancipation Period.* DeKalb: Northern Illinois University Press, 1995.

———. *Possessed: Women, Witches, and Demons in Imperial Russia.* DeKalb: Northern Illinois University Press, 2001.

Wortman, Richard. *Scenarios of Power: Myth and Ceremony in Russian Monarchy from Peter the Great to the Abdication of Nicholas II.* Volume 1. Princeton: Princeton University Press, 1995.

Zaslavskaya, Tatyana I. "The Correlation between Healthy and Ill Forces Is Not in Our Favor." Interview by Fredo Arias-King. *Demokratizatsiya* 13, no. 2. http://www.findarticle.com. Accessed May 14, 2008.

Zguta, Russell. "Witchcraft Trials in Seventeenth-Century Russia." *American Historical Review* 82, no. 5 (December 1977): 1187–1207.

Zhurzhenko, Tatiana. "Strong Women, Weak State: Family Politics and Nation Building in Post-Soviet Ukraine." In *Post-Soviet Women Encountering Transition: Nation Building, Economic Survival, and Civic Activism,* edited by Kathleen Kuehnast and Carol Nechemias. Washington, D.C.: Woodrow Wilson Center Press, 2004.

INDEX

BARBARA EVANS CLEMENTS

was born and raised in Richmond, Virginia. She received her B.A. from the University of Richmond and her M.A. and Ph.D. from Duke University. From 1971 to 2000, she was a member of the History Department of the University of Akron, where she taught Russian and European history and did research on the history of women in Russia. Some of her publications are listed in this book's bibliography. After retirement in 2000, she and her husband Jerry Newman moved to Ellensburg, Washington. In 2004, she decided to change her last name to Newman, but to continue using Clements as her professional name.

✣ ✣ ✣ ✣ ✣

Printed and bound by CPI Group (UK) Ltd, Croydon, CR0 4YY

13/04/2025

14656545-0004